The Founding of Israeli Democracy, 1948–1967

THE
FOUNDING
OF
ISRAELI
DEMOCRACY,
1948–1967

PETER Y. MEDDING

New York   Oxford
OXFORD UNIVERSITY PRESS
1990

Oxford University Press

Oxford   New York   Toronto
Delhi   Bombay   Calcutta   Madras   Karachi
Petaling Jaya   Singapore   Hong Kong   Tokyo
Nairobi   Dar es Salaam   Cape Town
Melbourne   Auckland

and associated companies in
Berlin   Ibadan

Published by Oxford University Press, Inc.,
200 Madison Avenue, New York, New York 10016

Library of Congress Cataloging-in-Publication Data
Medding, Peter.
The founding of Israeli democracy, 1948–1967
Peter Y. Medding.
p.   cm.   Bibliography: p.   Includes index.
ISBN 0-19-505648-5
1. Israel—Politics and government.   I. Title.
JQ1825.P3A443   1990   320.95694—dc20   89-32699   CIP

2 4 6 8 9 7 5 3 1

Printed in the United States of America
on acid-free paper

For My Children

Preface

The political history of the modern State of Israel can be divided into two distinct periods: 1948 to 1967 and post-1967. These periods are distinguished both by the nature and interplay of the problems that the state faced, and by the characteristic functioning of the latter's democratic political structures in coping with those problems.

This book deals with the first period, which I have termed the founding period. At one level, it seeks to provide an interpretative political history of that period as a whole: by focusing on the establishment and operation of new political structures; problems of statehood and social integration; relations among political parties; the aspirations and actions of political leaders; and the role of the electorate. These topics, portrayed in their contemporary context, are set against the background of the social, economic, and political structures inherited from the pre-state era.

At another level, the book has a clear analytic and comparative perspective, focusing upon Israel's newly established democratic political structures. It seeks to explain how these structures functioned both individually and as a system, in the light of the experience of other democracies. The two perspectives come together in the book's central theme: how the political structures and leaders coped with the major issues and problems of the founding period.

The book reaches the conclusion that during the founding period Israel's democracy generally managed to overcome the problems that it faced immediately after its establishment and those that developed in the ensuing years. Israel's relative success during the founding period stands in sharp contrast to its experience in the post-1967 period. Although this period began with a sweeping military victory in the Six-Day War, new and seemingly intractable problems arose in its wake.

The post-1967 period is characterized by three major developments. First, the political leadership was found wanting by an increasingly critical public as a result of its seeming inability to cope with, much less resolve, the interlocking problems that overloaded Israel's political agenda. Second, the previous balance between political and social forces was disturbed; as the former became weak and the latter gained in strength, the political system lost much of its capacity to control, direct, and set goals for society. Third, the same political structures that had existed previously now operated very differently; consequently, the overall pattern of democratic government in Israel changed significantly.

These developments raise many intriguing questions that fall beyond the scope of the present volume; they must await the interpretative political history and analytic study of the post-1967 period that hopefully will be completed in the not-too-distant future.

Over the years I was ably assisted by the following individuals in researching this book: Ayelet Baron, Shimon Hazenwald, Eliyahu Keren-David, and Amnon Layish; their help is gratefully acknowledged. I should also like to thank Barukh Tur-Raz, at the Archives of the Israeli Labor Party (Bet-Berl), and the librarians and archivists at Hamakhon Lemoreshet Ben-Gurion (Sedeh-Boker), the National and Hebrew University Library (Givat-Ram), and The Hebrew University Library (Mt. Scopus) for their assistance. The Ministry of Absorption is also to be thanked for providing a grant supporting the early stages of my research.

The manuscript was read by Mitchell Cohen, Avraham Diskin, Emanuel Gutmann, Arend Lijphart, Moshe Lissak, Michael Shalev, Yonatan Shapiro, and Ira Sharkansky, as well as two anonymous readers for Oxford University Press. Their comments and criticisms were of enormous assistance in preparing the manuscript for publication, thereby saving me from many an error, and I am greatly indebted to them.

Thanks are also due to Amy Lederhendler for preparing the index and to Odedah Zlotnick for help in producing the final version of the manuscript.

My wife, Ruth, happily assisted in reading the page proofs. Any public appreciation I can offer for this is but a small measure of my affection and gratitude to her for so much. This book is dedicated to our children in the hope that they will be witnesses to the resolution of Israel's problems and the realization of the ideals embodied in its Declaration of Independence.

Jerusalem   P.Y.M.
Erev Yom Kippur, 5790
October 8, 1989

Contents

The Founding of Israeli Democracy, 1948–1967

1

The Structures of Democratic Government

The Founding Period of States and the Maintenance of Democracy

In the historical development of states there is often a distinct founding period during which the political order is established, fundamental decisions are taken about who shall govern, and in what manner; and choices are made from among a variety of possible alternatives.[1] These actions set the terms and boundaries of subsequent political behavior, decision making, and of adaptation to social and political change. The founding period thus provides its political leaders with unique opportunities to imprint their values on state institutions.

Although Israeli political life had developed considerably in the previous forty years, 1948 to 1967 constitutes the founding period of the Israeli state. The political structures established then remain in place and still delimit the parameters of the Israeli political process today despite considerable political and social change. This fact not only makes it clear that these structures are deeply rooted but also explains why institutional reform has not occurred even though governmental capacity and effectiveness have declined markedly in recent years.

The Israeli state was founded as a democracy and is still a democracy, which makes it something of an exception in a world in which nondemocratic regimes far outnumber democracies. A study conducted in 1980, for example, rated fifty-one countries as basically democratic, and these accounted for approximately 37 percent of the world's population. But when more rigorous standards of democracy were applied, the total was reduced to thirty countries. Significantly, the list included very few of the new states founded after 1945; after democratic beginnings, most of them are now autocratic, one-party, or military regimes.

Not all thirty countries have maintained democracy continuously since World War II. Some—India, Greece, and Costa Rica—had nondemocratic interludes, while others—Jamaica, Spain, and Portugal—only recently became democratic. According to Arend Lijphart, in only twenty-one countries has democracy persisted without interruption during the entire period.[2] Israel is

3

the only new state among them. What is more, its stable democratic regime was set up under adverse conditions: substantial immigration; severe social dislocation; the introduction of ethnic, cultural, linguistic, religious, and national differences; rapid economic growth; a permanent security threat that led to six major wars; and a population that, in the main, had no personal knowledge or experience of democracy, having come from nondemocratic countries.

Not surprisingly, scholars of comparative politics have been puzzled by Israeli political development. After examining its party system, Giovanni Sartori concluded that "Israel is a most baffling case—and this quite aside from the fact that it is a microcosm of all the conceivable complexities." It was difficult to explain why "one finds, over the period 1949-1973, a remarkable stability," and "why Israel is, in spite of its fragmentation, a 'moderate' (i.e., nonpolarized or only semipolarized) type of polity." It was particularly exceptional; as he put it, "Israel is more *sui generis* than that" because it does not display the usual systemic and institutional features of moderate democratic party politics. Israel "is very definitely a case by itself to be understood as such."[3]

This book examines this "baffling case" and explains how the system was established and maintained during the period 1948-67, which we have called the founding period. It focuses upon the political conditions that gave rise to this distinctive period, the pattern of relations that characterized it, and the changes in the balance of political forces that brought it to an end.

Our approach is also analytical. It not only examines the founding of Israel's democratic political structures but also analyzes their foundations—the central elements and operating principles inherent in the institutional choices that were made—in order to determine which type of democracy emerged. It is set in the comparative perspective of the functioning of similar political structures in new states and other contemporary democracies.

The historical and analytical thrust of the book has three foci: the establishment and development of Israel's political structures and processes during the founding period; the major political actors—the political parties and their leaders—whose interests, goals and interaction determined the operation of those structures and processes; and the major policies, particularly those that related to the establishment of the political structures and state-building.

Democracy

As used in this book, the term *democracy* is taken to be both a set of normative ideals and a pattern of rule. Central to it are such key values as liberty and equality, which are simultaneously ends in themselves and means for attaining government by the people in the sense of responsiveness to popular preferences. Democratic systems, therefore, need political structures and processes that will facilitate responsiveness to popular preferences and provide institutional guarantees for liberty and equality, such as freedom of organization, freedom of expression, the right to vote, free and fair elections, public competition for political support and votes by leaders, and institutions for making policies depend on votes and other expressions of public preference.[4]

The book's major emphasis is centered upon the structures and processes of Israeli democracy, but some attention will also be paid to democratic values and to the rights and liberties of individual citizens. Discussion of the institutional pattern of Israeli democracy will be set in the context of Arend Lijphart's two diametrically opposite models of democracy—the majoritarian (or Westminster) model and the consensus model—and his comparative analysis of the twenty-one continuously democratic countries in terms of these models.

The Majoritarian Model and the Consensus Model

The essence of the majoritarian model, according to Lijphart, is that the translation of public preferences into policies and the resolution of political differences are determined by political structures that directly express the views of the majority, as, for example, in simple majority decisions. Apart from the majority's need to defeat the minority or opposition, there are no formal structural restraints over its power and authority to act and decide, except for the limitations that derive from the imperative of maintaining the democratic rights and liberties of all individuals.

The consensus model, by way of contrast, seeks more than a bare majority in the making of political decisions; it aims at broad participation and broad agreement, and tries to maximize the size of the ruling majority. In short, it emphasizes agreement rather than opposition. The differences between the two are highlighted in Table 1.

The aim of the consensus model as Lijphart points out, is to restrain "majority rule by requiring or encouraging the *sharing of power* between the majority and the minority (grand coalitions), the *dispersal of power* (among executive and legislature, two legislative chambers, and several minority par-

TABLE 1. Lijphart's Models of Democracy

Majoritarian Democracy	Consensus Democracy
Concentrated executive power: single-party majority cabinets	Executive power sharing: broad coalition cabinets
Executive dominance of the legislature	Separation of powers
Unicameralism	Balanced bicameralism
Two-party system	Multiparty system
One major issue dimension	Multidimensional issue cleavages
Single-member district plurality elections	Proportional representation
Unitary and centralized government	Federalism and decentralization
Parliamentary sovereignty	Written constitution, minority veto, judicial review

Source: Based upon the discussion in Arend Lijphart, *Democracies: Patterns of Majoritarian and Consensus Government in Twenty-One Countries* (New Haven: Yale University Press, 1984), pp. 1–30.

ties), a *fair distribution of power* (proportional representation), the *delegation of power* (to territorially and nonterritorially organized groups), and a *formal limit on power* (by means of the minority veto).[5]

These are abstract theoretical models, and no contemporary democracy incorporates all the elements of either model in its pure form. Rather, all existing democratic systems include elements from both. Nevertheless, some are much closer to one or the other model, whereas others are clearly in intermediate positions, mixing the various elements of the two models in different combinations. Structurally, Israel is such a hybrid. It posseses four majoritarian elements—a cabinet-dominated parliamentary system; unicameralism; a unitary and centralized government; and parliamentary sovereignty—and four consensual elements—proportional representation; a multiparty system; multidimensional issue cleavages; and a coalition government. As a result, the overall pattern of government can vary, depending upon the relative importance of particular elements under different political and social conditions.

Our analysis will seek to determine the pattern of Israeli democracy during the founding period, that is, the interrelation and balance between its majoritarian and consensus elements. Briefly stated, it will show that the pattern of government during the founding period was closer to majoritarian democracy than to the consensus model, mainly as a result of the character and practices of the coalition governments which operated almost as if they consisted of single-party majority cabinets. It will also show its dependence upon certain political and social conditions; as these changed or began to weaken in the latter part of the founding period, the balance shifted and the mixed pattern of Israeli democracy veered toward the consensus model, a process that has continued ever since.

Historically, it is of significance that these developments did not result from, and were not accompanied by, structural change or institutional reform. Israel still retains the structures established in the founding period, but they operate very differently and, many would argue, with far less effectiveness in meeting the greater demands made upon the political system since the end of the founding period. Its institutions, structures, and processes seem to be less capable of responding to the needs of the population, resolving internal social conflict, settling the external security issue, determining priorities, allocating resources, and formulating and implementing coherent and unified policies. It is also frequently suggested that in some respects there has been a decline in the level of adherence to democratic values and standards. Clearly, knowledge about how these structures performed during the founding period is essential for an understanding of their present state.

The book's argument can be briefly outlined. We begin with an analysis of the political legacy of the prestate period, the period of transition, the problems of independent statehood, and the founding of the new democratic political structures (chaps. 2 and 3). This is followed by discussions of the main political actors, namely, the political parties, and their policies, sources of support, organizational features, and electoral performance. The party system—issue structure; relations among the parties; the character of political rivalries; and the impact of the electoral system—is also examined (chaps. 4 and 5). In succeeding chapters we show how the practices of coalition government promoted majoritarianism and how this gave the leading party control over policy-making in many key areas, which are analyzed in depth (chaps. 6 and 7). We then return to the process of state-building and the establishment of centralized, unified, neutral state structures which stripped the political parties of important functions, and the development of a new ideology combining values of democracy and statehood (chap. 8). This is followed by an examination of the changing balance of political forces during the latter part of the founding period in the context of leadership struggles and disunity on the Left and growing unity and strength on the Right. In the last chapter we present our analysis of Israeli political structures in a comparative perspective, in which we summarize the distinctive elements of the founding period and the changes that led to its end, concluding with a brief examination of what has ensued (chap. 9).

Notes

1. Carl J. Friedrich, *Man and His Government: An Empirical Theory of Politics* (New York: McGraw-Hill, 1963), pp. 389–405.

2. See Arend Lijphart, *Democracies: Patterns of Majoritarian and Consensus Government in Twenty-one Countries* (New Haven: Yale University Press, 1984). In another analysis of twenty-nine nations with democratic regimes in place for at least five years (1958–76), Israel is again the only new state; see G. Bingham Powell, Jr., *Contemporary Democracies: Participation, Stability, and Violence* (Cambridge: Harvard University Press, 1982), p. 5.

3. Giovanni Sartori, *Parties and Party Systems: A Framework for Analysis* (Cambridge: Cambridge University Press, 1976), pp. 151–55.

4. Robert A. Dahl, *Polyarchy: Participation and Opposition* (New Haven: Yale University Press, 1971), pp. 1–14.

5. Lijphart, *Democracies*, p. 30. Emphasis in original.

2

Founding an Independent State

The Legacy of the Yishuv Political System

Strictly speaking, the founding of the political order in the new State of Israel did not begin on May 14, 1948. Israel embarked on the transition to independent statehood with an already functioning set of voluntary political arrangements developed by the Jewish community in Palestine (the Yishuv) during the British Mandate (1920–48). But during the founding period, fundamental decisions were made that effectively determined which of the existing Yishuv political arrangements would be maintained and which would not.

The Yishuv as a political community existed within the parameters allowed by the British Mandate, and internally was organized on a voluntary basis.[1] Although it lacked sovereignty and legitimate coercive power, its central structures enjoyed considerable authority based upon common ideological goals, political mobilization, and institutionalized patterns of attaining agreement and support.

Probably the single most distinctive characteristic of the Yishuv was the primacy of politics. Political forces were stronger than social forces; politics controlled and directed society, and, as a result, social structures had little or no autonomy. This was the result of two unusual historical sequences in the development of the Yishuv. One was that party preceded society. The other was that labor preceded and was stronger than capital.

The major institutions of political power in the Yishuv were created in a social vacuum, as it were, *ex nihilo*, by political parties, which were voluntaristic and ideologically motivated movements and organizations. They expanded their political power by increasing the support, resources, and geographic area that they controlled and utilized, both by direct importation from overseas and by access to the collective resources of the society. The political parties' direct and indirect performance of a wide range of social roles and functions can be characterized as the *partification* of significant sectors and activities of the society. Nevertheless, despite intense ideological disagreements and direct competition for control of the limited resources available, most parties were sufficiently united by the common goal of national independence and political sovereignty to enable them to operate institutions on the basis of power sharing. Partification was given its most direct institutional expression in the system of proportional representation employed in elections to Zionist and Yishuv institutions, and the distribution of scarce resources and administrative offices according to a party key determined by electoral results.

The precedence of labor over capital in the Yishuv reversed the characteristic process in Western societies. In the latter, labor arose as an organized response to the power of capital, and reflected the inability of the worker to compete against the forces of capital as an individual. There labor first attempted to combat capital in the economic sphere, to gain a greater share in distribution of the economic product. When it failed to achieve this by purely industrial and economic methods, it began to organize politically.

In the Yishuv, the party as political labor effectively preceded industrial labor, and eventually organized it into one national union—the Histadrut—that assumed responsibility for catering to all the workers' needs: employment opportunities, trade union representation, housing, education, health, culture, information, sport, and more. At the time of its establishment in 1920 by agreement of a number of parties, the Histadrut was stronger and more prestigious than any of the constituting parties. But from 1930 onward, it was effectively controlled by one party, Mapai, which won an absolute majority of votes in Histadrut elections and could thereby retain all the most important executive positions. Nevertheless, Mapai followed the party key in distributing collective resources and minor executive posts, and ensured that important collective decisions (such as defense) were fully discussed and approved in the broader representative bodies.

The Yishuv, and later the Israeli, model of party–union relations is one of competition among parties within the trade union organization, at all levels, leading to legitimate, highly centralized, and hierarchically organized party control of trade unions. Trade union leadership and trade union policies were determined and selected by parties in accordance with party criteria and interests.

Even if labor did not literally precede the existence of capital, the organization of labor preceded and outpaced that of capital. What is more, labor in the Yishuv created capital. It established a significant public capital sector to provide employment and to promote nation-building. Although private capital imports in the Yishuv exceeded those of public capital, the organizational discipline and industrial concentration of the labor economy and the public sector more than compensated for the relative economic weakness. This was further underlined by the integral connection of labor as capital with the organized strength of labor as trade union.

This developmental sequence resulted in the *politicization* of large and important sectors of society, and in labor leadership of the major institutions. Politicization meant the allocation and direction of many of the scarce resources of society according to party criteria and tests. Labor controlled and directed these processes through its leadership in the Yishuv, Zionist, and Histadrut institutions, and within labor, the major party was Mapai.

The legitimacy of the Yishuv's political institutions derived from the national struggle, and from democratic elections contested by the major parties and groups to determine the institutions' composition and leadership. There was, however, a major problem: how to make decisions binding upon an opposition minority, or upon organizations that boycotted the elections in protest. This presented considerable difficulties because of the lack of control by the Yishuv's institutions over the legitimate use of the means of coercion and violence, which in sovereign political systems is available, in the last resort, to enforce political decisions.

The political struggle for public support in the Yishuv was conducted by a multiplicity of groups, parties, and movements. The most highly organized of these, generally on the labor side of the political spectrum, created almost total social environments for their members, enclaves that were relatively autonomous spheres of action for the parties. Thus, the cost of being outside the central political institutions of the Yishuv was relatively low; to the contrary, being so conferred considerable independence and freedom of action. Groups that rejected specific decisions or policies could always withdraw, pursue counterpolicies, or undertake independent action. They could also establish their own separate bodies and institutions, not only to compete with their opponents but to challenge directly the right of the central institutions to operate on behalf of the collectivity.

No single party in the Yishuv ever received a majority in the elections, and hence the leadership of its executive and quasi-legislative institutions was always subject to formation of a coalition combining a number of parties and groups. This, in itself, made for decisions based upon wide consensus and agreement rather than on narrow majorities, and was reinforced by the voluntary nature of the Yishuv's political system. The threat of exit gave potential minorities considerable veto power. On the other hand, once decisions were made that encompassed a greater than minimum majority, they were regarded as binding upon all those who accepted them.[2]

In its main features the political system of the Yishuv incorporated many of the main features of Lijphart's consensus democracy. (Significantly, it possessed no majoritarian features at all.) Despite the lack of a formal structure and a written constitution, its open-ended, informal set of federative arrangements enabled competing groups to act together to pursue common goals, and simultaneously catered to diversity by enabling the groups to promote their own distinctive values both within their own enclaves and in society at large. In the absence of sovereignty of a state, the party, the movement, the enclave generated both primary and ultimate loyalty, and was the locus of higher authority for members than were the central political institutions. Those institutions were established and operated on the basis of agreement among the constituting parties. Their legitimacy was neither above, nor independent of, that of the parties and movements to which they owed their existence, their continued maintenance, and whatever degree of public support they enjoyed.

The political development of the Yishuv had significant implications for the transition to statehood. On the one hand, Israel had the advantage of being able to establish the new political and administrative institutions of the state on the basis of existing structures. Moreover, its leaders had gained vital political experience and had learned two important political lessons: how to exercise and share political power. Thus, they faced the task of setting up an independent political system with more than a theoretical knowledge about government and democracy.

The acquisition of sovereignty demanded that the new state develop sufficient authority, legitimacy, and capacity to govern effectively. It was not enough simply to take over and maintain existing institutions and political agreements. The political parties, movements, and sectors would have to recognize the superior authority and legitimacy of the state, assist it in developing its own independent sources of authority and legitimacy, and cede to it some of their activities and functions—all of which were potential sources of conflict because they related to political interests and ideological viewpoints. Much depended upon the parties' willingness to relinquish control over activities that gave them political advantages. Much depended, also, upon how a particular issue was affected by the beliefs of the political actors—the state and party leaders—about the desired role of the state in society. This necessitated a delineation of functions that the state should undertake and those that it should not, as well as those that might, or should, or should not, be carried out by other bodies, including parties, or party-controlled organizations.

The resolution of these questions would determine whether the new state would be neutral, that is, the extent to which the partification and politicization of society that characterized the Yishuv might be reversed. Neutrality means the removal of all partisan criteria, not just those that confer advantages on one party but those that confer advantages on all or a number of parties. The latter also infringe upon neutrality because persons without partisan affiliation are disadvantaged.[3]

We turn now to the transition process. First, to an analysis of its constitutional and political aspects—the institutional framework that was established to cope with the transfer of the formal power and authority inherent in independent statehood. Following that, to an examination of how the newly established political institutions dealt with problems of recently acquired statehood, particularly those that involved conflict with the entrenched patterns of the Yishuv.

The Transition to Independent Statehood

The formal legal basis for the establishment of the Israeli state lay in the United Nations Partition Resolution of November 29, 1947, which specified the stages and processes of transition, and laid down the major outlines of the political institutions and procedures to be included in the constitution. The resolution called for setting up a provisional council of government to act in consultation with the democratic political parties and other public organizations during the transition stage, leading to democratic elections for a constituent assembly. The latter was to elect a provisional government and draw up a constitution, *regulations for legislative elections.*

the major provisions of which were also specified. These included a "legislative body elected by universal suffrage on the basis of proportional representation, and an executive body responsible to the legislature"; and "guaranteeing all persons equal and non-discriminatory rights in civil, political, economic and religious matters and the enjoyment of human rights and fundamental freedoms, including freedom of religion, language, speech and publication, education, assembly and association."[4]

Transition to independent statehood was to have been supervised by an international implementation commission of the UN Assembly, but this did not come about due to British obstruction. Highly conscious of the historic opportunity, and apprehensive that it might slip from their grasp or be taken from them at the international level, the recognized political bodies in the Yishuv, led and directed by the political parties, quickly moved into the breach and began to prepare for the assumption of sovereignty.

On March 1 the National Council of the Jewish Community (Va'ad Leumi) decided that the elected representatives of its executive (Hanhalat Hava'ad Haleumi) and those of the Zionist executive (Hanhalat Hasochnut)[5] would jointly constitute the core of a provisional council of government. This, in turn, was empowered to co-opt delegates from groups and organizations not represented on either of the two constituent executives. Because of British objections to establishment of institutions of the Jewish state while the Mandate was still in force, the provisional council of government was renamed Moezet Ha'am (People's Council).

political parties

The composition of these bodies reflected the party distribution resulting from the Yishuv elections. On the left were Mapai, the largest party, and Mapam. To the right were the General Zionists, the Women's International Zionist Organization (WIZO), and Aliyah Hadashah (representing German immigrants). The religious sector of the population was represented by Mizrachi and Hapo'el Hamizrachi, and the Oriental communities by the Yemenite list. Not represented, because they had boycotted the previous Yishuv elections, were the ultra-Orthodox Agudat Yisrael, the Revisionists, the Sephardim, and the Communist party. The unrepresented groups were co-opted in April, thereby increasing Moezet Ha'am to thirty-seven members: Mapai, ten; General Zionists, six; Mapam, five; Mizrachi and Hapo'el Hamizrachi, five; Agudat Yisrael and Po'alei Agudat Yisrael, three; Revisionists, three; and Aliyah Hadashah, WIZO, the Sephardim, the Yemenites, and Communists, one apiece. This was the legislative body, and it was complemented by an executive of thirteen, Minhelet Ha'am (People's Administration).

The party distribution of Minhelet Ha'am did not replicate that of its parent body. It consisted of four Mapai members, two General Zionists, two Mapam, and one each from Mizrachi, Hapo'el Hamizrachi, Agudat Yisrael, the Sephardim, and Aliyah Hadashah. Thus, even before statehood, co-optation resulted in the inclusion in the executive of two groups—Agudat Yisrael and the Sephardim—that previously were outside the representative bodies of the Yishuv. On the other hand, two other such groups, the Revisionists and the Communists, were included in the legislative body but not in its executive.

leftist mapai (largest) mapam

communists were not included

Right zionist Giral zionist Women's InitNl Zionist Organization Aliyah hadashah

There was never any question about the exclusion of the Communists, but whether to include the Revisionists was the subject of intense discussion. The Revisionist party was not acceptable to the Left because of its ideological and organizational associations with the two separatist military organizations, the Irgun Zvai Leumi (Ezel) and the Lohamei Herut Yisrael (Lehi), that had refused to accept the collective authority and self-discipline of the Yishuv's central institutions, and had carried on an independent armed struggle against the British in defiance of the agreed policies of those institutions. (In fact, as later events made clear, the Revisionists were not held in high regard by the Ezel and the Lehi, and relations between them were rather strained.)

The discussions about inclusion of the Revisionists in Moezet Ha'am and Minhelet Ha'am paralleled negotiations between the Haganah and the Ezel over unification of the Jewish defense and fighting forces under the command of the new bodies, and the dissolution of separatist military formations. For both sides, the decision about inclusion in the new political bodies hinged upon agreement on the military question.

Haganah Kibbutzim

For the political and military leaders of the Yishuv who commanded the Haganah, agreement would indicate renunciation of the path of separatism and willingness to accept the political authority of the Yishuv's executive bodies, particularly on the crucial question of military policy. For the Ezel, agreement with the Haganah would indicate a measure of acceptance, after years of having been regarded as illegal terrorists by the representatives of the majority of the Yishuv.   צ people's administration

The membership of Minhelet Ha'am was discussed at a meeting of the Zionist executive on March 5, 1948. The Mizrachi delegates formally suggested that a place be given to a representative of the Revisionists. This was rejected by Ben-Gurion because the Revisionists were the mother party of the Ezel, and their presence in the future Provisional Government would make constant political crisis and conflict unavoidable in light of sharp political and ideological differences. This would seriously damage the new state's chances of gaining badly needed international support and recognition.[6]

Initial rejection was not regarded as final by the Revisionists or by the proponents of their inclusion. It was made final and mutual by the Revisionists. Their Central Committee discussed participation in Moezet Ha'am and Minhelet Ha'am but was divided. It was opposed by those who regarded it as tantamount to acceptance of partition, which the Revisionists vehemently rejected. The Revisionists finally decided to participate in Moezet Ha'am, and negotiated successfully to increase their membership from two to three. On the other hand, they maintained their refusal to participate in Minhelet Ha'am, the future Provisional Government, because its very basis until future elections was the UN Partition Resolution.[7]

The UN resolution specified that the Jewish state be established no later than October 1, 1948, and outlined specific transition steps, which necessitated full cooperation by Britain and international supervision. Britain refused to play the role allotted to it, and serious reservations were expressed at the UN about the desirability of proceeding with the plan for partition. Fear that the international doubts and hesitations might permanently prevent establishment of the Jewish state impelled the Jewish political leadership to take the initiative and press on.

On April 12 the Zionist General Council (Hava'ad Hapo'el Hazioni) announced that the Jewish state would be declared immediately upon termination of the British Mandate on May 15. With the fundamental substantive decision already made, Moezet Ha'am and Minhelet Ha'am, despite some last-minute second thoughts, turned their attention to the actual process of transition, the declaration of the state, and the guidelines for its government and administration.

Establishing the State: May 1948–January 1949

The formal declaration establishing the State of Israel was made on May 14, 1948, at a meeting of Moezet Ha'am, and was immediately followed by a proclamation setting forth the basic guidelines of government. Together, the declaration and the proclamation incorporated the main institutional outlines of the future Israeli political system. They also reflected, and gave formal expression to, agreements and understandings about many of its fundamental values that had already been arrived at.

Moezet Ha'am became the Provisional State Council (Moezet Hamedinah Hazemanit), and Minhelet Ha'am, the Provisional Government (Hamemshalah Hazemanit). Political decision making in the new state was made the joint responsibility of the two bodies, with the former designated as the legislative body, and the latter as the executive body. Parliamentary government, the fusion of legislative and executive power, was thus in broad outline instituted from the outset. This was made more patent by the Law and Administration Ordinance 1948, which provided that the "Provisional Government will act in accordance with the policy lines drawn up by the Provisional State Council, execute its decisions, report on its activities, and be responsible to it for its activities."[8]

In actuality, the Provisional Government had neither been chosen by the Provisional State Council nor approved by it. Both derived their authority from the political institutions of the Yishuv, and were created simultaneously by the declaration. The council, therefore, could neither express confidence in, nor withdraw its confidence from, the Provisional Government. In this respect, it departed from the conventional pattern of parliamentary government, in which the executive derives its authority directly from the legislature, is responsible to it, and is dependent on its confidence.

The declaration proclaimed Israel to be a Jewish state, and indicated that it was to function according to democratic principles, maintaining fundamental rights and freedoms, and guaranteeing basic equalities. Although an early draft of the declaration explicitly stated that "the Jewish state will be democratic,"[9] the final version put it more generally:

The State of Israel will be open to the immigration of Jews from all countries of their dispersion, will promote the development of the country for the benefit of all its inhabitants; will be based on the precepts of liberty, justice and peace taught by the Hebrew Prophets; will uphold the full social and political equality of all its citizens, without distinction of race, creed or sex; will guarantee full freedom of conscience, worship, education and culture; . . . and will dedicate itself to the principles of the Charter of the United Nations.

Legislative and executive authority was given to these institutions until appropriate units to exercise such authority were established by the Constituent Assembly (Asefah Mekhonenet), which was to be elected by October 1. The declaration contained no guidelines for the constitution or for elections, other than the general values and criteria cited above; consequently, guidelines were formulated by the Provisional State Council and the Provisional Government.

Immediately following the UN resolution of November 1947, the Jewish Agency had begun formal preparation of a draft constitution. The task was continued by the Constitution Committee of the Provisional State Council chaired by Z. Warhaftig (Mizrachi), whose members represented all the major parties, including the Revisionists and the Communists. The committee held a general debate on basic issues of constitutional significance and included a draft constitution in its report. Writing the constitution itself was left to the Constituent Assembly.

The matter of elections could not be left to the Constituent Assembly, for without them there would be no Constituent Assembly. The timetable laid down in the declaration was not met because of the war. Not until October 28, 1948, did the Provisional State Council consider a report from its previously established Elections Committee, chaired by David Bar-Rav-Hai (Mapai).

The committee was conscious of the historical uniqueness of its role in paving the way for the Constituent Assembly, which would be a major turning point for the nation and the state, the culmination of the process of becoming, the step symbolizing the transition to normality. It was also aware that it did not function in a vacuum but was heir to an existing and widely accepted tradition of democratic institutional politics as practiced in Zionist and Yishuv institutions. Under the circumstances, the committee did not decide upon the electoral provisions of the future constitution but limited itself to formulating electoral regulations for the Constituent Assembly. It thereby avoided fundamental questions of principle, and set as its goal making speedy elections technically possible.

The committee considered a number of electoral systems: single-member constituencies based on the majority principle; multimember constituencies with proportional representation; and national-constituency proportional representation. The last was preferred, and was accepted by the Provisional State Council because it was familiar, having been employed in Zionist and Yishuv elections. It would enable early elections with a minimum of controversy, the prime objective.

Four proposals were submitted for the number of members of the Constituent Assembly; 71, for reasons of efficiency; 101; 171, to permit wide representation of organizations and views; and the number chosen, 120. It was a compromise between the two extremes that carried the imprimatur of tradition as well: it was the number of members of the Knesset Gedolah in ancient times.[10]

The elections were set for January 25, 1949. Just prior to that date, the Provisional State Council considered the Constituent Assembly's term of office and its constitutional functions. Influenced by the Provisional Government, the council voted not to set any limits on the term of office or to fix a deadline for approval of the constitution, on the grounds that it was inappropriate for a nonelected body to constrain the first democratically elected legislature. The council also decided that to avoid a hiatus in government and executive authority, the Provisional Government would continue in its transitional capacity until the Constituent Assembly elected a new government.[11]

Coping with Statehood

Establishment of the formal operational framework was accompanied by political disagreements and conflicts that raised some of the characteristic problems of new states: capacity, inclusiveness; identity; legitimacy; and effectiveness. In the long run, as the experience of other new states confirms, these are the acid test for newly independent states because failure to cope with them can lead to the breakdown of democratic constitutional structures.[12]

Capacity

Political independence involves a vast expansion in the sources of political power available for conversion into a unified national authority structure. Areas of political and societal responsibility, such as the economy, defense, foreign affairs, education, health and welfare, the judiciary, and police power, become the province of the newly independent sovereign government. Their management necessitates the establishment and integration of differentiated structures.

Exercising independent and sovereign political authority for the first time means adaptation to an unaccustomed role, often after years of opposition to colonial rule. Crucial to adaptation is the bringing into being of a single, national authority and the disbanding of the competing political structures claiming the right to use violence or physical coercion. The government of a newly independent state must ensure that it remains the sole possessor and user of legitimate coercive power.

Particularly important in the establishment and integration of the political structures are the constitutional arrangements and practices that govern relations among them, their norms of behavior, and their relations with society at large. In older political systems, these have usually been settled and generally are not the subjects of fundamental conflict. The problem for the new state is not that of a challenge to the constitution but the absence of a constitution— the need to put a constitution in place, often under conditions of conflict and disagreement.

Inclusiveness

Newly independent states often face the problem of inclusiveness of participation, that is, the ability of the political structures to include all potential political actors. The leaders who accede to power do not always represent the entire population. Political and ideological opposition to the nationalist struggle for independence and its leaders may result in nonparticipation, refusal to cooperate, or active opposition and the pursuit of a separate struggle for independence by rival nationalist elites. In each case, they will be outside the circle of those who led the struggle for independence and consequently gained power. Failure to include all members of the population within the political system is glaring from a democratic point of view, and undermines legitimacy. Rival nationalist elites face the option of either continuing to challenge and oppose the system as a whole, or of accepting it and competing with other elites according to the new rules, which may mean disbanding their existing organizational forms.

Identity

The problem of identity in new states arises from the need of the new political system and its participants to define what and who they are, and how they differ from other systems and their participants. Significant identity problems commonly arise from sharply divided sentiments about territory, and the relationship between geography and nationality. At base, national identity (and nation-building) rest upon acceptance by the inhabitants of a state's geographic boundaries of shared ultimate ties.

Identity remains a problem if significant groups refuse to associate with the governing system, or when a majority does not accept minority group claims to identification with the system. Similarly, disagreements over the rightful territorial boundaries of the political community may engender identity problems.

Ethnic, religious, or national identity divisions limit the effectiveness of the state as a political unit if they are accorded higher loyalty than is the new state. This can be minimized by incorporation or by accommodation based upon the acceptance of plural identities.

Legitimacy

Legitimacy involves the recognition and acceptance of the authority exercised by the various political structures. It emanates from the population and derives from the population's views as to what is right, appropriate, and acceptable. In newly independent states, there is a particular need to develop the legitimacy of the constitutional structure, and the claims to leadership of those in authority. Failure to do so is almost certain to lead to crisis and violent regime change.

Legitimacy will be absent if the basis of the claim of governmental leaders to authority is not accepted by the public or if it is challenged by other sources of authority. An erosion of legitimacy is also likely following a failure of ideological belief, when the political leadership's claims to authority based on connections with the past, or on promises of a new world, are rejected.

Effectiveness

New systems of government must also survive the test of effectiveness. Although legitimacy may be gained initially by achievement of independence, to be lasting, it must be converted into popular support for the regime. But popular support may evaporate if the system cannot "deliver the goods," rule effectively, or satisfy public demands and interest claims. Effectiveness thus depends greatly upon establishment of suitable structures to deal with these problems.

Challenges to Capacity: Developing and Exercising State Power

The capacity of the political system to cope with the expansion of political power, and of the constituted authority to gain and use force legitimately were tested in a number of ways. At issue was the creation of an efficient executive power that could operate decisively. The question was how political power could be concentrated and exercised by the state. This was particularly acute in view of the wide distribution of political power in the Yishuv among the various political forces, which limited the authority of the central federative structures.

The actual process of transition to independence served to facilitate the development of capacity in a manner that suggests that the political leadership was aware of its importance. Independence was accepted by the collectivity, organized in its centralized decision-making bodies, and not by a single elite, group, or party. Moreover, the concentration of political power occurred through direct transfer of authority from centralized national bodies (whatever their limitations) to a single authority that embodied the newly gained sovereignty and political independence.

The political parties and movements entered the state with direct and indirect responsibility for a wide range of societal roles. Hence, the nature and extent of the societal roles to be retained or undertaken by the parties and movements in the new state needed to be authoritatively decided in the relevant state institutions. So, too, was it necessary to determine the degree of government's involvement in society—the limits to its formal authority, and that of its agencies and instrumentalities.

Aspects of this authority could be conferred on or delegated to nongovernmental bodies, and conversely, societal roles and functions could be taken over or removed from nongovernmental bodies. But these were all matters of partisan disagreement that needed to be resolved by authoritative political decisions. The nongovernmental bodies entered the state without formal powers or constitutional rights beyond those enjoyed by all citizens. The societal roles they retained or performed had now become contingent upon the political process and the balance of political forces.

Despite the elments of continuity, it was widely believed that a fundamental break with the past had occurred. The granting of independence and sovereignty constituted a political revolution with regard to Jewish political power. Although everything seemed the same, in fact, everything was different. The state, its institutions, and its symbols were enveloped in awe and reverence, and a seemingly unbounded willingness on the part of most citizens to accord them loyalty and obedience. This was reinforced by the feeling that the course of Jewish history had been changed fundamentally, and that those who participated in this change or witnessed it were privileged as had been no other Jewish generation.

At a more mundane level, capacity was demonstrated in the setting up of the governmental administration to take over the functions vacated by the Mandate, as well as those that it had not fulfilled. Preparation had begun after the UN resolution, so when the Mandate ended, offices were soon operational. Foreign relations were conducted, war was waged successfully, and responsibility was taken for the whole range of economic and social functions.

The Ezel and the Altalena Affair

A fundamental test of the capacity of the new state to exercise sovereign political power occurred over the *Altalena*, and the disbanding of the Ezel as an autonomous military organization. At stake was the government's capacity to establish and institutionalize the sole and legitimate control of the use of force by constituted political authority. Effectively, the Ezel was involved in an attempt to renegotiate the terms and conditions of its participation in the state, after it had been established, even to the extent of appearing to threaten secession.

The Revisionists, as we noted, had made their participation in Moezet Ha'am conditional upon the outcome of negotiations between the Haganah and the Ezel for incorporation of the latter into the armed forces of the future state. The Ezel agreed to cooperate but refused to disband its separate organization until after the state was declared. Mapai, Mapam, and Aliyah Hadashah opposed acceptance of this accord, but it was approved by the Zionist General Council with a majority made up of the General Zionists, Revisionists, Mizrachi, and Hap'oel Hamizrachi.[13]

On May 26, 1948, the Provisional Government established the Israel Defense Forces (IDF, also known by the Hebrew acronym Zahal), declared a general mobilization, and prohibited the establishment or continued existence of any other armed force. The Lehi immediately declared that it was disbanding and that its members would join the IDF as individuals. The Ezel, on the other hand, continued to negotiate. On June 3 agreement was reached between Yisrael Galili, representing the Provisional Government, and Menahem Begin, the Ezel commander. Under its terms, the Ezel command would of its own free will cease to exist or operate in the State of Israel and in the areas under the territorial control of the government of Israel. Ezel members would join the IDF collectively in distinct groups as part of larger military formations on the various fronts, at the direction of the army authorities. A temporary staff of Ezel officers was to be set up within the framework of the General Staff to speed up the mobilization of Ezel members into the IDF. The Ezel undertook to hand over all its arms and equipment to the latter, to refrain from separate purchasing activities, and to make its contacts available to the IDF.

In the Ezel's view, the agreement accepted the separate maintenance of its fighting units in Jerusalem, which had not been liberated, and was not under control of the Provisional Government. Although the latter disagreed with this interpretation, conditions in besieged and beleaguered Jerusalem facilitated the de facto presence there of the Ezel and Lehi forces. Neither did the Provisional Government seek to raise the question of Jerusalem, which under the UN resolution was to be internationalized and not under Israeli sovereignty.[14]

The agreement was put to the test by the approach of the *Altalena*, carrying arms purchased by the Ezel in Europe. As it sailed toward Israel, the Ezel leadership negotiated with the Provisional Government about the unloading and distribution of the arms. At first the Ezel agreed to hand over the weapons to the Provisional Government, but subsequently it sought to renegotiate the terms of the agreement to gain recognition of its role in their procurement. The Ezel proposed that its members be permitted to participate in the unloading of the arms, 20 percent of which would then be distributed to the Ezel forces in Jerusalem, and the balance to its units in the IDF. When the proposals were rejected, it dug in with regard to the unloading. But no agreement was reached, because the Ezel would not accept the Provisional Government's claim to undivided authority and control over the unloading, storing, and distribution of the weapons.

The Ezel defied the government and twice attempted to unload the vessel by itself, first at Kfar Vitkin and later at Tel Aviv. It ordered its members to leave their army units to assist, which many of them did. The Provisional Government demanded that the Ezel surrender the arms, and used force when met with noncompliance; there was a short battle at Kfar Vitkin and the ship was blown up by artillery shells at Tel Aviv, with loss of life on both occasions.[15]

This chain of events dramatically signified the transition to the use of state power that had been absent in the Yishuv. For the government, the sovereign authority of the state and its capacity to exercise political power and to govern were under challenge, and it reacted accordingly. It refused to recognize the right of any armed organization to negotiate with it as an equal, and insisted that its authority be accepted and respected.

Although at various stages of the negotiations some members of the Provisional Government had brought pressure to bear to reach a compromise solution in the spirit of the political arrangements of the Yishuv, when these came to nought the Provisional Government unanimously decided to use force if necessary in order to have its authority accepted. It treated the actions of the Ezel as a threat to its authority and a rebellion, and as an attempt to maintain an army within an army. The majority in the Provisional Government, particularly its labor component, believed that the Ezel wanted the arms to bolster its position as an independent political authority in Jerusalem, and later to use this position as a means of pressuring the government to make concessions to the Ezel's political viewpoint.[16] As David Ben-Gurion put it to the Provisional Government, "There will not be two states and there will not be two armies, and Mr. Begin will not do as he pleases. We must decide whether to hand over the government to Begin—or to tell him to stop his secessionist actions."[17]

The Ezel's immediate response was to declare that it no longer recognized the authority of the Provisional Government, which was controlled by a "crazy dictator and a spiritual pigmy." It demanded that this government of "criminals, tyrants, traitors and fraticidal murderers" be tried by the people. Ezel soldiers could no long serve in an army that received its orders from such a government, and the previous instruction to them to enlist and swear allegiance to the government was rescinded. They would rather be imprisoned in the concentration camps, which the Ezel was sure the crazy dictator maintained. Still, Ezel soldiers were ordered not to use arms against their Jewish brethren under any conditions because of the war against the Arabs.[18]

Although many Ezel soldiers involved in these events were arrested, the organization still retained its independent existence in Jerusalem. This issue became particularly acute when the Provisional Government decided on July 25, 1948, to apply Israeli law in Jerusalem, without incorporating the territory within Israel, and thereby deprived the Ezel of whatever legal justification it could adduce in support of its position. The Provisional Government continued to demand that the Ezel disband and accept its authority unconditionally.

Under pressure from the General Zionists and the religious parties, who had earlier tried to get the government and the Ezel to settle their differences by negotiation, and despite Ben-Gurion's opposition and belief that it was futile, the Provisional Government nevertheless established a ministerial committee of seven (all from these parties). Because they were not identified with the hard-line position of Ben-Gurion and the parties of the Left, they believed that they could resolve matters and iron out relations with the Ezel.

In light of his future treatment of the Ezel's successor organization, Ben-Gurion's attitude toward the Ezel during this period is instructive. Its continued existence undeground did damage but did not represent a great danger. "If it rebels it will be repressed by force, and the Ezel is making a mistake in judgement if it believes that those opposing it are 'weak liberals.'" Ben-Gurion and his supporters did not seek conflict and were prepared to allow the committee to try to negotiate a settlement, even though they did not believe in its chances. If, on the other hand, it proved necessary, the Ezel "would be put down by force, never to raise its head again."[19]

Negotiations between the ministerial committee and the Ezel dragged on but did not produce an acceptable compromise. However, immediately after UN mediator Count Folke Bernadotte was assassinated by the Lehi in Jerusalem in September 1948, the Provisional Government seized the initiative. It formally notified the Ezel that the laws of the state apply in Jerusalem, instructed the IDF to enforce them, and authorized it to use all necessary force to do so. On the instructions of the government, the General Staff issued the Ezel an ultimatum to disband, which was accepted by the Ezel commander just a few hours before it was due to take effect. With acceptance of the ultimatum, the Ezel effectively ceased to exist in Israel, and shortly afterward disbanded overseas.[20] The Ezel was disbanded because its continued existence as an armed underground alongside the IDF directly challenged the government's sole control over the legitimate use of force, and thereby diminished the capacity of the political system to harness and use political power for collective purposes.

Inclusiveness: Democracy and Pragmatism

In keeping with democratic values, prior to establishment of the state, a concerted effort was made by the political leadership to maximize inclusiveness. In the transition from a voluntary to a sovereign political system, the effort also contributed to legitimacy and effectiveness. These considerations were given great weight by the war, which made it desirable to maximize internal cooperation and unity.

A consensual approach to inclusiveness was prominent in the negotiated agreements between the major political groups about the new institutional structures. Groups that stood outside the institutions heading the negotiations were invited to participate despite their past history of separation, ideological opposition, and boycott. The invitation and its acceptance indicate a recognition by all concerned that the separatism that was possible under the voluntary arrangements of the Yishuv was no longer tenable in a state whose existence obliged all members of the population. The most striking example was the inclusion of Agudat Yisrael.

Including the Non-Zionists

Agudat Yisrael was founded in 1912 with the express goal of combating Zionism as a secular and nationalist enemy of true Orthodox Judaism, which the Aguda was pledged to promote and defend. It banned all forms of cooperation with the Zionist movement and adopted a separatist approach to all aspects of Jewish community organization and political activity, both in Europe and in Palestine. It boycotted elections to Yishuv institutions and was not represented in the Jewish Agency or the World Zionist Organization.

Agudat Yisrael did not restrict its promotion of Orthodoxy to schools, yeshivot, and synagogues. It was politically active in Europe, where it was represented in a number of parliaments. Approaching statehood forced it to rethink its separatism and its refusal to be involved with Zionists and seculatists. The question was the degree of recognition to be accorded to a Jewish and Zionist state. Was it a state like the Gentile states in which Agudat Yisrael had been active politically, or as a Jewish state, was it disqualified because it was dominated by secularist and nonbelieving Zionists, on the one hand, and in religious and theological terms represented a heretical view of Jewish redemption, on the other hand? Or put more positively, could what was rejected in the past because it implied a voluntary act of involvement be accepted because it emanated from the binding obligation and legitimate but ultimately coercive authority of a state? Moreover, there was the question of pragmatic politics: the impact upon Agudat Yisrael's institutions of continued separatism and refusal to be included in the state, particularly in light of the almost complete destruction of its major centers and sources of support in Europe during World War II.

The process of including Agudat Yisrael began in 1947 with the conclusion of an agreement between the major elements of the Zionist movement in the Jewish Agency and the Aguda. Despite the strongly held convictions of nonreligious Zionist leaders that the new state should be secular and not institutionalize Orthodox Judaism or make it the established religion, the need for maximal national unity and cooperation took precedence. The terms of the agreement were set out in a letter to the Aguda leadership from the Zionist executive and signed by Ben-Gurion as its head, by Rabbi Yehudah Leib Fishman (later Maimon) of the Mizrachi, and by General Zionist leader Yizhak Gruenbaum.

The agreement dealt with four main areas of concern: Sabbath observance; Kashrut; marriage laws; and education. It specified that in the new Jewish state the legal day of rest would be Shabbat. Food prepared for Jews in kitchens in all state institutions would be kosher. In matters of personal status—marriage and divorce—everything would be done to satisfy the religious needs of the Orthodox and to prevent the division of the Jewish people. This meant the application of Jewish religious law to everyone in matters of personal status because only this was acceptable to the Orthodox. In the sphere of education the full autonomy of the various existing streams would be recognized and maintained. There would be no infringement by the government in matters of the religious outlook and conscience of any part of the Jewish community. The right of the state to demand and supervise a program of minimal compulsory studies was accepted.[21]

The agreement guaranteed the status of religion in the future state and enabled the strictly separatist Aguda to be incorporated. It formalized and institutionalized a situation that had begun to develop in the Yishuv under the Mandate, although it went beyond it somewhat in specificity and detail. It was also of fundamental importance to the Orthodox Zionist elements, such as the Mizrachi parties, who on all these issues were in full agreement with the Aguda. Now that they were about to lose the protection of religious practice granted by the Mandate, the Orthodox, Zionist, and anti-Zionist alike were fearful that secular and nonreligious political leaders would use the political power of the majority in the new state to impose arrangements in accord with their ideological viewpoint. Instead, the secular Zionist parties and their leaders went in the opposite direction, granting the Orthodox somewhat more than they had before. This resulted mainly from the overriding need for maximal national unity in order to accomplish the huge tasks that confronted the new state. Concessions were made to gain support, particularly on a question that was of the utmost salience and intensity to the religious groups, and of less significance to the secularists.

Indeed, the outcome had an impact beyond that of the immediate issue, inclusiveness. For one thing, it settled some central aspects of the question of identity: the public character of the state. Moreover, it incorporated a fundamental element of Lijphart's model of consensus democracy—minority veto— in order to gain and ensure the political participation of all Orthodox Jews. This soon became perpetuated as "the status quo" because certain minimal undertakings and agreements effectively placed these issues permanently outside the power of the majority. The cost of weakening them was to run the risk of splitting the state and the Jewish people. The agreement became a baseline from which, for many years, change went in only one direction.

For inclusiveness to proceed smoothly, it must be mutual. It is not sufficient for the political leadership to want to include a separatist or previously excluded group; the latter must also seek incorporation. In the case of Águda, not only did it seek incorporation to promote its interests and to influence policies but—even more significant, given its history and past attitudes—many of its leaders and members were subject to the same historical processes as the rest of Jewish society in Palestine. Under the influence of the Holocaust, they had come around to the idea of an independent Jewish state. Then, when it actually arrived, they shared in the excitement and wonder. Despite their ideological position, they were swept up in a surge of fundamental national feeling and believed that they were witnesses to, and participants in, events that bordered on the miraculous.[22]

For the first few years after Israel's establishment Agudat Yisrael's commitment to, and involvement in, the state, contrasted sharply with its history of intense antagonism toward Zionism. The most outstanding expression of this sense of partnership and participation was its agreement to serve in the Provisional Government and in subsequent governmental coalitions.[23]

Including Non-Jews: The Arabs

The question of inclusiveness also arose prior to the elections to the Constituent Assembly with regard to the participation of the Arabs in Israel. As a result of the War of Independence, the Arabs in Israel in 1949 numbered about 160,000 (compared with some 750,000 in 1947), just under 15 percent of the population. (Most of the others had fled to neighboring Arab states and were mainly found in refugee camps.) Israeli decision makers were torn between the democratic goal of integrating them as citizens and the pressure to isolate and control them for security reasons, reinforced by nationalist sentiment and strong emotional antipathies.[24]

The desire to integrate the Arab citizens was given clear expression in the Declaration of Independence, in the call to "the Arab inhabitants of the State of Israel to return to the ways of peace and play their part in the development of the State, with full and equal citizenship and representation in all its bodies and institutions, provisional or permanent." The security need to isolate and control Israeli Arabs was institutionalized by subjecting them to military government, which imposed severe restrictions on their freedom of movement and economic opportunities, and placed them under surveillance and military law. In the first years of the state, the security need was also given expression in the sequestration of abandoned Arab property, which was then handed over to Jewish immigrants and agricultural settlers (later compensation was paid), and in the government's policy of seeking to keep the number of Arab citizens as low as possible by refusing to allow the return of Arabs who had fled during the war, except for qualifiers under a policy of family reunion (although it was prepared to take in larger numbers as part of a peace treaty). During and immediately after the hostilities many refugees sought to return by slipping across the border, which was treated as illegal infiltration, and if caught, they were sent back.

Just before the 1949 elections Ben-Gurion assembled a group of advisers on Arab affairs (not all of whom were Mapai leaders and members) to discuss "Was it better that the Arabs participate or not?" that is, whether there was any justification to deprive them of their right as citizens to vote. Second, "If they were to participate, was an Arab, Jewish, or mixed list desirable?" Some of the advisers argued that it would be safer if the Arabs did not participate in the elections. The war had not yet ended, it was not clear whether those who remained would stay, and if they stayed whether they would be loyal to the state. To permit the Arabs to participate in the elections under these conditions was undesirable because it would heighten their sense of citizenship and lead to further demands for the return of property, the right of return for those who had left, and for general freedom of movement. To prevent this, one suggestion was to tighten the restrictions of the military government. Another suggestion was to minimize the influence of Arab participation, if it proved to be unavoidable, through splitting the Arab vote by establishing a number of Arab lists, none of which would gain enough votes to ensure representation.

Other advisers took the pragmatic view that to prevent Arab participation was impractical, for election preparations had already begun, and many of the parties including Mapai, the Communists, Mapam, and even Herut, had campaigned among them. Even if the Arabs did not vote, there was no way to prevent the parties from building political and ideological support among them. So as not to hand the Arabs over to other parties, particularly the Communists, it was desirable to build upon earlier trade union cooperation by creating partners and allies among them in the form of a Mapai-affiliated list, or a number of Mapai-affiliated lists to reflect the interests of the various subgroups within the Arab population. It was also argued that it would be beneficial to have Arabs in areas in which Jewish control was tenuous, such as Galilee, campaigning to leave such areas under Israel control.

In response to the assertion that ideological support could be gained among the Arabs, the most outspoken opponent of Arab participation on security grounds declared that "the Arabs are like matter in the hands of the Creator. This is not a question of ideology—but rather, who is the master." In his view, the appropriate action was to stifle Arab political participation by tightening military restrictions, but those in favor of Arab participation, as we shall see, recognized that their control of the political and administrative structures to which the Arab citizens were beholden could produce partisan gains for Mapai.

Ben-Gurion believed that there were two binding considerations. The first was the ideal of inclusiveness and integration: the Arabs should not be deprived of their right to vote because neither the character of the state as a whole nor its boundaries had been determined, and "we must not begin with national discrimination." The second was pragmatic: Arabs would, in any event, be elected on the Communist list by Jewish voters, and this internal and external danger could not be met by splitting the Arab vote.

The decision made followed Ben-Gurion's position and reflected both the principled desire to include Arabs and the pragmatic possibility of benefiting politically from the high degree of administrative control; in short, a policy that combined the alternatives of integration and isolation. Arabs were not to be denied the right to vote, subject to a population census and to safeguards against legalizing infiltration through the franchise. It was also decided to include on the Mapai list at least one Arab (who was not to be bound by party discipline on the refugee question), and to establish two Mapai-affiliated Arab lists.[25]

The decision set the pattern for the whole of the founding period, and what is more, as a political strategy, paid dividends for Mapai: Mapai and its affiliated lists received 61.3 percent of the votes in Arab districts in 1949, and two-thirds of the votes in 1951. After this, the pro-Mapai Arab vote fell steadily, but even toward the end of the founding period, in the 1965 elections, which were the last held under military government, it still garnered just over half of the votes.[26]

Shaping Identity: What Is a Jewish State?

The democratic and liberal identity of the Israel republic, laid down in the declaration establishing the state, was an important element in ensuring that all groups were included and involved in the political system. What this entailed seemed to be clearly understood by both the political leaders and the populace. The Jewish identity of the state, on the other hand, was firmly entrenched in the declaration, but its meaning and nature were subject to considerable disagreement and conflict. That Israel was to be a Jewish state was widely accepted, but there were very divergent views as to what this meant.

Some of the differing views were apparent in the agreement between the Zionist executive and the leadership of the Aguda about the place of religion in the society. They were partly settled by acceptance of the notion that in important areas of public and private life the Jewish nature of the state meant acceptance of Jewish religious law as the authoritative and binding criterion.

Who was to interpret this law, who was to apply it, who was to be responsible for maintaining these standards, to whom did they apply, and who would control the administration of services where freedom of choice was guaranteed were questions left in abeyance.

Identity proved contentious in the drafting of the declaration establishing the state. In view of its historical importance and significance for all Jews, not just those living in Palestine, the religious parties demanded explicit reference to the Jewish people's faith and trust in God, and their gratitude for the reestablishment of Jewish statehood. The nonreligious, secularist Zionist leaders, mainly on the left, opposed an explicit reference to God as offensive to their consciences. A compromise formula expressed trust in the "Rock of Israel." Because this was an accepted synonym for God in prayer and elsewhere, it met the needs of the religious parties. In not making explicit reference to the deity, the declaration satisfied the nonreligious. Yet at the last moment, even this seemed to be going too far for the secular leaders. Aharon Zisling of Mapam suggested that it be removed because it imposed an expression of faith upon those who did not believe.

Ben-Gurion took a middle position. While publicly expressing personal identification with Zisling's point of view, he argued strongly for retaining the formula, which he regarded as a fine example of compromise based on Jewish comradeship: "We must be extremely careful not to sharpen such disagreements" on the threshold of independence. He knew exactly the meaning of the term at issue for the religious parties but believed that he could, with a clear conscience, justify to the nonreligious his signature on a document in which it appeared. He went out of his way to ensure that the drafting committee received a clear directive from Minhelet Ha'am that the phrase be retained in the final draft.[27]

Undermining Legitimacy: The Ezel After Altalena

The process by which the decision to declare independence was made, the inclusion of all groups in the society that wished to participate, the continuity with the familiar institutions and practices of the Yishuv, the support of world Jewry and its institutions, and the imprimatur of the UN resolution, all contributed to the legitimacy of the new state and its provisional institutions.

The only really serious challenge to that legitimacy came from the ranks of the Ezel after the *Altalena* incident. In its public response, the Ezel accused the Provisional Government of crimes against the people and against humanity, and of being set upon a path of terror and mass murder. Consequently, "Ezel soldiers no longer recognize the Provisional Government, and demand that it be brought to trial by the people: in an army that is commanded by such a government, Ezel soldiers are unable to serve." The Ezel canceled its order to its members to enlist in the IDF and to swear allegiance to the government. Ezel soldiers, on the other hand, were given unconditional instructions not to resort to arms within the territory of the State of Israel.[28]

The Ezel's challenge to the legitimacy of the Provisional Government quickly passed over. First, the Ezel accepted the directives of the authorities as enforced by the IDF. At about the same time it transformed itself into a conventional political party that contested elections and sought to gain power through the ballot box.

Thus, by January 1949 the basis had been laid for founding the political order in Israel. The formal problems of transition had been resolved, and some of the problems of independence had been overcome. By that date also, the prime test of effectiveness—defending and securing the political order from external threat—had been more than successfully passed. The War of Independence had concluded, and although the human losses were high, toward the end the army had performed with increasing efficiency and skill, and the territorial boundaries of the state had been extended far beyond those laid down in the UN resolution.

The longer-term aspect of effectiveness—the ability of the government to make decisions and implement them in dealing with the country's problems—remained unknown. In this regard much would depend upon the structures established, the processes adopted, and the goals and beliefs of the political actors. With the war concluded and the elections approaching, it was widely expected that the Israeli political order would move from the transitional phase to a more permanent phase.

Notes

1. The major work on the Yishuv as a political and social system is Dan Horowitz and Moshe Lissak, *The Origins of the Israeli Polity: Palestine Under the Mandate* (Chicago: University of Chicago Press, 1978).

2. For a formal analysis of the political institutions of the Yishuv in the context of their Zionist and British origins, and as forerunners to those of the state, see Samuel Sager, *The Parliamentary System of Israel* (Syracuse, N.Y.: Syracuse University Press, 1985), pp. 1–21.

3. Clearly, I do not define this concept as do Marxists, for whom, by way of contrast, neutrality is a question of class, not party. Consequently, the state cannot be neutral so long as it protects private property and therefore the inequality of property. It thus acts to translate economic power into political power, and protects it through maintaining law and order.

4. UN General Assembly Resolution on the Future Government of Palestine (Partition Resolution), November 29, 1947, sec. 10.

5. Strictly speaking, this is the Jewish Agency Executive.

6. David Ben-Gurion, *Yoman hamilhamah: milhemet ha'azma'ut*, 3 vols., ed. Gershon Rivlin and Elhanan Orren (Tel Aviv: Ministry of Defense Publications, 1982), 5.3.1948, p. 280, and 15.8.1948, pp. 648–49.

7. *Haaretz*, 7.3.48.

8. Law and Administration Ordinance, No. 1, 1948, para. 1, sec. 2(b).

9. See Zvi Berenson, *Megilat ha'azmaut: hazon umeziut* (Jerusalem: Ministry of Education and Culture, 1988), p. 7.

10. *Moezet Hamedinah*, 28.10.1948; Asher Zidon, *Haknesset* (Tel Aviv, 1950), pp. 40ff.

11. *Moezet Hamedinah*, 13.1.49.

12. See, for example, Leonard Binder et al., *Crises and Sequences in Political Development* (Princeton: Princeton University Press, 1971), which examines these problems in depth. My formulation of these problems is derived from their general approach, although I do not deal with all the crises they analyze, and at times the definition diverges somewhat.

13. Dubi Bergman, "'Tnu'at Haherut'—Meirgun mahteret lemiflagah politit," *Kivvunim* 21 (November 1983): 59–60. See also the references cited there. This article is based upon a masters thesis completed at Tel Aviv University.

14. Ibid., p. 58.

15. For full details of the chain of events, see Shlomo Nakdimon, *Altalena* (Jerusalem: Idanim, 1978): Uri Brenner, *Altalena: mehkar medini uzevai* (Hakibbutz Hameuhad, 1978): David Ben-Gurion, *Medinat yisrael hamehudeshet* (Tel Aviv: Am Oved, 1969), pp. 145–46, 179–91; Natan Yanai, *Mashberim politi'im be'israel* (Jerusalem: Keter, 1982), pp. 25–50.

16. The government's viewpoint was most sharply expressed by Ben-Gurion both in cabinet meetings and in public addresses, and these are amply elaborated in Ben-Gurion, *Medinat yisrael hamehudeshet.*

17. Cited by Michael Bar-Zohar, *Ben-Gurion*, 3 vols. (Tel Aviv: Am Oved, 1975–78), p. 783.

18. *Hamashkif*, 24.6.1948, p. 1.

19. Ben-Gurion, *Yoman hamilhamah*, 15.8.1948, pp. 648–49; see also Ben-Gurion, *Medinat yisrael hamehudeshet.*

20. Ben-Gurion, *Medinat yisrael hamehudeshet*, pp. 281–90; Bergman, "'Tnu'at Haherut,'" pp. 59–66.

21. Eliezer Don-Yehiya, "Pitaron ha'status quo' bithum yahasei dat u'medinah be'israel," *Medinah mimshal vihasim benleumiyyim* (Summer 1971); 100–112. The text is translated into English in Daniel Shimshoni, *Israeli Democracy: The Middle of the Journey* (New York: Free Press, 1982), p. 478.

22. See, for example, the speech of the Aguda leader and minister of social welfare, Rabbi I. M. Levin, in *Divrei Haknesset*, February 12, 1951, 1051; *Bet Yaacov*, Tishrei 5709 (1948) editorial: "The state of Israel has been resurrected supernaturally, and is built up by all sections and streams of its population from within and without. Agudat Yisrael participates in this upbuilding no less than the members of other movements and organizations"; *Hamodi'a*, 13.10.1950: "The resurrection of the Jewish state is a wondrous miracle which the leaders of the Left deny."

23. Later, as we shall see, it moved back toward its traditional position, and adopted a more separatist and critical view of participation in government, remaining outside the coalition by choice for twenty-six years.

24. See the discussion in Tom Segev, *1949: Hayisraelim harishonim* (Jerusalem: Domino Press, 1984), pp. 20–104. On policies toward the Israeli Arabs in general, see Jacob M. Landau, *The Arabs in Israel* (London: Oxford University Press, 1969); Ian Lustick, *Arabs in the Jewish State* (Austin: University of Texas Press, 1980).

25. The discussion is reported in Ben-Gurion, *Yoman hamilhamah*, 18.12.1948, pp. 882–84. All the direct citations are to be found there.

26. From table in *Encyclopedia Judaica* (Jerusalem: Keter, 1972), 1031.

27. *Minhelet Ha'am*, 13.5.1948.

28. Cited in Bar-Zohar, *Ben-Gurion*, p. 794.

3

Founding Democratic Political Structures

The Structures of Democracy

As we noted in chapter 1, the basic principle of the majoritarian (or Westminster) model of democracy is to facilitate and enhance rule by majority; that of the consensus model is to restrain and limit bare majority rule. The structures of Israeli democracy established during the founding period produced a hybrid of these opposing principles, with considerable inbuilt tension between them.

With one major exception, all the *structural* choices made in founding the political order in Israel were majoritarian. However, they were introduced into an existing social and political reality that exhibited some of the key elements of the consensus model, such as multidimensional social and issue cleavages, and multipartyism. The only structural element of consensus democracy introduced into the system was proportional representation (PR). PR is not necessarily a majority-restraining device because in principle it does not itself preclude achievement of an electoral majority. (In the Histadrut, Mapai and its successor parties consistently attained an absolute majority despite PR.) In practice, though, the use of PR in national elections with a gamut of political views and issues and extreme multipartyism makes a single-party majority highly unlikely. To that extent the fourth key consensus structure present in Israeli democracy since the outset—coalition cabinets—was not a matter of choice but political necessity. Unlike pure consensus democracies, Israeli democracy has no formal rules or agreed practices that make coalitions mandatory or specify their composition.

The inbuilt tension between the majoritarian and consensus principles was strikingly apparent in the failure to agree on a written constitution. This was, of course, contrary to the express provisions of the UN resolution, and of the Declaration of Independence. The substantive issue, however, was not whether the constitution should be written or unwritten but whether there were to be *formal* structural restraints upon rule by simple majority by giving institutionalized voice and representation to specific minorities and diverse interests, as in the consensus model.

30

The issue could not really be avoided because a formal written constitution would need to reflect agreements on legitimacy and identity, institutional guarantees of democracy, the structures of government and their respective powers, and limitations on government vis-à-vis the citizens, such as a bill of rights. It would authoritatively settle the question of the power of the majority, and the extent to which it would be limited, restrained, or dispersed. As we shall see, the debate over a constitution did not proceed very far. It foundered almost immediately due to intense disagreement over its very legitimacy, and over the identity and character of the state to which it was intended to give expression.

Paradoxically, while the process of deciding not to adopt a formal written constitution was the epitome of consensus decision making—the restraint in not using majority power to impose such a constitution and the specific concern to cater to the minority—the long-term impact of the decision was majoritarian. It left the political system without explicit restraints upon the power of the parliamentary majority, and cleared the way for the initial incorporation of majoritarian principles by means of regular legislative acts. These were at first thought to be temporary and transitory measures, but somewhat later, when it became clear that they were likely to last much longer, they were given special status as Basic Laws. In a few instances, as we shall see, amending them needed special parliamentary majorities. The net effect was that both rule by majority and limitations on its power rested on political, not constitutional, foundations. However effective these limitations were, they would always be subject to changes in the balance of political forces and dependent upon the partisan interests of the political actors.

The adoption of a formal written constitution could be delayed indefinitely, but other decisions could not. Choices had to be made and alternatives selected to enable the new state to function. Under these conditions, the founding of the political order was conducted in a piecemeal manner, never extending beyond urgent institutional requirements. Still, the institutions and processes thus established were not improvisations or radical political innovations derived from other political systems or theoretical treatises. To speed up acceptance, where possible the general tendency was to build upon or continue the familiar institutional patterns and practices of the Yishuv, with one or two major exceptions, for which the Westminster system served as the model.

We have already noted how these considerations affected the democratic elections that brought the provisional period to an end. The pressure of problems and events prevented anything more than a cursory consideration of possible alternatives, and led to the speedy decision to retain the familiar system of PR. Yet nothing proved to be more permanent or critical for the future operation of the Israeli political system than these "temporary" institutional choices and decisions. Even though they were hastily adopted at the beginning of the founding period, they subsequently underwent little change. For example, initial decisions were made about the form of the electoral system, the number of legislative bodies, the powers of the legislature, the location and type of executive authority, and the role of the judiciary in the political process. Although technically necessary to make the system opera-

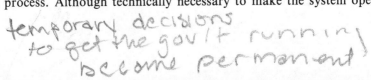

tional, they were, at the same time, of the utmost long-term substantive significance because they determined how political power was exercised and structured political choices and alternatives.

The Transition Law

[handwritten marginal note: majoritarian principles]

[handwritten marginal note: defined powers & functions of the major structures]

The Transition Law of 1949 provides a striking example of the permanence of the temporary and the critical significance of the transitory in the adoption of majoritarian principles. Immediately following its election, the Constituent Assembly took up the pressing institutional questions. In accordance with expectations, the first item was the draft constitution embodied in the report of the Constitution Committee of the Provisional State Council. But political realities foiled the intention that the Constituent Assembly's only business prior to its dissolution would be adoption of a constitution. Government and administration had to be maintained even though there was no formal constitution, and legislative and executive bodies could not wait for it to be passed. Moreover, significant opposition to a formal constitution had developed, and it became increasingly clear that drafting and passing a constitution would be a long and difficult process, and might never reach a conclusion. Interim arrangements were needed to carry on the basic political functions; a government had to be constituted and the structures through which it operated had to be established and their powers defined.

On February 16, 1949, the Constituent Assembly passed the Transition Law, which provided the legal basis for the government to carry on in the interim. It defined and clarified the powers and functions of the major structures in the political system: the legislature, the executive, and the presidency. Despite the speed with which the law passed and its temporary nature, its provisions have been subsumed in the Basic Laws and hence still determine how the political system operates in its most distinctive and characteristic elements. For this reason it is sometimes known as the Small Constitution.

The Transition Law stipulated that the legislature would be called the Knesset, and the Constituent Assembly was renamed the First Knesset, thus transforming it into a regular legislature. It was the first formal indication that the constitutional issue might not be resolved quickly, and that in any event new elections would reproduce the same distribution of public support. The law did not fix the term of the First Knesset, provide a method for its dissolution, or a method for the calling of new elections, which were left for the formal constitution. Subsequent amendments to the Transition Law defined the rights, duties, privileges, and immunities of Knesset members.

The Presidency *[handwritten note: mainly ceremonial role.]*

The precise provisions relating to the duties and powers of the president suggest that the leading political figures had clear ideas about his mainly ceremonial role. His political power was extremely limited. He was to be chosen by the Knesset in secret ballot, needing an absolute majority of all Knesset members on the first and second ballots, and an absolute majority of those present on the third ballot. His term was set to coincide with that of the First Knesset plus an additional three months from the date of assembly of the Second Knesset.

The president's functions were to include the signing of laws and treaties, appointment of diplomats, acceptance of credentials of diplomats, and granting of pardon. His major political role would be to set into motion the process of forming a government; after consulting with the representatives of the parties in the Knesset, he would commission one of them to form a government. The president was given no power to veto legislation or to refuse to countersign it, to dissolve parliament, to call it into special session, or to initiate a referendum. For all intents and purposes he was cast as a symbolic figurehead with ceremonial functions, without even limited powers to intervene in the ongoing political process.

The law relating to the election of the president was elaborated in a separate law in 1951, but the functions and powers remained part of the Transition Law of 1949. The two were combined in 1964 in one of the Basic Laws, President of the State. It added a provision that enabled a majority of Knesset members to oblige the president to commission a particular member of the Knesset (MK) to form a government. This was to cover the possibility that the president would either fail or refuse to commission that particular member. It also stipulated that the MK commissioned would become prime minister, which theretofore had not been necessary. Apart from these changes the 1964 legislation added little of substance to the provisions of the 1949 law.

Legislative and Executive Powers

The Transition Law stipulated that the Provisional Government was to resign immediately after the president's election but would continue to function until a new government, consisting of the prime minister and a number of other ministers from within the Knesset or outside its ranks, was constituted by a vote of confidence. The government was also to be collectively responsible to the Knesset, but what this entailed was not spelled out.

Far-reaching changes were thus made in the practices that had characterized the Provisional Government. Previously, the legislative body could determine governmental policy and specifically require the Provisional Government to carry out its decisions. The new law made retention of office dependent upon maintaining the confidence of the legislative body. To express no confidence in the government was to compel it to resign, which gave the legislature power that it did not possess under the Provisional Government. In practice, however, under the new law the government enjoyed greater leeway to initiate and make policy, without being completely free of legislative control. In this way, some of the key elements of majoritarian democracy were introduced into the major structures of the Israeli political system. These were a parliamentary system of government with a fusion of executive and legislative powers and effective cabinet dominance; unicameralism; and parliamentary sovereignty.

Although in theory the legislature controls the cabinet because it can withdraw its confidence, in practice a cohesive cabinet backed by a parliamentary majority maintains effective dominance of the legislature. Cabinet cohesion and the concentration of executive power vary with the party composition of the cabinet majority. Both are strengthened by the existence of a single-party cabinet majority and by collective responsibility. Coalition government weakens both, but some of its effects will, under certain conditions, be alleviated by collective responsibility.

Briefly mentioned in the Transition Law, collective responsibility was spelled out in greater detail a few weeks later when the government was presented. Similarly, parliamentary sovereignty, another key element of majoritarianism, was at first implicit in the absence of formal limitations on the power of the parliamentary majority in the Transition Law. It became explicit when the Knesset refused to adopt a formal written constitution, thus leaving the Transition Law as the only relevant authority on parliamentary sovereignty.

Following the procedures laid down in the Transition Law, the Knesset elected Chaim Weizmann as the first president of Israel, and the Provisional Government duly resigned. After consulting with the political parties, Weizmann commissioned David Ben-Gurion, the leader of Mapai, the largest party in the Knesset, to form a government. At the end of three weeks of negotiations with possible coalition partners, Ben-Gurion presented his ministry and its program to the Knesset, which accepted them by a clear majority.

The procedure followed then established a constitutional and institutional pattern that still remains a central element in the Israeli political system. Particularly significant was the presentation to the Knesset of a statement of "Basic Principles," upon which the coalition partners had agreed. Because this was the first such statement and had been drawn up prior to the acceptance of clear constitutional guidelines, Ben-Gurion used the opportunity to enunciate and reinforce agreements about the general political and constitutional principles that would guide the government and the state. The "Basic Principles" had two parts: a specific government program in the areas of foreign policy, defense, immigration, economic development, education, rehabilitation of demobilized soldiers, labor regulations, and administration; this part was preceded by two paragraphs that directly addressed major constitutional questions.

Democracy and Liberties

The second paragraph of the "Basic Principles," entitled "Freedom, Equality and Democracy," declared the government's intention to pass a "law that would establish the basis for the democratic and republican form of government in the State of Israel." This was the first formal, specific declaration that Israel was to be a democracy. The rest of the paragraph was mainly a reiteration and elaboration of the relevant clauses in the Declaration of Independence. Guarantees of equality of rights without regard to nationality were specifically added to similar guarantees in regard to race and religion, and the equality of women was spelled out in greater detail. Freedom of association, speech, and written expression were made subject to the need to maintain the security, freedom, and independence of the state, and respect for the rights of others. Equality of obligation was placed alongside the equality of rights promised in the Declaration.[1]

Collective Responsibility

The first paragraph of the "Basic Principles," with which all the coalition partners had agreed, dealt with collective responsibility, and effectively established new fundamental operating rules for the government. Ministers were deemed collectively responsible for their own behavior and that of their parliamentary party in connection with the agreed-upon coalition program and future government decisions. Nevertheless, Knesset members of the coalition parties retained freedom of debate on any issue, and freedom to criticize the government if it deviated from the principles that had been set by the Knesset or the coalition.[2]

Adopted from the Westminster model, collective responsibility means that all ministers are bound by the collective decisions of the cabinet. They may disagree during cabinet discussions, but once a decision is made, they must either stick by it or resign. The doctrine of collective responsibility restricts public utterances of individual ministers to statements of, or support for, government policy. There is no warrant for criticism of government policy, other ministers, or the activities of their departments.

Collective responsibility as the fundamental operating principle of the Israeli government, made binding by law, was a striking departure from the voluntary political arrangements of the Yishuv in the majoritarian direction. The Yishuv institutions had operated on the basis of voluntary cooperation, consensus formation, and persuasion. Where this failed, members of the governing coalition had had the right to discuss publicly disagreements and differences, in the hope that they might thereby gain support for their point of view, even if it was in the minority. Collective responsibility meant withdrawal of that right and the concentration of legitimate and unchallenged executive power in the hands of the cabinet majority, irrespective of its party composition.

Ben-Gurion made acceptance of collective responsibility a central theme of the 1949 election campaign and of the coalition negotiations as part of his emphasis upon the need for government to be based upon a stable majority. A stable majority, in his view, did not necessarily mean single-party government. Because of the overriding need for national integration and political unity, Mapai would form a coalition government, even if it received an absolute majority.[3] To be effective, both forms of government needed the support of a stable majority. It was the function of collective responsibility to provide it, particularly when there were a number of parties in the coalition.

Ben-Gurion's awareness of the advantages of collective responsibility was sharpened by a frustrating and unhappy experience as prime minister in the Provisional Government. During that period the capacity of the cabinet to govern had been severely hampered by some members of the government, particularly from Mapam, who simultaneously played the role of government and opposition. As he put it: "The first condition was collective responsibility. It was clear to me, and it seems to me that it was also clear to the large majority in the state, that the pattern of rule in the Provisional Government must not recur; it is impossible to be both in government and in opposition. The government should not be made up of a federation of autonomous departments, but be based upon an agreed plan of action and mutual responsibility."[4]

The application of the principle of collective responsibility was tested twice over the next few years. In February 1950, in protest against the government's education policies in the immigrant camps, three ministers of the United Religious Front, Rabbi Yehudah Leib Maimon, Rabbi Yizhak Meir Levin, and Moshe Shapira, boycotted cabinet meetings while continuing their other ministerial activities. Ben-Gurion demanded that they attend meetings of the cabinet or resign. Despite his desire that they remain in the cabinet for reasons of national unity and political effectiveness, it was on constitutional grounds that Ben-Gurion refused to let pass such a serious breach of collective responsibility. Their behavior, he explained to the Knesset, undermined the fundamental principle upon which the government rested. There could be no collective responsibility without joint discussion; a minister who did not wish to continue to sit in the cabinet could not head his ministry.

The government as a whole, not the individual minister, bore responsibility for governmental acts. Ministers could resign if they felt that they could not continue to bear the collective responsibility of the government, but they could not be both in the government and outside it. The implications of their behavior—that the government had no recourse or sanctions to use against them—were totally unacceptable to Ben-Gurion, for they led to the untenable conclusion that a minister dissatisfied with government policy could force the government to resign, if this were the only means to remove him. But, in fact, the power to force the government to resign had been vested only in the Knesset as a whole.

The cabinet met (with the three religious ministers still boycotting its deliberations) and decided unanimously that in accordance with the principle of collective responsibility passed by the Knesset on March 10, 1949, a minister who refused to participate in cabinet sessions or to implement a government decision could not remain a member of the government or continue to run his ministry, and would be regarded as having resigned.[5] Whereupon the three ministers resumed participation in cabinet.

The second aspect of collective responsibility that was further refined in the early years concerned replacement of individual ministers due to resignation or death. Because the cabinet was collectively responsible and the Knesset's expression of confidence was given expressly to the ministers presented to it, any change in the ministerial lineup was at first interpreted as necessitating the resignation of the entire cabinet and its reconstitution according to the procedures laid down in the Transition Law. To avoid the technical and procedural complications that arose from this interpretation, the Knesset amended the Transition Law in 1952 and empowered the government to make individual changes in the cabinet on the basis of an announcement to the Knesset and its vote of approval.[6]

The first coalition encountered severe difficulties in maintaining its internal unity and stability. After a series of cabinet crises, the prime minister handed in his resignation and that of his government in February 1951, following the defeat of its education policy in the Knesset. Although a similar crisis in October 1950 had been weathered and a new government established, on this occasion the president, advised by the parties, reached the conclusion that it was impossible to reinstate stable government on the basis of the existing Knesset, and that new elections should be held. Because there were no established procedures for dissolving the Knesset, and no election law to govern voting procedures for any but the First Knesset, the Knesset had to pass legislation to dissolve itself, schedule elections, and adopt an election law.

The Knesset passed the Transition Law, Second Knesset, 1951, which not only established the procedures for the immediate transition but also introduced a degree of continuity by stipulating that where relevant, the procedures would apply to all future transitions. It set the Knesset's term at four years.

Later, an election law was passed, and this also contributed to continuity by incorporating all the major principles and procedures of the elections to the Constituent Assembly. In an attempt to limit the splintering effects of PR, it made two important innovations. One, it stipulated that a list would achieve Knesset representation only if it exceeded 1 percent of the valid votes cast, and, two, it adopted the largest remainder system for distributing remainder votes.

The Constitutional Question

The constitutional issue had direct bearing on the majoritarian and consensual character of the Israeli political structure. By and large, the absence of a formal written constitution goes hand in hand with parliamentary sovereignty as key elements of the majoritarian model, with the British example being most prominent. Conversely, written constitutions are a key element of the consensual model because they place significant formal limitations on the power of the parliamentary majority in at least three ways. The amendment of written constitutions usually involves special majorities and other more elaborate procedures that in effect constitute a minority veto. The explicit constitutional determination that certain categories of political arrangements, law, or politics are outside the scope of the regular political process puts them beyond the reach of a parliamentary majority. Judicial review takes constitutional interpretation completely out of the hands of the legislature. The limitations may be reinforced by provisions for direct democracy involving popular minorities, such as referenda.

The Transition Law established functioning parliamentary government and enabled the system to operate, even without a solution to the constitutional question. It also bought time by allowing the constitutional debate to proceed without being subject to the pressure of the need for effective institutions. Thus, in April 1949 the whole constitutional issue was referred to the Knesset's newly established Constitution, Law and Justice Committee.

The expectation that Israel would have a rigid, formal, written constitution was for the first time open to serious question. Doubts were expressed as to its advisability and desirability, but they did not gain enough support from a parliamentary majority for abandonment of the idea of a constitution. To avoid an impasse, an alternative, piecemeal approach was proposed. A series of basic laws would be introduced over time, each dealing with a separate constitutional issue, and eventually they would be consolidated into a single constitutional document. The committee remained divided after nine months of debate, and the issue was brought before the Knesset plenum in February 1950.

The debate over adoption of a rigid, formal, written constitution that would not be subject to amendment by a simple parliamentary majority took place on two levels. One was political: the relations among the political parties, and between government and opposition. The other was formal: Was there a binding legal obligation to adopt a constitution, or was it merely a popular expectation that might be delayed if it proved inconvenient?

The political level of the constitutional debate had consensual and majoritarian aspects. The parliamentary opposition pressed the consensual arguments, seeking to limit the power of the parliamentary majority by the adoption of a written constitution. Consistent with the principles of the Transition Law, the leading parties in the governmental coalition were opposed to constitutional rigidity, and saw no need for formal limitations on the power of the parliamentary majority—particularly in view of the obvious political and coalitional difficulties in achieving agreement on the substance of such limitations.

The leading proponents of limiting the power of the parliamentary majority were Mapam, on the left, and Herut, on the right. One recurrent theme was that a written and rigid constitution was needed as protection against the actions of the government, and a defense against the power of the parliamentary majority. Nahum Nir (Mapam) pointed out that the existing juridical position permitted the government to use emergency regulations to disperse the Knesset, cancel the results of the previous elections, call new elections, and have the new Knesset ratify all such acts retroactively, provided it did so within three months. Although he did not believe that the government would ever use these powers, a constitution would make this certain.

Yisrael Bar-Yehudah (Mapam) suggested that a constitution would inject stability and permanence into lawmaking, protecting it from the whims and fancies of those in power. It was also necessary in order to specify and delimit the powers of the legislative, executive, and judicial bodies. But above all, a written constitution was needed to protect the rights of citizens from legislative, executive, and judicial infringement; in short, to restrain authority.

Another Mapam leader, Meir Yaari, suggested that the government's attitude left the state's guiding principles at the mercy of some future random parliamentary majority. He attributed the government's stance to its desire to prevent the establishment of meaningful parliamentary authority over the executive.

The strongest attack upon the government's reluctance to adopt a written constitution came from Herut. Menahem Begin compared the situation in Israel with his preferred minimal "night-watchman" state, and found that the government acted like "a thief in the night," sought to expand the authority of the state bureaucracy into all areas of life, and used detectives, inspectors, policemen, and officials to deprive citizens of their freedom. A written constitution would prevent the government from doing whatever it pleased in the future and from placing itself and its parliamentary majority above the law, as it had already done.

Not adopting a constitution was further specific evidence, in Begin's view, of the government's intention to ignore the law and place itself above the expressed will of the people. It sought to ignore a direct mandate from the people, who in electing the Constituent Assembly had placed a specific obligation on all its members to adopt a constitution. The elections had been conducted on the understanding, rejected by no party, that this was to be the legislature's major function. It was therefore a breach of trust and a betrayal of the will of the people not to go ahead with a constitution. Only a referendum could discharge the government of the people's mandate and free it to act differently.

Speaking on behalf of the government, Ben-Gurion rejected these arguments vigorously. The people had not demanded or expected a constitution merely by virtue of electing the Constituent Assembly. Originally, such a body had not been decided upon by the people but by the Provisional State Council. The latter had also decided not to bind the Constituent Assembly but to allow it to choose whether to adopt a constitution or not. The assertion that the elections had made a constitution mandatory because this discussion had taken place during the election campaign was not valid. In Ben-Gurion's view, the Knesset was free to decide.

He went on to provide a classic defense of government by parliamentary majority. Freedom was not protected merely by being proclaimed in a constitution; it could be guaranteed by only one principle, the rule of law, to which everyone in the state was subject and according to which they acted. Only in a state in which there was no arbitrariness on the part of ministers, representatives, and officials would individual and collective freedom be secured. But the existence and successful application of the rule of law depended on the rule of democracy, on agreement of the people to the laws.

Democratic rule, Ben-Gurion pointed out, is the rule of the majority, its capacity to make decisions while maintaining the right of the minority to freedom of thought, opinion, and conscience; to oppose and to criticize; and to choose representatives who are subject to the will of the people and not the reverse. On the other hand, democracy does not amount to anarchy because the decision of the majority is binding and becomes the law of the land. Thus, in response to the various arguments in support of a constitution to limit and restrict the government's capacity, Ben-Gurion maintained that democratic government could not survive if it was weak, inactive, and lacked executive power, and was deprived of effective means of self defense.[7]

The religious parties were the other main opponents of a written constitution. They argued formally, but at the level of highest principle, against a constitution. The Torah was the constitution of the Jewish people, and the only one they could support. "We regard a secular constitution as an attempt to give a bill of divorce to our holy Torah, for which all generations had sacrificed their lives."

Lacking the political power to ensure that a constitution would be to their liking, they feared that it would incorporate antireligious principles, which once accepted could never be removed. The difficulties they had encountered in attempting to express thanks to the deity in the Declaration of Independence, could not have been too far from their minds. Under prevailing conditions, therefore, the absence of a formal and written constitution was desirable from their point of view; it enabled them to protect and secure their religious interests politically by becoming part of a parliamentary majority, where the intensity of their commitment could be employed to counteract some of their numerical weakness. The stance of the religious parties was immediately demonstrated in the debate surrounding the constitution, which came on the heels of bitter debates on the issue of religious education for immigrants. It presented the government with a major political problem, for any government attempt to adopt a written constitution would lead to the breakdown of the coalition.

In principle, there was nothing at all in Ben-Gurion's arguments to preclude a written constitution that would entrench and give formal expression to the principles of majority rule and the rule of law. On the other hand, neither was there a principled commitment to a written constitution. Under these conditions, the choice was political. The thinking of the religious parties generated a pragmatic opposition on Mapai's part to a rigid, formal, written constitution.

Mapai MKs argued that to engage in a Kulturkampf about matters of conscience would weaken national resolve and threaten national unity at a time when the country already faced major problems of security, the ingathering of the exiles, and land settlement. Moreover, it was too early to decide about a constitution, which should reflect the end of the process of national renewal, and preserve the values that had been achieved. Israel was still at the beginning, its fundamental values had not yet crystallized, and a rigid, written constitution was therefore premature. Finally, it was suggested that it was not right to make such weighty decisions for the future, decisions that would be hard to change, when only about 10 percent of the Jewish people for whom the state had been established lived in Israel.

Some asserted that there was no need for a constitution because to all intents and purposes the state already had one. The basic patterns of governmental order and the rule of law had been established in legislative acts and institutionalized in practice. The declarative aspect of the constitution was missing, but this should be dispensed with rather than reduced to a set of platitudes, as would occur if a constitution were adopted at that stage.[8]

Mapam and Herut moved that the Knesset instruct its Constitution, Law and Justice Committee to prepare a constitution and to present it to the First Knesset. Effectively, this not only sought to ensure that a constitution would be adopted but also set a time limit—the duration of the First Knesset. The motion was referred to as the "proposal of thirty-seven MKs" because neither party wished to be seen publicly to be associated with the other, in view of the ideological chasm separating them.

During the debate, many members had argued that there was little substantive difference, in the long run, between the opposition motion and that of Yizhar Harari of the Progressive party. He had proposed that the constitution consist of separate chapters, each a Basic Law in itself, to be adopted separately but to be joined together later to form the constitution. This received the support of Mapai and was passed.

The religious parties, released from collective cabinet responsibility and given a free vote, abstained because they did not want to support any approach that could eventually lead to a constitution. They did not oppose it because they did not want the government to be defeated. The resolution reflected a readiness by Mapai to continue the process of constitution making, so long as the government was neither tied to a strict timetable nor obliged to produce a single, complete document.[9]

Subsequent Constitutional Developments

With the passing of Harari's resolution, the formal legislative and constitutional process associated with the establishment of the state ceased. The adoption of Basic Laws proceeded slowly. By the end of the founding period only four Basic Laws had been adopted, of which three related to the structure and process of government: The Knesset (1958); The President of the State (1964); and The Government (1968). The three Basic Laws added little of substance to the Transition Law. Their main function was to introduce order into the existing situation by elaborating sections of that law as separate laws, by paying greater attention to legal formulation, and by incorporating some of the accumulated experience of the preceding years.

Occasionally, the Basic Laws included elements of other laws. The most significant of these is the electoral section included in the Basic Law: The Knesset (1958), which came from the Election Law, not the Transition Law. It specified that the "Knesset was to be elected in general, national, direct, equal, secret, and proportional elections," and that this could be changed only by a majority of Knesset members. This meant a special, absolute majority of at least sixty-one members of the Knesset, and not a simply majority of those present. It also specified that no part of the law could be altered or suspended under emergency regulations, and that a majority of two-thirds of the members of the Knesset was necessary to change that stipulation.

both structure s.

The Hybrid Structure of Israeli Democracy

Israel was established as a hybrid democracy combining major features of both majoritarian and consensus models of democracy, confronting political actors with mixed alternatives. The potential was there to tip the balance of the system in either direction, but the extent to which it moved and the precise direction depended upon social and political factors, such as the electoral strength of the parties, the number and substance of issue dimensions, and the salience, intensity, and party distribution of opinion on these issues. Their impact upon the system was mediated, and to a large degree determined, by the goals and decisions of the major political actors: the parties and their leaders. It is to these that we now turn.

Notes

1. *Kavei Yesod*, para. 2.
2. *Divrei Haknesset*, 8.3.1949, pp. 55–61.
3. See his election speech as reported in *Haaretz*, 13.1.49.
4. David Ben-Gurion, speech at the end of the debate at the Histadrut Veidah, 29.5.1949 (in *Hazon vederekh*, 5 vols. [Tel Aviv: Mapai, 1951–57], 1:158), explaining the more oblique position that he had presented in a radio address after the elections on 29.1.1949 (ibid., 51–52). In the radio address he called on every party that was to participate in the government to "decisively choose one or the other: either it participates in the government—and in collective responsibility, or it stays out and retains the freedom to oppose and attack the government incessantly. Doing both is not possible." His diary reference following the elections sets out three principles for coalition formation; the first: "collective responsibility—not like the deeds of Mapam—both in government and in opposition." David Ben-Gurion, *Yoman hamilhamah: milhemet ha'az-ma'ut*, 3 vols., ed. Gershon Rivlin and Elhanen Orren (Tel Aviv: Ministry of Defense Publications, 1982), 26.1.1949, p. 962.
5. *Divrei Haknesset*, 8.2.1950.
6. Transition (Amendment No. 2) Law, 1952, enacted 24.6.1952.
7. The whole debate is to be found in *Divrei Haknesset*, 1.2.1950–20.2.1950, pp. 714ff. Significant excerpts are to be found in Emanuel Gutmann and Yehezkel Dror, *Mishtar medinat yisrael: osef mekorot* (Jerusalem: Academon, 1969), pp. 70ff.
8. *Divrei Haknesset*, op. cit.
9. *Divrei Haknesset*, 13.6.1950.

4

Parties and Policies

The State of Israel, as was pointed out in chapter 1, inherited from the Yishuv a working multiparty system that reflected social diversity and intense ideological differences over a whole range of issues. What is more they were anchored in separate and distinctive political subcommunities or enclaves. Ideology per se was of great significance as the parties struggled to imprint their particular weltanschauung upon the identity and character of the future state.[1]

Many of these ideological and issue differences were carried over into the state and became the basis for the policies advocated by the various parties, although as time passed some waned and others were resolved. During the founding period, there were four major issue dimensions. One was socioeconomic: the relative weights of the public and the private sectors in the organization of production, and the question of economic equality and social justice. The second was security: the defense of Israel's existence, territory, and inhabitants amidst the hostility of the neighboring Arab states. The third was foreign policy: Israel's relations with other states and international bodies, its attitude to the East–West conflict, and the general significance of diplomatic activity. And the fourth was the question of religion and state: the status of the Jewish religion in state and society.

This chapter focuses upon the ideological views and policy positions of the parties on these major issues in the context of electoral competition, their bases of social support, their internal social, organization, and factional structures, and their external responsibilities. These are closely interrelated; for example, ideological differences may stem from, or give rise to, internal factions and affect the organizational structure as well as policy outcomes. Similarly, various internal party groups or interests may favor policies that are unalike. Conversely, parties may adopt or modify particular policy positions for reasons of electoral popularity, to retain the support of previously identified groups, to resolve internal conflict, or in deference to the wishes of particular leaders. So, too, parties in power operate under different policy constraints than do parties in opposition.

The Parties of the Left

Mapai

Mapai, the leading party in the Yishuv, retained its share of the electorate during the founding period but did not manage to increase it. In the last elections in the Yishuv in 1944, Mapai won 35.9 percent of the votes for the Elected Assembly. In the six elections between 1949 and 1965 it consistently gained between 32.2 percent and 38.2 percent of the votes (with a mean of 35.8 percent!), giving it between forty and forty-seven seats in the Knesset. In short, while the electorate tripled in size during this period the Mapai vote more or less kept pace with it.[2]

As a party, Mapai grew fivefold, from 40,000 members in 1948 to 196,000 members in 1964. Mapai members constituted about 10 percent of the eligible voters in the Israeli electorate in 1949, and over 16 percent in 1964. Increased membership without a concomitant rise in public support may be the result of unreliable party membership records and a desire to show large numbers even if the membership is merely formal, or sometimes even nonexistent. It also bears witness to the significance of party membership in the allocation of scarce resources, on the one hand, and Mapai's need for increased party membership to enable it more effectively to penetrate and control other organizations (such as the Histadrut), on the other. As ideological commitment waned and instrumental considerations became more significant in attracting individuals to parties, membership increased.

Membership growth was accompanied by a radical restructuring of the party's social basis. A party in which pioneering agricultural interests were ideologically and numerically dominant was transformed into a predominantly urban workers' party. Members of kibbutzim and moshavim who together made up nearly 50 percent of the party's membership in the early 1940s, and 36 percent before the establishment of the state, dropped steadily to 11.6 percent by 1964. Urban membership increased commensurately.

Mapai's expansion and diversification were the result of a highly aggregative, rather than narrowly doctrinaire, approach to membership recruitment. The aggregative approach produced considerable internal social diversity within the urban sector. Economic development and modernization involved occupational differentiation, and the creation or heightened significance of new socioeconomic categories. The trade union sector became diversified, professions assumed increasing importance, and artisans and small business groups became a significant electoral force. Immigration introduced ethnic diversification, and heightened consciousnesses gave added weight to groups based on sex, age, and religious practice. Mapai not only sought to incorporate members of these groups but adopted separate organizational approaches in each case to facilitate their incorporation.

Mapai incorporated members of agricultural settlements (kibbutzim and moshavim), urban workers, professionals, artisans, women, youth, ethnic groups, and the religiously observant, often giving them specific representation within party bodies, while simultaneously gaining or maintaining Mapai influence in or control of their organizations. As a result, Mapai effectively controlled a kibbutz federation (Ihud Hakvuzot Vehakibbutzim),[3] a moshav federation (Tnuat Hamoshavim), and artisans' organizations, trade unions, health services, cultural activities, industrial enterprises, cooperatives, professional associations, and so forth, much of the last, of course, by means of the Histadrut.[4]

Moreover, throughout the founding period Mapai was a party of government and administration. It stood at the head of every governmental coalition and most local government authorities, controlled the Histadrut, and was the dominant element in the Jewish Agency and the World Zionist Organization. Clearly, the impact was two-way. It permitted Mapai to set the policies and provide the personnel of these bodies, but at the same time its policies had to take their different needs into account.

In this chapter we shall deal with the substance of Mapai's policies in only the broadest outline. Because so much of this is closely intertwined with governmental action and the operation of the political system as a whole, we deal with the content and decision-making processes relating to some of the more important policies, and with other aspects of its internal structure and leadership conflict in much greater depth in later chapters. Conversely, the policies and internal structures of some of the other parties come in for relatively more detailed analysis in this chapter.

Policies. During the founding period, Mapai's policies were shaped and influenced by the fact that the party bore the major governmental responsibility. It gave priority to what it defined as the country's most urgent needs and objectives, and in most cases its policies became government policies, with the result that it is difficult to distinguish where the policies of one left off and those of the other began. At the very outset, Mapai defined its priorities extremely broadly as security, the ingathering of the exiles, land settlement, population dispersion and economic development, and establishing Israel's legitimate place in the international arena.

More specifically, security related to Israel's relations with its Arab neighbors, the resolution of the War of Independence, and the resulting borders. Economic development involved, in particular, the instruments to be used and the approach to be preferred. And establishing Israel's place in the world arena translated at first into the question of foreign policy orientation: Israel's position on the conflict between United States and the Soviet Union. But once basic security was assured, hostilities had ceased, and the border question was resolved by the various armistice agreements, Mapai gave top priority to the ingathering of the exiles. Although security, economic development, and sound foreign relations were important, Ben-Gurion and other Mapai leaders emphasized that they should be viewed through the prism of their impact upon the ingathering of the exiles because this was the reason that the state had been established.[5]

Throughout the entire period, Mapai was moderately activist on security matters. This was particularly apparent before the election for the Constituent

Assembly in January 1949, when security and foreign affairs were the major issues in a low-key campaign held at the end of the war and just as peace negotiations with Egypt got under way. Mapai headed the government, which had taken the initiative in the later stages of the war to extend Israel's borders and to drive off the invading forces, but when hostilities ceased and there developed the possibility of some settlement with Israel's neighbors that might eventually lead to peace, Mapai chose the peace option.

Mapai's activist pursuit of peace was reflected in the slogan "Peace—but not at any price." Mapai's policy was based upon the belief that without military strength Israel would not survive, but that it could not survive on military strength alone. It was not enough to have a policy of war; it needed a policy of peace. Only such a policy would enable it to enjoy the necessary support of the international community—particularly the United States, the Soviet Union, and the UN. At the very least, it did not want to alienate them and incur their steadfast opposition. At the same time it kept open the possibility of normal relations with its neighbors. This led it to reject using the army to extend the borders and take control of the whole of the historic Land of Israel, including the Old City of Jerusalem, which some of its opponents on the right and left advocated.

Mapai's moderate or controlled activism on security policy was also quite prominent in the mid-1950s, most noticeably with regard to the policy of retaliation for terrorist incursions across the border. Despite internal differences, criticism from some within Mapai and outside that the policy was too activist, and others on the right and left that it was not activist enough, by the mid-1950s Mapai's policy had jelled into a decisively activist response, as epitomized by the preemptive Sinai War of 1956. (Discussed later.)

On the large questions of foreign policy and the East–West conflict, Mapai at first advocated a neutralist position in response to Soviet support for Israel's establishment, and the large number of Jews in Eastern Europe, and despite fundamental sympathy for Western democratic government. But as the cold war developed, Mapai policy became strongly pro-Western.

In economic matters, Mapai supported a mixed economy and a welfare-oriented policy. The contentious issue was that of socialism and nationalization, and the general role of collective economic effort, on the one hand, and of private enterprise and private capital investment, on the other. As a Zionist socialist party, Mapai might have been expected to implement socialism, while its connections with the Histadrut and the collective sector should also have predisposed it to give strong preference to the latter in its development plans.

In fact, in the early years of the state, following the policies and priorities it adopted in the Yishuv, Mapai, while not denying socialism, placed greater emphasis upon class cooperation and political and social compromise and agreement than on class conflict as the means to achieve the goal of national and Zionist upbuilding.[6] Similarly, it favored planning in broad outlines rather than centralized planning that would involve close supervision and direct control of the economy. Again, it acted pragmatically, for example, being prepared to utilize private and foreign capital if this was the only way in which the Israeli economy could be developed quickly, rather than adopting a dogmatic or doctrinaire approach to socialism. It did not nationalize industries when it had the governmental means to do so because it did not possess the capital to do so, and did not want to frighten away private investors when the country's needs were so great.

Its pragmatic, middle-of-the-road orientation figured prominently in electoral programs, coalition negotiations, government policies, and specific actions. It was strikingly evident in the negotiations to establish a government after the 1949 elections. Mapam sought a clear commitment to socialism; the General Zionists sought a declaration that socialism and Zionism were antithetical, better conditions for private enterprise and private capital, and a commitment not to give preference to the collective and public sectors. Mapai's response was to demand acceptance of its policies and program. These encouraged the import and investment of private and international capital, side by side with collective and governmental capital, and in the context of a planned and regulated economy, in which some preference would still be given to the collective sector.[7]

In the sphere of religion, Mapai continued with the general approach that had led it to make the agreement with Agudat Yisrael in 1947. It was willing to have the state take account of and, where necessary, supply the religious needs of the population, so long as there was no coercion of either the religious or the nonreligious sections of society. But the extent of this provision, the policy areas it applied to, the precise definition of needs and interests, and the specific meaning of religious and nonreligious coercion were not spelled out. Different understandings of these by the religious parties made some religious issues—education, the integration of the observant into the army—the source of major political conflicts.

Mapai's policies were set within the broad parameters of an ideological approach known as *mamlakhtiut*—literally, "statism."[8] Briefly described, it consisted of three main elements: the necessity for state frameworks to provide universal services, including those previously undertaken by political parties; the exclusiveness of state activity in certain areas of public life, thereby giving them a unitary character; and the depoliticization of state structures to render them impartial, that is, neutral to political party considerations, in policies, personnel practices, and administrative procedures.[9]

The specific policies were presented by a party that had a clear and strong image of itself and its decisive role in the establishment of the state, its successful defense, the ingathering of the exiles, and all other processes of development. Mapai projected itself as being mainly, but not solely, responsible for the progress that had occurred. It appealed to the public on the basis of its past achievements and its record rather than on the basis of promises for the future. Thus, although it did not precisely identify itself with the state, which within the ideology of *mamlakhtiut* it raised above party, it did claim credit for itself and its leaders for the state's achievements, which had been accomplished despite what Mapai depicted as the obstruction of the opposition parties.[10]

Mapam

Mapam was founded on January 24, 1948, by the merger of Hashomer Haza'ir, based around Hakibbutz Haarzi, and Ahdut Ha'avodah-Poalei Zion, mainly centered in the kibbutzim of Hakibbutz Hameuhad but with a significant urban membership. The ideological basis for the merger lay in common acceptance of Marxist socialism, and a similar *haluzic* (pioneering) approach. Shared admiration for the Soviet Union and its contribution to the defeat of Nazism, together with its support for the partition of Palestine, reinforced the merger process.

The UN Partition Resolution provided the political basis for the merger. Previously, both groups had rejected partition strongly, although for very different reasons. Hashomer Haza'ir was opposed because it sought a political solution to the national question based on cooperation between Jews and Arabs in a binational state. Ahdut Ha'avodah was opposed because it believed in a socialist Jewish state in the whole Land of Israel, not in part of it, which would provide a focal point for Jewish nationality. The UN decision enabled both to offer tactical support for partition while maintaining opposition in principle. Participation opened up the possibility of peace between Jews and Arabs, and could be viewed as transitional to a later stage, in which each might find greater scope for its own favored solution. Finally, as loyal members of the Zionist movement they felt obliged to take into account the majority support for partition.

Mapam aspired to a major role in making policy in the future state and in the Histadrut, where its constituting parties held 38.4 percent of the votes as against 53.7 percent for Mapai. In the elections to the Zionist Congress in 1946, they had received about 24 percent of the votes cast in the Yishuv. The aim of the merger was to create a revolutionary socialist and *haluzic* alternative to replace Mapai at the head of the political system.

The foundation program of Mapam clearly reflects its origins. It accepted the historic function of revolutionary class war, and the establishment of workers' rule in liquidating capitalism and all forms of national and social subjugation. Mapam saw itself as an indivisible part of the revolutionary workers' movement struggling to repel the forces of capitalist-imperialist reaction, which endangered world peace, and to root out fascism, racism, and anti-Semitism. Its goals were the political and social rise of the masses, their capture of key economic and political positions, the defense of the new People's Democracies, and a true covenant between all peace- and freedom-loving peoples. It pledged its support for the Soviet Union, and for the goals of the October Revolution.[11] At the same time, it supported the upbuilding and defense of a Zionist and *haluzic* Jewish state, and Zionist commitments to the Jewish people with regard to aliyah, settlement, and uniting the Diaspora. To achieve socialism within the Jewish state, Mapam would oppose the forces of reaction and aggressive clericalism, and seek to remove fascism in all its internal manifestations.[12]

At its founding, Mapam had some 24,000 members, and approximately the number of votes its constituent groups had received in Yishuv and Zionist elections. About 60 percent were in Hashomer Haza'ir, and 40 percent in Ahdut Ha'avodah-Poalei Zion. To assure these constituting groups equal status in the new party, the framing of an internal constitution was shelved and party institutions were initially based upon parity. It was hoped that unification would melt the old divisions and party identifications, and replace them with loyalty to the new larger and united party, but this never eventuated. In fact, the opposite occurred: original loyalties jelled, and prior organizational and institutional affiliations were reinforced.

Mapam emerged as the second-largest party in the 1949 elections, winning just over 64,000 votes (14.7 percent) and nineteen Knesset seats, significantly less than the nearly 25 percent of the votes won by its constituent parties in 1946. Clearly, it had failed to make gains among the new groups and voters in the electorate. (Mapai, it will be recalled, succeeded in retaining its Yishuv proportion, about 35 percent.) The decline continued in the 1951 elections, when Mapam, with 47,000 members, gained only 86,095 votes, 12.5 percent of the votes cast, which gave it fifteen seats.

Mapam's failure to increase support outside its own immediate circles is further demonstrated by comparison with the electorate: the electorate increased by 60 percent; Mapam's vote, by 26 percent. (Mapai increased its vote by 65 percent.) As a result, in 1951 Mapam lost its place as the second-largest party; it was now equal third, together with the United Religious Front, but behind the General Zionists. Most of Mapam's support came from the kibbutzim. In the populous urban areas, only in Haifa did it match its national average. In three sections of the population where it had hoped particularly to increase its electoral support—olim, Arabs, and Tel Aviv—it failed.

At about the same time, the tenacity of the basic internal differences was made manifest in the party's internal elections held in 1951 in advance of a party conference (*veidah*) to adopt a party constitution and platform. The elections demonstrated that the party was divided into a Hashomer Haza'ir majority of 65 percent, and an Ahdut Ha'avodah minority of about 35 percent, each of which acted as cohesive factions with independent institutions. They disagreed, as will be seen, on a multitude of issues. Cooperation between them became increasingly difficult and conflict more intense. In a series of smaller splits, some members, mainly urban workers, moved to the right and rejoined Mapai; others went left and ended up in the Communist party. Finally, in 1954, the party split again into its constituent parts, with the majority retaining the name Mapam, and the minority Ahdut Ha'avodah.[13]

While the internal differences and disagreements between Hashomer Haza'ir and Ahdut Ha'avodah continued, the issues on which they agreed and that formed the basis of their merger dominated Mapam's public stance and distinguished its policies from those of the other Zionist–socialist parties. In general, until about 1952 the differences between them were mainly centered on internal and organizational questions, or on those on which immediate policy choices did not need to be made and could therefore be shelved. On the other hand, on the major external policy questions there was a greater degree of agreement. It was only when the two kinds of questions became interwoven, and when Hashomer Haza'ir used its majority position both to impose its views on the minority on the external questions and not to allow the minority to maintain either an independent position or autonomous organization that the split took place.

Apart from the internal organizational questions, particularly the respective organizational rights and duties of the majority and minority, the major issues of disagreement were over the integration of Arabs into the party and the Histadrut, and the question of defense policy. On the Arab question, Hashomer Haza'ir advocated a territorial basis of organization that would have led to the integration of Arabs as full members, and to a binational party. Ahdut Ha'avodah opposed the membership of Arabs in the party and the Histadrut, and consequently advocated the establishment of a separate Arab socialist sister party.

The question of borders and the national character of the state seemed to have been settled for the time being, and these receded as a source of issue differences. But as relations with bordering Arab states worsened and Israel adopted an increasingly activist reprisal policy, sharp new disagreements developed. Ahdut Ha'avodah maintained its activist approach and criticized government security policies for not being activist enough. Hashomer Haza'ir, on the other hand, criticized government policies for being militarist and not sufficiently oriented toward securing peaceful relations with Israel's Arab neighbors, and not conducive to true amity and cooperation.

On the major questions of foreign policy and of economic and social policies, Mapam presented a united front. It advocated Israel's neutralism in international affairs, but in practice this meant support for the policies of the Soviet Union and opposition to those of the United States. The Soviet Union was "the second motherland," the leader of progressive forces and peace-loving peoples, and the model to be followed except on Zionism and the Jewish national question. The United States was militaristic, capitalistic, and imperialistic, if not fascist—the major threat to world peace. Thus, Mapam opposed Israel's agreement to accept U.S. loans, its pro-Western orientation, and its vote to support UN intervention in the Korean War.

So long as memory remained of Soviet support for the establishment of Israel and for Czechoslovakian arms supplies, and of Soviet opposition to Nazism, and while its traditional opposition to Zionism was muted, Mapam was united in maintaining its pro-Soviet orientation. The development of the cold war, increasing evidence of Soviet opposition to Israel and Zionism, Soviet support for the Arab states, mounting and violent anti-Semitism in the Soviet Union and other communist countries, and finally the Prague trials and the "Doctors Plot" in the Soviet Union split Mapam in its approach to foreign affairs.

Most members of Ahdut Ha'avodah leaned more to the Jewish national and Zionist approach, and increasingly distanced themselves from the pro-

Soviet line. A small minority of the party from both constituent elements, led by Moshe Sneh, moved in the opposite direction, and eventually joined the Israeli Communist party. The majority tried valiantly to maintain its traditional position of support for the Soviet Union and for Zionism at one and the same time. This became particularly difficult during the Prague trials, in which not only Zionism but a leading member of Mapam, Mordekhai Oren, were on trial. The simultaneous effort not to criticize the communist regime and to support a party leader proved to be impossible, and was a major factor in the 1954 split. Only later did Mapam, now constituted mainly of Hashomer Haza'ir, finally distance itself from the Soviet Union, and publicly acknowledge that Soviet policies were outrightly anti-Israel, anti-Semitic and anti-Zionist.

In matters of economic policy, Mapam advocated socialist policies that included nationalization of basic natural resources, land, transport, and communications. It gave clear preference to the public and collective sectors, opposed the import of private capital, sought to extend Histadrut activities in all spheres, and proposed a high degree of government control that would eventuate in a socialized, that is, fully planned, economy.

Mapam's attitude toward the ongoing activities and policies of the Histadrut was two-sided. On the one hand, it fully supported the idea and the ideals of the Histadrut and sought to increase its role and the scope of its societal functions, and wherever possible to use the principles of pioneering and voluntarism to achieve national goals. On the other hand, the policies and institutions of the Histadrut were closely controlled by Mapai. Mapam therefore embarked on a course of militant and radical opposition within the Histadrut.

Mapam sought to maintain Histadrut membership in international trade union federations that became communist-dominated, and opposed affiliation with the noncommunist federation that was set up in the early 1950s. It consistently adopted populist tactics within the Histadrut, and in relation to employers. For example, it regularly suggested much higher wage increases and cost-of-living adjustments than those that Mapai and the government believed were within the capacity of the national economy and of industry. It organized militant public marches and demonstrations against the government's and the Histadrut's economic policies under the general theme of "bread and work." In some of the key workplaces in which it had influence, it used its influence to organize or encourage shop-floor militancy, and this often eventuated in militant strike activity against the employer without the requisite Histadrut authorization, and often in defiance of its decisions. A dramatic example of such activity was the seamen's strike of 1952. The strike was initially against the paternalism of the Histadrut institutions in Haifa—as evidenced by the fact that their workers did not choose their own trade union representatives and officials—and an attempt to improve the working and living conditions of Israel's merchant marine. Mapam support in the context of the cold war and the influence of international communist unions, and their effect upon Israel's merchant marine changed the nature of the strike and gave it direct and clear political overtones. Although it had not instigated the strike, Mapam did support it strongly, using it to attack Mapai, the government, and the Histadrut, and to defend workers' demands. The clash was made even more dramatic by the decision to break it by police and military force.[14]

In this sphere too, as the years progressed, the Ahdut Ha'avodah wing of the party came much closer to Mapai and developed increasing reservations about the policies pursued by Mapam under the influence of the Hashomer Haza'ir majority. Among other things, this was a major factor in the breaking away from Mapam in 1951 of the Lifshitz-Lamdan group of urban workers within Ahdut Ha'avodah, which rejoined Mapai.

These various threads came together in Mapam's coalition behavior. In 1949 Mapam, a member of the Provisional Government, now with nineteen seats in the Knesset, might have been expected to join the cabinet and together with Mapai form a government based on a workers' majority of sixty-four seats. Both before and after the elections Mapai and Mapam expressed willingness to enter into coalition negotiations, and did so. But when it came to a decision, Mapam voted not to enter the cabinet on Mapai's conditions. Eventually, the two parties conducted coalition negotiations on five occasions between 1949 and 1954, and five times Mapam voted not to enter the coalition. In every instance the Hashomer Haza'ir majority opposed entry, and outvoted the Ahdut Ha'avodah minority, which supported it. These consistently divergent approaches stemmed from differing self-images. Hashomer Haza'ir regarded Mapam as an alternative to Mapai; Ahdut Ha'avodah regarded itself as a corrective. With its Marxist commitment and loyalty to the Soviet Union and its policies, Hashomer Haza'ir was concerned about ideological purity and did not see its way clear to cooperate with the "reformist" policies of Mapai, particularly in the area of foreign policy.

Ahdut Ha'avodah, on the other hand, had previously been part of Mapai, and regarded its rightful place as being at the center of power. It saw itself as part of the "spinal cord" of Zionist activism, and had always undertaken responsibility and played a leading role with regard to defense and security until the dissolution of the Palmah command. As time passed, the bitterness engendered by that affair continued to recede.

On a whole series of issues Ahdut Ha'avodah was much closer to Mapai than to its partner. Compromise with Mapai was therefore not only desirable in order to enable it to reassume its rightful place but also much more feasible. For Ahdut Ha'avodah, joining the cabinet would, in the short run, get it out of an impossible position—an opposition minority faction within an opposition minority party—and in the long run, bring it closer to assuming the position of national leadership that it had once shared, and to which it continued to aspire.

The party split more or less into its constituent parts, now called Mapam and Ahdut Ha'avodah, and they fought the 1955, 1959, and 1961 elections separately. They did better apart than together, and on all three occasions exceeded their share of the vote when united by a few percentage points and gained more seats than in 1951. Their best performance was in 1955: Ahdut Ha'avodah gained 8.2 percent of the vote, and ten seats; Mapam, 7.3 percent and nine seats. In this election Ahdut Ha'avodah benefited from the significant rise in public support for activist policies in response to the security situation on the borders, which on this occasion enabled it to gain more seats than Mapam. In 1959 and 1961 Mapam retained its nine seats, whereas its erstwhile partner received seven and eight, respectively.

By the mid-1950s Mapam had distanced itself from its pro-Soviet orientation and toned down its Marxist economic and international revolutionary outlook. Ahdut Ha'avodah had thrown these off completely and become much more strident in its military activism now that it was no longer restrained by Hashomer Haza'ir. As time passed, the differences between them and Mapai on these questions narrowed, and the similarities in their Zionist orientations became more pronounced.

These developments facilitated the participation of Mapam and Ahdut Ha'avodah in the coalition in 1955 and 1959; only the latter agreed to join in 1961. Their consistent governmental cooperation with Mapai further reinforced the process of convergence. In the case of Ahdut Ha'avodah, it paved the way for a joint list in the 1965 elections and led in 1968 to the formation of a new party, Mifleget Ha'avodah, the Israeli Labor party. The narrowing of differences also had its effect on Mapam, which returned to the coalition in 1965 and formed a joint list with the new party in 1969.

Maki

An openly anti-Zionist Communist party had existed in Palestine since 1923. It had not been very successful among the Jewish population, even in times of severe economic crisis. Yet despite outright support for extreme and often reactionary Arab positions, it had not made any inroads among Arabs either. During World War II, the party became less intensely anti-Zionist because of the common fight against the British, fascism, and nazism. Among Arabs, by way of contrast, considerable fascist and nazi sympathies developed. In 1943, the party split into Jewish and Arab sections.

Following establishment of the Israeli state, Maki, the Israeli Communist party, was set up on the basis of a reunification of the various Jewish and Arab communist groups. As we noted above, the Communists participated in the Provisional State Council despite a long history of intense opposition to Zionist goals, policies, parties, and organizations; this was in accordance with Moscow's line at the time. Maki called on its members and militants to take part in the war in 1948, which it regarded as a defensive war. It approved the Israeli capture of the Negev, and at first supported incorporation of Jerusalem within the Jewish state because the United States demanded internationalization. When the Soviet Union supported internationalization, Maki followed suit, as it did again in 1950, when the Soviet Union once more reversed its policy and opposed internationalization.

Maki contested the 1949 Knesset elections and received 15,134 votes (3.5 percent), giving it four seats in the First Knesset. Over the years it improved its position slightly, gaining 27,334 votes (4 percent) and five seats in 1951. For a short period in 1954–55, the party had seven Knesset seats following the union with the Left Socialist party led by Sneh, which had been expelled from Mapam. Maki did not manage to hold onto both of these seats in 1955, although it did better than in 1951, gaining 38,294 votes (4.5 percent) and six seats in the Third Knesset. It dropped to three seats in 1959, but by 1961 it was back at five seats. A split in the party mainly on national lines and the formation of a new communist party, mainly Arab, which gained three seats in 1965, reduced it to one seat.

Maki's support in the 1950s came in about equal proportions from Jews and Arabs. After the early period of support for the newly independent state, Maki reverted to its traditional anti-Zionist role, on the one hand, and became the champion of the rights of the Arab minority, on the other. In particular, it supported abolition of military rule. It was also the only party at the time into which Arabs were integrated at the membership and leadership levels. Of the more than four thousand members, about one-third were Arabs; on the Central Council, four of the fifteen places were held by Arabs, a proportion that was maintained in all party bodies. Popular support from Arabs was proportionately stronger, providing about 50 percent of the party's vote. In its stronghold, Nazareth, it got 50 percent of the total votes cast.

Among the Jews, Maki received greater support from new immigrants than among the Israeli-born or those who had immigrated prior to 1939. These included some who had been Communists and sympathizers in their countries of origin. Others had grievances with regard to housing, food, and working conditions, and turned to Maki in the hope that it would ameliorate them. Overall, Maki received more support among Jews from the lower middle class than from workers.[15]

In both domestic and foreign policy Maki followed traditional Communist approaches as expressed by the Soviet Union, and supported the latter even when it was openly anti-Jewish. It accepted Marxism-Leninism as interpreted by the Comintern, and advocated international and domestic class struggle to destroy capitalism and Western imperialism. Zionism was a tool of imperialism and reactionary capitalism, and the Arabs were the main victims of its exploitation.

As we noted above, Maki followed Soviet policies in the international sphere loyally, and supported it unquestioningly on all matters dividing East and West. Before 1955 the Soviet Union had not yet made its own inroads into the Arab world and advocated direct negotiations between Israel and the Arab states as the solution to their differences, which was the policy advocated by Maki. The adoption of Soviet policies was made easier in the Israeli context by the existence of diplomatic relations between Israel and the Soviet Union for most of the period, although over time these deteriorated rapidly.

Center and Right Parties

Progressives

The Progressive party, founded in September 1948 in preparation for the elections for the Constituent Assembly, was located just to the right of center in the Israeli political and ideological spectrum.[16] Its constituent elements were Aliyah Hadashah, about 45 percent of the membership; Ha'oved Hazioni, 30 percent; and General Zionists 'A' (Hitahdut Zionim Klaliyim), 25 percent—all of which had participated in Yishuv and Zionist elections.

Varied motivations came together in the establishment of a center party. The new party enabled Aliyah Hadashah to go beyond the framework of an immigrant association and play a more general role in the political system. It also enabled the General Zionists "A" to make up for the failure of their 1946 unification with General Zionists "B," which had moved it and its Histadrut wing, Ha'oved Hazioni, to the right and away from their traditional cooperation with the labor parties and their settlement movements. The Progressive party was solidly middle class, having a heavy representation of university educated, independent, and employed professionals, and a few businessmen.

The party name indicated its founders' desire to represent and promote the values of progressive liberalism. Its electoral policies emphasized the protection of individual rights; depoliticization, the reduction of the direct influence of political parties over health, transport, and labor exchanges; the protection of private property and the promotion of private enterprise, together with support for the welfare state; recognition of the contribution of skilled workers, academics, and professionals through selective wage differentials; cooperation with the labor movement; and support for the preservation of the coalition system.

The Progressive party advocated a single national educational system, and strongly supported establishment of an independent judiciary and independent civil service. It proposed a moderate foreign policy and more liberal treatment of the Arab minority. Close examination of its policies and Knesset behavior suggests that on most important issues of domestic, economic, and foreign policy, the party position was close to that of Mapai.

The Progressive party was Mapai's most loyal and dependable coalition partner and served in all coalitions between 1949 and 1961, except for the period between October 1951 and December 1952. It generally went along with Mapai policies, and its cabinet stance was marked by absence of the threat of crisis or failure to support the government. Similarly, in coalition negotiations it generally proved amenable. Thus, in 1949, despite considerable General Zionist pressure, it refused to form a joint negotiating front and would not make its entry into the Cabinet conditional upon Mapai's being able to reach agreement with the General Zionists. The latter strongly criticized the Progressive party for entering the cabinet without holding out for its declared policies, particularly on individual rights and economic issues. The Progressives justified their entry on the grounds that it was in the interests of private industry and agriculture.

By the time of the Second Knesset elections in 1951, the Progressive party responded to consistent attacks that it had been a Mapai satellite by forming a broad negotiating front with the General Zionists. This indicated a move to the right on economic questions. The strength of the change that had taken place can be gauged from the fact that the party remained outside the cabinet formed in October 1951 because Mapai and the General Zionists had not reached agreement on these questions. It did not return to the cabinet until the General Zionists finally entered it in December 1952. During this period, however, the Progressive party did not see itself as being in opposition to Mapai; its MKs abstained on the vote of confidence when the coalition agreement was presented to the Knesset, and generally sought to play an independent role above coalition–opposition conflict.

The Progressives' coalition strategy was governed not only by general policy agreement with Mapai but also by its electoral weakness and its relative failure at the polls. On the basis of the performance of its constituting parties at previous elections, the Progressive party had confidently expected to approach 15 percent of the votes in 1949; it was bitterly disappointed when it received only 17,786 votes (4.1 percent) and five Knesset seats. Nor did it do much better in subsequent years: 22,171 votes (3.2 percent) and four seats in 1951; 37,661 (4.4 percent) and five seats in 1955; and 4.6 percent and six seats in 1959. In all these elections it was clearly the smallest of the three parties at the center and right of the political spectrum.

One reason for the party's modest electoral performance is that many potential supporters, particularly those who were both middle class and Zionist in outlook, voted for Mapai, which they perceived as the leading party of national struggle and the party of the state. Their positive view of the achievements of Mapai and its leaders' foreign and defense policies was reinforced by a negative evaluation of Aliyah Hadashah's prominence among those who doubted the prudence and necessity of declaring the state.

A second reason is that the members of the middle classes who saw Mapai as an economic threat to private enterprise, trade, commerce, and the free professions turned to the General Zionists, who more stridently sought to defend the interests of private capital and individual enterprise, and took a firm stance against the collective aspects of the government's economic polices and the entrepreneurial activities of the Histadrut. For these voters, the economic policies of the Progressives looked like a prescription for a planned economy, and had the effect of making the party seem like a copy of Mapai. Finally, its success in obtaining cabinet representation may have been a contributing factor to its electoral weakness because it was hard for voters to pinpoint its influence on government policy.

The experience of the Progressive party is illustrative of three fundamental aspects of the dynamics of the Israeli party system. One, there seems to be no necessary relation between electoral achievement or failure and cabinet representation. Parties may succeed electorally and not participate in the cabinet, or fail yet be included in the cabinet, and perhaps even increase their representation and influence within it. Two, although cabinet membership confers instrumental advantages upon the participating party, it may also create electoral disadvantage through too close identification with the government and its policies. Potential supporters may thus be encouraged to vote for the leading government party because there appears to be little difference between government parties, or for the leading opposition party to emphasize their disagreement with the leading government party. In either instance, a small party like the Progressives loses out.

A third reason for the Progressives' modest support from the voters is the difficulty associated with trying to occupy the center of the political spectrum and still carve out a distinctive position and image. The party doing so is constantly under attack and in danger of being whittled down by the major parties, particularly the senior coalition partner. To this day no center party has successfully held onto the central position on the party continuum; it has always been captured by a party either to the left or right of it.

General Zionists

In the Diaspora before 1948, General Zionism was the strongest Zionist party. In Palestine, by way of contrast, it remained relatively weak. For the most part it was divided into "A" and "B"' factions that cooperated only fitfully during the years leading to the establishment of the state. When General Zionists "A" became one of the founding elements of the Progressive party, General Zionists "B" (Brit Hazionim Haklaliyim), with which it had previously been united, was left on its own.

The General Zionists had been represented as such on the Provisional State Council, and had had two ministers in the Provisional Government, both from the "B" faction. When most of the "A" faction and Ha'oved Hazioni left to form the Progressive party, the General Zionists were more or less reduced to a small group of leaders prominent in Diaspora Zionist affairs prior to their arrival in Palestine who had not yet become fully integrated. They lacked indigenous roots and support, were weak in local organization, and had little impact on the new generation that had grown up in the Yishuv. These weaknesses became particularly pressing with the approach of the elections to the Constituent Assembly. To mobilize political support the leaders united with Haihud Haezrahi to form Histadrut Hazionim Haklaliyim, known as the General Zionists. Haihud Haezrahi had been organized in the 1930s to represent citrus producers, industrialists, merchants, shopkeepers, and craftsmen in the cities, towns, and rural settlements in Yishuv elections. From the outset the General Zionists promoted the interests of private property and private capital, and maintained the strong antilabor economic outlook that both founding groups had espoused prior to 1948.

The new party went into the 1949 elections on a platform of conservative and free-enterprise economic policies. It opposed governmental economic controls and regulation of free enterprise, and advocated the curbing of labor's (Histadrut's) economic enterprise and activities by the nationalization of its basic industries. The importation of private capital was to be encouraged, and the use of collective or public capital restricted.

Similarly, the General Zionists proposed the handing over of the Histadrut health services to the state, the nationalization of labor exchanges, and the provision of a unified education system, all of which would make severe inroads into the labor parties' hold over their constituencies through their control of the Histadrut. In general, the party sought to limit the role of political parties in social and economic affairs. Its foreign and defense policies hardly differed from those of Mapai. On the question of religion, however, the General Zionists did not adopt the stridently secular stance of the Progressive party, in an attempt to avoid alienating religiously observant middle-class voters.

In the 1949 elections and in subsequent years the General Zionists conveyed the clear image of the party of property, the party of the citrus growers and the owners of real estate. It did rather poorly in 1949, finishing in fifth position after receiving only 22,861 votes (5.2 percent) and seven seats in the First Knesset. Not surprisingly, its votes came mainly from Tel Aviv and its environs—Ramat Gan, Petah Tikvah, Netanyah—and from the moshavot. Although it had been prominently represented in the Provisional Government, it did not participate in the first government established by Ben-Gurion in 1949.

Ben-Gurion made it clear to the General Zionists that he regarded them as suitable coalition partners and that he was prepared to include them again, provided they accepted the major points of Mapai's program, including its economic policies. The negotiations did not succeed, despite agreement on the major issues facing the country, particularly defense and foreign policy. But on economic questions Mapai's approach appeared too much like socialism and was unacceptable to the free-enterprise-minded General Zionists. Moreover, for internal political and personal reasons the General Zionists continued to insist on three cabinet posts, which, given their relative weakness in the Knesset, was more than Ben-Gurion was prepared to give. As he continually pointed out to them, if arithmetical logic was applied to their demands, it would give Mapai fourteen ministers and increase inordinately the representation of other parties as well as the size of the cabinet.[17]

The General Zionists went into opposition and continued to criticize the government's economic policies as being too restrictive of private initiative and too reliant on controls, regulations, and government direction and supervision. At first, they made little headway and had little impact upon the public, which was neither impressed with their leadership qualities nor with their individual-istic policies aimed at defending private property. Mapai's policies and its leadership were, it seems, preferred at first, even by many members of the independent middle classes, the natural reservoir of support for the General Zionists.

By mid-1950, economic problems overtook the dynamics of independence and development. The lack of resources, the immigration influx, the absolute shortages of many basic commodities, a burgeoning black market, the spread of immigrant camps and *ma'abarot* (transit camps), and the adoption of stringent austerity measures and strict rationing of commodities by the government, all contributed to rescuing the General Zionists from obscurity. Their criticisms that bureaucracy was inefficient, if not corrupt, that regulation strangled initiative, and that the preference for the Histadrut frightened off private investment and prevented the importation of much-needed capital fell on receptive ears, particularly among those who felt disadvantaged by the government and discriminated against by the regime and its economic policies. In particular, the General Zionists appealed to many members of the middle classes who previously had voted Mapai because of its foreign and defense policies.

This was dramatically emphasized at the municipal elections in November 1950 when the General Zionists received over 80,000 votes. Compared with the results in the Knesset elections twenty months earlier, the rise was phenomenal. The party had gained an additional 60,000 votes to increase from 5.2 percent to 24.6 percent, whereas Mapai went from 35.7 percent to 27.3 percent. The vote was interpreted by all, including Mapai leaders, as a decisive vote against it and the policies of the government that it led. Overnight the General Zionists had become the second-largest party and the main opposition party. It quickly exploited the momentum that it had gained from the municipal elections to establish branches all over the country and soon claimed over 25,000 members, more than the number of voters who had supported it in 1949.[18]

The party's newfound strength was quickly put to the test by the early elections in July 1951, which were fought mainly over economic questions and were clearly a contest between Mapai and the General Zionists. Mapai, shocked by the public expression of lack of confidence at the municipal elections, reacted quickly. It adopted new policies and administrative measures aimed at increased efficiency, more effective coordination, and stamping out the black market.[19] Its election program emphasized greater and more open encouragement to private capital and free enterprise.

The General Zionists continued to hammer away at economic problems and policies, and called for an end to Mapai rule: "Maspik vedai beshilton mapai." The party's leaders predicted that the party would receive a majority, or at the very least would be the largest party, and be able to form a government. But to many observers the General Zionists seemed to promise too much, and consequently had difficulty in getting a clear message across to the voters. As one person put it, "*Pele sheainam mevakshim leshanot et mezeg haavir*" (It's a wonder they don't seek to change the weather).[20]

In the elections, the General Zionists maintained the momentum and became the second-largest party, gaining 111,394 votes (16.2 percent) and twenty Knesset seats, but they fell far below their hopes of having a majority, or even of becoming the largest party. Again, their greatest successes were in Tel Aviv (25 percent of the votes), Ramat Gan (27 percent), and Haifa, Petah Tikvah, and Netanyah (over 20 percent), and similarly in many of the older moshavot. Clearly, they had gained the support of many middle-class and more-established voters who had previously voted for Mapai, Herut, the Progressives, or the religious parties, all of which lost votes. These voters, it seems, preferred parties promising economic management. Herut lost because this did not seem to be offered by those whose experience was as underground leaders. The religious parties and the Progressives declined because they were identified with the government. Although Mapai had lost one seat, it had nevertheless slightly augmented its proportion of the vote from 35.7 percent to 37.3 percent. But its increased support came mainly from new immigrants and from those disgruntled with the pro-Soviet policies of Mapam, and not from the established urban middle classes, among whom it lost appreciable support.

Mapai negotiated with the General Zionists regarding entry into the coalition, but once again agreement was not reached over economic policies, and over the General Zionists demand for the Ministry of Trade and Commerce. As a result of their electoral success, they felt in a position to set minimum demands in regard to economic policies, but Mapai rejected them. However, when the narrow coalition based on Mapai and the religious parties broke down at the end of 1952, a wider coalition was established, including for the first time the General Zionists, together with the Progressives and some of the religious parties.[21]

The inclusion of the General Zionists was made easier by the fact that Mapai's economic policies had moved closer to those advocated by the General Zionists, and the latter's bargaining position had improved because Mapam had moved further to the left. The General Zionists received four ministries: Trade and Commerce, Transportation, Health, and Interior.

The coalition was maintained when Moshe Sharett became prime minister in January 1954, and held together until the General Zionists refrained in mid-1955 from supporting the government on a no-confidence motion moved by Herut in the wake of the Kastner affair and were forced to resign for having broken the rules of collective responsibility. Their behavior was directly linked to the approaching elections for the Third Knesset, and some strong indications that Mapai was losing popularity.

The General Zionists hoped to escape blame for any governmental failure. While in the government, they had not made a great impact or been able to influence matters from within; hence they sought to be free of responsibility in order to be able to criticize the government. This, they hoped, would enable them to retain their Knesset representation, now twenty-three, following the addition of three MKs elected in 1951 on ethnic lists. Their strategy did not pay off. They had sensed correctly that Mapai was going to be taken to task by the electorate—it garnered only 32.2 percent of the vote (losing 5 percent and five seats)—but the General Zionists lost even more heavily. They won 10.2 percent of the vote (down from 16.2 percent) and only thirteen Knesset seats, and lost their place as the second-largest party. The chief gains were made by Herut and Ahdut Ha'avodah.

Economic questions on which the General Zionists had for so long staked their claim were no longer the issue uppermost in the public mind. Public concern now focused on the security situation on the borders and on the policies to be pursued in order to remove the threat. What is more, the General Zionists' participation in the government had convinced many previous supporters that they did not possess any rapid or miraculous solution to the economic problems.

The General Zionists stayed in opposition after these elections. After 1955 the Mapai-led coalition adopted a more activist security policy, culminating in the 1956 Sinai Campaign, promoted steady economic progress and development, and overcame many of the acute social and cultural problems resulting from the tremendous and rapid influx of immigrants in the early 1950s, and coped with further immigration without undue strain. The distinctive General Zionist economic message became less convincing as the government continued to prove its own effectiveness. This was amply demonstrated in the 1959 elections, when support of the General Zionists again declined significantly: they won only 6.2 percent of the votes and eight seats.

The 1959 elections gave the General Zionists two more Knesset seats than the Progressives, whereas before the 1955 elections they had nineteen more. The relative balance between the two parties, together with considerable policy convergence, led to their unification in 1961 as the Liberal party. The new party emphasized the liberal themes in the economic, social, cultural, and religious policies of both parties, and in the atmosphere of the 1961 elections it made some progress, gaining seventeen seats, three more than the total of their separate efforts in 1959.

The union of the two parties was very short-lived. Many of the former General Zionist leaders had viewed it as a means of getting back into the coalition, and at the very least of becoming the largest opposition party. Even in the atmosphere of 1961, when Mapai was in the midst of a crisis due to the Lavon Affair (discussed later) when Ben-Gurion had lost considerable public prestige and authority because of his handling of the affair, and when the party was internally deeply divided, the Liberal party failed on both counts. It received the same number of seats as Herut (but fewer votes), and Mapai chose not to enter into a coalition with it, preferring Ahdut Ha'avodah.

Within months of this rejection by Mapai, the Liberal party entered into negotiations with Herut that produced a joint parliamentary bloc (Gahal) in time for the 1965 elections. It was formed over the opposition to cooperation with Herut of most of the former Progressives, who split off and formed the Independent Liberal party. At the 1965 elections, Gahal won twenty-six seats (21.3 percent) and the Independent Liberals, five seats (3.8 percent), as against the thirty-four they had together before the elections.

Herut

Origins: From Underground to Political Party. In mid-1947 Ezel leader Menahem Begin told the UNSCOP (UN Special Committee on Palestine) delegation that when the sovereign Jewish state was established the Ezel would disband. It would give up its underground and armed struggle, Begin declared, "because bad government in a Jewish state was preferable to the best government under foreign rule."[22] What it would do politically after that, however, was not made clear.

Begin's view was not the only one. At the end of 1947 four alternatives were discussed within the Ezel: establishment of a government for the whole of Eretz Israel; not to recognize the government to be established by the UN Partition Resolution and to maintain the Ezel within the partition boundaries as an underground organization; to apply all the force available to the Ezel to capture Jerusalem; and to dissolve the underground organizational framework within the partition state and establish a party to participate in the elections to the Constituent Assembly while still maintaining its underground military organization and activities in Jerusalem and overseas. The Ezel command in Palestine preferred the last option. Although it would never accept the

> agreement of any Jewish authority to the dismemberment of the homeland, armed force would never be used against any Jewish authority, but only against external enemies. Thus the battle to reunite the torn-off parts of the homeland would take place under new conditions that would demand new methods. This would be in the form of a new popular freedom movement that would arise from the depths of the underground and would place before the people a program for its free decision that would be based upon the eternal principles of the indivisibility of the homeland, the return to Zion, freedom, equality and social progress.[23]

The Ezel command overseas opposed any course of action that accepted partition and Jewish political authority deriving from it, and therefore saw no need to disband the Ezel and establish a political party. They proposed the establishment of a supreme council for freeing the people to represent the people before the world. Some supported maintenance of the Ezel as a fighting underground within the borders of the partition state. Its task would be to extend the borders, and to conduct foreign policy in line with the Ezel point of view.[24]

Begin's basic position won out, although he also agreed to the continued existence of the underground outside the borders of the sovereign Jewish authority, which meant both in Jerusalem and overseas.[25] This served to mollify his more extreme followers and to maintain unity within the ranks while at the same time keeping alive the Ezel option to strive for its full program.

Organization. Within twenty-four hours of the establishment of the state, Begin announced the disbanding of the Ezel within its boundaries, and the formation of Herut to fight for the Ezel's ideals within the framework of Hebrew law and democracy.[26] Organizational preparations began immediately after Begin's announcement. Despite common ideological beliefs and organizational roots, the formation of Herut was characterized by refusal to merge with the Revisionist party.

Ezel leaders accused the Revisionist party of collaboration with the Jewish Agency during the "*saison*" in 1946, in handing over Ezel members to the British, and of not supporting them sufficiently in the *Altalena* Affair. By participating in the Provisional State Council, the Revisionist party had betrayed the Ezel's ideals through acceptance of the partition boundaries. There was also a clear age and generational gap between the leaders of the Revisionist party and those of the Ezel: the former were in their fifties and sixties; the latter, their twenties and thirties.

Although Herut appeared to agree to a merger, it did not come about because Herut was not willing to accept the ultimate authority of the world executive of the Revisionist party over the new Israeli party. In essence, the merger never eventuated because Herut sought to take over and gain control of the Revisionist constituency in its own name and to found a new party, which the Revisionists could join if they wished, so long as they accepted the leadership of Menahem Begin and the Ezel command.

As a result of the failure of these merger attempts, Herut was the first new party founded in Israel. As Begin later put it: "We are the only movement which was established in the homeland and which was not a reflex image of the movement from the diaspora. The movement was established there because the rebellion was in Eretz Israel." [27] This had a significant impact upon its self-image, as a completely new party that was not burdened by the traditions and agreements of Diaspora and Yishuv politics, which encumbered the Revisionists. He saw it in revolutionary terms as the direct offshoot of the Ezel, which "had liberated the homeland from British subjugation." [28]

Herut's immediate organizational and ideological efforts were directed toward the 1949 elections. It enrolled members, established branches, published a newspaper, and submitted a list for the elections. These were directed by a pyramidal and hierarchical decision-making structure that gave formal legitimation to the decisions of the inner leadership of Ezel commanders, with Begin at the helm. The personnel who composed these bodies were selected at the top rather than elected from below; for example, the list of Knesset candidates and the Central Committee that approved it were both personally chosen by Begin. [29]

The pivotal and dominating role of Menahem Begin as leader of Herut was thus clearly imprinted upon the party from the outset. It was not weakened by the subsequent establishment of a series of national representative and executive bodies, and by provisions for party referenda; in fact, these were subject to the dominant influence of Begin and served as the instruments of his control. Begin's position and sway were accepted willingly and unquestionably for the most part by most fellow party leaders and by the membership. The few challenges that occurred in the 1950s and 1960s were quickly put down, and the persons involved were generally either shunted aside or made a quick exit from the party. [30]

The origins of Begin's mastery lay in the transformation of an illegal and banned underground into a legitimate political party. Although Begin as commander of the Ezel had become chairman of a political party, for most of his collaborators, subordinates, and the rank and file, he remained "the commander." His decisions and position obligated them, and demanded much the same degree and type of loyalty that they had exhibited as soldiers in the underground united in the task of ridding the country of the British and establishing a Jewish state in the whole of Eretz Israel. What is more, he possessed considerable rhetorical, oratorical, and polemical talents, which he used to good effect to gain the support of his followers, and to criticize and attack his external rivals. He utilized those talents with even more withering effect to silence and defeat internal opponents.

Policies: Activism, Populism, Statism. The three major characterizing elements of Herut's policies from 1949 onward were military activism, populism, and state action. Although there were variations over time, the main elements elaborated in Herut's lengthy 1949 electoral program were subsequently repeated in the Knesset and in later election programs and campaigns, and in broad outline were still there until 1965.

In foreign policy, it aimed to restore the entire territory of Palestine, including both sides of the Jordan, to the State of Israel. Partition and agreements with Jordan based on partition or territorial compromise were Munich-like policies of appeasement, and Ben-Gurion was a Chamberlain. The only way to achieve a stable peace was to use force to drive out the Arab and British invaders.

Herut consistently claimed that the Ezel (and not any other group or organization) had ejected the British by force and thus been responsible for the establishment of Jewish sovereignty and independence. It continued to advocate the use of force and militarily imposed solutions in Israel's relations with its neighbors, in pursuit of Israel's undisputed historical rights to the territories on both sides of the Jordan, and in particular, to recapture the whole of Jerusalem. Israel's rights in the part of the city under its control should immediately be asserted by declaring it the capital of the state, despite all UN and great-power plans for internationalization.

Herut's political populism is evident in its reliance on "the people" and direct democracy to curb a government whose rule was not in the people's interests. It suggested a constitution with a bill of rights, and direct democracy to decide important questions by referendum and to elect the president. The term of office of representatives was to be cut to a minimum, and provision made for recall. All British and "Israeli" emergency laws that had turned Israel into a police state were to be revoked, and the secret political police, inherited from the Mandate, and the government's detention camps, which Herut termed concentration camps, were to be dismantled. The party key, which had turned the state into the private property of a single party or a conspiracy of parties was to be abolished.

Herut's socioeconomic policies aimed at social security and improvement of the living standards of the weaker sections of the population. The economy was to be directed, regulated, and coordinated, with the major role given to national–public capital, but with ample opportunity for private initiative and enterprise within the boundaries of public and national need.

The socioeconomic populism of Herut is particularly prominent in its attacks upon the Histadrut's "trusts and monopolies," which were to be broken up. Its health fund was to be handed over to the state, and its economic enterprises were to be given to the workers, who would then be organized in independent corporative societies. Similarly, trade unions were to be made independent, and freed from party control. This was to be accompanied by industrial democracy—workers' participation in ownership, management, and profits.

Although Herut was on the right of the Israeli political spectrum in its opposition to the Left's policies and institutional structures, it did not advocate conventional conservative or free-enterprise economic policies. To the contrary, it saw itself as the representative of the underdog—the underprivileged, deprived, and discriminated against. Thus, in the first few years of its existence, Herut poured scorn on General Zionist economic policies for seeking to enrich the already wealthy. Similarly, in 1949 Begin suggested that if the people were hungry, then the property and capital of the bourgeois classes should be expropriated.[31]

Socioeconomic populism was also a major element in Herut's attacks upon the leaders of the Yishuv for policies of superiority and discrimination against the Oriental immigrants (*'edot hamizrah*), which had caused severe social problems. It called for the integration of the various groups, the breaking down of the divisions among citizens, and for dissolving ethnic distinctions in the melting pot of the nation. It proposed abolition of the independent party streams in education, which fractionalized the populace into "political tribes," and their replacement with a uniform state education system. All this was mixed with appeals to traditionalism, not as a matter of belief and practice but as a national attribute. Special emphasis would be placed upon the Torah as the basis of a constitution. Because of their special social significance, the Shabbat and Jewish festivals would be binding upon the state and its institutions, as well as a matter of right for Jewish citizens of Israel.[32]

Herut advocated the breaking up of the existing centers of power and dismantling the established institutional structures in order to improve the lot of the people. In doing so, it did not adopt an individualist and conservative opposition to government intervention. On the contrary, such advocacy foreshadowed an even greater role for the state in the administration and regulation of the economy and society than existed under Mapai's policies and practices. The point of Herut's critique was not to destroy the institutions but to remove them from the control of left-wing political parties and hand them over to the state in the name of the people. It was a policy of statism and state corporatism to replace the corrupt and repressive Mapai regime.

Party of Opposition. The purpose of Herut's 1949 election campaign was to rid the country of the Mapai regime, and it declared its readiness to establish an alternative government. It believed that its chances were good; Herut officials estimated that they would receive approximately one-third of the votes, as against 45 percent for the whole Histadrut sector. Optimists among them predicted that they would do even better, enabling them to unite the antilabor forces to form a coalition.[33] In the event, Herut received 49,782 votes (11.5 percent) and fourteen Knesset seats, and the rival Revisionist list, 2,892 votes (0.7 percent).

Herut turned its attention to the task of becoming a responsible parliamentary opposition. It quickly integrated into parliamentary life and procedure, and led by Begin, fulfilled the role in a demonstrative and formal manner, and sought wherever possible to emphasize its commitment to parliamentary practices and behavior. Although Herut received the chairmanship of a parliamentary comittee, its members felt that the animosities and antipathies of the past had not been forgotten. They asserted, for example, that parliamentary procedures were manipulated to preclude their supplying one of the deputy speakers, when numbers seemed to qualify them for such a post,[34] and resented being referred to by political opponents in the Knesset as an "enemy" rather than as a rival. They complained of economic disadvantage and deprivation on the grounds that former Ezel members were not given civil service appointments, and that because of Ben-Gurion's adamant opposition, Ezel fighters wounded or disabled in Ezel military actions prior to the establishment of the state were not granted by law the same benefits as Haganah veterans injured before the state was declared (this was later rectified administratively).[35]

Initially, there were strained social relations between Herut MKs and other MKs, but the processes of institutional socialization soon left their mark. The Herut members adapted their behavior to the parliamentary arena and proved that they were not different from other members; collegial relations developed despite the past and the lines of division.[36]

Herut members of the Knesset were active in all areas of legislative debate, but their main focus during the first few years was foreign policy and security issues. Herut perceived itself, and was perceived by the public, as the voice of military activism and the critic of the government's weakness, appeasement, collaboration (with the arch-enemy Britain), refusal to exercise military force to assert Israel's rights, and pursuit of futile peace and negotiating efforts with Israel's neighbors—these only weakened Israel's position and led to the sellout of its rights. In short, Herut was regarded as the war party.

Prior to the 1951 elections Herut underwent a change of image. Its stance on socioeconomic questions became less radical. In general, it became routinized and sought to convey more of an image of middle-class respectability and solidity. In those years economic and social problems were uppermost in the public mind. The dramatic upsurge in support for the General Zionists at the 1950 municipal elections resulted in a slight decline in the Herut vote. As a consequence, Herut reframed its economic policies in the direction of a more traditional right-wing approach and placed greater emphasis upon individual enterprise and private capital, seeking thereby to hold the members of the independent middle classes to whom Herut in the past had appealed on nationalist grounds but who now looked toward the General Zionists to solve the country's economic ills. Herut's critique, however, remained relatively unchanged; it continued to attack Mapai and Histadrut trusts and monopolies, the dependence of citizens upon party-controlled bureaucracies, and a system of government based upon shortages, discrimination, disadvantage, and favoritism.[37]

Because of the increasing similarity between Herut's economic policies and those of the General Zionists, Herut's activist defense policies were the most distinctive element in its public political image. According to Begin during the election campaign, "The bullet which killed Abdullah destroyed all of Ben-Gurion's and Sharett's foreign policy. If a week ago a trustworthy government had stood at the head of the state and not the government of a false prophet, we would be over the walls of Jerusalem and on the Jordan, and all the nations would approve."[38]

Herut attacked the General Zionists for their obvious willingness to join in an antinational coalition with Mapai, "the dismemberers of the homeland and the trust owners." It presented itself as the only force remaining to preserve national integrity, and reiterated its belief that it would achieve power in the state within a few years. Consistent with this point of view, Herut consistently declared that it would never join a coalition headed by Ben-Gurion, even if invited.[39]

The equation of nationalism and the concern to maintain national integrity with antileftism, antisocialism, and opposition to the labor parties that made up the Histadrut became an increasingly important component of Herut's political stance. The labor parties were not true to the national ideals because they compromised on defense and foreign policy questions, and protected their own sectional party-controlled economic interests at the expense of, and to the detriment of, those of the "people."

The electorate in 1951 was neither impressed with Herut's new image of economic and social respectability and solidity nor with its militant national-ism. Herut's proportion of the vote was reduced by almost half, to 6.6 percent, and it received fewer votes in absolute terms (45,651) than in 1949 from an electorate that had expanded by nearly 60 percent. Herut leaders regarded this as a severe blow, and Begin, together with two other leaders, took it as a vote of no confidence and evidence of failure, and made plans to retire from politics. They attributed their defeat to the people's tiring of the period of heroism. The people appreciated all that had been wrought but did not want the national revolution to continue; they sought peace and quiet, housing, a satisfactory income, and food. In such a state of mind, they were not interested in radical change. What is more, the many new immigrants from backward societies who had difficulty in accustoming themselves to modern society were unaware of Herut's contribution and message:

> If in the future, after years of education and information, they will one day assist Herut to overthrow the existing regime, currently they prostrate them-selves before the vehicles, military police, loudspeakers and flowing hair of the Messiah, the King. They worry about a crust of bread, a day's work, housing and settlement, are intimidated by even the most minor Mapai official or civil servant who controls the camp or ma'abarah, upon whom they are totally dependent and to whom they are therefore loyal, and before whom they wait in line to have their vote for the government entered into their identity documents.[40]

The Reparations Agreement: Threat to Democracy? Begin's intention to retire was not realized, and he was cast back into the center of the political limelight by the government's announcement in January 1952 that it intended to conclude a reparations agreement with West Germany. For Herut, this was tantamount to concluding an agreement with the Nazi murderers and their heirs, and was equivalent to trading in the blood and lives of slaughtered Jewish brethren. It was totally offensive to its national pride.

Just before the Knesset debate, Begin addressed a public rally and urged his supporters to march upon the Knesset to express their opposition while the debate was in progress. He vowed to do everything to ensure that the agreement would not eventuate, and made it clear that Herut would go underground and even be prepared to resort to arms, if this was necessary, to stop the agreement. "When you fired upon us with the cannon, then I gave an order: No! Today, I will give the order: Yes! This will be a war for life or death."[41] The crowd stormed the Knesset and stones were thrown through the windows. The police used batons and tear gas to disperse the crowd and prevent it from entering the Knesset chamber. Inside, near-chaos ruled, insults were traded freely, and at times it appeared as if members would come to blows. The speaker called a number of recesses because of the pandemonium.[42]

During the debate Begin repeated some of the threats that he had made outside. When asked by the speaker to leave the podium, he refused, saying that if he "could not speak, nobody would speak"—which had ominous overtones in view of what was happening outside the building. Subsequently, he was expelled from the Knesset for three months for unparliamentary behavior.[43]

Ben-Gurion treated "Begin's tragic and despicable, but failed attempt at a putsch"[44] as a direct attack upon the foundations of Israeli democracy and an endeavor to use force to undermine rule by parliamentary majority. In a radio broadcast to the nation the next day, he explained that these dangers had been averted by the loyal actions of the army and the police, and that he would not hestitate to use those forces in the future to protect Israeli democracy from similar attacks.

For three years Herut had worked hard at being a responsible parliamentary opposition and at demonstrating its full integration into the parliamentary system by becoming its defender par excellence. The foregoing events set the process back and aroused the old apprehensions. They also reinstated Herut as the major opposition party, even though the General Zionists, with two and one-half times as many Knesset seats, opposed the agreement, too. Its status as the leading opposition party was reinforced when the General Zionists joined the coalition some months later.

The events also enabled Herut to consolidate its claim of being the defender of national honor and national pride, willing to sacrifice material advantage for nationalist vision and values, in sharp contrast with the other parties. Over the next few years it sharpened this oppositionary stance by simultaneously attacking all parties in the coalition, both on the left and the right. In this way Herut was able to continue to present itself as the *only* alternative to the existing regime. Its position was strengthened by the change in the political agenda that made security the major issue as relations between Israel and its neighbors, particularly Egypt, worsened. The blockade of the Suez Canal, frequent terrorist incursions into Israel with increasing civilian casualties, an escalating pattern of Israeli retaliation raids, and Communist bloc arms supplied to Egypt generated a full-scale debate within Israeli political and military circles about various policy alternatives.

Herut called for more active policies, and criticized the government for weakness and neglect, which led to lapses in security and permitted terrorist incursions. Mapai was accused of cynically using defense issues for electoral gain. Thus, just before the 1955 elections Begin attacked Ben-Gurion for intimating that Israel might use force against Egypt. When Herut had suggested such policies, he said, Ben-Gurion had rejected them as the height of irresponsible adventurism and militarism. For Ben-Gurion publicly to adopt them now was, in Begin's view, the height of irresponsibility. It could be explained only by the cynical use that Mapai made of such important issues for its narrow electoral needs. Instead of remaining silent about such options, Ben-Gurion had made the threats to gain votes and popular support by calming down a tense and insecure public. This Begin characterized as "votes for blood." Because the element of surprise was lost, Israeli soldiers would now die needlessly; Mapai, he charged, "did not hesitate to use the blood of Israeli soldiers to grease the wheels of its regime."[45]

In the 1955 elections Herut made extensive gains, virtually doubling its share to a high of 12.6 percent (107,190 votes) and winning fifteen Knesset seats. Most important of all, Herut for the first time had become the second-largest party, which served to underline its claim of being the major opposition party and the only real alternative to Mapai. Its sense of victory was heightened by Mapai's loss of five seats, which it described as the beginning of the decline of Mapai. In contrast, Herut saw itself moving "from unvanquished opposition to victory, government, and the realization of its aims."[46]

Herut's success was explained at the time by an astute observer as stemming partly from its activism, and partly from a revolt of the petty bourgeoisie against the Mapai-General Zionist coalition, which represented large capital, both public and private. But in the main it was attributed to the growing support of voters from 'edot hamizrah in the development towns and transit camps. Begin's emphasis upon the issue of ethnic discrimination had clearly begun to appeal to those whom Mapai's policy of absorption had failed. According to this analysis, even though most Oriental (Sephardi) immigrants had work and housing, a social gap and a sense of inferiority to Ashkenazim had been created. These growing feelings of disadvantage and animosity against the pre-1948 Yishuv were now being expressed at the ballot box.[47] Thus, the party of the political outsiders had begun to represent the social outsiders.

For the next ten years Herut made very little further electoral progress. Its proportion of the vote rose by about 1 percent in 1959 and 1961 to 13.6 and 13.8 percent, giving it seventeen seats on each occasion. Even the ethnic riots in Wadi Salib in 1959 did not seem to help it appreciably, and neither did Mapai's problems in 1961. Although it remained the second-largest party, it seemed to have reached a plateau. Mapai's effectiveness in meeting the security problem, and the steady absolute rise in the standard of living of the Oriental immigrants appeared to have stopped Herut's advance by cutting the ground out from under its main electoral issues.

Herut began to look elsewhere to strengthen its political position, and found a positive response from the General Zionist section of the Liberal party to the idea of a joint parliamentary bloc. As noted earlier, the bloc was not a great success initially, gaining twenty-six seats in 1965. But the agreement to form it and the attendant decision to present a joint Herut-Liberal list in the Histadrut elections were a major turning point in Israeli politics in the founding period, and are separately dealt with in a later chapter.

The Religious Parties

In the first six Knesset elections, the religious parties won a remarkably consistent proportion of the votes that over the years increased somewhat. In the first two elections, they gained in the vicinity of 12 percent, giving them sixteen and fifteen seats. From 1955 they averaged close to 14.5 percent with a range of 13.8 to 15.4 percent, regularly gaining either seventeen and eighteen seats. In the 1949 elections, the four religious parties appeared on one list, the United Religious Front. In 1951 the parties disagreed about the allocation of places on the list and some policy issues, and ran separately. The United Religious Front was reconstituted after the elections in order to join the government coalition but split again after a year. From 1955 until 1965, the parties usually ran on two lists, reflecting the division between the Mizrachi parties, which gained about two-thirds of the votes and seats, and the Aguda parties, which gained about one-third (although on occasion the two Aguda parties ran separately).

The Mizrachi Parties

The Mizrachi was established at the beginning of the century to mobilize and represent religious Jews within the Zionist Organization. Its distinctive ideological claim was that political activity by Jews to reestablish an independent Jewish political entity was not in opposition to Jewish religious laws and principles but was the fulfillment of religious yearnings for the return to Zion. To cooperate in Zionist work, therefore, was religious obligation and mitzvah, and would enable the full restoration of ancient Jewish traditions and institutions. In participating in the Zionist movement, the Mizrachi leaders rejected the separatist and segregationist point of view in Orthodoxy, which steadfastly refused to participate in any Jewish communal endeavor necessitating cooperation with nonobservant Jews.

From the 1920s onward there were actually two Mizrachi parties. The Mizrachi party had attracted to its membership a strong middle-class element: traders, shopkeepers, educators, lawyers, academics, and other professionals, united under the slogan that came to epitomize its ideology: "*Eretz yisrael, le'am yisrael al pi torat yisrael*" (The land of Israel, for the people of Israel according to the Torah of Israel). Its economic and social policies were clearly identified with those of the Right and center in Zionist and Yishuv politics. The other Mizrachi party was a labor movement, Hapo'el Hamizrachi, whose position was neatly summed up in the motto "*Torah Va'vodah*" (Torah and Labor). It acted in parallel with the Histadrut to provide a whole range of services to its working-class members, and eventually developed a series of economic enterprises. A *haluzic* sector established kibbutzim and moshavim.

In the Yishuv, the Mizrachi parties, loosely joined in a world federation, received 16.6 percent of the votes to Asefat Hanivharim in 1944, and 12.4 percent to the Zionist Congress in 1946. By this time Hapo'el Hamizrachi, although established later, was more than twice as large as the Mizrachi. Both cooperated closely with Mapai in the various executive bodies of the Yishuv. In return for their support, they had been granted the dominant, if not sole, voice on questions of religion, and they controlled the organizational and institutional frameworks for promoting religious services for the Jewish population, such as the Chief Rabbinate, the Religious Councils, and the religious educational stream. Given this historic tradition of partnership with Mapai, it is not surprising that the Mizrachi parties received two ministries in the Provisional Government. Somewhat more unusual was the agreement of the Mizrachi parties and Aguda parties to constitute the United Religious Front in the 1949 elections.

The initiative and impetus for unity came from the leaders of the Mizrachi, while within Hapo'el Hamizrachi there was considerable uncertainty and opposition. The establishment of the state seemed to offer a sound basis for realizing long-cherished hopes of religious unity in view of that event's vindication of religious Zionism rather than the anti-Zionism of the Aguda. Under these conditions, the Mizrachi parties sought to create and lead a much larger camp.

Opposition to the merger derived from concern about the loss of distinctiveness in a larger body united solely on the basis of religion, and the consequent inability to be involved in the broader social, political, and economic affairs of the state. Affiliation with the Aguda in one united front was likely to create a separatist religious ghetto that would cut off religious Jews from contact with the nonreligious majority, and would thus, in the long run, lessen their influence and divert them from the path of religious Zionism. In the end, because of these doubts and the historical rivalries and disagreements, it was decided to be satisfied, at first, with a joint list and a united parliamentary bloc, and a federation of parties rather than a merger of the four into a new party.[48]

The distinctive role of the religious Zionist parties in the political system was reflected in their participation in all government coalitions between 1948 and 1965, except for about a year in opposition in 1958–59 after resignation from the government over a religious issue. This enabled them to control the institutions and administration of the official and public practice of the Jewish religion in Israel. They gave particular emphasis to establishment of a ministry of religions for the administration, supervision, and promotion of religious services. Their emphasis was also evident in their support for, and dominance of, the Chief Rabbinate, the religious courts, and the local Religious Councils, as well as in their early but unsuccessful demands that separate religious units be set up in the army for the purposes of ensuring that the religious needs of observant soldiers would be fully met.[49]

The religious Zionist parties also aimed to strengthen the role of religion in the life of the individual and the nation, preserve religious values, and where possible endow the state with a religious character in its practices. In these matters it was fully supported by the Aguda parties, which often took a more extreme position. By and large, on these questions the Mizrachi parties sought to find the common ground and the possibility for compromise between the needs of religion and the views of the nonreligious parties; the Aguda parties tended to emphasize nonagreement and to highlight the differences and the distinctions.[50]

The provision of kashrut in state and military institutions, marriage and personal status, and Shabbat observance were salient in the thinking of the religious parties. In these areas they succeeded in having many of their policies accepted and their needs met, generally by means of coalition negotiations. Mapai was prepared to grant such policy concessions in order to establish coalitions, maximize national unity, and prevent a Kulturkampf. Much more controversial were education of the new immigrants from Asia and Africa and conscription of women. The religious parties were far less successful in having their demands met on those issues, which led to a series of cabinet crises and governmental resignations between 1949 and 1952. Thus, although the religious parties were among Mapai's most steady coalition partners, they were also the most troublesome.

The inability of the religious parties to reestablish the United Religious Front prior to the 1951 elections reflected the resurgence of many of the traditional differences between the Zionist and non-Zionist religious parties in their attitude toward the state and its needs. Despite agreement on the education issue, the religious parties were divided on the question of conscription of women. The Zionist parties recognized conscription's importance for the state and the nation, and agreed to an alternative form of national service for women who did not wish to serve in the armed forces for religious reasons. The Aguda parties took the traditional view that for women to serve in the armed forces was against the Torah, and that alternative forms of national service would not solve the problem, for it was no different from army service in taking women out of the closed home environment and exposing them to grave moral danger.

Mizrachi was somewhat closer to the Aguda position, and was therefore more inclined to reconstitute the United Front, which would have implied acceptance of many of the Aguda positions; Hapo'el Hamizrachi was staunchly opposed, arguing that the experience of the previous two years had vindicated its original opposition to the United Front. In particular, it had deprived the religious Zionist parties of the opportunity of influencing events in the direction of their distinctive policies, and had forced religious Jewry into a ghetto with the forces opposed to Zionism, and put paid to any attempt to come to grips with modern society in a synthesizing manner. Hapo'el Hamizrachi was also dissatisfied with the distribution of seats within the United Religious Front, suggesting that the Aguda parties had received more than they deserved electorally, and that it had received far less than its share. When one of Hapo'el Hamizrachi's leading factions threatened to run its own list, the Mizrachi parties decided not to participate in a United Front rather than face an internal split.[51]

Running separately permitted electoral reflection of the major change that had taken place in the relative strength of the parties, and in the balance of forces within the religious camp. Hapo'el Hamizrachi proved that its complaints about insufficient parliamentary representation were well founded, and added two seats to the six that it had won in 1949, whereas Mizrachi won only two seats, compared with four at the previous elections. This was a clear indication of the dominance of the labor-oriented, *haluzic* elements in religious Zionism as opposed to the more traditional and bourgeois elements.

By the time of the 1955 elections, a process of merger and unification between them was well under way, occasioned in part by the decline in strength, influence, and leadership capability of the Mizrachi, particularly with the passing from the political scene of the leading rabbis, such as Yehudah Leib Maimon, Meir Bar-Ilan, and Ze'ev Gold, who had previously stood at its helm. In 1955 the Mizrachi parties ran on a joint list and increased their combined strength slightly, to eleven seats. Not long afterward the merger was completed and the National Religious Party (NRP) was established.

During the period of the Second Knesset, the forces pulling the United Religious Front apart became stronger. At first an agreement was reached after the elections for the United Religious Front to be reconstituted and to enter the coalition, which it did in October 1951, on the basis of Mapai's agreeing to a moratorium on the issues of religious education and conscription of women. The Aguda parties sought a two-year moratorium, which was agreed to by Ben-Gurion with regard to education, but on conscription he was prepared to agree to only one year. Thus, when in September 1952 Ben-Gurion sought to introduce legislation to provide for alternative forms of national service for women in place of army service, the Aguda parties left the cabinet and went into opposition. This was the end of the United Religious Front; it left the Mizrachi parties as the only representatives of religious Jewry in the cabinet.

From this juncture onward, the Mizrachi parties took up what became their traditional stance of loyal and reliable coalition partner, what was later termed "*hashutafut hahistorit*" (the historic partnership). In this regard, their capacity to seek and reach compromises on religious questions rather than take extreme and uncompromising positions, as did the Aguda parties, stood them in good stead. Because of their involvement in all aspects of the state's development and their strong Zionist ideological stance, they were able slowly but surely to assume political responsibility for the formal and official status that the Jewish religion assumed in the new state, as outlined earlier and as expressed in a steadily widening body of legislation.

The task of the Mizrachi parties was made easier by the departure of the Aguda parties from government because, although this meant a decline in religious representation in the coalition, it also meant that they did not have to fight intrareligious battles and did not have to make compromises to maintain religious unity. This was particularly relevant to the questions involving state-administered religious facilities, and the quest to extend these both in breadth and depth, on which the Aguda parties with their anti-Zionist and anti-Mizrachi past, were, to say the least, still somewhat ambivalent.

By the time the full merger between Mizrachi and Hapo'el Hamizrachi had been achieved, the religious Zionist approach had become a religious *mamlakhti* approach. It accorded positive religious value to the state and its institutions, and regarded all forms of service to the state and nation as fulfillment of a religious obligation. Moreover, it had clearly become the dominant trend in representing the Jewish religion in politics.

The strength of Hapo'el Hamizrachi and its success in absorbing, integrating, and gaining the support of the new immigrants in its settlements is also reflected in the distribution of voters in the 1955 elections. In that year, 32 percent of the total Mizrachi vote came from rural areas, which included many of the new moshavim established in the previous six years. Among these were many voters of Sephardi origin who had come to the Hapo'el Hamizrachi settlements as a result of the operation of the party key. Although the absolute numbers remained more or less stable, the rural proportion of the NRP dropped to about 19 percent by the end of the founding period as a result of its strengthened urban vote.

Much of the increased urban vote came from younger voters and reflected the success of the NRP's affiliated educational institutions—the high schools, yeshivot, and university—and its youth movement, which had instilled national religious values in a younger generation. Many of this generation carried these values with them through their army service, and in that way expressed their joint commitment to religious and national goals. Particularly important in mobilizing these commitments in a party direction was a youth section of the party that became increasingly influential in party affairs. The sheer weight of the absolute numbers of youth and the demonstrated capacity of the religious Zionist sector to hold onto its youth educated in Israel and now fully participant in all aspects of national life and society were radically new developments in a party that had experienced considerable difficulty in this direction in the past and considerable loss of youth due to secularization.

NRP politics and policies between 1955 and 1965 can best be described as the politics of the status quo. After the initial crises and advances of the early 1950s, the NRP settled down to preserving its gains and strengthening its institutional hold over the official bodies that it controlled. Little attempt was made to extend the reach of religious legislation, and in some areas the NRP was barely able to maintain the status quo established and was forced to retreat. The politics of the period was symbolized by two issues: "Who is a Jew?" and Sabbath legislation.

The question "Who is a Jew?" came to public attention in 1958 when the minister of interior Yisrael Bar-Yehudah (Ahdut Ha'avodah), issued administrative regulations to the effect that for purposes of registration of nationality in the Population Register, and for determining Jewishness for the purposes of the Law of Return, a personal declaration of Jewishness would suffice. Such a personal declaration would be accepted even if, according to Jewish religious law, the person making it was not regarded as Jewish.

The NRP objected to the regulations on three grounds: they violated the existing coalition agreement; they infringed on the exclusive jurisdiction of the rabbinical courts in matters of personal status; and they threatened to split the Jewish people into two groups, only one of which was Jewish according to Jewish law and tradition. By one action three basic elements of the NRP's political stance were undermined; it dismantled the status quo, undercut the official rabbinate, and challenged the NRP's ideological commitment to the ethnic unity of the Jewish people on which it based its policy of Zionist cooperation and involvement.

When the government majority backed Bar-Yehudah, the NRP believed that it had no alternative but to resign, and it had to wait until after the 1959 elections to bring about the withdrawal of these administrative regulations by insisting upon, and gaining, control of the Ministry of the Interior. This resolved the immediate political issue, although it became a major judicial question during the 1960s and reasserted itself politically in the 1970s.

The coalition agreements of 1955, 1959, and 1961 all included provision for a bill banning the conduct of business on the Sabbath, which would join existing legislation forbidding the employment of Jews on the Sabbath. The latter also had provisions for the exemption of essential services, which were broadly administered by the minister of labor. The NRP wanted the new projected law extended to cover employers, particularly the self-employed and the cooperatives, and to give the minister of religions a much greater say in the granting of exemptions. Suffice it to say, no Sabbath bill was presented to the Knesset between 1955 and 1965, and from the NRP's point of view this was a significant failure. This, and the widespread granting of exemptions, were clear evidence of regression from the agreed upon status quo.

The Aguda Parties

For Agudat Yisrael, rabbinic authority was, from the outset, the decisive locus of authority. Over the years, this developed into the informally constituted Moezet Gedolei Hatorah (Council of Torah Sages), which consisted of leading rabbis and chassidic rebbes whose decisions provided the guidelines and often the specific details for the political activities of Aguda leaders. Democratic organization based upon the votes and views of the members had little impact. At best, they could be brought to the attention of the rabbinic authorities by the Aguda political leaders, who were not, however, members of the party's authoritative decision-making body.

The operation of the Yishuv structures and the pattern of events in Europe led the Aguda parties into a *modus vivendi* of cooperation with the Jewish authorities in the Yishuv. This eventuated in a split and the secession from their ranks of some groups from the old Yishuv who demanded total separatism and total opposition to any form of secular Jewish political authority. The mainstream of the Aguda, by way of contrast, recognized the need for Jewish unity and cooperated in order to promote and pursue its interests, but remained separate from the decision-making bodies.

Participation in a Jewish and Zionist state, however, presented acute ideological problems. It could be construed as according recognition and legitimacy to bodies that were constituted and behaved in ways that were anathema to the Aguda parties and in whose policies, decisions, and moral considerations they did not wish to be implicated. This was the fundamental dilemma of the Aguda: how to respond to constituted nonreligious Jewish political authority.

The dilemma was resolved before the establishment of the state. The Aguda leadership, rather than adopt the traditional separatist position that had, for example, kept the Aguda for the most part outside the official frameworks of the Yishuv and the Jewish Agency, and from participating in elections for Knesset Yisrael, came to terms with the reality of the Jewish state, and decided to participate in it as a party. The letter sent by Ben-Gurion and Rabbi Maimon on behalf of the Jewish Agency setting out the minimum religious provisions in the new state (discussed earlier) enabled the party to join the Provisional State Council, to take a ministry in the Provisional Government, to participate in the elections for the Constituent Assembly, and to be a member of the coalition between 1949 and 1952.

The transition came about, first, for pragmatic reasons. To promote and pursue Aguda interests, the leaders had no alternative but to participate in the political process. They could not, as in the days of the Yishuv, refuse to participate in the official Jewish and Zionist bodies because in the state there were no others. They thus set minimum religious demands for participation. Ideologically, however, the Aguda maintained its traditional opposition to Zionism as a political and national ideology, and made no moves toward recognition of its legitimacy.

On the other hand, the establishment of the state as both a Jewish and democratic state facilitated the Aguda's integration into the political system without the need to accord legitimacy to Zionism as an ideology. Clearly, the fact that the state was an existing entity solved part of the messianic dilemma. Moreover, the fact that it was a Jewish state provided an impetus and encouragement to participate. At the very least, it was no different from any other state. More positively, to participate provided the Aguda with an opportunity to influence events in the state, and to fight against that which it opposed. The democratic nature of Israeli society permitted it to pursue its own goals and interests freely, with minimum demands for strict ideological conformity.

The events of the Holocaust and the impact of the actual establishment of the state also played a significant role in creating an atmosphere that facilitated entry of the Aguda parties into the mainstream. Aguda leaders at the time were moved by the recognition that events of major historical importance had occurred of which they were part.[52] This was particularly critical in the move toward unity in the religious camp and the formation of the United Religious Front, which was influenced by the belief that together the parties might achieve more for Orthodox Judaism, might add a spiritual dimension to the physical exodus from the *galut* and the physical settlement in Israel.[53]

Thus, Aguda politicians participated in the state and its affairs, without regarding the affairs as holy, sanctifying, or even of positive ideological value. Large sections of the Aguda, moreover, remained neutral or lukewarm to the state, and some remained implacably opposed, viewing it with contempt or disdain. As the years passed and the immediate impact of the historic events faded, the latter attitudes strengthened, and received particular impetus from the withdrawal of the Aguda from the cabinet in 1952 and its retreat into opposition.

The Aguda parties went into the 1949 elections as part of the United Religious Front but without any previous record or experience in elections in Palestine. The Aguda proportion of the URF was fixed at 37.5 percent, but the division between the two Aguda parties was the subject of considerable disagreement, with Po'alei Agudat Yisrael demanding parity. Eventually, after rabbinical arbitration and threats of breakaway, it received 45 percent of the Aguda share, but when the final distribution was made, each of the Aguda parties had three seats. The parties ran separately in 1951, Aguda winning 2.0 percent and three seats, and Po'alei Aguda, 1.6 percent and two seats. In 1955 they again ran together, winning 39,836 votes (4.7 percent) and six seats. This was more or less where they remained. Although they managed to raise their proportion to over 5 percent, whether they ran together (1959, 1961) or separately (1965), they consistently won six seats.

The Aguda vote was very much an urban vote, with only about 5 percent coming from rural sources, although the rural proportion among Po'alei Aguda with its settlements was higher, about 14 percent. In the urban areas, the Aguda parties did best in Jerusalem and Bene-Berak, where there were strong concentrations of Orthodox Jews. The Aguda regularly gained over 40 percent of its total vote in these areas. The vote came from the same groups that had constituted the Aguda in Europe: the chassidim; those educated in the Lithuanian-type yeshivot in Israel, which from the early 1950s onward grew rapidly in strength, self-confidence, and influence; many who had migrated from Hungary and their offspring; and the old, established Jerusalem traditional Orthodoxy. Noticeably absent were Orthodox Jews of Sephardi origin. Nor were there any rabbis of Sephardi origin represented on Moezet Gedolei Hatorah.

During its period in the cabinet, the Aguda held the Ministry of Social Welfare, and its representative was Rabbi Y. M. Levin, a leader of the Aguda from Poland and a relative of the Rebbe of Gur. The Aguda's characteristic tendency was to take a stand on principle and to highlight differences between it and the secular parties, as well as those distinguishing it from its Mizrachi partners in the United Religious Front. Despite a tendency not to go out of its way to seek compromise, it remained in the government for over four years, through various conflicts and crises, notably over education.

But finally, an issue arose to which the Aguda was deeply opposed in principle on religious, moral, and social grounds: the conscription of women. Its intransigence led it out of the cabinet while it publicly proclaimed the values that distinguished it from the rest of the society, including the religious Zionist parties, which were prepared to make concessions because of the needs of the state.

In opposition, the Aguda's stance hardened, and it directed much of its criticism against the NRP for a weakness and lack of religious conviction that led to the compromising of religious standards and values. On the other hand, because of the Aguda's unwavering commitment to the letter of the Halakhah, it began to exert an influence over sections of the NRP. But overall, its experience in the state during the founding period led it away from the state rather than toward it. Instead of being willing to bend, it tended to make increasingly inflexible demands. Rather than becoming more integrated, it became more stridently separatist and isolationist, and not a trifle contemptuous and disdainful of state and national values.

Notes

1. For an analysis of the significance of ideology in the Yishuv in general, and of the major axes of ideological issue differences, see Dan Horowitz and Moshe Lissak, *Origins of the Israeli Polity: Palestine under the Mandate* (Chicago: University of Chicago Press, 1978), chap. 6.

2. These figures and much of the subsequent discussion of Mapai is based upon Peter Y. Medding, *Mapai in Israel: Political Organisation and Government in a New Society* (Cambridge: Cambridge University Press, 1972).

3. This was after the split in the kibbutz movement in 1951 against the background of the conflict between Mapai and Mapam. Prior to that date Hever Hakvuzot was overwhelmingly loyal to Mapai, whereas the Hakibbutz Hameuhad was split between Mapai and Ahdut Ha'avodah, which after 1948 became part of Mapam (see later discussion). Thus, in 1949 and 1951 Mapai received about 42 percent of the votes in Hakibbutz Hameuhad.

4. See Medding, *Mapai*, pp. 19-81.

5. A characteristic statement of this position is to be found in the speech Ben-Gurion made to the Knesset on 8.3.1949, in presenting the first government together with the basic principles. The speech is reprinted in David Ben-Gurion, *Hazon vede-rekh*, 5 vols. (Tel Aviv: Mapai, 1951-57), 1:61-72.

6. For a detailed analysis of Mapai's economic and social policies in the early part of the founding period, see Izhak Yanai, "*Haidiologiyah hahevratit shel mapai leor mediniyutah bamedinah uvahistadrut bashanim 1948-1953*" (Ph.D. diss., Tel Aviv University, 1987).

7. David Ben-Gurion, *Medinat yisrael hamehudeshet* (Tel Aviv: Am Oved, 1969), pp. 362-78.

8. The theoretical dimensions of *mamlakhtiut* and its application to policy and structure are the subject of chapter 7.

9. For a somewhat different analysis of *mamlakhtiut* in its more general cultural and symbolic senses, se Charles S. Liebman and Eliezer Don-Yehiya, *Civil Religion in Israel* (Berkeley: University of California Press, 1983), pp. 81-122.

10. See, for example, Mapai election publicity in the newspapers, as in *Haaretz*, 11.7.1951.

11. Moshe Braslavski, *Tnu'at hapo'alim haerez yisraelit*, 4 vols. (Hakibbutz Ha-meuhad, 1962), 4:106ff.

12. Ibid.

13. The split in Mapam is analyzed in detail in Yael Yishai, "Si'atiut bitnu'at haavodah beyisrael" (Ph.D diss., The Hebrew University, 1976).

14. See Zvi Segal "Iggud hayamaim 1935-1953: meiagudah mekomit le'igud arzi" (Master's thesis, Tel Aviv University, 1976); Levi Kantor, *Lelo maso panim: hitpathut*

yahasei' avodah beyisrael (Tel Aviv: Yahad, 1977), pp. 127–56, particularly pp. 144ff.; Yosef Almogi, *B'ovi hakorah* (Jerusalem: 'Idanim, 1980).

15. Walter Z. Laqueur, *Communism and Nationalism in the Middle East* (London: Routledge and Kegan Paul, 1956), p. 119. In general this is a good source for a brief analysis of Maki.

16. The best analysis of this party is Khayyam Zev Paltiel, "The Progressive Party: A Study of a Small Party in Israel" (Ph.D diss., The Hebrew University, Jerusalem, 1961).

17. Ben-Gurion, *Medinat yisrael hamehudeshet*, pp. 362–78.

18. See "Poles," "Hazionim Haklaliyim Beyisrael," *Miflagot baarez erev habehirot laknesset hashniyah* (Tel Aviv: Pirsumei Haaretz, 1951), p. 19.

19. For example, see the long discussion in Ben-Gurion's unpublished diaries for 26.11.1950, at Ben-Gurion Archives, Sedeh Boker, in which he clearly attributes the results to a protest against Mapai and the failure of its policies, and concludes that if the movement to the General Zionists is to be stopped or reversed, the government and Mapai will have to correct and improve their economic policies.

20. *Haaretz*, 17.7.1951.

21. Both these coalition negotiations are described in Ben-Gurion, *Medinat yisrael hamehudeshet*, pp. 411–13, 424–26.

22. Dubi Bergman, "'Tnu'at Haherut'—Meirgun mahteret lemiflagah politit," *Kivvunim* 21 (November 1983): 67.

23. Article in *Herut*, no. 81 (November 1947), cited ibid., p. 69.

24. Bergman, "'Tnu'at Haherut," pp. 69–70.

25. Ibid., p. 70.

26. The text of Begin's announcement, "Dvar mefaked haelyon shel ezel la'am bezion," "Shidur Bkol Herut," 15.5.48, is to be found in Shmuel Eisenstadt, Hayim Adler, Rivka Bar Yosef, and Reuven Kahana, eds., *Yisrael-hevrah mithavah: nituah soziologi shel mekorot* (Jerusalem: Magnes Press, 1972), p. 240.

27. Bergman, "'Tnu'at Haherut," p. 82.

28. These themes recur in almost every issue of the party newspaper *Herut* for the month of January 1949 leading up to the elections.

29. This is described in Yohanan Bader, *Haknesset veani* (Jerusalem: 'Idanim, 1979), pp. 18–21.

30. Some of these are dealt with in Yoram Lichtenstein, "Tnu'at haherut: mivneh vetahalikhim pnimi'yim" (Master's thesis, The Hebrew University, 1974).

31. Yohanan Bader, personal interview, 23.3.68, in archives in Oral History Division, Institute of Contemporary Jewry, The Hebrew University, interview 6, p. 8.

32. The program appears in full in *Herut*, 21.1.49.

33. Bader, *Haknesset veani*, pp. 21–22.

34. In fact, what happened was that the number of deputy speakers was fixed so that the numerical line was drawn before it reached them, the positions being occupied by larger Knesset factions.

35. Ben-Gurion, unpublished diaries, 8.9.49, 22.9.49; Bader, *Haknesset veani* p. 25–26.

36. Bader, *Haknesset veani*, ibid; David Hacohen, *'Et lesaper* (Tel Aviv: Am Oved, 1974), pp. 201–2.

37. See Aryeh Ziv, "Hademut shel Herut," *Miflagot baarez erev habehirot*, p. 48; *Herut*, July 1951; *Haaretz*, July 1951; Bader, 51.ff. *Haknesset veani*, pp. 51ff.

38. *Haaretz*, 29.7.51.

39. Ziv, p. 49; *Haaretz*, 27.7.51, 14.8.51.

40. This appeared in *Herut* 3.8.51, and was written by Yohanan Bader; It also appears in Bader, *Haknesset veani*, pp. 54–55.

41. From Begin's speech, as it appears in *Herut*, 8.3.52.

42. See the reports in the daily press for 8.1.52, particularly *Haaretz* and *Davar*. See also the description in Michael Bar-Zohar, *Ben-Gurion*, 3 vols. (Tel Aviv: Am Oved, 1975–78), pp. 920ff.

43. *Divrei Haknesset*, 7.1.1952, pp. 907–64.

44. David Ben-Gurion, "Yoman Ben-Gurion," unpublished diaries, 11.1.1952.

45. *Herut*, 11.7.55. The press report is headed "Mapai mukhanah la'asot midam hayaleinu shemen legalgaleha."

46. *Herut*, 15.8.55, which reports Begin's speech summing up the elections under the heading "Meioposiziyah bilti menuzahat lenizahon, leshilton, lehagshamah," a direct quotation from his speech. The latter was published in full on 19.8.55.

47. Amitai Etzioni in *Haaretz*, 11.8.55.

48. This is dealt with in great detail in Moshe Unna, *Bidrakhim nifradot* (Jerusalem: Moreshet Yad Shapira, 1983).

49. See Gary S. Schiff, *Tradition and Politics: The Religious Parties of Israel* (Detroit, Mich.: Wayne State University Press, 1977); Charles S. Liebman and Eliezer Don-Yehiya, *Religion and Politics in Israel* (Bloomington: Indiana University Press, 1984).

50. For evidence and discussion of this difference, see Unna, *Bidrakhim Nifradot*.

51. Ibid.

52. See, for example, the speech made by Rabbi I. M. Levin, *Divrei Haknesset*, 12.2.51, at p. 1053; see also *Hamodiy'a*, 25.9.50, 29.9.50, 13.10.50.

53. Unna, *Bidrakhim Nifradot*, notes the impact that this had upon Aguda politicians.

5

Issue Structure, Electoral Response, and Coalition Politics

The capacity of the major political actors—the political parties and their leaders—to influence events and exercise political power in democratic societies is, in the last resort, dependent upon winning public support in electoral competition. Ideological and issue differences are usually important elements in elections, and in policy conflict within political institutions between elections. Particularly in coalition systems such conflicts must be resolved if governments are to be constituted and political decisions are to be made. These, in turn, are dependent upon the structure and intensity of the issue differences, and the overall ideological or issue distance between the parties.

The ideological distance between parties derives from the distribution of party opinions and policies on the relevant issue dimensions. Large and consistent differences between parties on all major issues result in maximum ideological distance. Conversely, the overall ideological distance or polarization will be attenuated if parties that are distant from one another on some issues are close on others, or if large parties are situated close to the center of the political spectrum.

There is a second element: the intensity with which issue positions are held. Although it is almost inevitable that maximum ideological distance will give rise to and reflect intense rivalry and political competition, it is also not uncommon for parties that are by and large on the same side of the continuum and relatively close to each other to differ intensely on a whole range of specific issues. In this instance, proximity and even shared values will create intense differences, as, for example, in the case of conflicts between socialist parties, in which the contest is over ideological truth and over the same segment of the electorate.

Our analysis is based upon the issue positions of the parties and their leaders, which clearly are the most significant for the operation of the political structures, and particularly of coalition cabinets. It should be noted, however, that the intensity of issue differences and the ideological distance between party members and supporters may be greater or lesser than between the leaders, and this has an influence on the overall level of polarization. Party leaders who are more extreme than their followers may have difficulty in gaining support for

81

their positions, whereas party leaders who are more moderate than their followers are in danger of losing support for having abandoned the party's true ideals.

It is difficult to take this factor into account because there are no data on the issue positions of party followers and supporters in Israel before the early 1960s.[1] Figures collected then indicate that differences when measured by the policies of the parties and the views of party leaders were somewhat greater than those between the views of party members and supporters. That is to say, the latter were less consistent or more moderate in their espousal of party policy. This was probably also the situation in the 1950s, when, as we shall see immediately, differences between party positions and leaders were even wider and more intense than they were in the 1960s. There is certainly no evidence to indicate that rank-and-file differences were even greater, such as rank-and-file criticism of party leaders for being too moderate or conciliatory. If anything, in both periods rank-and-file members, whatever their views, tended to fall in line behind their party leaders on policy matters, particularly those involved in coalition negotiations, with regard to which they had little incentive and even less opportunity to intervene.[2]

The Structure and Intensity of Issue Differences

The previous analysis of party policy positions examined four main issue dimensions: security; foreign policy; economic organization and policies; and religion and state. For some of the period, positions on foreign policy and economic organization were interconnected because of the international ideological debate of the cold war: communism and democracy in the political order; communism, democratic socialism, and free enterprise in the economic order; ideological collectivism and freedom in the social order; East and West in foreign policy. These manifested themselves in particularly intense partisan disagreements, of which the most significant were between Mapam and Mapai (and all other parties to the right of it).

Another set of issues led to intense partisan differences between Herut and Mapai (and the parties to the left of it). Mapai therefore fought an intense political battle on two fronts. As a leading Herut politician noted in his biography: "Ben-Gurion's style did not change. At every opportunity and also when it was not relevant, he attacked the Ezel and the Palmah, Mapam and us."[3]

The ideological and partisan struggle between Mapai and Mapam lasted until the second half of the 1950s. It manifested the intensity and ambivalence of ideological proximity, shared goals, common party origins, a long period of Zionist and haluzic cooperation, and the belief of both that theirs was the right path, and that the others were not real political enemies but mistaken comrades who had strayed from the path of truth, and who therefore could and might be persuaded by ideological arguments to recognize the error of their ways. It was a struggle for the hearts and minds of the elite youth, the future leaders of the country, and hence was a struggle to determine the political identity of Israeli society.

Its first and most immediate focus was the institutions of the labor movement, within which Mapam hoped to defeat Mapai and thereby replace it at the helm of the state. Mapai's electoral majority enabled it to control the Histadrut's affairs without any real sharing of power, but Mapam, with over 40 percent of the vote, was a more than credible threat. Within the Histadrut, in particular, Mapam sought to win adherents on the basis of ideological conversion and conviction, by demonstrating the correctness and purity of its socialist vision. Mapai was especially concerned about the inroads Mapam had made and might make among the more idealistic, politically conscious youth, many of whom were the sons of Mapai leaders and members, and themselves potential leaders, as had occurred in the case of the Palmah.[4]

Such a direct ideological confrontation was also at the heart of the struggle within the kibbutz movement. Those loyal to Mapai resisted the Mapam demand for majority imposition of ideological collectivism, which amounted to acceptance of Marxism-Leninism and the whole Mapam line. The kibbutz occupied a central symbolic position at the apex of the *haluzic* and Zionist value structure. For Mapai to be defeated there meant more than Mapam control of a few more kibbutzim; it would be interpreted as an ideological victory for Mapam's ideas over those of Mapai, and therefore threatened to erode Mapai's position everywhere.

In the Histadrut, Mapam projected itself as the spearhead of a class-conscious proletariat. It consistently adopted militant tactics in opposition to those proposed by Mapai, the most dramatic example being the seamen's strike, and consistently employed extreme policies of wage outbidding.

In this ideological battle Mapai defended its policies by criticizing and opposing Mapam rather than by proposing a coherent counterideology. It staunchly opposed all manifestations of communism, the pro-Soviet orientation, Marxism-Leninism, and fully socialist economic organization in Mapam's policies. This bitter and uncompromising struggle against Mapam was conducted in intense ideological tones. Terms like *communist slaves, hidden communists, Yevsekim, loyalty to the Cominform, preferring the Kremlin to Jerusalem, totalitarians, double standards*, and *Stalinists* were freely applied. Time and time again the message was hammered home that Mapam's policies would result in replacement of the Zionist democracy of Israel with a "people's democracy," which was really a communist dictatorship, and that in the last resort there was little difference between Mapam and Maki except the honesty of the latter in declaring their aims openly.

Occasionally, doubts were expressed about Mapam's ultimate patriotism and loyalty to the state: "a party which makes the pretense of Jewish Zionist patriotism—a position replete with hypocrisy and contradictions."[5] This was taken seriously at the practical level as well; Mapam leaders were kept under surveillance by the security services, and their offices fitted with listening devices.

Mapam responded in kind. Mapai were revisionists who had strayed from the path of true socialism and Zionism, had betrayed the workers by supporting the international class enemy, had given in to the internal bourgeois and clericalist forces, and had lent support to imperialism, the enemies of world peace, and the reincarnations of fascism, and so forth.

The concerns of both sides were manifest in an exchange between Ben-Gurion and Mapam leaders in 1950. The latter sought to find out whether he believed that "one could rely on the loyalty of Mapam members to the people of Israel, or not." His response was most revealing: "If the Jewish people ask for my opinion, I will recommend that it not give a single vote to Mapam—for the Knesset, the Histadrut, the Kibbutz, or anywhere. I negate Mapam's existence—but it is strange that they ask me about their loyalty—when they deny my haluzic, working-class, and often my Zionist, loyalty."[6]

The ideological conflict with Herut, by way of contrast, was not within a common ideological tradition. Despite the shared Zionist consensus, it was a conflict between political enemies, rather than comrades, across clear ideological boundaries. It is perhaps most aptly captured in the application of the terms *fascist* and *fascism* to Herut, its leaders, and its policies, by the left parties in Israel. These were not simply labels or terms of disapprobation used unthinkingly or in passing; they summed up and expressed deeply held beliefs about the dangers Herut and its policies represented.

An allied and consistent theme in the political and ideological battle against Herut was to depict its policies and actions as empty jingoism, irresponsible, declamatory, demagogic, and dangerous to the security of the state because of Herut's refusal to recognize political reality. It was in a sense a continuation of the previous battle in the Zionist movement between the power of deeds and the power of words. As Ben-Gurion put it, in response to Herut criticism in the debate after presenting his first government in March 1949: "I must tell you that there is a fundamental difference between us and you. And this is not only with regard to the question of Jerusalem, but on all questions. We do not have much faith in the value of declarations and declamations, even if they are about great, holy, historical and vital matters such as borders, a capital city, an eternal city etc, if this is not attached to hard and arduous routine activity, and if the activity does not lead to the realization of the declamation."[7]

Mapai criticized what it saw as Herut's irresponsibility, its inability to distinguish rhetoric from acceptable political responses, its emphasis upon armed force to solve Israel's problems with its neighbors. For Ben-Gurion, the irresponsibility and fascism, and the threat to security and democracy went together, and the *Altalena* and the reparations debate were constantly used as examples. Later in the 1950s, Begin's habit of arriving at election meetings preceded by a motorcycle escort and welcomed by lines of uniformed Betar youth group members were exploited as evidence of the fascist image.

Ben-Gurion's attitude to Herut and Begin was deep-seated and changed little over time. Only weeks before his retirement as prime minister in 1963, Ben-Gurion attacked Herut and Begin in a highly polemical speech in the Knesset, parts of which were later removed from the official record by order of the speaker. He strongly reiterated these views in private correspondence. Not for the first time Herut and Begin were compared with Hitler and accused of Hitlerism: despite their hatred of Hitler, they would bring dictatorship and absolute rule, and use any means if they thought them justified by the ends. Their political adventurism endangered the state. "If Begin ever gets into power, it will spell the destruction of the State of Israel. In any event his rule would turn Israel into a monster." "Herut, that is to say, Begin, represents a danger to the moral standing of Israel." [8]

The use of such strong language and epithets to describe political opponents was not confined to Mapai and Ben-Gurion. Throughout the period, Begin used his not inconsiderable rhetorical powers to return the criticism in kind. Some striking examples of this were encountered in Begin's reactions during and after the *Altalena* and reparations crises, and they were prominent in Herut electoral campaign speeches. Particularly significant and representative of Begin's attitude is a long speech made after the 1955 elections in which he rebutted Mapai charges that he and Herut were fascist. His response was that the only fascist party in Israel was Mapai because of its worship of the single leader. And to forestall the argument that Mapai was not fascist because it was socialist, he reminded his audience of the National Socialist Workers Party in Germany.[9]

The polarizing impact of these conflicts was tempered by the widespread acceptance of overarching values, on the one hand, and by a series of specific crosscutting interparty policy agreements, on the other. The fundamental agreement that tempered the partisan ideological conflict was consensus regarding Israel as a Jewish state, to which all parties except Communist and Arab were believed to be committed. Not only was the legitimate existence of an independent Jewish state no longer challenged but the constant defense effort needed to maintain it in the face of external threat generated an overriding national and patriotic value commitment and unity. Ben-Gurion expressed this in 1954:

> We are witness in this country to a pathological exaggeration in party controversy and to the blowing up amongst the people of totally non-existent differences. If we exclude the open and the disguised communists, who are slaves to the Kremlin, and operate according to the orders of the Cominform, the people are fundamentally united on the major questions of the state: security, the ingathering and integration of the exiles, upbuilding the land and economic independence.[10]

Furthermore, the issue differences were crosscutting, not mutually reinforcing. That is to say, parties that disagreed on some issues agreed on others. For example, the religious parties, General Zionists, and Progressives basically accepted Mapai's approach on security and foreign policy. On the other hand, Ahdut Ha'avodah and Herut agreed on activist military responses. On economic questions, Mapai shared some agreements with Mapam and Ahdut Ha'avodah, and other agreements with the religious parties and the Progressives, and at times with the General Zionists. On the role of the Histadrut,

Mapai, Mapam, and Ahdut Ha'avodah were ranged against the General Zionists and Herut, with the religious parties and the Progressives somewhere in the middle. On the religious issue, the religious parties were fundamentally divided from all the other parties, none of which accepted their *Halakhic* claims. Some rejected them root and branch; others were prepared to enter into various degrees of pragmatic compromise on coalitional, electoral, and national grounds.

The issue differences between the parties lessened in intensity over time. By and large the historical evidence suggests that all these major questions had reached some degree of resolution and settlement by the middle of the 1950s, or at the very least, that the lines of conflict had been clearly defined. International and regional developments beyond Israel's control left it with only one viable position in the East–West conflict. The Sinai Campaign seemed to have determined the security and border question. The mixed and highly regulated economy appeared to be achieving positive results. Private capital had been increasingly encouraged and the preference for public and collective capital progressively reduced. Moreover, significant Histadrut activities had been transferred to the state, and others were in the process. A *modus vivendi* had been arrived at on religious matters, and no party seemed intent upon disturbing the status quo by a major extension or repeal of religious legislation.

In a sense the theretofore prominent matters had ceased to be issues in Israeli politics. Apart from the question "Who is a Jew?" none of the coalition crises between 1955 and 1965 related to them. Nor were they involved in the major disagreements between the government and opposition. One recurring issue was that of relations with Germany, which was more a moral and Jewish issue than one of East–West relations. Another dealt with the obligations of collective responsibility. Others dealt with ethnic disadvantage, and the continuation of military rule over the Arab citizens of Israel. Even the major crisis, that engendered by the Lavon Affair of 1960–61 and 1964–65, which raised many contentious questions, did not involve these fundamental value conflicts.

The Pattern of Electoral Response

In the elections for the Elected Assembly in 1944 and those for the Zionist Congress in 1946, the parties of the Left received about 60 percent of the votes, those of the center and the Right about 23 percent, and the religious parties close to 14 percent. Remarkably, the same general distribution of support was to be found at the end of the founding period, despite an influx of new voters that tripled the electorate.[11]

Thus, from 1949 to 1965 the parties of the Left (including the Communists) consistently received between 52.5 and 54.6 percent of the vote; those of the center and the Right, between 23.6 and 27.4 percent; and the religious parties, between 11.8 and 15.4 percent. By 1955 the ethnic lists that had received about 4.5 percent in 1949 and 3.5 percent in 1951 were wiped out electorally. The Arab lists maintained a steady proportion ranging from 3.1 to 4.9 percent.

Overall, the left parties lost the most support after independence, but when viewed individually, a different picture emerges. Mapai retained the support that it had had in the Yishuv, and may even have increased it slightly in 1959. The loss was borne by Hashomer Hazair and Ahdut Ha'avodah, which declined from over 24 percent in the Yishuv to between 12.5 and 15.5 percent in the state.

These ideological camps—left, right, center, and religious—existed on paper but not in reality. They did not act collectively nor did they blunt extreme multipartyism as manifested in high fragmentation and fractionalization. Fragmentation was reflected in the large number of parties and lists contesting elections. In the six Knesset election campaigns between 1949 and 1965, the number of lists competing for the electorate's support ranged from 14 to 24, with a mean of 18.5. Knesset representation was somewhat narrower but still highly fragmented, ranging from 11 to 15, with a mean of 12.5. If lists that existed for electoral purposes only and had no permanent extraparliamentary organization are excluded, the mean number of parties in the Knesset was still more than 11.

The large number of parties was associated with high fractionalization. Between five and ten parties, and on average seven, secured 1–5 percent of the votes; from three to five, and on average four, gained 5–15 percent. The most extreme case was in 1951; ten parties had less than 5 percent and thirteen parties had less than 15 percent. At the other end of the scale, from 1949 to 1965 no party ever exceeded 40 percent of the votes or seats.

Mapai's share of the vote held steadily between 32.2 and 38.2 percent, averaging 35.8 percent. It did slightly better in seats, winning between forty and forty-seven, and an average of forty-four. Four parties achieved second place, averaging 15.3 percent, the highest being 16.2 percent in 1951, until 1965, when Gahal received 21.3 percent. Thus, before 1965 the largest party regularly exceeded its nearest rival by over 20 percentage points, and was at least two and one-half times larger than its nearest rival.

Fragmentation was closely related to the multidimensional issue structure. Proportional representation did not create policy and issue differences, but it did facilitate their expression and afforded them relatively easy parliamentary access. One percent of the votes was all that was needed for a seat in the Knesset. So long as differences in ideological nuance could achieve public recognition, there was little incentive for compromise. To the contrary, the possibilities available by means of electoral competition magnified partisan differences and heightened their intensity.

Rather than aggregate into a few large political parties in which they would be obliged to make value compromises, many smaller political parties preferred to promote their views on the issues independently. Thus, ideological and value conflicts during the founding period were by and large fought out between parties, not within them. Moreover, the mere existence of separate party organizations within which, in addition, leaders and activists satisfied their material interests and psychological needs further exacerbated fragmentation.

A large number of contesting lists does not necessarily result in fractionalization. Neither, on the other hand, does it prevent it, as does the plurality system. Rather, fractionalization is a consequence of the distribution of public support. In theory, the electorate could vote for a few parties, which would then be sizable, and ignore the others. But when public support is spread over a large number of alternatives, proportional representation produces fractionalization.

Polarization, fragmentation, and fractionalization all had to be confronted directly if stable and effective coalition government was to be established. One way of coping with such problems is to base coalition formation upon policy agreement, which may oblige some participating parties to compromise on their stated positions and goals. Coalition government, once established, may therefore counteract some of the effects of proportional representation and a multidimensional issue structure. Moreover, the capacity of coalition government to counteract them was greatly enhanced by adoption of a number of majoritarian political principles: parliamentary sovereignty; the fusion of executive and legislative powers; cabinet dominance, unicameralism; and a centralized unitary system. During the founding period these were reinforced by the practices of parliamentary government followed by the main political actors—the parties and their leaders.

The Dynamics of Coalition Formation

The politics of coalition formation during the founding period was dominated by Mapai, as a result, in the first place, of its electoral plurality. Mapai won between forty and forty-seven Knesset seats in every election, but for the purposes of coalition calculations we should add the automatic support of its affiliated Arab parties, thereby bringing its starting total to between forty-five and fifty-two seats, making it at least twice as large as its nearest opponent. It was taken for granted by the political leaders that no majority coalition government was possible if Mapai was excluded.[12]

In terms of simple arithmetic, it was, of course, theoretically possible for other parties to form a majority without Mapai. This never occurred, partly because it was much harder to unite six or seven parties to create a coalition majority without it than it was for Mapai to join with one or two parties in order to form a majority government. Just as significant was Mapai's location in the center of the ideological spectrum and the issue map, or what scholars have called its pivotal position. For other parties to form a government without Mapai would necessitate agreement among parties that were at opposite ends of the spectrum, often at its extremes, and were strongly opposed to each other ideologically. It would have meant joining far left and right, collectivist and free enterprise, religious and secular. In practical political terms this was most unlikely.

Mapai's centrality on all but the important issues enabled it to represent a majority opinion or consensus without relinquishing its claim to political leadership and ideological goal setting. It did not merely register the balance of opinion; rather, it sought to shape and mold opinion in line with its views and policies. Neither did its centrality derive from a belief that its task was to discover and follow public opinion; rather, it derived, somewhat paradoxically, from the distribution of opinion and the pattern of opposition to its policies.

Mapai's ideological and political centrality provided it with the support of a number of other parties on all important questions. On questions of defense and foreign affairs, it could count on the center and moderate right parties, and the religious parties. On economic matters, it took a decidedly centrist, mixed-economy position between the Marxist Left and the free-enterprise Right, and was thus able to count on them alternatively, depending upon the specific issue. For example, in promoting collective or public economic activity, it enjoyed the support of the Left; in encouraging the import and investment of private capital, that of the Right; and on most economic questions, that of the religious parties. On religious questions, it reached a broad accommodation with the religious parties about the Jewish character of the state in the public sphere, which met their policy requirements, and which also was representative of the broad consensus of opinion of the majority of the population.

Mapai used its electoral plurality and policy centrality effectively in coalition negotiations. The pattern was set by Ben-Gurion in 1949. His goal was to create a viable core of policy agreement upon which he could base the support of a parliamentary majority. His very first step was to heighten the possibility of policy agreement by narrowing the degree of ideological distance. A range of possible policy accommodation was established by excluding extreme ideological positions and those that generated intense opposition among some of the potential coalition partners. Certain ideological positions were excluded from consideration because they involved intense and unbridgeable policy and ideological differences.[13] Consequently, the parties identified with them were excluded as potential coalition partners. Conversely, this served to highlight the basis of possible agreement among the remaining potential coalition partners.

This basic position was formulated in a number of different ways, but the net effect was the same. After the 1949 elections, Ben-Gurion invited "the constructive and productive forces from the General Zionists to Mapam"[14] to unite with him in forming a coalition, and proceeded to negotiate with them. But there were "two parties, 'Maki and Herut,' which a priori did not come into consideration in forming the government, for understandable reasons."[15] He followed the same line after the 1951 elections, distinguishing clearly between the coalition potential of Mapam and the General Zionists, on the one hand, and Maki and Herut on the other: "During the election campaign we rejected two outlooks. We did not disqualify parties . . . we rejected their outlooks. We rejected two things: Mapam's foreign policy . . . and . . . the economic policies of the General Zionists who seek to establish a 'new regime.'"

The fact that the electorate also resoundingly rejected these policies, constituted a basic element in his strategy of coalition formation, enabling him to join the two elements that formed the basis of his coalition strategy throughout the founding period: the possibility of policy agreement, and the claim of democratic legitimation for Mapai's policies.

> And if we rejected Mapam's foreign policy approach and the General Zionist economic approach,—and together with us the majority of the people rejected these approaches—we did not disqualify these two parties. And if they accept the majority decision, they are able and welcome to join the government—on the basis of the policy which was approved by popular majority. This basis is laid out in the Mapai program, not in every clause in it, but in its political and economic principles.[16]

Because Mapai did not have a majority, coalition government was necessary. However, "two parties are in our view unfit . . . Maki and Herut with whom we see no possibility of cooperation." All other parties were able and were requested to join the government, and to make the effort to establish a coalition as wide as that of the Provisional Government.[17]

Although Mapam and the General Zionists were expected to alter their policies to conform with those of Mapai on foreign policy and economic questions if they wished to participate in the coalition, on certain issues Mapai accepted the policy stand of other parties, in whole or in part, as the basis for joint coalition policies. This was particularly noticeable in the case of the religious parties, for which religious questions were so salient that they insisted on a policy minimum as a precondition for their entry into the coalition. In return, they offered loyal support on major questions of foreign, defense, and economic policies. Mapai's acceptance was possible if two of its conditions were met. The first was that the particular religious question was not salient to Mapai,[18] which therefore espoused no specific policy with regard to it. As Ben-Gurion put it: "I had to make concessions to the religious parties in some spheres in order to gain their support in others that seemed to me to be of more immediate urgency. . . . I refused to compromise on issues that I place at the top of my order of priorities . . . but when there was an agreement on what was vital to me, I was ready to make concessions on what was vital to others."[19]

Second, the policy needs of potential coalition partners were more likely to be met if this did not entail Mapai's having to accept policies and actions that conflicted directly with its preferences, even on less salient issues. But when this occurred, as in the case of education in the immigrant camps, which impinged directly upon its political interests, or that of conscription of women, which conflicted with its commitment to universal criteria and to the role of the army in socialization and nation-building, the pattern of policy accommodation broke down.

Considerations other than the degree of policy flexibility were also significant in coalition negotiation and formation. On the question of religion, for example, Mapai had a small but growing number of religiously observant members; to maintain their support, it needed to adhere, at the very least, to a policy of neutrality. At the national level, Mapai sought to maximize national unity and avoid a Kulturkampf by including some religious parties in the coalition and by meeting some of their policy demands. For this reason, Ben-Gurion often stated publicly that he would include the religious parties in a coalition, even if Mapai had a majority.

The dynamics of coalition formation were governed by a number of organizational principles. The first was that whatever the size of the parliamentary majority that supported the coalition, Mapai MKs always constituted at least a majority within it. The second was that parties received ministries in proportion to the size of their coalition membership. The third was that Mapai always had an absolute majority in the cabinet. Although the third followed logically from the first two principles, operationally it was the most significant, and very quickly became an ultimative principle of Mapai's coalition strategy.

Ben-Gurion did not plan this from the outset. In the broad coalition he initially suggested in 1949, Mapai did not have a majority, and consequently he proposed a cabinet of twelve ministers, of whom only five were to be from Mapai.[20] But when both Mapam and the General Zionists refused to join the coalition, Mapai ended up with both a coalition and a cabinet majority. However, after Mapai had gained experience of its controlling impact upon coalition operation, a Mapai majority was made a precondition in all subsequent coalition negotiations, even when large coalitions in which Mapai did not have a Knesset majority were proposed.

Throughout the founding period, proportionality was maintained for both large and small coalition parties with only minor variations in both directions. For example, Mapai's proportion of the ministry ranged from 56 percent to 69 percent, as often understating its precise coalition proportion as exceeding it, in the range −3 percent to +3 percent, although in the first coalition it was understated by over six percentage points. In terms of political realities and coalition dynamics, the absolute numbers were far more significant: depending on cabinet size, which ranged from twelve to sixteen ministers, Mapai membership was seven, 1949–51; nine, 1951–61, and eleven, after 1961. Other parties each had from one to three ministers, except for a short period in 1954–55 when the General Zionists had four.

The fourth principle was that Mapai consistently held the most important ministries. From 1949 to 1965 it received prime minister, Defense, Foreign Affairs, Finance, Agriculture, Labor, Education, and for most of the period, Commerce and Industry, Communications, and Police. The other parties had to be content with the minor ministries. In some instances, these were the ministries that they desired; the Mizrachi parties made the establishment of the Ministry of Religions a condition of joining the first government and subsequently ensured that one of their ministers would head it. The specific division of portfolios and the number allocated were often a significant factor in determining the success or otherwise of coalition negotiations.

In 1949 the General Zionists insisted on at least two portfolios, which was what they had had in the Provisional Government. Having only one minister, they maintained, would cause severe internal, factional problems, and in addition would underrepresent the social significance of the middle class. Ben-

Gurion refused because applying to other parties the same ratio of ministers to Knesset members would lead to a cabinet of twenty-five, twice as large as that which he intended to establish. The refusal played a major role in the decision of the General Zionists not to join the Cabinet.[21]

Occasionally, potential coalition partners sought high-level bureaucratic positions for party members in ministries controlled by other parties, as part of the coalition agreement. A particularly notable example was Mapam's demand in 1949 to be given top bureaucratic positions in a number of key ministries, particularly Foreign Affairs, Defense, and Finance, over and above a proportion of positions within others. In its view, this was necessary to ensure that it would not be in a "policy ghetto," wherein its influence would be restricted, at best, to the ministries that it headed. Ben-Gurion rejected these demands, and in particular the view that the heads of departments within all ministries be allocated on a party basis.[22]

The Dynamics of Coalition Operation

The fifth, and the single most fundamental, principle of coalition organization was collective responsibility, which, as noted earlier, was from 1949 incorporated into law. Its effect upon the operation of coalition government cannot be overstated because it served to mute and overcome one of the major structural elements of the consensus model of democracy, executive power sharing, and in many ways it led to a high degree of concentration of executive power. What is more, it laid the groundwork for strengthening another key structural element of majoritarian democracy: centralization (discussed later).

Collective responsibility (1) provided for the creation of a government that spoke with one voice and acted in unison, (2) facilitated coordinated policy-making and implementation, and (3) specifically sought to prevent the government from becoming a federation of officeholders. It did not operate alone but in conjunction with the other principles of coalition formation—particularly the permanent Mapai cabinet majority, and responsibility for the major ministries—to produce significant measures of cabinet control and concentration of executive power.

These factors alone enabled Mapai to translate coalition government into a close approximation of government by single-party majority. But Ben-Gurion took additional steps to reinforce this. He sought to ensure that the government would have the capacity to make decisions and that these would be binding upon his coalition partners, thereby promoting stable government free of crises, on the one hand, and not prone to immobilism, on the other.

Ben-Gurion perceived his role and that of Mapai to be the provision of decisive leadership, the setting of national goals, and the determination of policy priorities. The roles were facilitated in part by the transformation of Mapai's ministers, known as Sareinu, into a separate functioning collective body. They were underpinned in no small measure by the party's organizational structure, and in particular by development of the doctrine of the primacy of party (discussed later). The underlying element of both was that by and large the policies for which the Mapai ministers were responsible were first discussed and worked out in internal Mapai forums.

In 1948 Ben-Gurion was defeated on a critical decision relating to the conduct of the war by a majority of the Provisional Government made up of some Mapai ministers and some from other parties. After that he decided that it was necessary to assemble Mapai ministers prior to cabinet meetings at which critical or controversial subjects were to be discussed.[23] Accordingly, Sareinu became a regular feature of Mapai decision making, particularly after Moshe Sharett became prime minister in 1954. These preparatory gatherings enabled Mapai ministers to enter cabinet meetings with a united front. Decisions made there became government policy through Mapai's cabinet majority and the operation of collective responsibility. Sareinu was thus the cornerstone of Mapai's pattern of party government, concentrating executive power and serving to convert coalition government into an approximation of majoritarian single-party government.

Sareinu's significance was underlined after Ben-Gurion returned to the portfolio of minister of defense in February 1955 under Sharett as prime minister. During that period their policy differences on security and foreign affairs issues were sharp and frequent, and the question arose as to where and how to resolve them. The problem was that on a number of occasions Ben-Gurion's proposals were defeated in cabinet, even though it was clear that they enjoyed the support of a majority of Mapai ministers.

Sharett refused to use a cabinet majority based on other parties and a minority of Mapai ministers to gain support for his policies against those of Ben-Gurion. When he had taken office, the party had nominated a core group of five ministers to make decisions on security and foreign affairs issues, and in this group he was in a minority of one. He decided that "in this situation I will not attempt in any way to gain a majority in the Cabinet against the majority of the group authorized by the party. I will not dismantle the arrangement fixed within the party. . . . The party is above all else. . . . I will not exercise my authority as Prime Minister in opposition to my party."[24]

Discussions in the core group were also important in facilitating coordination of policy among the key government ministries represented in it. In addition, the group could refer to the authoritative party institutions if there were doubts whether the steps proposed were in line with party policy, or if they were thought likely to engender significant intraparty opposition. In both cases, the questions needed to be resolved prior to being brought before the coalition partners at the cabinet table.[25]

Ben-Gurion further reinforced the concentration of executive power and the development of single-party-like government by pursuing two strategies designed to maintain stable government. By lessening the likelihood that coalition partners could bring down the government, or be able even to utilize this as a threat, he would limit their capacity to put the kind of pressure on

Mapai that weakened executive power and cabinet dominance. The elimination of the threat of crisis and instability would prevent the system from moving in the direction of the coalition politics of the consensual model.

The first strategy was ideological balance, which utilized paired opposites: balancing the presence of secular parties by religious parties, and of left-wing parties by right-wing and center parties. Moreover, in the choice of paired opposites, the balance was further maintained by avoiding extremes and favoring the moderate parties. No coalition ever included a more extreme party from any one camp while leaving a moderate party from the same camp in opposition. A moderate party might be included by itself, but a more extreme party was included only with a moderate party from the same camp alongside it.[26] The second strategy was oversized cabinets containing one or more parties in excess of the number needed for a minimum majority coalition. Such cabinets are the opposite of the minimum winning coalitions that are predicted by some theorists as likely on the grounds that coalition formation is easier when cabinet size is kept down because in this way fewer payoffs have to be made to the participants, particularly if the minimum coalitions consist of ideologically adjacent parties.[27]

Ben-Gurion strove to exercise both strategies simultaneously in all the cabinets he established, for example, in his consistent proposals to set up coalitions including all parties from Mapam to the General Zionists. His ideal coalition was therefore a good deal larger than the minimum, with a Knesset majority dependent upon support for Mapai from at least *three* other parties from different parts of the political spectrum. His ideal coalition also had a Mapai majority in the cabinet.[28] Ben-Gurion's logic was simple and impeccable. Oversized cabinets and ideological balance provided Mapai with considerable freedom of action and enabled it to use its other coalition advantages to the full to determine major government policies: on the one hand, contradicting theory, they kept Mapai's policy costs or payoffs to a minimum; on the other hand, the capacity of the smaller parties to influence and pressure Mapai was also greatly limited.

Of the two strategies, somewhat surprisingly, cabinet size seems to have been the most important to Ben-Gurion, precisely because it maximized Mapai's policy-making capacity. In a minimum winning cabinet a Mapai majority and ideological balance could not prevent the small coalition partners from exercising their blackmail and veto potential, that is, their power to bring the government down by resigning. He gave clear expression to his strategy in criticizing the coalition of sixty-eight set up by Mapai in 1961, based on Mapai (forty-two), the NRP (twelve), Ahdut Ha'avodah (eight), and Po'alei Agudat Yisrael (two), supported by the affiliated Arab parties (four). This led to

a coalition of blackmail—each one of the two lesser parties can undermine the government—in opposition to my opinion to include within the government the 'club of four' whose combined total was the same as the party's representatives, but such a combination would have prevented extortion, as the government coalition would have numbered 92 members, and no party of the 'club' would have been capable of undermining the government, and we would have been guaranteed that in economic and social questions no decision would have been taken in opposition to the needs of the workers, and in foreign policy and defense no 'leftist' decision would have been accepted.[29]

Ben-Gurion's strategies were facilitated by postelection coalitions. Prior to the elections, parties generally did not declare with which other parties they would or would not agree to join in order to form a majority. In most cases, parties ran separately rather than in large blocs or preelection coalitions. Government coalitions were thus formed on the basis of negotiations held *after* the elections, in a fluid and open process involving a large number of parties. These factors restricted the freedom of action of the other parties and maximized that of Mapai. Its membership in the coalition was certain, but that of all the others was in doubt. Under such conditions, its size and ideological centrality enabled Mapai to play off one side against the other.

Once such a coalition was established, small coalition parties were ill-advised to leave the cabinet if this did not bring the government down. In fact, as the NRP learned when it resigned in 1958 over the question "Who is a Jew?" it could prove to be counterproductive, increasing the political influence of partisan and ideological opponents in the cabinet. The NRP relinquished the ministries it held, and although it reentered the coalition after the 1959 elections, Ben-Gurion demonstratively refused to return to it the Ministry of Religions, which was important for the NRP's control of official state religious institutions. (The NRP did, however, gain the Ministry of the Interior, which administered the issuance of identity cards and the Population Register, and this gave it control over the registration of religious identity.) The Ministry of Religions was not returned to the NRP until 1961, when under the coalition conditions at the time its bargaining position was at its strongest.

The strategy of building coalitions that gave only minimal blackmail or veto potential to the minor parties created considerable latitude for the prime minister to use aggressively the power of resignation as a means of maintaining coalition discipline. Because his resignation would automatically bring down the government, often the anticipation or threat of it was sufficient to bring coalition partners into line. The minor partners were under continual pressure to compromise because under conditions of postelection coalitions, it was never clear who would join Mapai in the next Cabinet, and at what price. This was reinforced by the actual use of the weapon of the prime minister's resignation to enforce coalition discipline, as occurred with the General Zionists in 1955, and with Mapam and Ahdut Ha'avodah in 1957 and 1959.

The evidence shows that Mapai consistently established oversized coalitions during the period 1949–65, always including at least one and often as many as three excess parties (that is, more than were necessary to create a bare coalition majority). Despite this, from 1949 to 1951 and 1961 to 1965 (about 40 percent of the period) the coalition was still not large enough to avoid being a "government of blackmail," that is, its majority could be undermined by the resignation of one partner.

The Israeli evidence relating to the stability or durability of these "black-mail governments" is mixed. Between 1949 and 1952, such a coalition structure proved highly unstable. The government fell three times over religious questions. Twice, the religious bloc, which held sixteen of the seventy-three seats, voted with the opposition. On the first occasion, the same coalition was reconstituted, but the government treated the second defeat as a vote of no confidence and resigned, and early elections resulted. On the third occasion, the religious bloc held fifteen of sixty-seven seats. The prime minister resigned after three religious parties in the bloc with seven Knesset members left the coalition, which, including the five seats of Mapai-affiliated Arab parties, had the support of only sixty MKs. But within days a new and broad coalition with the support of eighty-four members received the confidence of the Knesset.

In the coalition from 1961 to 1965, as we noted above, the NRP held twelve seats out of sixty-eight; Ahdut Ha'avodah, eight; and affiliated Arab parties, four. Yet there was not a single cabinet crisis. Neither does the record indicate unusual NRP legislative or administrative successes on religious questions. It seems that the NRP had learned the lesson of 1958–59. Ahdut Ha'avodah was intent on cementing close relations with Mapai as part of its rapprochement, and it, too, was a consistently supportive coalition partner.

Coalition Formation, 1949–1961

In both 1949 and 1951 Ben-Gurion sought to reestablish the broad coalition of the Provisional Government: Mapai, Mapam, the religious parties, the General Zionists, the Progressives, and the Sephardim. Such a coalition, enjoying the support of more than ninety-five members of Knesset, met all the criteria of his coalition strategy elaborated earlier. But on both occasions he failed to establish this broad coalition. Despite his many public utterances in its favor he adamantly rejected a coalition based upon a two-party majority, either with Mapam (1949, 1951) or the General Zionists (1951). In his view, this was the least attractive alternative of all. It would create major problems of reaching policy agreement on central questions, and would put pressure on Mapai to make unacceptable policy compromises if the partner did not accept Mapai's policy outlines. Thus, there would be neither ideological balance nor much chance of policy agreement. Moreover, a two-party coalition would give the minor party high blackmail and veto potential. The other two parties set their sights on the two-party coalition, but Ben-Gurion did everything he could to avoid it.

Ben-Gurion's priorities in coalition formation come through powerfully in his speech to the Knesset on October 7, 1951, in response to the debate that followed his presentation of the government. His first preference had been for a Mapai majority, which would meet all the criteria for stable government and clear policy direction. Failing this, his next preference had been a stable coalition majority based upon maximum coalition unity and internal consolidation, to ensure national integration and unity. A coalition with Mapam alone, constituting a workers' front or a workers' government, would not fulfill this goal; it would be too sectional and likely to arouse considerable national disunity, particularly with regard to defense and foreign policy. Neither would a coalition with the General Zionists alone contribute to cabinet unity or national consolidation; the policy differences between them were certain to lead to considerable instability.[30]

An absolutely fascinating and authentic firsthand insight into Ben-Gurion's coalition strategies and the considerations involved appears in his diary for September 12, 1951, recorded during the negotiations to form a government after the elections for the Second Knesset.

I sought to clarify for myself the problem of whether a coalition with the General Zionists or with the religious parties was desirable.

The advantages of a coalition with the G.Zs are: (1) a large majority—72 Jews (against 40) plus another 5 Arabs (against 3). With the religious parties only 62 Jews (against 50). (2) A solid majority: one party has 23 members, whilst the religious parties have only 16 members, and they are three factions. (3) A coalition with the General Zionists ensures the cooperation of the Progressives. It is doubtful whether the Progs will go only with the religious parties. (4) A government with G.Zs will give satisfaction to Zionists overseas. (5) Perhaps it will prove effective in attracting capital. (6) Perhaps it will ensure the cooperation of the property owning circles in Israel. (7) It will guarantee freedom of conscience and religion and prevent religious extortion. (8) It might possibly cure the situation in Hapo'el Hamizrachi and reinforce Lamifneh. (9) It is hard to know whether it will increase stability.

The disadvantages: (1) the General Zionists will demand a large payoff in terms of portfolios—the religious parties will accept 3-4 unimportant portfolios. (2) There will not be a uniform line on economic questions. Despite a uniform program—the G.Z. ministers will act as they wish. (3) There will be no possibility of an honest partnership—the G.Zs are headed towards rule by the right. (4) Their participation in the government will strengthen the right— only in a coalition with the religious parties alone will we be able to attract the middle classes to us. (5) Partnership with the G.Zs will reinforce the left in Mapam and will unify Siyah Bet with Hashomer Hazair in opposition to the government. A coalition only with the religious parties will strengthen the ferment in Siyah Bet and will move many Mapam sympathisers from their party. (6) Partnership with the General Zionists will reinforce the incitement against the government amongst the workers, and every evil will be blamed upon this partnership.—In a coalition with the religious parties alone the government will be regarded as a workers' government and they will take it into more positive consideration. (7) Rule by the G.Zs will attract to them many workers who are becoming middle class, members of cooperatives to whom the partnership will give a stamp of approval [*hekhsher*]. (8) Every economic improvement will be credited to the Right. (9) The G.Zs will act on behalf of interested parties from within their circle at the expense of the state and the public—the religious parties will restrict themselves only to matters of religion. (10) The G.Zs whole interest is to turn into a majority or into that force without which it is impossible to rule in the state.—The religious parties are not capable of taking over the government. (11) This partnership will drive the religious workers away from us—a coalition with the religious parties, will have the opposite effect, especially if Lamifneh will also participate in the government. (12) Such a partnership will reinforce the right-wing in Zionism, and is likely to arouse conflict with non-Zionist Jewry. (13) If the partnership is broken—it will then be difficult to establish a coalition with the religious parties, whilst as against this, partnership with the religious parties leaves an opening for widening the coalition. (14). If such a partnership were to fail—it would also represent a moral failure. Our moral position would not be undermined in a partnership with the religious parties. (15) There is the question of education—in a coalition with the G.Zs it would be necessary to hand education over to them. There is no such necessity in the case of the religious parties. (16) Towards the next elections we will be able to acquire a majority if we join the middle classes to us, there is no such possibility before the elections after a coalition with the General Zionists.

Conditions for success in a coalition with the religious parties are: a clear economic line, the implementation of which will be guaranteed, coordination between the economic ministries, additional strength to the government ([Perez] Naftali, [Levi] Eshkol), refining the administrative machine, regular weekly meetings of the economic ministers.[31]

In the event, after fifty-five (!) meetings between Ben-Gurion and the potential coalition partners, a narrow coalition was established between Mapai and the religious parties, which together with the Mapai-affiliated Arab lists enjoyed the support of sixty-seven Knesset members. The General Zionists declined to enter into a coalition with Mapai because they were not satisfied with the portfolios they would receive in a broad coalition.

But within a year, after the Agudah parties resigned, the General Zionists agreed to join a Mapai-led coalition together with the two Mizrachi parties and the Progressives. For the first time, Mapai's criteria of ideological balance and more than minimal size were met. In policy terms, considerable progress had also been made, for Mapai was prepared to compromise more to meet the demands made on behalf of private enterprise. But the major concessions were made by the General Zionists; they received far less in policy and portfolio terms than they had demanded in 1951, when they had held out for Development, Commerce and Industry, Rationing and Supply, Interior, and Education—which would include many services administered by Welfare—and possibly Transport; this had been rejected by Ben-Gurion. But by 1952 they were prepared to accept Commerce and Industry (without Development), Health, Interior, and Transport. What had changed was the General Zionists' willingness to enter the coalition, even if it meant lowering their demands.

The partnership with the General Zionists survived one cabinet crisis in 1953, on the education issue (discussed later), but was dissolved in June 1955. The General Zionists abstained in a no-confidence vote in the Knesset, and Prime Minister Sharett effectively dismissed them by resigning and reconstituting the same cabinet but without them. This took place a month before the previously scheduled elections, and there can be no doubt that the General Zionists used it as an opportunity to try to detach themselves from overidentification with what they perceived to be an unpopular Mapai-led government. As we noted earlier, their resignation did not stop their suffering a major electoral defeat.

The 1955 elections proved to be a major turning point in coalition formation. Ben-Gurion again sought to establish a broad coalition of eight parties, but the General Zionists and the Agudah parties quickly refused to participate. Consequently, for the first time since the Provisional Government, the parties of the Left, Mapam and Ahdut Ha'avodah, agreed to participate in a Mapai-led coalition together with the two Mizrachi parties and the Progressives. This was made possible by the split in Mapam and the distancing of the two parties from their previous pro-Soviet foreign policy and Marxist economic policies. This enabled them more easily to make the necessary policy compromises, and highlighted the shared Zionist consensus upon which the coalition rested.

The cabinet was close to Ben-Gurion's ideal: it was oversized, enjoying the support of another four parties and a total of 80 Knesset members; it had ideological balance; it provided a firm base for policy coherence; Mapai had a majority and the most important ministries; and no party had veto or blackmail potential. The internal cohesion of the cabinet was reinforced by the resolution of internal Mapai differences over defense and foreign policy, which led to the resignation of Sharett as foreign minister (discussed later) and by the success of the activist policies that culminated in the 1956 Sinai Campaign.

The utility of this coalition strategy was amply demonstrated over the next four years, during which time it successfully withstood three major cabinet crises. In December 1957 Ben-Gurion demanded that Ahdut Ha'avodah ministers resign for their breach of cabinet secrecy by publishing and criticizing in the party newspaper a secret decision to send a top military figure on a mission to Germany. When they refused to resign, he brought down the government with his own resignation. But it was reconstituted on exactly the same basis within a week, with more stringent agreements for collective responsibility and the maintenance of cabinet secrecy.

The conflict over the question "Who is a Jew?" involved a head-on collision between the religious parties and the secular parties, particularly Ahdut Ha'avodah and Mapam, with some support for the latter from within Mapai and the Progressives. What is more, it was an issue that lay within the jurisdiction of the responsible Ahdut Ha'avodah minister, with whose views Ben-Gurion sympathized in principle. He refused to back the NRP because doing so would have entailed a head-on collision with three other parties that together had veto power and the capacity to bring the government down, and hence he sought to defuse the issue by doing nothing pending broader theoretical clarification by leading Jewish thinkers throughout the world, which clearly would take a considerable time. When the NRP ministers resigned on the grounds that this was a matter of conscience to be resolved only by returning to the status quo through rescinding the offending administrative order, the government continued with the support of sixty-nine Knesset members.

After the 1959 elections, the cabinet was reconstituted on the original 1955 basis, and held office until Ben-Gurion resigned in reaction to the government's majority decision over the Lavon Affair in January 1961 (discussed later). After the 1961 elections, he was once more unable to reestablish his ideal coalition and was forced to be satisfied with a narrow cabinet enjoying the support of sixty-eight Knesset members, although he was able to maintain the other principal elements of his coalition strategy. But what is most significant about the events of 1961 was the concerted attempt, for the first time, of four parties—Mapam, Ahdut Ha'avodah, the National Religious Party, and the Liberals—to prevent Mapai from maintaining its traditional coalition strategy. The Club of Four, as they were to become known, sought to exploit internal conflict in Mapai, the widespread public and internal party criticism of Ben-Gurion, and his loss of authority to dictate coalition terms to Ben-Gurion. Their lack of success reveals a great deal about the dynamics of the Israeli coalition system as it was operated by Mapai, even from a position of relative weakness.[32]

The results of the 1961 elections gave Mapai forty-two seats (forty-six, with the affiliated Arab parties) as against forty-six for the other four parties combined. Having fought the election campaign in terms of bringing an end to Mapai rule, and of protecting Israeli democracy from what they declared were the dangers of Ben-Gurion's autocratic rule as demonstrated in his handling of the Lavon Affair, and particularly in his insistence that the party strip Lavon of his post as Histadrut secretary-general, the four parties sought to pursue their parity with Mapai by forming the Club of Four to negotiate coalition arrangements with it as a bloc. Above all, they sought to bring an end to the practice of a Mapai majority in the cabinet, which enabled Mapai effectively to determine cabinet policy by itself. It was, in their view, undemocratic for a party that was a minority in the Knesset to constitute a majority of the cabinet and thus enjoy all the advantages of a majority party. Moreover, they wanted to ensure that Mapai would no longer retain all the major portfolios.

The Club of Four did not succeed in gaining a single one of its demands. It failed for the simple reason that in order to be able to make real its threat that none would join a Mapai-led coalition unless their terms were accepted, it needed to demonstrate that it could prevent Mapai's establishing a government by establishing one itself. It could do this only by joining forces with Herut to create a coalition that would enjoy the support of sixty-three MKs. After some months of deadlocked negotiations in which neither side gave way, Mapam and Ahdut Ha'avodah made it plain that they would not join forces with Herut in order to bring an end to Mapai rule.

If the four disaffected parties could not succeed in bringing about a coalition with Mapai in which the latter did not enjoy a majority, they would rather a Mapai-led coalition with a majority and based on a core of workers' parties than a coalition with Herut but excluding Mapai. In such a coalition, in their view, the left parties would be an insignificant minority; it would be dominated by a united bloc of the Right, on which Herut would put its stamp, economically and politically.

Mapai exploited the failure of the bloc to accept its compromise offers due to internal differences, and informed the president that it would make a last effort to establish a coalition by negotiating with the parties individually. A continued stalemate—no government with Mapai on Mapai's terms, and no government without it—heralded the unwanted prospect of new elections. The Club of Four quickly disintegrated under this pressure; the NRP, the Liberals, Mapam, and Ahdut Ha'avodah all agreed to negotiate, but as we noted earlier, contrary to Ben-Gurion's advice, the Mapai Secretariat decided to establish a narrow coalition without the Liberals and Mapam. Little did they know it at the time, but this rejection of the Liberals proved to be extremely significant for the future development of Israeli politics, as we shall discover later.

The Legislative Process

The Knesset had been established as a unicameral legislature with almost unbounded legislative supremacy. It was not subject to the limitations of a second chamber, judicial review of legislation, or executive veto. So long as it followed the correct procedures and mustered the requisite majority, it could pass almost any legislation it wished. By law, the prime minister had to be a member of the Knesset, and by convention and practice most other ministers were. The executive was responsible to the legislature and dependent upon its continued support.

In majoritarian democracies, the government enjoys the almost automatic support of the majority party in the legislature; in multiparty systems, control of the legislature is a function of coalition formation. It does not inhere in the system, as in the majoritarian case, but must be constructed. Governmental stability and durability depend, therefore, upon the manner in which coalition politics is conducted.

Control of the Knesset was built into the practices of coalition government. First and foremost, Israel had no experience at all of minority government, that is, of a cabinet that rested on less than a majority of the members of the legislature but was maintained in office by the passive support of, or absence of opposition by, additional members, as was quite common in a number of other multiparty democracies.[33] On the two occasions when such a possibility existed— in 1950, when Ben-Gurion proposed a minority government until new elections could be held, and in 1961, when the Club of Four could have established one with the passive support of Herut—it was vigorously rejected. Majority coalition cabinets were accepted as the norm of Israeli executive-legislative relations.

Executive control of the legislature by majority coalition cabinets was maintained strictly by collective responsibility, coalition discipline, and internal party discipline. Provided that the government could retain the support of its own constituent parties, it had no trouble in controlling the legislature. Thus, whatever the formal relationships, in practice the Knesset was controlled and directed by its executive, the government. Steady and predictable control of the legislature, not unlike that of government by single-party majorities, was the distinguishing mark of Israeli parliamentary government, as evidenced by the fact that no Israeli government was ever removed by a formal vote of no confidence (although in September 1951 the government did treat a vote on its education proposals as a vote of confidence, and resigned when defeated).

Knesset legislative initiative was clearly in the hands of the government. Of the 1,366 laws passed in the period 1949-68, 93 percent were initiated by the government, 5.3 percent by private members' bills, and 1.7 percent emanated from committees.[34] In effect, then, the government enjoyed a virtual monopoly over the legislation discussed and enacted during this period. Its majority in the Knesset committees that determined the parliamentary agenda and procedures also conferred on it control of the conduct of the Knesset.

Members could raise issues by asking ministers questions, and by agenda motions. Although both could be availed of by all members of the Knesset, in the early period of the first Knesset Mapai members were not sure whether they, as part of the governmental coalition, should even ask parliamentary questions. Consequently, these were utilized more by the opposition parties. For example, during the Second Knesset 476 agenda motions were moved, of which 70 percent were by members of Mapam, Maki, Herut, and the General Zionists. Similarly, nearly 80 percent of the 1,786 questions submitted to ministers in the Second Knesset came from the same four parties, 60 percent of which came from Mapam and Maki.[35]

Governmental control of the conduct of the Knesset was also facilitated by the coalition's operating as a single unit with preexisting policy agreements spelled out in the coalition agreement and in its Basic Principles, as laid out by the prime minister when presenting the government and seeking the Knesset's vote of confidence. The opposition parties, by way of contrast, were spread all along the political spectrum, and were more divided among themselves than some of them were from the government. Thus, although there was a single government, there was not a single opposition or even an informal opposition coalition. A striking example of the opposition's incapacity for cooperation occurred during the debates over the constitution in June 1950. A legislative proposal was termed "the proposal of the 37" because its sponsors, Mapam, Herut, and Maki, did not wish to be seen to be joined together as its sponsors.

Governmental control of the Knesset was also maintained by means of the committee system. The Knesset was divided into nine permanent standing committees, each with clearly defined areas of jurisdiction. The membership of the committees was allocated more or less in proportion to the strength of the parties in the Knesset. This gave each party equitable representation but also ensured that the coalition parties had a majority in each committee. Often, however, it was not possible to give exact representation to the smaller parties because of inadequate numbers. The statistical difficulties were exploited in the Second Knesset to exclude the Communists from the two most important and sought-after committees, Foreign Affairs and Defense, and Finance, because they handled sensitive and classified information. This was done by deciding that parties with fewer than eight Knesset members would not be represented on the committees.[36]

The operation of the committees and their internal dynamics, on the other hand, created greater opportunities for influence upon government policy by opposition members. First, although Mapai retained the chairmanship of four of the nine committees, including the most important ones, the other five were chaired by members of other parties from both within and outside the coalition. Second, the actual functioning of a committee in the legislative process encouraged the full participation and contribution of all committee members irrespective of party. The committee's task was to discuss proposed legislation in detail after the general debate in the Knesset, which followed the first reading. The less public, collegial atmosphere of the committee was more conducive to consideration of proposals on their merits. This was reinforced by the tendency of committee members to develop expertise and experience in particular fields, which enabled them to suggest amendments unrelated to party programs and competition.

Amendments proposed by members of noncoalition parties had a much greater likelihood of being accepted at the committee level than in the plenum, and this sometimes led to committee votes across party lines on amendments moved by noncoalition members or by backbenchers from the minister's party. All amendments were voted on at the committee level, and both majority and minority proposals came to the full Knesset at the third-reading stage for final approval. Ministers and officials often appeared before the committees to explain and defend their proposals, and were subject to questioning by committee members.

Overall, joint action for the best legislative solution, rather than strict party competition, was more likely to occur if amendments did not oppose the essence of the government's proposal or question its main purposes but sought to improve and refine it. In the case of the former, the government used its majority both in committee and in the plenum to ensure passage of the proposals. Generally, this form of influence was greater when combined with public attention aroused by a debate in the full plenum.[37]

The Primacy of Party

The practices of coalition politics resulted in a pattern of government not very different from government by a single-party majority. The concentration of executive power and effective cabinet ascendancy developed because Mapai dominated the coalition cabinet and the coalition cabinet dominated the legislature. These in turn rested upon Mapai's capacity to maintain structures and processes of decision making, policy coordination, and conflict resolution that amounted to a strong form of party government. This derived from a doctrine of the primacy of party that in essence enabled party government to be translated literally into government by the party.

Mapai's practice of party government during the founding period was an essential element in overcoming many of the disaggregating or power-dispersing tendencies of coalition government at the policy level—the inherent desire of the various coalition parties to prevent the development of single-party-like majority rule by striving for policy and bureaucratic autonomy within the sections of the government apparatus that they controlled, in short, to turn the cabinet into a federation of divergent interests. Mapai adopted a number of different patterns of internal organization during the founding period aimed at coordinating its complex relationships with government and other external bodies, particularly the Histadrut.[38] Despite their variations, all were embodiments of the doctrine of the primacy of party, which had four basic elements.

The first basic element was a clear division of authority. Cabinet ministers were not solely the delegates of the party; they owed responsibility to the cabinet, the Knesset, and the electorate, and consequently were entitled to decide and implement policies in the state sphere without specific supervision or direction, but they were not given complete freedom of action.

The second basic element determined the legitimate role of party institutions, the conditions under which they would exercise a significant influence. Thus, differences of opinion within a ministry, or between a ministry and Mapai's Histadrut leaders, were brought for discussion to party institutions. In principle, the party took the view that a minister was the party's delegate, and that all matters within a minister's jurisdiction (except operative security details) were therefore fitting subjects for party discussion. In practice, intervention was consciously limited. It was not thought to be necessary for party institutions to "follow ministers around like shadows."

The third and decisive element in the primacy of party was that the party, not its representatives, finally determined party policy. When ministers and Histadrut leaders brought their differences to party institutions, what ensued was not an ad hoc discussion between two rival sets of leaders who somehow had to reach accommodation. It was a discussion within the framework of the party, whose authority and primacy both acknowledged, and whose deliberations both sought to influence, but whose decisions both regarded as binding and definitive. When they had not been able to decide, they agreed that the party decided for them. In this way, party institutions were both the coordinators and arbitrators of Mapai's manifold activities and representatives.

Initially, the fourth element in the doctrine of primacy of party was that elected party executive and representative institutions would fulfill the functions of deliberation, decision, arbitration, and coordination, but eventually the institutions were supplemented and sometimes replaced by nonelected, informal bodies. Although this had important implications for intraparty democracy, it made little difference to the doctrine of the primacy of party.

The practices of primacy of party were reinforced by Mapai's leadership selection processes. Both, in fact share common ideological origins in the belief that representatives are delegates, the bearers of the party's views and ideals, and subject to its instructions. The use of nominations committees (in Mapai nomenclature, appointments committees) to select and rank Mapai's Knesset candidates helped to maintain the delegate role. In addition, it made Mapai's Knesset members literally dependent upon party leaders and institutions for maintenance of their positions rather than, say, the party rank and file or the electorate. Similarly, Mapai's ministers, usually from seven to ten in number, were effectively chosen by the prime minister. Although after 1955 their selection was formally ratified in a party body, alternative candidates were never proposed and no election for ministers ever took place.

One way of assessing the impact of this strong pattern of party government is to examine the processes of decision making in a number of major policy areas, in an endeavor to discover the degree to which the concentration of executive power and the cabinet dominance by Mapai were expressed in practice, and further reinforced by centralized policy control. We shall pay particular attention as well to the processes of depoliticization, which related directly to this question. The capacity of the coalition government to develop single-party-like majority characteristics depended in no small degree upon the extent to which functions previously within the legitimate province of the parties were handed over to the state and made subject to its immediate control and direction.

Notes

1. The first data were collected in the early 1960s. See Aharon Antonovsky, "Idiologyiah uma'amad beyisrael," *Amot* 7 (August–September 1963): 21–8; Aharon Antonovsky, "'Amadot politiyot-sozialiyot beyisrael," *Amot* 6 (June–July 1963): 11–22; Alan Arian, "Voting and Ideology in Israel," in Moshe Lissak and Emanuel Gutmann, eds., *Political Institutions and Processes in Israel* (Jerusalem: Academon, 1971), pp. 257–86.

2. For an important analysis of polarization and fragmentation (discussed later) and their application to Western democracies that is based on mass attitudes, see Giacomo Sani and Giovanni Sartori, "Polarization, Fragmentation and Competition in Western Democracies," in Hans Daalder and Peter Mair, eds., *Western European Party Systems: Continuity and Change* (Beverly Hills, Calif.: Sage Publications, 1983), pp. 307–40.

3. Yohanan Bader, *Haknesset veani* (Jerusalem: 'Idanim, 1979), p. 61.

4. See Anita Shapira, *Mipiturei harama 'ad piruk hapalmah* (Hakibbutz Hameuhad Publishing House, 1985), p. 52.

5. David Ben-Gurion, 24.11.52, "Mishpat Prag," *Hazon vederekh*, 5 vols. (Tel Aviv: Mapai, 1951–57), 4:128.

6. David Ben-Gurion, "Yoman Ben-Gurion," unpublished diaries, 31.1.1950.

7. *Divrei Haknesset*, 10.3.1949, p. 135.

8. See Michael Bar-Zohar, *Ben-Gurion*, 3 vols. (Tel Aviv: Am Oved, 1975–78), pp. 1538–47; Zev Zahor, "Aherei 20 Shanah," *Monitin* (October 1983): 52–55, which quotes letters in a similar vein written by Ben-Gurion in 1963 to Sharett.

9. *Herut*, 19.8.1955.

10. Ben-Gurion, *Hazon vederekh*, 5:138–39. By the "open" communists he means Maki; by the "disguised" ones, it is important to note in view of the argument later, he means Mapam!

11. For a comprehensive analysis of the stability and major characteristics of the party system, see Emanuel Gutmann. "Miflagot umahanot—yezivut veshinui," in Moshe Lissak and Emanuel Gutmann, eds., *Hamarekhet hapolitit hayisraelit* (Tel Aviv: Am Oved, 1977), pp. 122–70.

12. Luebbert defines this situation as a "dominated system," and such a party therefore is in this sense the "dominant party." See Gregory M. Luebbert, *Comparative Democracy: Policymaking and Governing Coalitions in Europe and Israel* (New York: Columbia University Press, 1986), p. 72.

13. Luebbert calls this a "divergent-explicit" relationship in which one or both parties demand a preference change—mutual or unilateral—as a quid pro quo for coalition participation. For agreement to take place, parties would have to accept policies directly at variance with their issue preferences, and for that reason it rarely occurs. Ibid., pp. 62–63.

14. See, for example, Ben-Gurion, *Medinat yisrael hamehudeshet* (Tel Aviv: Am Oved, 1969), p. 371.

15. Ben-Gurion, letter to the president, 27.2.1951, in *Hazon vederekh*, 3:72.

16. Ibid.

17. Ben-Gurion, 8.8.51, *Hazon vederekh*, 3:183.

18. Luebbert calls such preferences tangential, that is, parties concentrate on issues that are unrelated and therefore are not considered incompatible. Luebbert, *Comparative Democracy*, p. 62.

19. Cited in Bar-Zohar, *Ben-Gurion*, p. 1423.

20. Ben-Gurion, *Medinat yisrael hamehudeshat*, p. 364.

21. Ibid., pp. 362–69.

22. Ibid.

23. Bar-Zohar, *Ben-Gurion*, pp. 826–29.

24. Moshe Sharett, *Yoman ishi*, 9 vols. (Tel Aviv: Sifriat Ma'ariv, 1978), 18.5.1955, p. 1007.

25. These features will be dealt with in greater detail later.

26. I am indebted to my colleague Dr. Avraham Diskin for this observation.

27. These concepts are discussed and data regarding the practice and experience of twenty-one democratic societies from 1948 to 1980, including Israel, are to be found in Arend Lijphart, *Democracies: Patterns of Majoritarian and Consensus Government in Twenty-one Countries* (New Haven: Yale University Press, 1984), pp. 46–66.

28. Bader, *Haknesset veani*, p. 97, recalls that Ben-Gurion once explained his strategy to him along these lines.

29. This forms part of Ben-Gurion's diary entry for June 16, 1963, the day of his final retirement. It is cited in Haggai Eshed, *Mi natan et hahoraah* (Jerusalem: 'Idanim, 1979), p. 301.

30. Ben-Gurion, *Hazon vederekh*, 3:215–27.

31. Sharett, *Yoman ishi*, 12.9.1951.

32. See Avi Milkov, "The Club of Four," unpublished seminar paper for my course Parties and Party Politics in Israel, Political Science Department, The Hebrew University, 1984.

33. Lijphart, *Democracies*, p. 61. Between 1945 and 1980, 68 percent of governments in Denmark and Sweden, 40 percent in the Fourth French Republic, 36 percent in Italy, and 25 percent in Finland were minority governments.

34. See Shevah Weiss and Avraham Brichta, "Private Members' Bills in Israel's Parliament—The Knesset," *Parliamentary Affairs* 23 (1969): 21–33.

35. Ibid.

36. Marver H. Bernstein, *The Politics of Israel: The First Decade of Statehood* (Princeton: Princeton University Press, 1957), p. 98.

37. Asher Zidon, *Haknesset* (Tel Aviv: Ahiasaf, 1950), pp. 150ff.

38. These patterns and their relationship with Mapai's internal organizational structure and development, and with its leadership selection processes are analyzed in depth in Peter Y. Medding, *Mapai in Israel: Political Organisation and Government in a New Society* (Cambridge: Cambridge University Press, 1972).

6

Coalition Cabinets, Party Government, and the Control of Policy-making

The concentration of executive power in single-party governments and cabinet dominance of parliament in unitary systems facilitate control over policy-making. Coalition cabinets, by way of contrast, even in unitary systems, tend to disperse power and to limit the capacity for control over policy-making. To establish and maintain the majority coalition, policy determination may be handed over to separate ministries controlled by different parties rather than retained by the cabinet as a collective body. The cabinet becomes a federation of government departments, or a meeting place of the heads of autonomous party fiefdoms. Under such conditions, overall policy coherence suffers as unrelated, divergent, or even directly conflicting policies are pursued.

Alternatively, policies may reach the stage of collective decision but be decided by ad hoc compromises between competing coalition partners, based upon constantly changing majorities, rather than according to a set of agreed-upon priorities and goals. The result may be a form of directionless consensus, which places more emphasis on the fact of policy agreement than on its content. Decision making takes place formally in the cabinet, but coherent overall policies are not arrived at. Such a situation demands the constant renegotiation of compromise and is therefore likely to be highly unstable.

Stable control over policy-making may, however, be achieved under coalition conditions if collective decision making is directed by a cohesive leadership with predetermined policy views. This is more likely to occur if the leading party is united and if it exercises firm control over its partners: the former permits overall policy coherence; the latter ensures that it can have its policy adopted as government policy.

In chapter 5 we analyzed Mapai's approach to party government and to coalition politics. In this chapter we examine the extent to which Mapai was able to utilize party government and coalition politics to gain control over policy-making during the founding period. We focus upon three major areas of policy-making: economic policy in general, and, in particular, wage policy; foreign policy; and defense policy. The evidence of these case studies supports the view that despite permanent coalition government, Mapai achieved a high level of control over policy-making, approximating that characteristic of single-party executive dominance.

The Centralization of Economic Policy-making

Despite uninterrupted coalition government, Israel is one of the most centralized democratic states in the world. Lijphart measured centralization in terms of the central government's share of total central and noncentral tax receipts. Whereas the average degree of centralization of the fifteen unitary states was 83 percent, and that of six federal states was 58 percent, the central government's tax share in Israel was 96 percent.[1]

The government played a major role in the Israeli economy, and exercised a considerable degree of control over it. During the founding period the economy was "to a large extent directly and indirectly government controlled, not only in its aggregative character, but also in many details." In fact, "if indirect means of control, such as import controls and customs levies, are taken into account, Israel emerges as the country with the largest amount of governmental influence on the detailed operation of the economy among all western-type democratic states."[2]

Centralized control over policy-making was promoted, rather than hindered, by the pattern of relations between ministers and civil servants. In the Israel of the founding period, which inherited and legitimated the tradition of administrative appointments according to a party key, many senior and not-so-senior civil servants owed their positions to their party affiliations. Consequently, they accepted fully the political authority of their ministers and perceived their role as assisting them in promoting and implementing the policies whose goals and guidelines were set by the minister and the party. They, too, shared the values institutionalized in the practices of the primacy of party.

Thus, during the founding period, ministers generally exercised political authority over their civil service advisers, both jointly and individually. In general, ministers and leading civil servants were not rivals but cooperated and intermingled as loyal members of the same party promoting its policies, with civil servants often being directly mobilized by the party to assist party bodies to make policy, even though they were not members of these bodies.

The specific historical circumstances of the establishment of the state and the struggle to consolidate it reinforced this pattern. There is considerable evidence from Europe and Britain to suggest that the policy-making influence of civil servants is at its lowest during periods of change and crisis, and of major reform, and that the major initiative for policy decisions comes from the political executive. According to Mattei Dogan, after the war in Europe, "the directing staffs of political parties were, at that time, the principle actors and enactors."[3] Similarly, politicians were found to play a larger role in public policy-making in Israel than in nearly all other modern states, and the influence of the professional staffs was very limited.[4]

This pattern was most developed in the case of Mapai. Its majority in the cabinet and its hold over all the major ministries specifically promoted economic policy centralization. It should be recalled that for all of the founding period in addition to the office of prime minister, defense minister, and foreign minister, Mapai held all the major economic portfolios: finance, labor, and agriculture for the whole period; commerce and industry, and development for most of the period. In fact, every major ministry that dealt with the *production* of economic goods and with the control of the allocation of resources was held by Mapai. This was reflected dramatically in the constantly rising proportion of the nation's already centralized budgetary resources at its disposal. Mapai ministries controlled a much larger proportion of the budget than was their proportion in the cabinet. From 1951 until the end of the founding period, the proportion of the budget spent by Mapai ministries steadily increased from 72 percent to 90 percent, whereas it never exceeded 70 percent of the cabinet posts.[5] Moreover, Mapai's retention of the same ministries for the whole period, while other ministries changed hands among different cabinet coalition partners, reinforced its control over economic policy-making, and with it the capacity for policy centralization.

The overall picture is of a high degree of centralization in the making of economic decisions by the government. This was reinforced from the first by the overriding importance of national goals, such as defense, development, agriculture, immigrant absorption, and housing, that had priority and were the subject of constant cabinet discussion. When industrialization was promoted from the mid-1950s onward, it occurred under a system in which the government was the leading actor and the major source of, or conduit for, capital investment. This of course fitted in with the pattern inherited from the Yishuv of public and Histadrut ownership and direction of capital.[6]

In the determination of policy the cabinet had the ongoing authority. The budget was used to impose an overall framework and guidelines. Ministries submitted line-by-line proposals to the Ministry of Finance, whose task it was to convert the various requests into an overall and detailed proposal that received cabinet approval before being sent to the Knesset, where it was legislated into law. So, too, did all other economic legislation and all significant changes in fiscal and monetary policy, as well as appointments to all senior economic positions, need cabinet approval.

Centralization was most characterized by a high degree of central control and direction of ongoing economic activities, as exemplified in the active and personal involvement of the key ministers, particularly the ministers of finance, and commerce and industry, at all levels of decision making, including specific details of policy and implementation. Furthermore, according to Shimshoni, the "organization and powers of the Ministry of Finance" gave it considerable capacity for control as a result of the following:

> The role of the minister—in party affairs, the Cabinet, and the Economic Minister's Committee

The budget and the size and scope of government investment and consumption

The ministry's use of the civil service and the government's role as employer

Foreign-currency control

Control of cash flow by the Accountant-General and the State Revenue Administration

The ministry's determination of many factor costs—fuel, electricity, water, land communications

Tax, customs, and excise management

Representatives on interdepartmental committees who accept the Finance view and bring back to the minister and the directors the opinions and situations in the other ministries

Representation on boards of directors, guidance of government financial institutions and of government corporations

Control and operation of the capital market.[7]

But above all, "the most important source of authority for central direction and control" lay in "the congruence of political and economic power"—the backing of the prime minister, the confidence of colleagues, and the support of the party and its institutions. Clearly, economic-policy centralization and control rested with, and was a prime manifestation of, Mapai's pattern of party government, and its capacity to operate a coalition cabinet and make economic policy as if it were a single-party cabinet. Only within these parameters could ministers from other coalition parties enjoy some limited autonomy to determine the policies within the ministries that they controlled.

Wages Policy

Wages policy is a major area of economic policy not easily subjected to direct cabinet control by law or policy decision. Rather, the determination of wages policy is essentially a publicly negotiated agreement that must meet the needs and resolve the separate interests of three actors: employees, employers, and the government. Nevertheless, given Mapai's highly centralized pattern of control and direction of all other aspects of the economy, it is not surprising that it sought to control the process of wage determination as well. But whereas the focal point of Mapai's control of the other aspects of economic policy was the cabinet and the Ministry of Finance, the focal point of the decision-making process Mapai adopted to coordinate and centralize wages policy was the party itself. Party government was even more direct in this sphere than it was in others. This was even more remarkable, given the historical circumstances at the end of the Yishuv in which wages policy had been decided in direct negotiations between the Manufacturers Association and the Histadrut, based upon changes in an official cost-of-living index, and then generally adopted by all employers. Had such a pattern been maintained after independence, the government would have been completely left out of the making of wages policy, in clear contrast with its central role in economic policy control and direction.

If the government wished to align wages policy with other elements of economic policy, it had to become involved in the process; the question became how to achieve this end. Rather than establish statutory bodies for wages determination, the solution that evolved was policy coordination within Mapai party institutions. This proved effective because both Mapai ministers and Mapai Histadrut leaders owed their positions to the party, were represented on party bodies, and accepted the idea of the primacy of the party in setting policy and resolving differences between them. Thus, the centralization of wages-policy decisions within the party became a distinctive element in Mapai's pattern of party government.[8]

After independence, the Histadrut gave full support to the government's austerity measures. In 1949 it agreed to tie wage increases to individual incentive payments based on production quotas. It also accepted automatic wage reductions that resulted from a decline in the cost-of-living index due to price controls. (Worker opposition to a second successive decline led the Histadrut to press for a reexamination of the index, and eventually a new, more accurate index was adopted.) Again in 1950 and 1951, despite worker militancy and opposition, the Histadrut supported the government's austerity measures, and continued to tie wage raises to increased productivity. On this occasion, however, some unions and workers' committees gained wage increases through militant action and direct negotiations with employers.

As a result of these developments, by the end of 1950 relations between Mapai economic ministers and Histadrut leaders were not good. Although the Histadrut leaders proposed only minor wage increases for 1951 in line with government policy, they were strongly opposed to a government proposal to exclude the Histadrut as the representative of government employees, and generally displeased with the government's lack of cooperation and failure to consult sufficiently with them on economic affairs in general.

Although the Histadrut trade union leadership did not wish to be dictated to by the government over wages or labor policies, neither did it seek autonomy or freedom of action. Rather, it proposed cooperation and joint activity between Mapai's ministers and Histadrut representatives, which meant that policy differences and disagreements would be resolved within the party's decision-making institutions. This would give the Histadrut the greatest opportunity to influence the policy process, while recognizing the government's right and need to be involved in it but without granting it the decisive say. Mapai ministers accepted the proposal because, for the first time, it institutionalized their influence over wages policy, and avoided the dangers of head-on conflict with the Histadrut leadership.

These general ideas were initially put into practice toward the end of 1951. During that year a major strike in the metal industry had secured a wage increase of 15 percent, and it was quickly followed by strikes in other industries, with similar outcomes. Inflation spiraled during the year, the black market boomed, and tax evasion spread. Early in 1952 a new economic policy was introduced. Its aim was to curb inflation, increase production, and encourage investment, and a key element was a major devaluation.

The Histadrut's wages policy was drawn up at the end of 1951 in conjunction with the framing of the new economic policy. In it the Histadrut reaffirmed its commitment to the linkage of wage increases to productivity. Some of its other demands, however, went significantly beyond its previous position. It sought to raise the ceiling for the payment of cost-of-living increases and to institute a new index. Moreover, the Histadrut proposed that workers who had not received wage benefits as a result of the strikes be given increases of 10 to 15 percent.

To assist in overall economic planning, the Mapai Secretariat had earlier established a special Economic Committee comprising ministers, Histadrut leaders, and leading members of the Knesset's finance and economics committees, and it played a major role in the formulation of the new economic policy. The original intention was that wages policy would form an integral part of the overall economic plan, but the committee could not agree on the issue of a wage increase, and the matter was brought to the Mapai Central Committee. Also present at the meeting were many Mapai trade union and workers' committee activists who, during the debate, put considerable pressure on the delegates to accede to the Histadrut's wage demands. The first two parts of the Histadrut's policy passed easily; the proposal for wage increases proved more controversial. Although opposed by all Mapai ministers except the minister of finance, it eventually passed by a very narrow majority, with many abstentions.

The Histadrut made a concerted effort to follow a policy of wage restraint for the period 1953–55, that is, no increase in wage levels. Cost-of-living increases were granted, and in 1954 the ceiling was raised to take account of the wage rises of the previous two years. By this time a definite pattern had emerged in the making of wages policy. It was discussed first among Mapai leaders in the Histadrut, and then brought to the party executive bodies for further discussion and final decision.

The arrangements were put to the test in 1954. Ahdut Ha'avodah and Mapam brought increasing pressure to bear within the Histadrut to raise wage levels by 15 percent. Mapai Histadrut leaders did not think that such increases were justified, but the political nature of the pressure from the minority parties made it imperative that they take action to maintain rank-and-file support for wage restraint and increases tied to productivity. A policy along these lines drawn up by a committee of the Secretariat won the support of both Mapai ministers and Histadrut leaders. Following this, an extensive campaign to gain support among local and national union, and workers' committee activists was launched. Only subsequently was the policy of a wage freeze brought to the Mapai Central Committee for final decision. There, the proposal of activists to raise wages 15 percent in order to match the other parties received no support, and the wage freeze passed without opposition.

The debate over wages policy in 1956 was protracted and complex, and took place in the wake of strikes by professional workers, investigation of their salaries by a committee, and a subsequent 15 percent increase. Industrial workers pressed for similar increases. Initially, the Mapai Secretariat, over the opposition of the minister of finance, Levi Eshkol, recommended a general increase of between 5 and 15 percent. Eshkol's argument that such an increase was inflationary was given added weight by the emergency security situation created by the Czech-Egyptian arms deal. In view of the security problem and the strong stand taken by Eshkol, Mapai's Histadrut leadership reconsidered its demands. It agreed to Eshkol's proposals to freeze wages for six months as part of an overall emergency plan, to levy a defense tax, and to cut government spending.

The opposition parties kept pressing for an increase of at least 10 percent, and the professionals, despite pressure from the government, refused to cut their promised increase by half. The Histadrut was caught in strong cross-pressures: from the government, on the one hand, and from professional workers, opposition parties, many of its own trade union activists, and rank-and-file workers, on the other. The matter was brought to the Mapai Central Committee for decision.

It had before it Eshkol's proposal for a wage freeze, and that of the Histadrut for salary increases of between 4 and 10 percent for all workers. Following an evenly balanced vote, it was sent back to the Secretariat, which after many consultations with the ministers, Mapai Histadrut leaders, and its own wages committee, finally opted for the Histadrut's recommendations, which were then ratified by the Central Committee. A compromise was also negotiated with the professionals after another strike.

Between 1957 and 1959 various technical changes were made in the process: automatic adjustments as calculated by changes in the cost-of-living index were extended from three- to six-month intervals; its ceiling was raised; the adjustments were made nontaxable; and the collective wage agreements were to be valid for two years.

The system worked quite routinely until a major devaluation and significant economic policy changes in February 1962 sparked a major conflict within Mapai over the payment of cost-of-living adjustments. The Histadrut pressed for April compensation for price rises, despite the fact that they would not be due until July, which was the position taken by Eshkol, who was still minister of finance. Various compromises were suggested that sought mainly to give special consideration to low-income groups, which would be especially hard hit by increased prices. The issue was discussed in Mapai's Economic Committee, the Secretariat, and the Central Committee. The compromise solution was to compensate low-income groups in April from national insurance funds, by the amount of the advance due to be paid by employers on the July cost-of-living increment. This met the need to look after the low-income groups, and the Ministry of Finance's desire not to add to inflationary pressures.

As July approached, it became clear that the rise in the cost-of-living index would be about 7 percent. To control inflationary pressures, Eshkol sought to delay payment by converting half the due sum into promissory notes to be redeemed at a later date. He held initial discussions with the employers' representatives, the Manufacturers Association, to test their reaction, and only then brought the scheme to the Secretariat of the Mapai Economic Committee. Here complaints were voiced that he had discussed the question with employers before Mapai's Histadrut leadership or the relevant party institutions had been consulted. Substantively, the Histadrut opposed the scheme.

An ad hoc Mapai committee was appointed to examine the proposal and to seek ways of preventing price rises. Significantly, from the point of view of policy centralization and party government, it consisted of Eshkol, minister of finance; Aharon Becker, the Histadrut secretary-general; the director-general of the Ministry of Finance; another leading Ministry of Finance official; the head of the Histadrut trade union department; and the director of its Social and Economic Research Institute. Eshkol raised the matter at a cabinet meeting in order to have it passed on to the Ministerial Committee for Economic Affairs. At the cabinet, he was criticized by non-Mapai ministers, who maintained that the matter should have first been brought before the cabinet before being discussed with the Manufacturers Association and the Histadrut.

The Ministerial Economic Committee decided against Eshkol's suggestion and proposed a compulsory savings loan, the details of which were worked out by Ministry of Finance officials. Only after it received the approval of Mapai's Economic Committee was it brought back to the cabinet. The Manufacturers Association agreed to hold prices in line, and as a result the Histadrut did not oppose the combined package.

Wage policies for 1963 were made for one year only. At first the Ministry of Finance sought a two-year wage freeze, but during discussions of Mapai's Economic Committee it was clear that one year was acceptable. The Economic Committee was widened for these discussions to include representatives of Mapai's parliamentary party and the Histadrut Trade Union Department, the secretaries of six major local Labor Councils, and a number of economic experts. Despite strong grass-roots pressure, the Histadrut leadership accepted a policy of wage restraint and a one-year freeze, provided that current tax and price levels were maintained, and that the compulsory loan was not reinstituted after it expired in April

Before the Economic Committee made a final decision, the Mapai Secretariat initiated an intensive grass-roots campaign to explain the necessity of the policy of restraint to the rank and file. Meetings were held across the country mobilizing Mapai's national-union, local-union, Labor Council, and party-branch activists in all the main centers of Histadrut concentration. Only after this campaign was concluded did the party Secretariat, together with the Mapai Economic Committee, the Mapai Histadrut leadership, and the Mapai members of the Knesset's finance and economics committees, "recommend to the government and the Histadrut" that the joint policy previously agreed to by Mapai's economics ministers and Histadrut leaders be adopted.

The wages policy for 1964–65 followed this pattern. The ministers opposed wage increases, and the Histadrut leaders pointed to the statistical evidence indicating a projected two-year growth of 8 to 9 percent in net national product, which, since 1960, was the measure that they followed. Ministerial opposition led them to lower their demands to 6 percent, spread equally over the two years, raised ceilings for the payment of cost-of-living adjustments, payment of the applicable rise in the cost-of-living index, and additional family allowances for low-income earners. The demands passed easily through the Mapai Economic Committee, the Secretariat (with enlarged parliamentary, Histadrut, and Economic Committee representation), and the Central Committee.

Two observations about the characteristic features and political implications of this centralized policy-making process emerge from the analysis. The first is the relative weakness of private employers in Israel, and their nonrepresentation at the critical stages of wages-policy formulation during the founding period. Effectively, they were represented by the government. Second, in view of the tremendous power potential of the Histradrut, one cannot help but be struck by the sense of restraint exhibited by its leadership, particularly in view of rank-and-file demands for increased wages and improved conditions, reinforced by the more extreme demands of the opposition parties. Even though the pattern of party appointment to top Histadrut positions partly insulated union leaders from the threat of being removed by the vote of the rank and file, the centralized leadership still had to withstand rank-and-file pressure, and explain why it did so. The explanation lies in the main in the Histadrut's self-conception that it was to serve the national interest, the well-being of the entire population, and the state as a whole, and therefore had to take into consideration the objective realities and problems of the economic situation, and the effects of the Histadrut claims upon society at large.

Thus, from the outset, the two main groups involved in wages-policy negotiations were not very far apart. The Histadrut was hardly less concerned about the economy than the government, and made this a major policy principle. Similarly, the Mapai-led government was deeply concerned with the fate of the workers, and was sympathetic to their needs and interests. This convergence was the basis upon which settlement of differences in wages policy rested.

The essential condition for bringing settlement about was the common party membership of the two sets of decision makers, and simultaneous Mapai control of both major institutions. Negatively, the potential costs of inability to reach agreement generated considerable pressure upon the participants to resolve their differences. Positively, simultaneous party control made it easier to reach decisions. Politicians who knew each other well, had worked together for many years, and shared ideals, goals, and loyalty to a party in power and a desire to keep it there made decisions within the confines of party bodies, away from the spotlight of publicity and public controversy.

Basically, there were two characteristic types of situation with regard to the making of wages policy. The more usual was for the Histadrut to take the initiative and make wage demands. This put the government in the position of having to indicate whether or not it supported them. Alternatively, the government would take the initiative and set the limits within which it would support future wage demands. Here the Histadrut was forced onto the defensive, and it either had to accept the guidelines or have them altered by the party institutions. Eventually, Mapai ministers and Histadrut leaders learned to have informal contact with each other prior to taking a policy position, and this enabled each to formulate policy on the basis of an informed projection of the other's likely response.

Open debate took place in Mapai party bodies as the final stage in the process of bargaining and negotiation, characterized by compromise and flexibility. The essence of the process was that there should be agreement between the government and the Histadrut. Once this was achieved, there was little room for any other group, and no scope for any other decision-making body to influence policy. Thus, the opposition parties in the Histadrut could not exert pressure directly in the actual process of wages-policy negotiation. They could, however, attempt to do so indirectly by applying pressure upon the Histadrut leadership. The minority opposition parties in the Histadrut, particularly Mapam and later Ahdut Ha'avodah, consistently demanded wage increases far above those demanded by the Mapai Histadrut leadership. Generally speaking, it felt politically vulnerable to the pressure exerted by the opposition parties. Having constantly to keep the political consequences of its wages policies in mind meant that the Mapai Histadrut leadership had to maintain the rank-and-file worker support that kept it in power in the Histadrut and enabled it to make these decisions. Strong campaigning by opposition parties coupled with general worker support for their position often pushed the Mapai Histadrut leadership into going further than it might otherwise have done.

Seemingly vulnerable to the political pressure of the opposition parties, the Mapai Histadrut leadership was more resistant to the views of Mapai trade union activists. It listened to their opinions and it enabled them to participate formally at various stages in the policy-making process, particularly the early stage of policy crystallization, but rarely, if ever, did it give in to this form of political pressure. When faced with pressure from below, the Mapai Histadrut leadership campaigned strenuously at the grass roots. Here it used the potentially damaging effects of excessive wage demands upon Mapai's political position in the government to persuade trade union activists to moderate them. In the last resort, it was only its capacity to maintain the loyalty of the rank and file in this way that enabled it to withstand the pressure of the opposition parties at election time.

Thus, Mapai utilized its approach to party government as embodied in the practices of the primacy of party to create a centralized process of policy determination in an issue area that was by nature public and involved many groups and interests. It excluded other political parties, including its coalition partners, from any formal or authoritative part in the process by transferring the effective decision making to internal party bodies. Once agreement was reached between the government and the Histadrut within Mapai party bodies, there was little scope, if any, for other groups, including the employers' representatives, to have any significant role in policy-making.

We turn now to two major fields of policy-making centralized in the hands of, and controlled by, Mapai's cabinet ministers and their leading administrative officials and advisers. Here, the party institutions are also generally excluded, along with cabinet partners, opposition parties, interest groups, and the public at large.

Foreign Policy

Of all the areas of policy-making in Israel in the founding period, foreign policy has attracted the widest scholarly attention. Both the substance and the process of such major decisions as that making Jerusalem the capital of Israel; the decisions to accord diplomatic recognition to the People's Republic of China but not to establish diplomatic relations with it; support for the United States and the Western powers and their stance at the UN Security Council regarding intervention in the Korean War; and the Reparations Agreement have all been studied in considerable detail.[9] So, too, have been the development of Israel's foreign policy orientation, the policy of nonalignment, and its eventual replacement by a declared pro-Western orientation.[10]

Our purpose here is not to examine these decisions in detail but to place them in the context of party government, control over policy-making, and coalition government. Some of these decisions enjoyed an overwhelming national consensus (Jerusalem), with the main interparty differences being tactical; others engendered bitter partisan dispute and disagreement (reparations and Korea); and some were subject to internal divisions within Mapai as well as interparty differences (the nonestablishment of diplomatic relations with China).

From Nonalignment to Support for the West

Nonalignment was neatly summarized in the Basic Principles of the first coalition in March 1949 as "loyalty to the principles of the United Nations Charter and friendship with all freedom-loving states, and in particular with the United States and the Soviet Union."[11] It had crystalized even before establishment of the state and was based upon three considerations: large concentrations of Jews in both blocs, with the greatest reservoir of potential *olim* in the Eastern bloc; the support of both the United States and the Soviet Union in Israel's establishment and defense, and the desire for future good relations with both to assist its future development; and the concern to minimize internal political conflict within the labor movement arising from Mapam's strident support for the Soviet bloc. Nonalignment was, therefore, a necessary precondition for any Mapai–Mapam coalition.

Nonalignment policy was discussed in internal Mapai bodies, and its formulation and implementation were agreed upon by the party's two major actors in foreign policy, Ben-Gurion and Moshe Sharett, who called this pragmatic approach, the "knock-on-any-door" policy, and it won overwhelming internal support. Its general principles, however, had to be applied to specific foreign policy questions, and here opinions in the party were divided.

At the ideological level, the question was whether the party should be neutral in the struggle between communism and democratic socialism, or should Mapai as a democratic socialist party take a stand against the oppressive nature of the Soviet regime? In foreign policy, this same debate was translated into the question of whether Israel should be neutral—equal friendship with both powers, or equal nonalignment and independence, that is, equal distance from both—or whether Israel should adopt a selective but pro-Western and pro-democratic stance.

The issues were debated within Mapai circles in the early years with regard to the Histadrut's international affiliations: Should it leave the communist-controlled trade union international or join the Western one, and should Mapai join the Socialist International? The issues were also the subject of the interparty debate with Mapam over coalition formation. The two were joined in the question of how Mapai publicists and newspapers should treat the issue. Despite the very strong opposition to the USSR and its policies, the real weight of Mapai's opposition was directed at Mapam. It was made clear that the enemy was not the USSR itself but what were termed the Yevsektsia, the Jews and Israelis who served communism blindly and consequently rejected Zionism, even when they purported to promote it.

The major and decisive element in Israel's pragmatic foreign policy of nonalignment in the early years was Ben-Gurion's political and strategic outlook, shared in substance, if not always in style and tone, by Sharett. Ben-Gurion had long entertained strong anticommunist views, but given the country's material needs, he was prepared temporarily to follow a course of nonidentification. It was a pragmatic and utilitarian approach, not one of ideological nonalignment. As he explained to Mapam leaders in November 1949, he would "refuse to give up his soul, but would give up his pants for the absorption of immigration."[12] He viewed the Soviet Union as the major enemy of Zionism and the free world, but for some years he followed a policy of no public antineutrality, and no public anti-Soviet statements. Eventually, this gave way under the pressure of events, particularly the decline in, and the increasing unlikelihood of, further Jewish immigration from the Eastern bloc countries; the noneventuation of military and economic aid, and the anti-Semitic campaign in the Soviet Union.

When the Korean issue erupted on the international scene in mid-1950, it added a further critical element: strong U.S. pressure upon Israel to support the Western position. Decision makers in Israel realized that they had come to a critical point in its foreign policy, that they were being called upon to stand up and be counted, and that they had to make a decision that would clarify where Israel stood. Mapam and the Communists urged that Israel not support the pro-Western Security Council resolution that branded North Korea the aggressor because a freedom struggle was going on with which Israel should sympathize. The General Zionists, Mizrachi, and Progressives all urged Israeli approval of the resolution. Herut regarded North Korea as the aggressor but opposed support for the resolution because of lack of faith in the UN as a guardian of the peace, and urged caution.

The government held an extraordinary cabinet session to discuss Israel's reply to the request of the UN to member states for assistance. On the advice of foreign office personnel and Israeli diplomatic representatives in the United States, mainly Eliahu Elath and Abba Eban, Sharett proposed that Israel offer diplomatic and political support. Ben-Gurion proposed the participation of Israeli troops in the UN command to show that Israel was serious in saying that North Korea was guilty of aggression, but he won no support at all. The cabinet did not formally vote because there was consensus on its statement of opposition to aggression and support for the Security Council's efforts to restore peace. The statement was debated in the Knesset, where the government easily defeated separate motions of no confidence from Mapam and Herut.[13]

Jerusalem

The UN Partition Resolution included provision for the internationalization of Jerusalem, which reluctantly had been accepted by the Jewish authorities as part of the partition package. During the war, the Israel Defense Force gained control of the western part of Jerusalem but was unable to wrest control of the Old City from the Jordanian troops. Despite Arab rejection of partition, the status of Jerusalem and proposals to proceed with internationalization were brought up regularly at the UN.

From the outset there was considerable pressure within Israel to act to confirm Israeli sovereignty over the part of Jerusalem under its control. Particularly vocal in this regard was Herut, which also sought military action to free the Old City and to reunite both parts under Israeli control. Within most of the other parties there were internal disagreements about the international repercussions of declaring Jerusalem as the capital of Israel, as well as doubts because of the security burden and the drain on resources.

Before the state was established, then, internationalization was thought to be one of the prices to be paid for independence. After it was established, the idea that Jerusalem would be internationalized lost acceptance, and it was replaced by the view that Jerusalem was within the borders of the Jewish state, regretfully without the Old City. As Ben-Gurion put it at a meeting of the Provisional State Council in June 1948, "There is no difference between Jerusalem and Tel Aviv, Haifa, Hanitah. They are all part of the Jewish State."[14] The problem was how to overcome the military, economic, and political difficulties.

Until the end of 1949 this was how matters rested with regard to Jerusalem. Israel slowly established its presence: it appointed a military governor, made Jerusalem the location of the Supreme Court, transferred some government institutions there, declared that it preferred partition to internationalization, convened the first sessions of the Constituent Assembly, and swore in the first president there. In the meantime, the UN continued to discuss various proposals for internationalization.

Matters came to a head at the end of 1949. Sharett cabled the cabinet from the UN that the General Assembly was about to discuss a resolution about the territorial internationalization of Jerusalem, and that it had considerable support. Thus, in mid-November Ben-Gurion urged the cabinet to act quickly and make Jerusalem the seat of government. But there was no decision, and when Begin a week later in the Knesset advocated a law to make Jerusalem the capital of Israel, Ben-Gurion, because of advanced negotiations with King Abdullah, had the proposal transferred to a Knesset committee rather than put to a vote.

On December 5, when it became apparent that the UN proposal for internationalization was assured a large majority, Ben-Gurion again urged the cabinet to act quickly to transfer the government to Jerusalem, and convened a special session of the Knesset. There he made a strong statement in which he affirmed Israel's right to Jerusalem, and declared that it would resist UN action to forcibly remove Israel from Jerusalem or interfere with its authority there, and that it regarded the November 1947 resolution on Jerusalem as null and void. Aimed at dissuading the UN from acting, Ben-Gurion's statement had the opposite effect; it resulted in an overwhelming UN vote in favor of territorial internationalization and immediate action to establish Jerusalem as a *corpus separatum*.

The very day after the UN vote the Israeli cabinet made Jerusalem the seat of government and the capital of Israel. It was a decision made by Ben-Gurion to prevent implementation of the UN resolution by presenting the UN with a *fait accompli*. Most ministers supported the decision, although at least two Mapai ministers were hesitant, and Sharett, in New York, dissented. He immediately cabled his resignation because he regarded the failure to anticipate the UN action as his responsibility, and because his view that Israel should not act directly against a UN resolution had not been accepted. The resignation never took effect because Ben-Gurion ignored it.

The government reaffirmed Ben-Gurion's earlier statement, announced that it would not cooperate with the UN resolution, which was unworkable; hastened the transfer of the government and ministers to Jerusalem; and declared that the Knesset would move permanently to Jerusalem. The Knesset approved these steps in a vote a few days later, and held a major debate on the issue early in January after Israel had been severely criticized at the UN. Begin attacked the government for its earlier failure to act, and a Herut motion of no confidence on the grounds that the government had prevented proclamation of Jerusalem as the capital was defeated. Mapam attacked the government for its acceptance of the de facto partition of Jerusalem, but this, too, was easily defeated.

Two weeks later the Knesset accepted Ben-Gurion's view that it did not need to pass a law to make Jerusalem the capital of Israel; this had already been done by King David. It therefore issued the following statement: "With the creation of a Jewish State, Jerusalem again became its capital." [15]

German Reparations

The decision to enter into direct negotiations with the West German government regarding reparations for plundered Jewish property in Europe was, as we have already noted, at the center of a dramatic interparty conflict. A year before the issue came to the Knesset, the government decided to seek German reparations indirectly through the occupying powers. When it became apparent that the West German government would not agree, the Israeli government decided to follow the path of direct negotiations.

In the period leading up to this decision, it was clear that Herut rejected any idea of reparations and all contact with West Germany, which in its view was a neo-Nazi regime. Mapam and Maki opposed reparations for the same reasons, and as well because West Germany was revanchist and endangered world peace. For the General Zionists, the question of negotiating with West Germany was morally unacceptable and, in addition, they did not trust its intentions.

Although the impetus for the raising of the question of reparations was economic, and they were perceived as an answer to Israel's pressing needs, the debate was conducted in moral, political, and historical terms. For the government, the lead was therefore taken by the foreign minister and the prime minister. There was complete agreement between them; immediate direction of the diplomatic negotiations was handled by Sharett; the main burden of convincing the party, the cabinet, and the public fell upon Ben-Gurion, who pursued it with his characteristic determination and polemical skills. In particular, he cast the debate in terms of Israel's need for security and survival. His arguments were particularly significant in swaying the waverers among the Mapai ministers, such as Golda Meir.

After winning support for direct negotiations within the Mapai leadership, Ben-Gurion brought the question to the cabinet, where it received the support of a majority, including the Mapai ministers who had previously not been supportive. It was then brought to a meeting of the combined coalition parties, where it again won approval, although the religious parties were completely divided on the issue. Because it was widely known that the opposition commanded fifty-one votes in the Knesset, the stage was set for a close and emotional debate, in which considerable effort would be made to win the support of the waverers.

The government proposed that the Knesset's Foreign Affairs and Defense Committee be empowered to decide what action should be taken, and this was passed sixty to fifty-one in a personal vote, with five abstentions, and four absentees. The government's majority consisted of forty-five Mapai MKs, five MKs from affiliated Arab lists, six Hapo'el Hamizrachi, three Progressives, and one Agudat Yisrael. The five abstentions were all from the religious parties. Among the opposition were three members of the coalition, one Mizrachi, one Progressive, and one Sephardi, together with all members of Herut, Mapam, General Zionists, and Maki. Not long after, the Foreign Affairs and Defense Committee authorized direct negotiations.[16]

These brief case studies indicate that control over foreign policy decision making rested upon three conditions. The first was agreement between the two key actors: Ben-Gurion, the prime minister, and Sharett, the foreign minister. The second was the support of Mapai ministers and parliamentarians, and, if necessary, of Mapai party bodies, to create and maintain the necessary majorities in the relevant institutions. Under these two conditions, the influence of other parties, whether in the coalition or in opposition, was extremely limited.

Problems developed in the area of foreign policy and defense policy because of an inability to maintain one of these conditions. Disagreements between the prime minister and the foreign minister, or between the prime minister and the defense minister, or the failure of the leading actors to take the necessary steps to ensure the requisite Mapai majority in the relevant institution enabled other parties to gain influence over policy. We shall examine some examples of this in the area of defense policy.

Defense Policy

The issues to be treated in this section are fundamentally different from the other examples of policy-making we have analyzed. Because of their sensitivity, they were discussed behind closed doors, and were at the time known to only very few persons beyond the actors directly involved. There was no press mention, no public discussion or debate. What we know now has in some cases only recently been revealed in diaries, memoirs, and government documents made available for public examination after the elapse of the requisite period of time, although some aspects were widely aired during the second and third stages of the Lavon Affair in 1960–61 and 1964–65. But when the actual events occurred, most MKs in the coalition as well as in the opposition parties were quite unaware of them, and within Mapai only a very small number of party leaders beyond the ministry were in the picture. Party institutions as such that had a defined and often decisive role on other questions were specifically excluded from discussing matters of security and defense.

In part, the closed circle stemmed from Ben-Gurion's very firm view that defense matters were not questions to be discussed by political party forums, and were not the proper subject of party intervention. (This was also a central factor in his insistence upon disbanding the Palmah and its independent command structure, as we shall see in the next chapter.) He also excluded Mapai party bodies from discussing these questions. As he later expressed himself, "I never brought security issues to my party . . . I always accepted a majority decision in the party, in the Histadrut, and in the Cabinet as self-understood. . . . But in security matters as I see them, there exists for me only my own conscience." [17]

Ben-Gurion did not intend to suggest that he decided these issues by himself but, rather, that defense and security questions were matters to be discussed and decided only in the proper state, not party, forums: the General Staff, the Ministry of Defense, and the cabinet. Moreover, he was sometimes overruled by a cabinet majority on actions and policies that he, as the responsible minister, proposed. For example, Ben-Gurion's policies on defense and the conduct of the war were often opposed, and on occasion were overruled during the period of the Provisional Government. His demands to disband the Palmah were not immediately accepted; they encountered what became known as "the revolt of the generals." The whole issue was discussed by a ministerial committee before Ben-Gurion finally got his way. Similarly, his proposals with regard to the banning of the Ezel after the *Altalena* Affair were delayed by a ministerial committee that sought to reach a compromise.

In terms of historical and political consequences in the long run, undoubtedly Ben-Gurion's most important defeat occurred on September 26, 1948, when the Provisional Government by a vote of seven to five rejected his proposal for an attack on Latrun that was intended to break through to Jerusalem and to remove the Jordanian army from control of the Judean hills. With the failure to approve that attack, the government left the Old City of Jerusalem in Jordanian hands, a decision that Ben-Gurion later termed "a historical tragedy." On the other hand, it has been suggested that he did not fight to have his point of view accepted, as he did on many other occasions.[18]

The political significance of the vote in the Provisional Government was that *all* Mapai ministers voted against Ben-Gurion's proposal. Ben-Gurion was surprised that his party colleagues voted against him, and, as was noted earlier, he decided that henceforth he would call meetings of Mapai ministers before cabinet sessions in order to decide upon an agreed position.

Thus, within weeks Ben-Gurion brought a proposal to renew hostilities against Egypt, to break through to the Negev, before a meeting of his party colleagues in the government, and a few other senior party members of its Political Committee. As he himself indicated later, this represented a departure from his previous habit of bringing military questions only to the General Staff and the government as a whole. This meeting of Mapai colleagues did not vote on the question, but it was clear from the discussion that the majority were strongly in favor. When the government met the next day, the proposal was carried with the support of all Mapai ministers except one, Eliezer Kaplan, who abstained.[19]

This chain of events set the pattern for the future: Mapai ministers usually convened before cabinet meetings to agree on policy; with Mapai having a majority, this was sufficient to carry the issue. The pattern held up well until Ben-Gurion's retirement in 1953, and was not upset by his differences with Sharett over the wisdom and scope of Israel's reprisal raids. Generally, these were managed between them on a case-by-case basis without reaching crisis proportions, and without involving other ministers or the cabinet.

During his long tenure in office, most of it as both prime minister and defense minister, Ben-Gurion followed a unique pattern of highly centralized and personal political control of defense matters. By law, the cabinet as a whole was the supreme and final authority in defense matters, and the "commander in chief." Its dealings with the armed forced were through the defense minister by way of the chief of staff. Clearly, the fact that the prime minister and the defense minister were one and the same could only enhance the authority of the defense minister and reinforce his control, and that of the entire cabinet over the military. Ben-Gurion's personal authority on defense matters was unique, stemming not only from these structural arrangements but from the historical development of his involvement in them from 1947 onward, when the defense portfolio was placed in his hands by the Yishuv institutions by virtue of his extremely clear and firm views about civil–military relations, of maximum political control and minimum partisan influence. His authority rested indirectly on popular and party political sources as well. Ben-Gurion's pattern of political control of defense matters has been characterized in this way: "At his peak, Ben-Gurion had the full confidence and support of the Mapai Party machinery and rank and file, of the General Staff and the Defense Ministry bureaucracy, and of the populace. Ben-Gurion did not always have his way in the Cabinet, but within the defense system the breadth of his sources of support, together with his personal characteristics, gave him almost complete authority, to the extent that he decided to use it." [20]

The Lavon Period, 1954–1955

The overall pattern of the Lavon period was one of the absence or loss of political control and the disintegration of the pattern that had been established by Ben-Gurion, as a result of his retirement to Sedeh Boker, which led to the appointment of Sharett as prime minister and foreign minister, and Pinhas Lavon as defense minister. Sharett continued to maintain his sensitivity to the diplomatic aspects of defense policies and reprisals, and consistently sought to limit the latter, if not do away with them, and to judge them in terms of their effect upon Israel's position in the region and in the world. Lavon adopted an extremely activist approach, far beyond that advocated by Chief of Staff Moshe Dayan. It was regarded by many of his colleagues, including Sharett, as dangerous and unrestrained adventurism.

In addition to the fundamental substantive differences between them, Sharett maintained that Lavon did not consult with him or report to him where necessary, that Lavon acted unilaterally without authorization, and that as prime minister he had often been placed in the wholly untenable situation of learning from the radio about actions over which he should first have been consulted.[21] There were even suggestions that after reprisal raids Sharett was given incomplete and false information.

Lavon succeeded in alienating not only those who, like Sharett, opposed activism but also those who, like Dayan, Shimon Peres (director-general of the Ministry of Defense) and Isser Harel (head of the Security Services) accepted the activist policy adopted by Ben-Gurion, and were among Sharett's strongest opponents on substantive policy grounds. This was a matter of policy difference as well as a matter of proper civil–military relations. Apart from serious disagreements over army purchasing requirements and priorities, which led to Dayan's resignation (later withdrawn), there were differences over the administration of the ministry and the respective functions of the minister and the director-general.

Lavon sought greater direct personal involvement on all these questions, and often went over the heads of the chief of staff and the director-general to establish direct relations with army officers and civil servants. Doing so was a clear and radical departure from the pattern of civil–military relations established by Ben-Gurion. It indicated lack of confidence in Dayan and Peres, and despite efforts to maintain working relationships, personal relations between them were bad, to say the least.

This was to prove critical after the security mishap in Egypt in July 1954. Lavon sought to prove that he personally had not given the direct order that led to activation of the intelligence group in Egypt, eventuating in its capture, the execution of some members, and the imprisonment of others. He asserted that it had been given by one of the officers with whom he had established a direct relationship unmediated by the chief of staff, Chief of Military Intelligence Binyamin Gibly. Gibly maintained that Lavon had indeed given him such an order. Neither Lavon nor Gibly was able to adduce written evidence in support of their assertions.

Dayan and Peres were not directly involved in the actual operation, but they clearly sided with Gibly. They were later accused by Lavon of being implicated in various activities, such as coaching witnesses and fabricating documents, aimed at demonstrating that Lavon had given the order. Similarly, Peres, in particular, used the opportunity afforded by the Olshan-Dori Committee of Enquiry to describe critically the state of relations within the Ministry of Defense, for which he blamed Lavon.

There were also serious differences during the year between Sharett, as foreign minister, and Dayan. Many of these related to Sharett's refusal to give Dayan authorization for proposed reprisal actions. But at the end of the year, the differences developed into a substantive major policy disagreement over the advisability and potential effectiveness of diplomatic actions to focus attention upon Israel's increasing encirclement and worsening security situation. It came to a head in discussions over whether Israel should attempt to send a ship through the Suez Canal in defiance of the Egyptian blockade, which was illegal in international law and had been condemned in the UN. Dayan strongly opposed this because Israel would not be in a position to use force to rescue the crew if the ship was stopped by the Egyptians and its crew arrested, which is in fact what happened.

At the party–government level Sharett responded to the crisis by establishing a committee of five ministers—Sharett, Lavon, Eshkol, Zalman, Aranne and Meir—to discuss and resolve all differences between himself and Lavon. He hoped to use these ministers, who supported him, to provide the backing to enable him to exercise his authority over Lavon. It seems that this worked with regard to specific policy proposals prior to the security mishap. In the longer term, Sharett hoped to work toward a situation wherein he could force Lavon to resign, but felt that the ground had to be prepared publicly and within the party. After the security mishap, this option was no longer available because

Lavon's resignation would universally be interpreted as Israeli acceptance of responsibility for what had gone on in Egypt, which was totally unacceptable before the trial had even taken place.

A second pattern of response to the crisis was the increasing practice of Mapai Leaders, ministers, and party officials and senior members of the party to go to Sedeh Boker to seek Ben-Gurion's advice, and to persuade him to return to active politics and clean up the mess. In the short term, this only made the situation worse. It may have served to convice Ben-Gurion that he had made a disastrous mistake in nominating Lavon as his successor, and as a possible future prime minister, but it did not succeed in bringing him back into active politics.

The visits did manage to unsettle Ben-Gurion's successor further. Sharett was aware that his inability to control Lavon and the latter's undisguised contempt of him in party and cabinet meetings had caused him a serious loss of political authority among his immediate cabinet colleagues, even when they agreed with him on policy. And the regular pilgrimages to Ben-Gurion only served to spread the news of his failure to his predecessor, whose policy support and personal backing he believed he lacked. Despite Ben-Gurion's public and formal noninvolvement in political affairs, the visits together with a series of Ben-Gurion initiatives regarding fundamental electoral change and new forms of *Haluziut* were all regarded by Sharett as acts to undermine him and his authority, and to prepare the ground for his replacement by Ben-Gurion.

The situation was exacerbated by increasing contact and closeness between Ben-Gurion, and Dayan, Peres, and a number of other leading younger members of Mapai. Sharett viewed this negatively for two reasons. It represented further support for the policies of activism, which he opposed. In addition, Dayan not only had openly involved himself in internal party affairs (which was against army regulations) but had taken a leading role in suggesting ways of renewing the party that seemed to imply replacement of the current leadership. Thus, Sharett saw his leadership position as being undermined with Ben-Gurion's blessing, if not inspiration.

These responses to the crisis into which Lavon's appointment plunged the party and the state represented increased politicization, and in many ways undid some of the processes of depoliticization that had occurred under the pressure of Ben-Gurion's drive toward *mamlakhtiut*. (This is dealt with in chapter 7). The party committee of five ministers to discuss the sensitive security issues in dispute between Lavon and Sharett infringed the rules of cabinet responsibility and the depoliticized pattern of decision making set up by Ben-Gurion in two major ways. The first was that security matters were decided there without being brought to the cabinet for formal discussion and approval. The second was that it was not a cabinet committee but an internal party committee, the existence of which was not known to the members of cabinet from other parties.

The dependence upon Ben-Gurion even in retirement, and particularly on important and sensitive defense matters, separated the head of the state from the head of the party and upset the careful balance between party and state encapsulated in the practices of primacy of party. It undermined the capacity of the ministers to carry out their governmental functions, and undercut the authority of legitimate internal party institutions by being based on personal authority completely outside institutionalized party control.

Dayan's active and open involvement in party politics at the level of seeking to replace the party leadership while he was chief of staff was a blatant infringement of the rules governing civil–military relations, and the military in party politics. Although earlier problems had stemmed from the involvement of political parties in military affairs, this represented a crossing of the line from the opposite direction. Military officers who were formally obliged to accept direction from their political superiors were engaged in activities to determine who those superiors might be, and in other open political activities that limited the political control and authority of their superiors.

The ramifications of the security mishap were so far-reaching that Sharett established a secret semijudicial commission of enquiry known as the Olshan–Dori Committee. Its primary purpose was to determine who had given the orders that resulted in the arrests in Egypt. The committee could not reach an unequivocal decision as to whether Lavon had given the order to Gibly, or whether the latter had proceeded to act without ministerial authorization. The response therefore had to be political. The leading Mapai ministers, after consulting with Ben-Gurion, came to the conclusion that Lavon had to go because he had not been cleared unequivocally. Lavon maintained that he need not resign because it had not been determined that he had given the order. He thereupon demanded that Peres and Gibly be removed from their positions, and that the Ministry of Defense be reorganized to give the minister greater authority to intervene in army affairs. Alternatively, he threatened to resign and to make it known publicly and through a parliamentary inquiry why he had done so.

For some weeks after the Olshan–Dori decison neither side would budge because the Egyptian trial had not ended. After it did, Sharett and other Mapai leaders were hesitant to act because of apprehension about the party and international consequences of Lavon's dimissal, and because there was no acceptable or agreed-upon replacement for him as minister of defense. On the other hand, a few tentative moves were made to get Peres and Gibly to move voluntarily, but these failed. It became clear to Lavon that the Mapai leadership was almost unanimous in its view that he should resign, and that Sharett had no intention of using his authority to have his, Lavon's, demands met. He therefore resigned. His public statement did not make the reason clear at all, but his statement to the government and the Knesset Foreign Affairs and Defense Committee cited as the reason Sharett's unwillingness to accept his recommendations for the reorganization of the Ministry of Defense.

The Mapai leadership proposed to Ben-Gurion that he return to the Ministry of Defense, and he accepted. His return to the government put an end to the chaos caused by Lavon, and retored the previous patterns of civil–military relations. However, it also brought with it renewed and heightened conflict with Sharett over defense and foreign policy priorities. In the past such questions had been resolved by agreement between Ben-Gurion and Sharett based on three key factors. The first was that Sharett was foreign minister and Ben-Gurion was prime minister as well as defense minister, and it was clear that the final authority and responsibility rested with Ben-Gurion. Under such conditions Sharett was prepared to make compromises once he had stated his case, and in this way to maintain the leadership coalition between them. Now, however, Ben-Gurion was defense minister and Sharett was prime minister and foreign minister. Although Sharett had the formal authority and responsibility, Ben-Gurion was still acknowledged to be the party leader and enjoyed superior prestige in general, and on defense questions in particular. For Sharett to return to the previous pattern of relations would be to abdicate the ultimate authority and responsibility inherent in the position of prime minister.

The second factor was that in the earlier period security and diplomatic considerations were more evenly balanced. The Soviet bloc had not yet taken an outright anti-Israel stance, the countries of Asia and Africa had not yet lined up in support of the Arab countries, and the bordering Arab states were somewhat less militant, less intransigent, and less involved in terrorist incursions into Israel. As the security issue became more central and pressing, the diplomatic option pursued by Sharett seemed less likely to prove effective.

The third factor was that after Ben-Gurion's return, the personal aspect in Sharett's differences with him became much more pronounced. As his diary makes clear, Sharett was consumed by the belief that Ben-Gurion lost no opportunity to denigrate, demean, and degrade him and the policies for which he stood. Whether this was actually so (and Ben-Gurion's diary does not confirm that he was possessed by an all-consuming hatred or contempt of Sharett) is quite irrelevant. The point is that Sharett believed it to be so and acted accordingly. This made policy agreement and compromise even harder to achieve, except by Ben-Gurion's imposing his point of view. Under the circumstances, this merely served to make relations worse. Thus, Sharett later asserted that Ben-Gurion had retained him as foreign minister after the 1955 elections only to be able to force him to resign in 1956.

The differences and conflicts between the two men mainly centered on policy toward Egypt. In April 1955 the cabinet rejected a proposal by Ben-Gurion to capture the Gaza Strip and to cancel unilaterally the armistice agreement with Egypt. Although Sharett was extremely pleased with the decision in substance, he was most concerned about the fact that the majority of Mapai ministers were in favor of the proposal. Again in May, the five Mapai ministers discussed a Ben-Gurion proposal for a large-scale reprisal raid, which Sharett opposed but he was outvoted four to one.

Ben-Gurion's suggestion to Sharett to use a cabinet majority to defeat this proposal and gain support for his own proposal for a raid much smaller in scale disturbed Sharett and highlighted his dilemma. As Golda Meir pointed out to him, to turn to the cabinet under those conditions would nullify the previous arrangements the party had made for settling such questions, and there was no way of knowing what the consequences would be. Ben-Gurion would not countenance the idea of a smaller reprisal raid, and a negative decision in the cabinet might result in a "serious explosion" on his part. Sharett wrote in his diary:

> I said that in this situation I would in no way attempt to gain a majority in the government against the majority of the authoritative party group. . . . I told her . . . that because of this decision now another question that relates to my future has been decided: but it will not be implemented now, because the party is above all else, and the most important thing now is to succeed in the elections. . . . I will not exercise my authority as Prime Minister against my party. It is better to resign than to follow this path. . . . My resignation now would be destructive for the party and the state. It would be a political resignation.[22]

Sharett not only gave adequate expression to the dilemma of decision making in defense and foreign policy but underlined the fundamental problem of the Israeli political system in the early years: What was the legitimate realm of authority of the new state, and what was the legitimate realm of the party?

Defense Policies After 1955

After Ben-Gurion's return to power in 1955, the process of centralization of policy-making in defense matters reached its height. At first, even as late as December 1955, Ben-Gurion was again defeated in the cabinet over a proposal from the General Staff to conduct a military raid into Egypt to gain control over the Straits of Tiran by a majority that included four Mapai ministers. Eventually, however, policy coherence was served by bringing foreign policy into line with the needs of security as understood by Ben-Gurion and supported by the Mapai majority in cabinet, which led in 1956 to Sharett's resignation and his replacement by Golda Meir. Significantly, the public explanation and the discussion in Mapai over the need for the resignation turned on the very question of the need to maintain policy coherence, even at the cost of the resignation of one of the party's top leaders because his views were out of line with the dominant opinion in the party, and therefore the government.

Sharett's departure put effective control of the defense policy that led to the Israeli agreements with France and Britain and the Sinai Campaign in the hands of a very small group. At its head, and clearly the decisive figure, was Ben-Gurion; the actual and final decision to go to war was made by him alone. He worked closely with Meir and Eshkol to ensure the support of the party core group and majority, and with Chief of Staff Dayan and the director-general of the Ministry of Defense, Peres, as well as a small number of civil servants.

The military and political arrangements that led to war were an extremely tightly kept secret; only after the decision had been made, did Ben-Gurion inform his cabinet colleagues. Apart from one minister from Ahdut Ha'a-vodah, Moshe Carmel, who had been involved earlier, none of the others knew anything until they were informed just prior to the cabinet meeting a day before the campaign, and just ahead of the opposition parties. Formally, of course, the cabinet could have withheld its approval, but all the basic decisions had already been made and Israeli commitments given without cabinet knowledge or authorization. Nor did Ben-Gurion reveal to his cabinet colleagues the real nature of the arrangements with France and Britain. The final decision more than any other epitomized the centralized control and personal authority of Ben-Gurion in defense matters, on the one hand, and the support that he generated for his policies in the General Staff, the defense bureaucracy, the cabinet, the party, and the public, on the other.

The decision to go to war was made in secret, but the decision to withdraw from Sinai and Gaza under tremendous U.S. and Soviet pressure could not be made in this manner; it was the subject of full-scale Israeli public and international discussion and concern. The cabinet met in a long and outspoken session, divided between those who counseled withdrawal and the hard-liners. Michael Brecher put it this way: "But the real power of decision lay with the 'Big Three' of Mapai at the time, Ben-Gurion, Meir and Eshkol, and in the last analysis with the Prime Minister himself—for the lines of division were vocal but not rigid. Rosen recalled: 'The Government decision was to leave the decision to Ben-Gurion.'" [23]

Ben-Gurion's prestige and authority in defense matters remained at their height after the success of the Sinai Campaign, and the negotiated withdrawal brought relative peace to Israel's borders. These qualities were not challenged until the Lavon Affair of 1960–1961, and the crisis over German scientists in Egypt and Ben-Gurion's German policy in 1962–63. In an attempt to influence policy in the late 1950s, Ahdut Ha'avodah published details in its own newspaper of a planned secret visit to Germany of the chief of staff, and Mapam and Ahdut Ha'avodah voted in the Knesset against the government's decision to sell light arms to Germany. In both cases they were forced to resign and secured no substantive impact on policy.

It is little wonder, then, that after more than a decade of experience of coalition government, Mapai's coalition partners depicted the cabinet as controlled by Mapai's centralized policy-making, leaving them no scope for influence. The Club of Four sought to break Mapai's cabinet majority and its control over the most important ministries, specifically in order to deprive Mapai of the capacity to make and implement policy without regard to the policies of its partners. In the past, in their view, Mapai had ridden roughshod over them. Policies were first determined in Mapai party bodies, and only then brought to the cabinet, where Mapai used its majority to do what it wanted. To prevent Mapai's being able to do this would, they argued, contribute to democracy, parliamentary responsibility and sound administrative practices:

> In order for the coalition partners to cease to serve as a pawn in Mapai's hands, they must decide collectively, not to agree again to grant Mapai a

majority in the government, whilst it is still a minority in the Knesset and the coalition. . . .

One must demand guarantees, which will ensure that all information, including matters of foreign affairs and defense will be handed to all ministers prior to the implementation [of any decision], and, as well, demand a guarantee that every decision will be taken in the government as a whole, and not in any place outside it.[24]

Control over policy-making in defense matters was made possible by the support of the majority of the party and its leadership for Ben-Gurion's initiatives, by the institutionalized practices of party government, by firm control over the cabinet, and by the unequaled leadership prestige and authority that Ben-Gurion enjoyed, particularly with regard to such matters.

In four major areas—economic policy in general, wages policy, foreign policy, and defense—Mapai was able to overcome the inherent limitations of coalition government and to centralize and gain control over policy-making to such a degree that it was able to govern like a single-party government in a majoritarian democracy. This actuality was reinforced by its efforts to create neutral and legitimate structures of public authority, which in some cases involved the dismantling of many of the partisan structures, functions, and arrangements that the new state inherited from the Yishuv. These came under the rubric of *mamlakhtiut*, to which we now turn.

Notes

1. Arend Lijphart, *Democracies: Patterns of Majoritarian and Consensus Government in Twenty-One Countries* (New Haven: Yale University Press, 1984), pp. 177–78.

2. Benjamin Akzin and Yehezkel Dror, *Israel: High-Pressure Planning* (Syracuse, N.Y.: Syracuse University Press, 1966), pp. 7, 24.

3. Mattei Dogan, "The Political Power of the Western Mandarins: Introduction," in Mattei Dogan, ed., *The Mandarins of Western Europe: The Political Role of Top Civil Servants* (New York: Halsted Press, 1975), p. 20, cited in Joel D. Aberbach, Robert D. Putnam, and Bert A. Rockman, *Bureaucrats and Politicians in Western Democracies* (Cambridge: Harvard University Press, 1981), p. 15.

4. Akzin and Dror, *Israel*, p. 7.

5. See David Nachmias, "Coalition Politics in Israel," *Comparative Political Studies* 7 (October 1974): 316–33.

6. See the extremely enlightening analysis of Israel's political economy in Daniel Shimshoni, *Israeli Democracy: The Middle of the Journey* (New York: Free Press, 1982), pp. 223–86.

7. Ibid., p. 244.

8. Most of the data here follow the discussion in Peter Y. Medding, *Mapai in Israel, Political Organisation and Government in a New Society* (Cambridge: Cambridge University Press, 1983), pp. 192–210, although the focus of the analysis is somewhat different.

9. See Michael Brecher, *Decisions in Israel's Foreign Policy* (London: Oxford University Press, 1974).

10. See Uri Bialer, *"Our Place in the World"—Mapai and Israel's Foreign Policy Orientation, 1947-1952*, Jerusalem Papers on Peace Problems, 33 (Jerusalem, 1981).

11. *Divrei Haknesset*, 8.3.1949, p. 55.

12. Cited in Bialer, *"Our Place in the World,"* p. 43.

13. See Brecher, *Decisions in Israel's Foreign Policy*, chap. 4.

14. Cited, ibid., p. 17.

15. Ibid., chap. 2.

16. See ibid., chap. 3.

17. *Davar*, 13.1.1961.

18. Michael Bar-Zohar, *Ben-Gurion*, 3 vols. (Tel Aviv: Am Oved, 1975-78), p. 826.

19. David Ben-Gurion, "Yoman Ben-Gurion," unpublished diaries, 5.10.48, 6.10.48; Bar-Zohar, *Ben-Gurion*, pp. 827-30; David Ben-Gurion, *Medinat yisrael hamehudeshet* (Tel Aviv: Am Oved, 1969), p. 294.

20. Shimshoni, *Israeli Democracy*, p. 197.

21. See, for example, the letter that Sharett wrote to Lavon on 25.5.1954, cited in Bar-Zohar, *Ben-Gurion*, pp. 1036-37.

22. Moshe Sharett, *Yoman ishi*, 9 vols. (Tel Aviv: Sifriat Ma'ariv, 1978), 18.5.1955, 4:1007.

23. Brecher, *Decisions in Israel's Foreign Policy*, p. 288. The Rosen referred to is Pinhas Rosen, minister of justice (Progressive party).

24. Meir Yaari, *'Al Hamishmar*, 14.8.1961. Similar sentiments were expressed by Yisrael Galili, *Lamerhav*, 13.8.1961; Yigal Allon, *Lamerhav*, 24.8.1961; and in the formal announcement of the establishment of the Club of Four, in *'Al Hamishmar*, 1.9.1961.

7

Mamlakhtiut: Partisan Interests and the Establishment of Centralized and Legitimate State Public Authority

In chapter 6 we were concerned with the capacity of the leading political party to control decision making within the political structures, which often involved a considerable degree of centralization. In this chapter, we examine another aspect of the same process: the establishment of centralized, that is, state, political and administrative structures to perform functions and provide services in place of other social frameworks, be they voluntary, partisan, or private. This was guided, justified, and encouraged by a broad set of principles known as *mamlakhtiut*, which has no exact English translation but is roughly equivalent to statism.[1]

Mamlakhtiut is best understood in the context of the historical development of the Yishuv[2] and the process of transition to independent political sovereignty. The general principles of *mamlakhtiut* are universal, but its specific demands and institutional applications, and the particular pattern of opposition to them were directly related to the social, political, and institutional inheritance of the Yishuv.

Upon establishment of the state, its new administrative structures took over functions from the Mandatory authority, and from Yishuv institutions, within which partisan considerations were legitimate and central. Thus, a major question in the founding period was, What was to be the place, if any, of such considerations in state structures, and how would the latter incorporate the basic values of democracy and the rule of law, such as universality, achievement, inclusiveness, neutrality, fairness, responsibility to the public, and the public interest?

Removing party and partisan considerations from administration and state services—depoliticization—was an integral part of a larger process of state-building and the centralization of power. Yet the transfer of functions from the parties to the state did not remove completely party influence or involvement. Parties remained a central and directing element in the structures and processes of parliamentary government and party government. However, a significant change occurred in the nature of party involvement. *Direct* party control on the party's own behalf gave way to *indirect* party control, formally responsible to parliament and the public. Compared with the situation in the Yishuv, parties in government increased their reach by providing the direction and content of a widened range of state policies, but at the same time their hold was diminished to the extent that the legitimacy of partisan considerations was limited by democratic, state, and national criteria.

Even though it had more general application, *mamlakhtiut* was the ideology par excellence of the founding period, standing in radical contrast to the principles and practices of the Yishuv. Its precise meaning is not completely captured in the term *statism*[3] because *statism* does not indicate anything about the concept or character of the state, and therefore is easily given to misinterpretation.[4] In my views, its meaning is best defined as legitimate state public authority. To understand the full meaning of *mamlakhtiut*, we must clarify how such authority is legitimated, and what is implied by the term *public*, and what is excluded by it.

The concept of the state that lies at the heart of *mamlakhtiut* is almost completely encapsulated by Ben-Gurion in a few brief sentences, and is highlighted by the contrast to the Yishuv. Despite their great contribution to national upbuilding, the capacity of the organizational instruments of the Yishuv were limited by their voluntary and partial character. But "with the establishment of the state, a superior and powerful, but not all-powerful, instrument has been created. . . . The state is a binding, all-inclusive and sovereign framework."[5] According to this view, three qualities characterize statehood and *mamlakhtiut*: the general interest; compulsion; and independence. The *mamlakhti* approach is distinguished by its universal and general nature, and its all-inclusiveness. All members of the society participate as citizens, and *mamlakhtiut* directs their attention "to the good of the whole," to the public interest, to "the good of the citizen," and to "the service of the state." *Mamlakhtiut*, therefore, is general; it means being prepared to accept "state responsibility," that is, "to cater for the interests of the state as a whole."[6]

The binding and compulsory nature of the state is the second defining characteristic of *mamlakhtiut*, adding to the citizen's relation to the state a "tie of obligation." This is expressed in the institutions of the state, which act by and provide "the power of law, in the government administrative apparatus, and the state budget."[7] Moreover, certain tasks and functions can be undertaken only by state action and state frameworks. Although never clearly specified or elaborated, they include defense, immigration, development, education, and health services, that is, those of general and national concern.[8]

The third characteristic is sovereignty and independence, that is, a people responsible for itself and its fate. A "*mamlakhti* nation knows how to carry the burden of the responsibility which independence thrusts upon every people. . . . This entails collective power, joint political responsibility and a unifying historical will."[9]

Clearly, *mamlakhtiut* promoted an instrumental and limited view of the state. It was not an end in itself but a useful and necessary framework for the achievement of important goals. The values embodied in the state rested upon more elevated ideals, which imposed limits on its power and provided criteria for its legitimate application. In the *mamlakhti* view, therefore, the state was an instrument for the achievement of collective tasks. Its purpose was to serve the citizens upon whom the state rested, and to be a bridge for the transmission of human, Jewish, and labor values.[10] Thus, the people as a whole are greater than the state, and the goal and the end "are not the state or the people, but the man."[11]

Even as a means the state was not self-sufficient. Although it enjoyed unique advantages in the pursuit of goals, the goals could not be achieved solely by employment of state power. Success depended upon the state's being able to inform its methods with some of the significant human and social motivations that had characterized the prestate period:

> With the establishment of the state, two schools of thought developed within the labor camp. There were those who negated the value of the state as a creative and innovative force, and relied solely on individual and collective activity. And there were those who relied totally on the state and regarded it as omnipotent, and placed all their demands upon the state, so that the citizen or organizations of citizens were relieved of a concern for the whole, and were solely self-concerned. Both these schools of thought are mistaken, misleading and harmful. The state is not omnipotent, and is not the only body upon which demands can be made. Moreover, even if in their private lives they act as *haluzim*, both the individual, and organizations of individuals, will fail if they do not put their *haluzic* activity in the service of the state, and if the state's financial, organizational and legislative power is not committed to the haluzic tasks that are thrust upon us.[12]

Ben-Gurion reiterated again and again that Israel could not succeed in the achievement of its tasks if it relied solely upon the power of law and the government administrative machinery. It needed the assistance of the values of *haluziut*, of pioneering and volunteering, and above all, of the willingness of individuals to make demands upon themselves for the benefit of others and for the general good.

On the other hand, this was not the *haluziut* of the past but a new form, one that accepted new tasks beyond the traditional *haluzic* tasks, and one that adjusted to the new circumstances, particularly the existence of a binding *mamlakhti* framework, which makes demands upon, and is the subject of the demands of, every citizen. That is to say, the state based upon external obligation had to incorporate some of the *haluzic* values of personal sacrifice and voluntary service to the public good, and the *haluzic* movement had to adjust to organizational frameworks that were superior in value to its own, even if based upon principles of compulsion and not upon voluntariness.

Mamlakhtiut in the sense of independent statehood could not be maintained without a high degree of national integration and nation-building. This was particularly urgent in view of the diverse national origins, languages, and cultural levels of the *olim* who arrived after 1948. What is more, "the state framework is not capable of turning a galut people into a *mamlakhti* nation, and parts of tribes speaking a mixture of many languages into a united, self-reliant people, consciously and effectively bearing its *mamlakhti* responsibility."[13] This demanded the combined efforts of state and social forces, educational efforts, and *haluzic* service. In particular, Ben-Gurion held up as an example the distinctive and significant contribution that the armed forces made to national integration, because they were "the only framework in the state in which all ethnic, party, class, and other barriers disappeared."[14]

Ben-Gurion's approach incorporated strong party government to provide the state with its values and policies. Thus, the state framework's content and the direction of its activity were "of necessity fixed by a political party. Without a directing and governing party the state is like a ship without a helm and without a compass."[15] In directing the state, of course, the governing party was obliged to follow the principles of *mamlakhtiut*.

These principles came through clearly in an informal discussion with some younger members of the party in August 1948 about the role and status of the party in the state. The discussion was opened by the party secretary-general, Aranne, who summed up the transition to statehood: "The values of the party are rising—the value of the party is falling." Ben-Gurion argued that in concentrating upon how, for example, Mapai could increase its slight majority over its nearest rival in the Histadrut (at the time 3.7 percent), his colleagues were taking a too narrow view of things:

> I reject the starting point of 3.7 percent. The only starting point is 100 percent—that is to say, a concern *for the whole*, not a concern for our power in the state, or the Histadrut, but concern for the power of the state, and of the Histadrut. We will fulfill our obligation to the state and the Histadrut, and if we do it capably, faithfully, with foresight, and with courage—there will be no need to worry about our power in the state. Concern for the state and the Histadrut means concern with both big things and small things. They go together. Let us not live off our past credits. And if we are instrumental in bringing about a full victory—let us not become dependent upon the victory.

Here Ben-Gurion explained the English people's rejection of Churchill at the polls in 1945, even though he had won the war for Britain. It was not due to ingratitude or lack of admiration; the elections were not about whether to give Churchill a reward but to determine the future of Britain. He went on:

> For our past good deeds we will receive a reward—but for that we do not deserve the government of the future. We wish to guide the state in the future—because, it is our belief that we have the way which the state must follow for its own sake, for the sake of its peace, existence, development, and historic mission. We shall fight for the way—not for a reward. . . . Four years ago we said a few things to the public. Most of them we fulfilled . . . but not all. We said: mobilization of the masses, their participation in thought, in decision, in implementation. We did not fulfill this sufficiently. We will do it

now, with the establishment of the state and with the laying of the foundations. It is not enough to do good things—but we should do them on behalf of
the public and with the involvement of its initiative. Not by the power of
government—but by the power of our central idea—service to the whole, and
by the whole.[16]

Mamlakhtiut was also to be understood in terms of, and to be limited by,
the fundamental constitutional principles laid down in the Declaration of
Independence, the Basic Principles of the First Government (March 8, 1949),
and as elaborated in the constitutional debate of 1950. In particular, their
emphasis on freedom and equality, and on the rule of law as the essential
components of Israeli democracy promoted the ideal of the neutrality of the
state and militated against granting preference to party, party members, and
partisan considerations. Only in this way could the commitment to the whole,
and the concern with the general welfare be given their due expression.

Only in a state in which everyone—citizen, soldier, official, minister, legisla-
tor, judge and policeman—is subject to the law and acts according to the law;
only in a state in which there is no arbitrariness, neither of ministers or rulers,
nor of representatives of the people, and also not of individuals and political
leaders—only in a state such as this is freedom guaranteed to the individual
and to the many, to the person and to the people.[17]

But if party preference and party considerations were arbitrary and infringed against equality and freedom, which demanded that the state be neutral
with regard to partisan considerations, this did not mean that party was to be
done away with entirely. To the contrary, as we saw, *mamlakhtiut*, in keeping
with the practices in other parliamentary regimes, reserved an important role
to party. It gave party the formal right to determine public policy—what we
know as party government—but within political structures that it operated on
behalf of the state and the public, to both of which it was ultimately responsible. In return for gaining the right to govern indirectly, *mamlakhtiut* demanded that parties relinquish their claims or practices of direct party rule
solely on behalf of their members, which was the situation in the Yishuv.

Because there are no absolute criteria, drawing the line between state and
parties to guide the transition from direct party rule to indirect party government may encounter disagreement on goals, or on the applicability of the
principles of *mamlakhtiut* to a specific structure or service. This is likely to
develop into open political conflict if the suggested changes threaten party or
institutional interests with the loss of existing partisan advantages. The relative
strength of the proponents and opponents, and in particular whether they are
in government or in opposition, will be critical in determining the outcome of
proposals to apply the principles of *mamlakhtiut*.

We turn now to examine how the principles of *mamlakhtiut* were applied to
the defense forces, education, employment exchanges, the civil service, health
services, and electoral reform. There are two major questions: What were the

specific principles of *mamlakhtiut* that were invoked in each specific case, and how were they put into practice? And, What were the political and partisan consequences of the changes involved in applying *mamlakhtiut*?

As a result of the political structure and processes of the Yishuv, and relations between the parties in the state during the founding period, the two are inextricably interwoven, giving rise to different possible interpretations of *mamlakhtiut* and its application by the actors themselves and, subsequently, by scholars. In the very simplest terms, varying interpretations arise not so much from ideological and theoretical disagreements about the meaning of *mamlakhtiut*, its legitimate place in the state, and its limitations as from the fact that the changes that went with it were proposed and carried out by Ben-Gurion standing at the head of a Mapai-led government. In many cases, the removal of services and functions from parties, and the exclusion of previously legitimate partisan considerations directly weakened competing parties and strengthened Mapai in the short term both relatively and absolutely. Through its governmental role Mapai still maintained indirect control and direction of these functions and structures.

Because the consequences of *mamlakhtiut* for the state structures and for Mapai were closely connected, it was always possible to explain the changes not in terms of the general and universal needs of *mamlakhtiut* but in terms of the advantages that accrued to Mapai. From there it was but a short step to the interpretation that the changes were *motivated* (solely or primarily) by Mapai's partisan interests—its need or desire to weaken its rivals and at the same time to strengthen itself. The universal claims of *mamlakhtiut*, therefore, were merely a facade behind which Mapai promoted its own particular partisan advantage and weakened its opponents.

The question is, however, whether there exists definitive evidence to support such a partisan interpretation of *mamlakhtiut*. However significant it might be to show that other parties lost more than Mapai, or that Mapai benefited in various ways from these changes, this would not provide sufficient evidence for the partisan interpretation because logically there is a clear distinction between intent or motive on the one hand, and results or consequences on the other. One can never infer intent simply on the basis of consequences, and definitive evidence of motive must therefore be found elsewhere. Nevertheless, the obvious political consequences of *mamlakhtiut* cannot be ignored, particularly if they were predictable, for there is every reason to believe that the political actors were aware of them. Thus, we begin with the assumption that the commitment to *mamlakhtiut* as a set of principles for state structures existed side by side with the political advantages it conferred, and that without further evidence we cannot assign primacy or exclusivity to either factor. We cannot exclude the impact of a commitment to *mamlakhtiut* as an ideal simply because it had certain consequences and conclude that these were *the* reason for its application. By the same token, it would be wrong to ignore the political consequences of the application of *mamlakhtiut* because these would have served to strengthen the commitment to apply the principles of *mamlakhtiut*, not weaken it. At the same time, we shall seek evidence capable of settling the argument conclusively one way or the other, for example, that Mapai applied the principles of *mamlakhtiut* even when it was clear that they would weaken its position vis-à-vis other parties, that is, when it was to its relative or absolute disadvantage, or conversely, that it refrained from applying them when it was to its relative or absolute disadvantage.

The Israel Defense Forces: Disbanding the Palmah

Because authority over the armed forces and the maintenance of security are integral elements of state-building and the establishment of legitimate political authority, and are of the broadest general concern, sole and direct state control over the military was central to the institutionalization of *mamlakhtiut*. Accordingly, the Provisional Government quickly subjected defense to its political authority. This necessitated the disbanding of all the separate paramilitary organizations that had existed in the Yishuv and their integration into the Israel Defense Force (IDF).

The continued existence of the independent Palmah command structure directly challenged the duly constituted political authority's control over the armed forces. It raised important issues of civil–military relations, in particular, that of political responsibility for the actions of the military. The Palmah sought to make governmental decisions about military matters subject to the agreement of some other body, which would severely limit the Provisional Government's capacity to exercise sole control over the legitimate use of violence. That the intervening body was closely tied to a political party greatly exacerbated the problem. The issue of civilian control of the military was injected with concerns about politicization: the effects of partisan loyalties, rivalries, and competition upon military decision making and personnel advancement, and upon the relations of the armed forces with the government.

The Palmah had been established in 1941 by the Haganah as a permanently mobilized countrywide unit subject to the supreme command of the Haganah. Its main focus of operation was Hakibbutz Hameuhad, where most of its bases were established. After the split in Mapai in 1944, Hakibbutz Hameuhad was divided in its political loyalties between Mapai and the newly formed Ahdut Ha'avodah, which held a majority in that kibbutz federation. Consequently, most of the top-level and middle-level officers in the Palmah were members of Ahdut Ha'avodah, which had become part of Mapam in January 1948.

From mid-1947 onward, Ben-Gurion set out to reorganize the Haganah, and to convert it from a voluntary militia that had become conservative, afraid of change, and an end in itself into an army that served the nation. His plan of reorganization had two major prongs: professionalization, and civilian control over the military. He sought to accomplish the first by introducing into the top command of the Haganah officers who had served in the British army, from which he derived a model of permanent and professional armed forces, with a large component of conscripts. He moved to accomplish the second through the active involvement of the minister of defense in military decision making;

by subjecting the military directly to the orders of the government as transmitted by the minister of defense to the chief of staff; and by disbanding and abolishing all intervening bodies and positions.

Ben-Gurion's plans for radical reorganization encountered strong resistance from the top command of the Haganah on both counts, and from the Palmah and its leadership on the second count. Although often intertwined, the sources of resistance were different. The General Staff of the Haganah and later the IDF were concerned mainly with three issues: the desire to carry over the egalitarian, nondisciplinarian ethos of the Haganah into the IDF, which would be lost if the model of the British army were to be adopted; Ben-Gurion's overinvolvement in military tactics, technical issues, and the placement and promotion of officers, which many regarded as meddlesome; and the deleterious effects of both upon the army and morale in the midst of a life-and-death battle for survival. The Palmah's concern was ideological and political.

As part of the plans and preparations for establishment of the state, Ben-Gurion at the end of April 1948 made his acceptance of the portfolio of minister of defense conditional upon institution of full and direct civilian control over the military. He insisted upon direct contact with the chief of staff, and the sole authority to present the government's views and instructions to the military authorities. The Mifkadah Arzit (National Command), the public political body in control of the Haganah that stood between the Jewish Agency executive and the Haganah command, was to be abolished because the public would be represented by the new government. This automatically did away with the post of head of the Mifkadah Arzit held by Yisrael Galili, a leading Palmah and Ahdut Ha'avodah figure.

Galili opposed Ben-Gurion's plans, and sought continuation of the previous practice whereby he stood between the minister of defense and the General Staff, and gave instructions to the chief of staff. He received some support from the Haganah command, particularly because the chief of staff was ill, and Galili's experience was thought to be vital.

After the state was declared and the IDF was established, the Palmah became integrated into the IDF but retained its own command structure, Mateh Arzi (National Staff), which coordinated and directed the separate Palmah units throughout the country. Integrating the Palmah command structure into that of the IDF quickly became the focal point of the opposition to Ben-Gurion's plans for the armed forces and for civil–military relations.

As a first step, Ben-Gurion ordered the General Staff to issue orders to the Palmah units directly, and not through the Mateh Arzi. To reassert its autonomy within the IDF, the Mateh Arzi notified all appropriate military authorities that Palmah units would not accept any order or any other material from any army body that was not transmitted through it and with its agreement. Ben-Gurion forced the Palmah to cancel this instruction, but even so its units continued to behave according to its spirit. The incident strengthened his resolve to bring to an end the independent existence of the Palmah and its command structure.

Ben-Gurion argued that security and defense were matters of state to be determined by duly authorized state officials, who received the political responsibility from the people through parliament and the government. Above all, these were not matters for party bodies, or party officials. Moreover, the duly authorized officials should ignore all party concerns and considerations in their deliberations because these were illegitimate in this context. Thus, according to Ben-Gurion, Galili and the separate Palmah command structure, and the distinctive unit structure, had to give way before the vital claims of the state. Not to remove them was to permit development of an army within the army, an authority between the minister of defense and the IDF General Staff, and particularistic party considerations to rank with universal state considerations, if not take precedence over them. Such apprehensions were heightened by the fact that 94 percent of the officers in the Palmah were members of Mapam.[18]

The issue, however, was not only that of the Palmah officers' party affiliation; it was this coupled with the close-knit discipline, the distinctive counter-ideology, the collective spirit, and the directive leadership that made them act together as a sect. The danger to unitary and nonpartisan state control lay precisely in the fact that they constituted a "private, factional military force, a type of party military formation, . . . which placed a section of the army under special conditions of party monopoly."[19] The primary loyalty of the Palmah to a political party contradicted the necessity for "loyalty to only one body: to the state and the government, not the party and not the Histadrut. The defense forces must be subject to only one authority, the authority of the state."[20]

The response of the Palmah and Mapam leaders was that the Palmah preserved valuable *haluzic* and class values, that it was an efficient fighting force, that an egalitarian form of army organization was desirable, that the special conditions of the Jewish national rebirth had created a special kind of military force, and that many tasks still awaited it. Only the Palmah could save the state from the militarism that would inevitably arise with a professional army. Moreover, it would always be available in the event of a threat from the fascist forces on the right. The leaders accused Ben-Gurion of being motivated by the desire to gain political advantage for Mapai by severing the nexus between Mapam and the highly admired Palmah, and of politicizing the army by establishing Mapai control over its personnel and promotions.

The Palmah units were among the most important military units in the IDF and engaged in many of the major battles, scoring some of the most notable military successes of the war. Consequently, the members of the IDF General Staff, even those who were not in Mapam, held up implementation of Ben-Gurion's plans on pragmatic and military grounds.

In October 1948 the chief of staff ordered that all staff functions of the Palmah command be transferred forthwith to the IDF General Staff. The Palmah protested, as did Mapam. In an approach characteristic of the Yishuv period, Mapam sought the intervention of the Histadrut to have the order reversed. Mapam's position was that the Histadrut should instruct its members in the army and the government to oppose implementation of the order and thus preserve the special pioneering and socialist character of the Palmah.

The Histadrut Council accepted the view of its Mapai majority that after establishment of the state, the Histadrut no longer possessed the right to intervene in defense matters. These were now the sole province of the government, and therefore it could not even discuss the issue, let alone overturn the decision. The orders of the chief of staff were implemented: the Palmah command structure was disbanded, and its units were integrated into the IDF's regular command structure. After the war ended, the Palmah units were disbanded as separate units.

Rather than continue their already distinguished military careers, the leading Palmah commanders who were most politically identified with Ahdut Ha'avodah resigned from the army in a demonstrative political protest.[21] On the other hand, a number of middle-level Palmah officers remained in the armed forces, and went on in later years to achieve the position of chief of staff.

Clearly, the requirements of *mamlakhtiut* as outlined by Ben-Gurion—inclusiveness, universality, and neutrality—had been met by the establishment of state control and the removal of partisan considerations. Direct party rule had been replaced by indirect party government. Did this, as Mapam asserted, mean the introduction by Ben-Gurion of a new Mapai-controlled partisanship? The evidence in the previous chapter suggests that this was far from the reality. Ben-Gurion himself as minister of defense played a dominant role, but Mapai as a party was relegated to the sidelines. Similarly, he sought to exclude partisan considerations from policy deliberations on defense and security issues.

In the elections in January 1949, there had been no restrictions placed upon soldiers' being candidates. In fact, Mapai placed three popular and successful officers, including Moshe Dayan, in prominent places on its list, on the understanding that they would resign after the elections, which they did. Following that, over the years the military were increasingly formally separated from party activity and electoral involvement. In 1949 the Knesset approved a law that permitted soldiers to join parties and attend meetings but not be candidates or politically active. Later, election propaganda in army camps and propaganda specifically directed at soldiers was almost completely restricted. Eventually, in keeping with restrictions on public servants in general, officers were obliged to resign at least one hundred days before running for the Knesset.

As minister of defense, Ben-Gurion also played an extremely active role in professional and administrative questions, and in appointments and promotions at the senior level. But the evidence does not add up to the heightened relevance of partisan considerations. To the contrary, it points to firm ministerial, political, and civilian control over the military, and the acceptance of political responsibility by the relevant minister and cabinet. The transfer to indirect party rule and party government brought about a clear reduction in the significance of partisan considerations, if not their complete removal.

Six chiefs of staff served under Ben-Gurion. All were nonpolitical, except for Dayan, who came from an active Mapai family background and was himself highly involved in party matters, even it seems, when such activity had been banned by law. But in his close relations with Ben-Gurion, party considerations were irrelevant. To the contrary, Ben-Gurion "was regarded by the Chief of Staff as the unshakable political authority, . . . based on professional and personal esteem." [22]

Nonpolitical senior officers and those with Mapai backgrounds were more prominent during the 1950s and early 1960s because of the refusal of most Mapam-affiliated Palmah officers to remain in the army, and the almost complete absence of officers who openly avowed an Ezel or Lehi background. Nevertheless, the steady progress up through the ranks of three former Palmah officers who remained in the army and their attainment of the rank of chief of staff indicate that negative political and party tests were not systematically applied. On the other hand, in the case of Yizhak Rabin there is evidence to suggest that even years later he was held back by Ben-Gurion because in 1948 he had participated in a Palmah gathering in direct contravention of Ben-Gurion's orders; he did not become chief of staff until after Ben-Gurion retired.

Thus, according to one analysis, "Ben-Gurion succeeded in avoiding both separate sectoral armies and party patronage in the uniformed ranks. Since that time, parties have not been able to control or seriously influence lower- or middle-level appointments, or to use them to strengthen a party's base and control, thus advancing or weakening specific ideological or class trends." [23]

We can also assess the gains and losses of the various political parties in the transition from direct party rule to state control, indirect party government, and the absence of partisan considerations. Mapam lost its direct control over military matters, and by remaining out of the government gave up the formal opportunity for influence over policy. The center and right parties gave up nothing. They gained the possibility of formal influence over policy-making to the extent that they participated in governmental coalitions, and also gained to the extent that a rival party lost its direct control.

Mapai as a party gave up nothing because previously it had had little direct control. Through the establishment of state control and party government, Mapai's leaders gained the legitimate right to determine security policy, and through the responsible minister, to exercise indirect control over all military matters. But as we noted above, this was kept by Ben Gurion within a very narrow group of ministers and professionals—officers and civil servants—that effectively excluded not only the leading members of the coalition parties but often the leading members of Mapai as well.

At the level of defense organization, initially Mapai probably gained directly.

> The civilian departments of the burgeoning Defense Ministry in the early days were deliberately staffed by Mapai or apolitical (but personal) loyalists referred to as *mishelanu*, or "one of ours." This was only partly in the ordinary party-key tradition, and was done mainly to ensure reliability in a period when the legitimacy of the government monopoly of arms had not been fully established and was still being questioned by Ezel and other groups. Later on,

the need for thousands of new employees in the defense industries offered
Mapai an unusual potential for patronage. This aspect has declined. . . . [24]

At the same time, there was more organized party activity and canvassing
within the army than was formally permitted, especially around election times.
These were carried out by a number of parties, but Mapai was the most
involved and active.[25]

Education

Education was central to Ben-Gurion's conception of *mamlakhtiut*. The acceptance of the responsibility for the whole and for the common interest needed to
be transmitted and perpetuated directly by an educational process, that is, in
the schools. This raised special problems of national integration because the
immigration process had brought hundreds of thousands of immigrants lacking the basics of Hebrew or an understanding of the goals and history of the
independent and sovereign Jewish collective entity in which they were living.
Only common education could lay the basis for national unity in the face of
tremendous social, cultural, ethnic, and linguistic diversity.

The assumption by the state of responsibility for education in Israel, as in
other modern states, was also part of state-building. This meant the establishment and control of the educational and administrative frameworks necessary
for the provision of education. Education was also perceived to be a prerequi-
site for economic growth, technological development, and scientific progress.
Mamlakhtiut looked to education as an integrative, unifying, and developmental factor, which, consequently, could be provided only by the state.

Immediately after independence, however, the reality was very different. In
1948 there were four separate educational streams within the Jewish community. As in so many other spheres, the educational institutions were closely tied
in with the political party structure. The general stream, closely affiliated with
the General Zionists, was the largest, with 43.8 percent of the total enrollment;
the workers stream, run by the Histadrut, had 24.8 percent; the Mizrachi
schools had 25.9 percent; and the Aguda schools had about 5 percent.

These educational streams were directly or indirectly controlled by political
parties, and were viewed as mechanisms for political and ideological socialization capable of creating long-term loyalties. Parties competed to recruit children into their particular schools, using the political resources at their disposal
to assist their efforts. What is more, the immigration process was controlled
and actually administered by officials appointed by, and loyal to, political
parties, which determined the recruitment of pupils and the progress of the
four educational streams.

Upon establishment of the state, the government assumed responsibility for
education. In 1949 it legislated compulsory education for all children aged
between five and thirteen, but left the existing situation intact. Parents were, as
in the past, free to choose an educational stream for their children. Exercising

this freedom of educational choice, however, became a major issue of political conflict because of the dependence of the new immigrants upon the government, the Histadrut, the settlement authorities, and the political parties. As a result, instead of fulfilling an integrating and unifying role, education became a major source of divisiveness and the focus of intense political competition and severe social conflict. Establishing a state educational system was therefore highly controversial and bitterly contested, and it took over five years before a solution was reached.

Absorption of immigrants in the early years—their initial temporary shelter, employment, and eventual permanent settlement in urban or agricultural settings—was carried out by the relevant administrative frameworks according to a party key. Thus, the numbers of various camps and settlements, instructors, and other services were allocated according to the proportions received by the participating parties in the Jewish Agency, Histadrut, and Knesset elections. Consequently, the immigrants were distributed according to the same key. The larger the party, the greater the number of immigrants sent to absorption facilities under its control, and, the greater the number dependent upon it and subject to its influence.

Initially, Mapai had over 50 percent in these allocations, and the religious parties close to 15 percent.[26] The majority of *olim* from Asia and Africa were religiously observant, and maintained a traditional way of life. The religious parties were hopeful that this would bring a considerable increase in their political support. Some of their leaders even entertained the possibility that the influx of religious migrants would change the political balance of power in the country and make their parties the dominant political force.[27] In practical terms, however, the religious parties were severely limited in material and human resources. Under these conditions, they pressed for an increased share of the party key rather than demand that the immigrants be given the right of self-definition because this would have entailed outright party competition, and the possible loss of previous gains.

The religious parties' tactic proved relatively successful. The religious Zionist parties were given 30 percent of the youth from North Africa, compared with the previous 15 percent. Hapo'el Hamizrachi was allocated 30 percent of the housing built by the Jewish Agency, and increased its proportion in agricultural settlements from 12 to 22 percent. Mapai agreed to these increases in the party key as part of its general policy of seeking to accommodate the religious parties for reasons of national unity and coalition management, and because it put a ceiling upon the proportion of immigrants directly dependent upon the religious parties.

The most vexing aspect of allocation was education. First, it involved a conflict between different criteria. Here, the religious parties sought to apply the principle of self-definition, as implied in the 1949 law. Because the two religious education systems already had at least 30 percent of the pupils, they were confident that self-definition would enable them to maintain, if not increase, their "market share." The labor parties, led by Mapai, sought to maintain the principle of the party key, which entitled them to about 50 percent of educational allocations, because their educational system at the time had only 25 percent of the pupils.

Competition between the religious parties and the labor parties was particularly strong. This was not only a battle to secure future party loyalty, as was that between the workers' and the general streams, but a battle for souls. The religious parties argued that the immigrants from Oriental countries were observant Jews whose children were entitled to a traditional religious education in keeping with their culture, practices, and beliefs. This was, in their view, an issue of freedom of conscience. They therefore demanded that the authorities upon whom these immigrants were totally dependent respect the integrity of the immigrants' tradition and culture rather than seek to impose new behavior patterns that directly undermined that tradition and culture.

The religious parties denied that the process of social and economic adaptation to the conditions of Israeli society necessitated rejection of the immigrants' traditional religious practices and way of life. Only education in a totally religious environment would, in the parties' view, enable the immigrants to maintain that tradition. Religious education in a nonobservant environment by irreligious teachers was not possible because it lacked the conviction of personal commitment. The demand that traditional immigrants be given a religious education meant, therefore, enrollment in one of the religious educational streams.

The religious parties' fears and apprehensions about the effects on immigrants of education in the nonreligious streams were exacerbated by the behavior and actions of some teachers and administrators within the labor education stream who avidly seized the opportunity given to them to "enlighten" the immigrants. They used material inducements and sanctions to get the migrants to enroll their children in the secular labor educational stream. Once there, ideological pressures, physical coercion, and administrative stratagems were employed to ensure that "archaic" religious practices, rituals, and modes of appearance and dress were dropped, and replaced with those of the new secular Hebrew and Zionist culture. In an effort to bring pressure to bear on the government to accede to their demands, the religious parties widely and emotionally publicized these incidents in Israel and the Diaspora, which greatly raised the temperature of the political debate.[28]

But "secularizing" the immigrants was not, it seems, the only motivating factor within Mapai. Most of its leaders were prepared to grant religious education to the immigrants. Their problem was how to permit this but avoid the party-political element, that is, handing the immigrants over to the religious parties, which would occur if those parties' demands for religious education of immigrants were met. As Zalman Aranne put it, "When we say that religious education, Kashrut, the Sabbath, etc., should be maintained—that does not mean that dealing with education should be handed over only to religious people . . . that becomes a religious monopoly. There are rumors that the government's policy is to place this matter solely in religious hands. The party cannot accept such a move."[29] That such was Mapai's main motivating factor was soon made abundantly clear.

To meet the arguments of the religious parties, Mapai, after considerable pressure, gave in on the question of self-definition. However, it immediately set up a rival Histadrut religious education stream to compete directly with those of the religious parties. In response, the religious parties withdrew their unconditional demand for self-definition, and a new compromise was reached to set up a single religious education system jointly controlled by the four religious school streams. Although this was specifically intended for Yemenite immigrant camps, the spirit of the agreement was that it should apply to all immigrant camps, and to the transit camps (ma'abarot) as well.

But here, too, Mapai educational policymakers sought to protect their party-political and organizational interests by interpreting the agreement narrowly, as applying only in immigrant camps but not in the transit camps, where they sought to introduce the stream system and free competition. But in many transit camps, only the labor stream was made available, and what is more, many immigrants were transferred from immigrant camps to transit camps. Attempts at compromise based on a ministerial committee recommendation to have a supervisory committee of three ministers and to establish religious schools where none existed were rejected by the United Religious Front. The front feared that both would institutionalize Mapai control, and its member parties consequently voted against the government in the Knesset in February 1951, which led to its resignation and new elections.

Education, therefore, was one of the major issues of the 1951 elections campaign, forcing Mapai to formulate an overall policy in this sphere. Consistent with his views on mamlakhtiut, Ben-Gurion was convinced that state control over education was the solution to the problem, with special provision for elements of choice to meet the educational needs of the religious sections of the society, as well as those of other groups seeking to promote distinctive values, such as the kibbutz movements. These principles were enunciated in the proposed education policy he put before the Mapai Central Committee in March 1951.

To avoid the continuation of "disintegration and endless splitting," he recommended the abolition of party control over education exemplified in the four streams; the institutionalization of the authority of the state over all schools, that is state education, but not uniform education; the certification of teachers and their appointment only by the Ministry of Education; the fixing by the state of a compulsory minimum curriculum in all schools; the right of parents and teachers to add to this compulsory minimum, provided that its basic principles were not undermined; and the guaranteed provision to religous parents of a religious school that included the compulsory minimum but added the religious studies and practices to give it a religious tone.

Initially, the Mapai Central Committee deferred discussion on Ben-Gurion's proposals to permit the Histadrut to formulate its views. Prior to the elections, the issue was aired again at the Central Committee during debate over its Second Knesset Election Program. Drafted by Ben-Gurion, the education policy was almost identical with his earlier proposals. The education policy aroused more controversy than any other because of opposition by leaders of the Histadrut's education stream. They supported continuation of the Histadrut system side by side with a state system. Full discussion of the issue was deferred once more, but some amendments were made to the draft that Ben-Gurion had proposed. The clauses demanding the severance of all party connection with schools were omitted. What remained was the minimum upon which agreement could be gained: state education for all children; the placing of elementary schools under the authority of the Ministry of Education; the right of parents to cater to special educational needs beyond the compulsory minimum; and guarantees of a religious way of life in religious schools.

Despite Mapai's electoral victory and the continuing educational crisis, which demanded legislative action, the government did not introduce legislation until 1953. Mapai was in no hurry to resolve the education issue while a coalition with the General Zionists was in the offing. Because the general stream was larger than the workers' stream, the General Zionists believed that this entitled them to the portfolio of Minister of Education. Ben-Gurion, who, as we saw earlier, recognized the validity of that claim, was not prepared, however, to part with control over the ministry because it held the key to the success of the reform and to the institutionalization of *mamlakhtiut* in the educational sphere. Moreover, there was still strong opposition to state control of education from Mapai Histadrut educational officials, and from Mapam and its kibbutz movements, which sought to maintain the unique and autonomous kibbutz education networks and were apprehensive of state control directed by Mapai.

Nor were the religious parties easily or quickly satisfied. After the elections, they placed tremendous pressure on Mapai, which resulted in a coalition agreement to establish a dual state-education system. Rather than leave religious education as an option to be offered in addition to the compulsory minimum, it was agreed to establish two sections within the Ministry of Education, one for general state education, and the other for state-religious education. Each would provide the minimum, but the religious section, to be staffed and administered by religiously observant administrators and teachers, would provide both religious content in the educational program and a religious way of life in the schools. Parents could choose between the two forms of state education.

The principles were discussed and agreed upon by the relevant Mapai party and parliamentary bodies, and Mapai Histadrut leaders. The latter ceased their opposition, in part because the proposed legislation made it clear that many of the values that had guided the Histadrut's educational system had been made part of the goals and values of state education. In fact, Mapai's leaders actively sought to hand education over to the state in order that the schools would imbue all Israeli youth with the major values of the labor movement, which, in their view, would be of benefit to the future development of the state.

Moreover, the coalition agreement would also solve some of the internal tensions and conflicts within the workers' stream. The conflict in the kibbutz movements between Mapai and Mapam supporters, and the differences within

Mapam had made it clear that in reality there were three workers' streams. In particular, Mapai members in some kibbutzim were concerned about the effects on their children of pro-Soviet Mapam indoctrination, and in some kibbutzim two schools existed tensely side by side.

Drafted by Ben-Gurion, the preamble to the legislation gave expression to the commitment to both universal human and scientific values, and to the values of the Jewish tradition, *mamlakhtiut*, and labor: "The aim of state education is to found primary education in the state upon the values of the culture of Israel and the achievements of science, upon the love of the homeland and loyalty to the state and the people of Israel, upon trust in agricultural labor and craftsmanship, upon haluzic training, and upon the aspiration to a society built upon freedom, equality, tolerance, mutual assistance and love of one's fellows." [30]

The kibbutz movements were satisfied by the provisions for additional education beyond the minimum, which enabled them to run their schools with a considerable degree of autonomy and ample scope for the transmission of their own ideological values. This solution suited the religious Zionist parties because their schools had steadily lost ground, from 25.9 percent in their stream in 1948–49 to 19.1 percent in 1952–53. What is more, the provisions of the legislation gave their educational network and personnel control over the new state–religious education system. The Aguda parties accepted the new arrangement because it guaranteed their autonomy, on the one hand, and considerable state financial support, on the other.

By the time Mapai introduced the legislation, the workers' stream was the largest, with 43.4 percent in 1952 and about 50 percent in 1953, replacing the general stream, which had declined to 27.4 percent nationally. Not surprisingly, its gains were in agricultural settlements, transit camps, immigrant camps, and smaller urban areas, including development towns, where instrumental dependence was at its height, but not in the three major cities, where the general stream remained by far the largest. Clearly, the children of many Mapai urban voters were not being educated in the workers' stream.

The growth in the workers' stream enabled Mapai to accept the long-standing support for state education of the General Zionists, who were now in the coalition, without being under pressure to give them the Ministry of Education. In effect, the workers' and general streams merged to form the state system, and the Mizrachi stream became the basis of the state–religious education system. Being in control of the ministry gave Mapai and Histadrut educational officials and educators more than an even chance of putting into practice within the state system the values that they had succeeded in introducing into the legislation.

Before the legislation had even passed the Knesset, disagreement by the General Zionists with one of its proposed clauses led to their resignation and a coalition crisis. It had been customary for the schools in the workers' stream to fly a red flag together with the Zionist (and later the state) flag, and to sing the workers' anthem. The Mapai parliamentary party accepted the view of the Mapai ministers that these practices should cease when the Education Law passed, and that because the schools were state schools, only state symbols should be permitted. Some Mapai MKs, more inclined to the workers' and class viewpoint of the Histadrut, appealed to the Mapai Central Committee.

Ben-Gurion defended the stand of the Mapai ministers. For him, two issues were at stake: first, the content and framework of education, about which there was no longer a debate within the party; and second, the historical strategy and symbolic tactics of the working class. This had been fundamentally transformed by the transition "from class to nation," so that for Ben-Gurion, in the final resort, the issue was simple: "Is there a state or isn't there a state?"

The Mapai Central Committee was not yet ready to go the whole way and completely remove the connection with class symbols. It decided by a large majority that it should be obligatory for schools to display the national flag and sing the national anthem, but that on May 1 and the anniversary of the Histadrut, it would be permitted to fly the red flag and sing the workers' anthem in schools where a majority of parents requested them.[31]

The General Zionist ministers resigned because to their mind this decision had nullified the strenuous negotiations to reach an agreed-upon coalition position about state education that would truly be state education. In view of Ben-Gurion's public announcement that he was bound by the decision of the Mapai Central Committee democratically arrived at, they felt that they had no other option. This put the education issue in a completely different light.

Having worked long and hard to create the coalition with the General Zionists, the Mapai leaders were anxious to preserve it, particularly in view of the country's grave economic problems. They therefore proposed to defer the matter for four to five months pending a special session of the Mapai Council, but the General Zionists would not accept such a vague undertaking, especially because Mapai leaders were not prepared to guarantee the outcome. Ben-Gurion committed himself to use his influence to have the decision reversed. In the meantime, they decided to go ahead with the special session of the council, to be preceded by widespread discussion of the issues in the party branches, and proposed a compromise to the Mapai Central Committee: immediate passage of the Education Law, but without reference to the question of the anthem and the flag. The diehards accepted this because the legislation could later be amended if the council decided to uphold the committee's original decision.

The Mapai Central Committee's action enabled the General Zionists to withdraw their resignation because the original decision that they had found unacceptable, although not rescinded, was not being implemented. When the Mapai Council met in November 1953, it decided that schools should adopt the practices of all other state institutions: the exclusive use of national symbols. With this, the battle for *mamlakhtiut* in education—the abolition of the party-controlled streams, the establishment of state education, and the introduction of a common minimum educational curriculum embodying essential values—was over.

In establishing a state educational system in line with the demands of *mamlakhtiut*, Mapai as a party gave up very little in the way of direct party rule. Unlike all other Histadrut institutions wherein its control was greater than its electoral majority, in the sphere of education Mapai's direct control was at its weakest. Because of the way in which the institutions of the workers' stream had been set up, the Histadrut political parties together provided only one-third of the representatives on these bodies; the rest were representatives of teachers and parents. Many of these represented the kibbutz movements where Mapam influence was particularly strong, and even Mapai kibbutz members had a separate kibbutz educational agenda of their own. Moreover, as noted, the workers' stream as a whole was particularly weak in the three big cities.

Mapai gave up at best tenuous direct party rule for indirect party government by means of its control of the Ministry of Education. More significantly, perhaps, in accordance with its avowed aims, it succeeded here as elsewhere in making *mamlakhti* and *haluzic* values part of the shared values of the whole of society by imprinting them on the guiding principles of the educational system, and directing their implementation.

Mapam gave up a considerable degree of direct party control for kibbutz autonomy. The religious parties gave up nothing, and strengthened the situation of their more or less autonomous educational systems. Not only was the direct and threatening competition of the secular parties removed but the Mizrachi parties institutionalized their control through the religious section of the Ministry of Education. In the case of the Aguda, at no cost they gained significant state financial support for their independent school network.

The general stream gave up everything, and in the short run seemed to gain nothing. On the other hand, its leaders might have felt vindicated that as years went by, labor and *haluzic* values seemed to play less and less of a role in the state educational system, and the schools were little different from a latter-day version of the general stream.

Employment

Before the establishment of the state, the trade union and labor organizations affiliated with the various political parties operated labor exchanges to provide employment for their members. Over time, agreements for cooperation were reached between the Histadrut and the trade union organizations of the General Zionist, Mizrachi, Agudat Yisrael, and Revisionist parties. These were institutionalized in the establishment of joint local labor exchanges and a Labor Exchange Center.[32] Each labor organization received a percentage of the administrative positions in the exchanges and of the jobs to be allocated, determined by agreement on a party key reflecting the electoral strength of each party. The Histadrut was by far the largest organization, and it effectively controlled the labor exchanges. As in other Histadrut bodies, this meant Mapai control.

The Labor Exchange Center operated under the general supervision of the Jewish Agency until 1948, when it was transferred to the Ministry of Labor. During and immediately after the period of extensive immigration, the labor exchanges played a significant role. Although the rules provided for allocating jobs on a first-come, first-served basis, in reality, membership in a political party represented in the labor exchange was helpful, and clearly that of Mapai was best. Resort to the same practices did not deter Mapai's political rivals from criticizing it for introducing partisan considerations and political favoritism into job allocation procedures. (There are many stories of immigrants producing a number of different party membership cards before they found the appropriate one.)

There was considerable tension between the central bodies of the Histadrut and the Labor Exchange Center. This stemmed partly from a basic rivalry within the Histadrut between its central national bodies and the local Labor Councils, which provided the Histadrut officials operating the local labor exchanges. There were also administrative disputes between them, such as the conflict in 1952 over the refusal of the labor exchanges to continue to collect trade union membership dues for all the affiliated trade unions as a condition of finding employment, on the grounds that it lacked staff to do so. Most of all, however, what rankled with the Histadrut leadership was that it had very little say over what went on in the Labor Exchange Center and in the local exchanges, despite the Histadrut's formal position of strength.

The real power in the labor exchanges lay with Mapai officials directly appointed by the party, working in close cooperation with the Mapai-controlled Ministry of Labor. Despite its direct interest in these matters the Histadrut had little control over them. Suggested changes in these arrangements, therefore, did not generate conflict between Mapai Histadrut leaders and Mapai government leaders, as did wages policies or education. The Mapai Histadrut leaders were not committed to the labor exchanges and had little ideological investment in them. The opposition came from Mapai's political rivals on the left, Mapam and Ahdut Ha'avodah, which portrayed the issue as another example of the ongoing process of stripping the Histadrut of its distinctive pioneering and collective character, and of diminishing its role in society in favor of the state that would eventually leave the Histadrut as a mere trade union.

Mapam's and Ahdut Ha'avodah's opposition was somewhat ironic because in 1948 Mordekhai Bentov of Mapam, the minister of labor, had suggested the nationalization of the labor exchanges, that is, their direct incorporation into the administrative structure of the Ministry of Labor instead of the existing indirect state supervision. This would have given Mapam considerable influence over the provision of employment, whereas under the existing arrangements, it had little say in the Mapai-controlled structure. Not surprisingly, in 1948 Mapai opposed nationalization because this would have terminated its effective control over the labor exchanges, but this factor became irrelevant after 1949, when Mapai took over the Ministry of Labor, and then retained it throughout the founding period.

The Basic Principles of the cabinet coalition in the First Knesset in March 1949 referred briefly to the establishment of a "single labor exchange that would provide work to those that seek it without ethnic, national, party, or any other discrimination."[33] However, nothing was done about it for over six years, and it was ten years before legislation was finally passed. Mapai's election platform in 1951 did not mention the issue, and the platform for 1955 even seemed to regress somewhat by calling for the retention of the existing system.

In the early 1950s immigration was heavy and the employment situation was difficult. This was a period of direct and active political competition for the support and loyalty of the immigrants, in which instrumental means of gaining and maintaining support were popular currency for all parties. Of all the instrumental benefits available for distribution, the capacity to provide employment was extremely valuable, and conferred upon the party that could provide it a considerable advantage. As a result, Mapai was content to maintain the status quo.

By the mid-1950s, however, the situation had changed. Unemployment was much less of a problem, and the relative instrumental political advantages to be gained from continuing control over employment opportunities declined in importance. Moreover, there was increasing dissonance between Mapai's commitment to *mamlakhtiut* in this sphere (as evidenced by the values of universality and equality embodied in the Basic Principles of 1949) and the partisan practices and political favoritism endemic in the labor exchanges. The labor exchanges as they were constituted simply did not, and perhaps could not, live up to these principles. As Pinhas Lavon, the secretary-general of the Histadrut put it in 1956, "There are organic faults in the labor exchange . . . rooted in the cursed fact that a bureaucracy divided according to percentages is naturally unable to allocate work on a first come first served basis."[34]

After the 1955 elections, the Progressive party made employment a central issue in its election platform, and an ultimative condition in its coalition negotiations. Ben-Gurion, who had drafted the 1949 Basic Principles, clearly regarded employment as a universal service meeting the criteria of *mamlakhtiut*. Accordingly, he eagerly seized upon the political opportunity presented to him to engineer its transfer to the state.

For his cabinet, Ben-Gurion sought the secularism of the Progressive party to balance the religious parties, and its more liberal economic policies to balance the socialist economics of Mapam and Ahdut Ha'avodah, which for the first time since 1949 appeared willing to enter the coalition. With only the passive opposition, and perhaps even the connivance, of the two labor parties that publicly were committed to retaining this service under the Histadrut's control, Ben-Gurion "gave in" to the ultimatum of the Progressives and reached agreement with them to transfer the labor exchanges to the state, and included it in their agreed-upon draft of the government's Basic Principles. This was now a *fait accompli*, and rather than turn it into an ultimative issue of principle, Mapam and Ahdut Ha'avodah went ahead and joined the coalition despite it. They did, however, express reservations about specific aspects of the proposal, which were not accepted but were recorded in an addendum to the Basic Principles.

The Basic Principles in 1955 thus committed the government to introduce legislation that would "guarantee a just allocation of employment without favor or discrimination, on a basis of first come, first served, and of seniority, and other rules that will ensure efficiency and fairness in the allocation of employment." The Ministry of Labor was to supervise the process, an appeals tribunal headed by a judge was to be established, the employees of the new labor exchange would receive appointments as civil servants and would be bound by civil service regulations. The labor exchange would be the sole employment service, its activities would be monitored by the state comptroller, and representatives of workers and employers would sit on various joint committees under the aegis of the ministry.[35]

The next stage took place within the Histadrut and Mapai. A general debate was held at the 8th Histadrut Convention in March 1956. Ben-Gurion addressed the issue in terms of *mamlakhtiut*: "Every service which is required by the citizens as a whole—the state must perform it. . . . Everything that was essentially a general state need dealt with by the Histadrut before the establishment of the state, because there was no basic state instrument during the Mandate, should no longer be carried out by the Histadrut, but must be handed over to the authority of the state." [36]

The Mapai Party Conference of August 1956 reiterated the main points of the 1955 Basic Principles in the context of Mapai's commitment to overall economic planning and its general economic policies.[37] Following this, a sub-committee of the Histadrut's Central Executive Committee met with officials of the Ministry of Labor to work out the legislative proposal in greater detail, and once it had their general approval it was brought before the Mapai Central Committee. The proposal enjoyed the strong support of Mordekhai Namir, former secretary-general of the Histadrut, and now minister of labor, and of Pinhas Lavon, the current Histadrut secretary-general, and it was passed with only two dissenting votes.

Now that Mapai was formally committed to transferring the service from Histadrut control with state supervision to direct state control, which enjoyed the strong support of the Mapai Histadrut leadership, Ben-Gurion pressed for a formal approval by the Histadrut prior to initiation of the legislative process. Although Mapam and Ahdut Ha'avodah were bound by coalition discipline to support the Basic Principles, they received Ben-Gurion's permission to oppose the change when it was discussed within the Histadrut. At the 70th Histadrut Council in December 1956, they moved that the Histadrut prevent "the expropriation of the labor exchange from the authority of the class and its transfer to the authority of the government." This and a number of more specific amendments were all roundly defeated, and Mapai's proposal was passed.[38]

The legislation to replace the party-controlled exchanges with a government employment bureau in keeping with the general principles agreed to earlier was brought before the Knesset in 1958 and passed a year later. With it, Mapai and the other parties lost their direct influence over the staffing and administration of the provision of labor. Through the Ministry of Labor, however, Mapai retained indirect but sole control over employment policies and their implementation, although staffing and personnel practices and the relevance of partisan considerations now came within the much broader framework of the civil service and its operative principles.

The Civil Service

Whether or not the transfer of functions to state structures fulfilled the purposes of *mamlakhtiut* depended upon what went on within the government frameworks providing those services. *Mamlakhtiut*—the commitment to general and common concerns—not only would not be served but would be damaged severely if the civil service employed partisan considerations and political favoritism in appointments and promotions, the administration of policy, and relations with the public. And even if political considerations were excluded from these matters, there still remained the more general problem of the partisan involvement of civil servants. Could a civil service achieve and maintain neutrality and impartiality if its officials in their capacity as citizens belonged to, or were active in, parties? What effect would such political involvement have upon their dealings with politicians, fellow civil servants, and the public? Was their involvement consistent with *mamlakhtiut*?

As in so many other areas, the Basic Principles of the first coalition government adopted by the Knesset on March 8, 1949, indicated the direction that future legislation would eventually take. At the instigation of the Progressive party,[39] they stated that "the government recognizes the need for an appointment system for civil servants based upon examinations to be administered by an impartial committee."[40] This committed the government to a civil service appointed on merit, a system that if carried out to the letter would leave no room for partisan considerations. But events had already passed the government by, and the task of establishing a civil service based upon these principles could not be attempted from scratch; it had to contend with practices inherited from the Yishuv, and applied with great dedication by the political parties immediately after the state was declared.

Political appointments to administrative positions in the Jewish Agency and the Va'ad Leumi were not only the norm but the very essence of the political system of the Yishuv. They were reserved for party activists and were both rewards for loyalty and the means to ensure application of party policy. Parties that gained control of departments in these bodies staffed them to the hilt with party members, and through the party members sought to promote the party cause within them.

After the state was declared, a civil service had to be established overnight. It was constituted from three main sources: whole departments of the Jewish Agency and the Va'ad Leumi were transferred intact, and many individuals who had previously worked for the Mandate were retained by the new government. These were supplemented by wide-scale recruitment of persons from the outside. Thus, within five years the number of civil service employees (excluding teachers) rose from a few thousand to over thirty thousand.[41]

The recruitment process differed significantly from that of an established civil service, which recruits slowly, according to a plan, and follows fixed procedures. In Israel, the number of civil service positions expanded dramatically and rapidly, without the direction of an institutionalized civil service. Formal recruitment procedures, general regulations, defined responsibilities, central organizational authority, and organs of personnel management did not exist at the beginning. As a result, initial recruitment was conducted at first directly by the ministries, and not by a general body, such as the Civil Service Commission established in 1951.

Under these conditions, civil service appointments were made on the basis of political and personal acquaintance, which were often synonymous. A significant proportion of the early appointees, particularly in the senior and most decisive positions, were placed there by their political parties. Others, generally at the less-senior levels, received them on the basis of family, friendship, and other personal connections.[42] Despite the legislative commitment to an impartial civil service based upon merit criteria, politicization was built into the structure of the Israel civil service at its inception, both in terms of the appointment process and of role expectations. The reality was that at the outset most officials owed their appointments to party, and were steeped in the partisan practices of the past. As the General Zionist leader Elimelekh Rimalt put it in the Knesset in 1959, "Restraining the party activity of civil servants is very important, insofar as the conception and birth of our civil service were according to a party key, and most of the veteran officials were put in by the parties. For that reason it is particularly important to restrict party activity."[43]

The political parties that formed the coalition governments in the early years systematically maintained and extended the practices of the Yishuv. They treated the ministries that they received as party spoils, and, as in the case of Mapai, established special committees and departments to oversee and coordinate the recruitment of party members into key civil service positions, for which there was keen competition among party members. Moreover, the party loyalty of civil servants was regarded as a key factor in maintaining a strong form of party government, and thereby of maximizing party influence over public policy.

Once initial recruitment had taken place on this basis, similar principles applied when ministries were transferred from one party to another. Although theoretically possible, the dismissal of civil servants of the "wrong" party was not a viable option because of strong trade union organization. After a change in the party affiliation of the minister it was quite common, therefore, for senior and middle-level officials voluntarily to move to ministries controlled by their own party. Because of both their ideological and policy commitments, and the greater possibilities of promotion, officials themselves seem to have instituted this "reverse spoils" system of bringing their party membership into line with that of the minister. On the other hand, if they chose to remain in a ministry headed by another party, they were vulnerable to a variety of bureaucratic stratagems designed to shunt them aside, and counteract their influence within the ministry.[44]

The government set up after the elections to the Second Knesset undertook in its Basic Principles to introduce a bill setting out the service conditions, rights, and obligations of civil servants, and laid down certain principles according to which it would be framed. Such a draft law was in fact made public in March 1952, but was withdrawn after some of its proposals encountered considerable criticism. When the coalition was reconstituted about a year later, with the return of the Progressives and inclusion for the first time of the General Zionists, the Basic Principles included an even more specific and detailed statement of coalition goals.

A revised comprehensive civil service law was given its first reading in the Knesset in June 1953. Although it was regarded by many as deserving of inclusion among the Basic Laws eventually to be included in the constitution, it was never designated as such. In fact, it was eventually divided into three laws: the Civil Service Law (Pensions); the Civil Service Law (Appointments), 1959; and the Civil Service Law (Restriction of Party Activity and Fundraising), 1959. The delay and its subsequent division into three parts were due mainly to the controversial nature of the provisions dealing with partisan considerations and political activity.

There were a number of fundamental questions. The first related to the role of partisan considerations and party affiliations in appointments. In this regard, there was a clear decision to adopt merit criteria in appointments, with examinations, public and internal competition for civil service vacancies, and decisions made upon the basis of qualifications, in which personal and party considerations were illegitimate and totally excluded. A number of major exceptions, however, were made to these rules by specification in the law of positions for which the rules of public announcement and competition did not apply, that is to say, for appointments to be made by the whole cabinet.

In some cases, the intention was to underscore and reinforce the political independence and neutrality of the position, such as the state attorney-general, the state comptroller, the civil service commissioner. In others, the opposite was intended, most notably with regard to the post of director-general in the various ministries. This was a political appointment, and partisan considerations were paramount. The idea was that party government would be strengthened and fulfilled if the minister were assisted and advised by a director-general in whom he had both personal and political trust, and upon whom he could rely to promote and implement party policy. This was also the rule for a number of other immediate personal assistants. Thus, when ministries changed hands, it was common for these officials to be replaced. But at all other levels officials were expected to remain in place because they were neutral civil service officials for whom partisan considerations were illegitimate.

The second fundamental question was that of promotion, and here, too, merit criteria were laid down by law, with provisions for seniority, experience, the demonstration of qualification by examination, and internal and public advertisement and competition for openings, and the award of positions to the most qualified.

The formal criteria for appointment and promotion could be circumvented within the general framework of the law to enable partisan considerations to be reintroduced. If a minister or a party that controlled a ministry sought to appoint a party member to a vacant position, he or it could do so by means of the public and competitive appointment procedures, provided that the candidate was suitably qualified. If there were some doubts in this regard, or if there was some apprehension that a more qualified candidate might also apply, other possibilities were available. Temporary appointments could be made first so that the candidate had the benefit of experience gained on the inside. Alternately, the job specification could be tailored to fit the precise qualifications of the desired candidate. The law also provided for term employment on special contracts that avoided many of these problems.

Parties and ministers were therefore able, in practice, to expand the number of political appointments permitted by law in a manner that was within the letter of the law even if not within its spirit. There were, however, a number of inbuilt limitations. One was the need for qualifications; an unqualified and unsuitable party appointee was not likely to get a job because parties would be held responsible for failure or lack of capability. Moreover, too many such appointments would cause internal unrest by slowing down and blocking the promotion of those already within the ministry, including other party members. On the other hand, suitably qualified party members already within ministries might find their promotion accelerated, particularly if ministries changed hands and there was an exodus of officials from other parties. Overall, active membership in the same party as the minister was not a disadvantage.

The third fundamental question was the role of partisan considerations and political favoritism in relations between the civil service and the public. There was no disagreement on this issue: neutrality and impartiality were universally accepted. The problem was how to ensure them in practice, particularly when the civil service had initially been widely staffed with party appointees.

One school of thought, led by the Progressive party and the General Zionists, sought total depoliticization: a complete ban on the party membership of all civil servants, and failing that, of those involved in the making and implementing of decisions that directly affected the public, particularly economic decisions. Their model was a career civil service like that in Britain. Merit criteria in appointments and promotions were not enough. Officials who were active party members would be under considerable pressure to give preference to party interests and favor party members, and the public would inevitably be influenced by this in its dealings with the civil service.

There was always the possibility that party-identified officials could be influenced by party members or leaders outside the department to make decisions that favored other party members. Even if bureaucrats did not apply such partisan considerations, members of the public would inevitably be convinced that they did so, and would act accordingly. They might feel constrained, for example, to express support for the party in various ways in order to improve their chances of gaining a favorable decision. In any event, the image of a neutral and impartial bureaucracy would be damaged by the party identification of officials, even when they behaved in a neutral and impartial manner.

The other school of thought, led by Mapai and supported by the National Religious party, argued that a complete ban on political and party activity was not necessary, possible, or desirable. In their view, the demands of *mamlakhtiut* could be served by merit criteria in appointments and promotions, and strict impartiality and neutrality in administration and relations with the public, supported by some restrictions upon public or conspicuous political and party activity by the senior ranks of the civil service.

A total ban on party membership and activity was not thought to be *necessary* to meet the demands of *mamlakhtiut* because the other criteria would ensure that partisan considerations and political favoritism were not applied. To reinforce this, and more important, to maintain public trust in the fairness and impartiality of the bureaucracy, it was sufficient merely to restrict the political and party activities of senior civil servants.

Neither was it realistic or *possible* to ban party membership and activity. Given the way in which the civil service had developed and the high degree of political involvement in the society, totally to restrict the civil servants in this regard would create dishonesty. As Aranne put it, "We were discussing the service of the state officials of the people of Israel. These state officials do not live in a political fog. They generally have a political consciousness and a political temperament. Minimum limitations—minimum falsehood; maximum limitations—maximum falsehood."[45] It was also impossible for structural reasons. Civil service workers were organized in the Civil Servants Union, which was part of the Histadrut. The elections to both were contested between the national political parties. Thus, those who sought to be involved in trade union affairs at any level could do so only as representatives of political parties.

To ban party membership and activity totally for civil servants therefore demanded a radical change in trade union and Histadrut organization among civil servants that would put them outside the existing structure, and the establishment of some new and unique nonparty trade union pattern for civil servants. Alternatively, it meant the denial of the rights of trade union organization for civil servants. Both were certain to encounter the strong opposition of the Histadrut and all labor parties. The latter insisted on regarding relations between the government as employer and the civil servants as employees as no different from any other labor relations. In fact, tentative indications in the 1952 draft of possible limitations upon the usual pattern of employer–employee relations and trade union representation for civil servants were vehemently opposed. The result was the eventual legislative protection of the role of the Civil Servants Union and the Histadrut as the recognized representatives of the civil servants.

To permit the normal Israeli pattern of trade union representation, accordingly, was to build parties, party competition, and partisan considerations into the structure of the civil service in a way that could not be evaded or avoided. Not only candidates for all trade union offices but voters in union elections as well were encouraged to declare their political identity and party membership, and once this was known to their superiors, subordinates, and the public, it could easily become a factor in their civil service activities.

A total ban on party membership and activity was not *desirable* either. It would deprive civil servants of the basic political rights of citizens. This not only was unfair but would deprive the civil service of access to talent by keeping out those with political views and commitments, who were regarded as being likely to have a concern for the common weal.

Mapai sought simultaneously to meet the criteria of impartiality and neutrality, the practices of party government, and the inbuilt politicization of trade union organization. Its proposals permitted party membership but proscribed certain types of political activity for all civil servants, and public party activity or officeholding by top civil service ranks. The general principle that underlay its approach was to exclude activities that led to an inevitable conflict of interest between civil servants' role and image as public servants and their party loyalty.

The Progressive party and the General Zionists went along with Mapai's partial depoliticization on the grounds that this was a necessary coalition compromise, a step in the right direction that was better than nothing. (Nevertheless, during the Knesset debates, Mapai spokesmen reminded the General Zionists that they did not practice what they preached and were quite proficient in making party appointments to the ministries under their control.) In the 1953 debate Mapam opposed all restrictions on the rights of political activity and party membership of civil servants, and attacked the legislation as designed to promote Mapai's partisan interests and to discriminate against the opposition parties. (By 1959 when Mapam was in the government its criticism had waned.) Herut supported complete depoliticization, and accused Mapai of abusing the existing system to further its own partisan interests.

The need for broad restrictions on certain political activities of state employees was generally accepted. The various formulations in the two drafts and the law were quite similar in this regard, and the amendments were technical rather than substantive. The amendments eventually included in the law covered (1) organizing, sitting at the head of, or speaking at, public political meetings; (2) organizing or participating in political demonstrations; (3) being involved with electoral propaganda; (4) publicly criticizing government ministries' policies; and (5) raising or receiving funds in an official capacity for any purpose except the state treasury.

The difficulties in passing the law revolved around three other issues: first, defining the level of membership activity in parties or other political bodies that was to be proscribed; second, specifying who would decide whether a particular organization was a party or other proscribed political body; and third, specifying which body would determine the classes of civil servants to be forbidden from engaging in the proscribed party and political activities. The 1959 law resolved the three issues. In addition to the political activities listed above, which had been generally accepted, membership "of the active executive of a party or political body" was proscribed. The government, in consultation with the Knesset's Labor Committee, would determine to which classes of civil servants or holders of state offices the proscriptions applied. Finally, the government would determine whether a particular body was a party or political body within the meaning of the law.[46]

The 1959 law represented a compromise between the earlier proposals. The first draft had outlawed the broader political activities for all civil servants, and left it up to the Civil Service Commission to determine which civil servants would not be permitted to be active members of a political party or engage in political propaganda, and to decide, subject to government approval, whether a given body was a party or political body within the meaning of the law. The second draft made these the responsibility of the government, and sought to make active party leadership off limits for civil servants whose "work is apt to lead to conflict or incompatibility between their duties as state employees and their activity in a party."

The need to show conflict of interest and incompatibility, and the intention to make the government responsible for determining to which parties and political bodies the law applied generated considerable unease and concern among the noncoalition parties, which opposed both, alleging that these discriminated against them. Civil servants belonging to opposition parties would be more likely than those who were members of coalition parties to face charges of conflict of interest and incompatibility. It also seemed to give the government power to proscribe parties, and not just activities, for certain classes of civil servants.

As the legislation makes clear, Mapai backed down somewhat. It sought to assuage the apprehensions of other parties by removing the condition of incompatibility and conflict of interest, and made the determination subject to the advice of the Labor Committee of the Knesset, which included representatives of the opposition parties.

As finally passed, the law laid down that the top three grades of the civil service and all state employees who had direct personal contact with the public, such as social workers, would be restricted with regard to the specified party and electoral activities, and that *all* state employees were forbidden to organize political demonstrations or publicly criticize governmental policies. In 1961 an amendment stipulated that civil servants who sought to become Knesset candidates had to resign from the civil service, in the case of senior officials, or take leave of absence, in the case of the lower grades.[47] Subsequently, senior officials were required to resign at least one hundred days prior to the Knesset elections.

The formal legal situation in Israel incorporated elements of both a merit system and a spoils system. Although its major thrust reflected an acceptance of the values and demands of *mamlakhtiut*, the law did not establish a completely neutral and nonpartisan senior civil service. As noted, it left room for, and legitimated at the very top level, some of the inherited practices of partisan appointment. What is more, these were further reinforced by informal and not entirely legitimate means.

The simultaneous operation within the Israel civil service of these two conflicting sets of principles raises the empirical question of their relative strengths over time. Did the principles of *mamlakhtiut* and merit win out, or did those of partisanship and spoils prevail? What was the long-term impact and success of the informal practices? Were initial appointments made along partisan lines? Did party affiliation or activity speed up advancement after initial appointment?

A study in 1968 by Donna Robinson of the career patterns of all ninety-eight civil servants in grade 19, the second highest level in "the Israeli administrative 'unified' classification and considered to be the single most influential grade of the civil service for policy formation and implementation" goes a long way toward answering these questions.[48] She found that seventy-five of the ninety-eight civil servants in this grade actually belonged, or had in the past belonged, to political parties.

Of these, forty-nine (65.3 percent of the politically affiliated, and 50 percent of the total) belonged to Mapai; seven to Ahdut Ha'avodah, two to Rafi, eight to the National Religious Party, five to Mapam, two to Po'alei Agudat Israel, and two to the Independent Liberal Party. There were *no* members of any of the opposition parties: the two component parts of Gahal—Herut and the General Zionists—or of Agudat Israel, the Communist party, or any Arab party.

As might be expected, the party members were concentrated in the ministries currently or previously controlled by their parties. In many ministries the only party members belonged to Mapai, and no senior civil servants were members of any other party. Thus, in the Prime Minister's Office, and the Defense, Foreign Affairs, Police, and Justice ministries, *all* civil servants in grade 19 were Mapai members. In the following ministries the Mapai proportions were as follows: Finance (68 percent), Commerce and Industry (60 percent), Posts (50 percent), and Tourism (66 percent), but the balance in each case was nonparty. In a number of ministries the civil servants were distributed among a number of parties: in Labor, between Mapai (83 percent) and Ahdut Ha'avodah (17 percent); in Housing (78 percent), Agriculture (40 percent), Transportation (25 percent) Mapai, and the balance consisting of Ahdut Ha'avodah, Mapam, and nonparty; in Education, Mapai (45 percent) and the balance NRP and nonparty. The NRP was the only party in Religious Affairs, and the NRP and Po'alei Agudat Israel were the only parties represented in Social Welfare. Interior was split among the two religious parties, Ahdut Ha'avodah, and nonparty; and Development between Mapam and the Independent Liberals. Health is the outstanding exception, being the only ministry in which nonparty members (60 percent) outnumbered the party members, in this case Mapam (40 percent).

On the surface, this seems to indicate extensive politicization and the victory of the spoils system over the merit system in a manner totally contrary to the spirit of the legislation. Yet on being specifically questioned, only one official stated that his political activities were instrumental to his rise into grade 19. To investigate this further, the contribution of party membership was compared with formal criteria, such as age, education, level of entrance, and speed of advancement. Of the party members only thirty-six (48 percent) had been active at any stage, and a few had held public or municipal office on behalf of the party before their entry into the civil service. But once in the civil service, their party activity tended to be scaled down, consisting mainly of help in organizing electoral campaigns and other tasks as requested by party leaders, within the range of the activities permitted by the law.

Somewhat surprisingly, those active in parties regarded their civil service employment as a more significant element in gaining status and influence within the party rather than the reverse. Some, in fact, had reached the top of the civil service before they became active in party affairs. On the other hand, not all who had been active in party affairs previously remained active while in government service. Pressured for time, about 30 percent gave up such activity, thus making clear their belief that it had no bearing on their advancement within the civil service. Consistent with the view of most of them that party activity was not a significant factor governing entry *into* or advancement *within* the senior ranks of the Israeli civil service, they concentrated upon acquiring university education, technical competence, and administrative experience.

The average age at reaching grade 19 was 45.38 years, but the differences among party activists, the not active, and those who had never belonged to parties were not significant. Neither did party activity appreciably improve the chances of rising to the top quickly. It took, on average, 7.81 years to rise to grade 19, with party activists taking 7.54 years, and nonactivists, 8.15 years. Mapai members needed 8.39 years; those of other parties, 7.31 years; and non–party members, only 7.09 years.

The biggest difference of all was that between the university educated and non–university educated; the former reached grade 19 at an average age of 43.9 years, compared with 46.2 years for the non–university educated. Similarly, those with a university degree before entry rose in 6.41 years; those without a degree on entry needed 8.04 years. Party activists with degrees were, on average, 43.61 years of age on reaching grade 19; those without degrees were 47.61 years.

Level of entry was also examined. Of the seventy-two officials who began their service at the top levels, thirty-three had university degrees and thirty-nine did not. Whereas only nine of the thirty-three with degrees were party activists (27 percent), seventeen of the thirty-nine without degrees were party activists (43.6 percent). Clearly, according to Robinson, party activity played an important role in compensating for the absence of university education. It gave activists prominence, and accorded them an opportunity to demonstrate their talents and competence.

There was a high degree of consonance between the party affiliations of ministers and civil servants on entrance; in only four cases did the party of the minister and that of the civil servant differ. On the other hand, there are twelve cases of officials' being accepted to serve in senior positions without their being party members, suggesting that party membership was neither a decisive nor sufficient qualification for entry into the senior ranks of the Israeli civil service.

Neither was political activity related to the speed of advancement. Four groups of officials were compared: university degree-rapid advancement; no university degree-rapid advancement; university degree-slow advancement; no university degree-slow advancement. The highest proportion of party activists was found to be in the fourth group: no university degree and slow advancement up the civil service ranks. Robinson concludes:

> The data analyzed . . . demonstrates that for the officials of grade 19 of the Israel civil service, political party activity has not been important for advancement, that political party activity has been a factor in the entry of officials into high administrative offices only on occasion and even then it has depended on the previous work experience of the candidate. It is clear, moreover, that while political party membership may have facilitated entry into specific ministries, political party membership is not as influential a consideration as level of education. In Israel, as in other countries, political affiliation and activity may, under circumstances still to be delineated precisely, aid entrance or advancement into the senior civil service up to grade 19, but political activity or party membership is no special shortcut to administrative power and is not a necessary precondition for access to top bureaucratic positions. Education, for one, seems a more important factor for entry into the senior civil service.[49]

The mutually reinforcing ideals of *mamlakhtiut* and merit became institutionalized in the Israel civil service during the founding period, and slowly replaced most of the partisan practices and considerations inherited by the state on its establishment. To the extent that party membership remained significant, it seems to have been due more to the career pressures of civil servants from below than to partisan design from above. Senior civil service positions created more advantages within the party than did party membership within the civil service.

In the process, Mapai gave up the advantages of direct rule: the opportunity to fill all administrative positions with party nominees, and the legitimacy of making administrative decisions solely according to partisan considerations. In return, party government was incorporated by means of legislation permitting political appointments to the top civil service positions, and was reinforced by the continued informal relevance of partisan considerations, both of which facilitated its hold over policy implementation. This was further enhanced by party government's retention of the key ministries that had the function of central control and coordination of other ministries, such as the Prime Minister's Office and Finance, from which the members of other parties were totally excluded at the senior level.

The parties that lost the advantages of the party key gained nothing unless they were in government. If they occupied the same ministries for long periods of time, they were able, as in the case of the NRP, to repeat the Mapai pattern and reserve senior civil service positions for members of their own party and keep out those of rival parties, and in this way emulated some of the advantages that accrued to Mapai.

Failures of *Mamlakhtiut*: Health Services and Electoral Change

The provision of health services, and electoral reform were frequently singled out by Ben-Gurion as integral elements of *mamlakhtiut*. Health care was a universal service previously undertaken by the Histadrut and other voluntary bodies for which the state should now accept responsibility. Replacing proportional representation with majoritarian-constituency elections to produce a two-party system was thought to be essential to enable the political parties to transcend their self-interested and narrow partisan considerations and act out of concern for the common weal.

Both issues figured prominently on the political agenda during the founding period and were widely discussed. Yet the supporters of *mamlakhtiut* consistently failed to gain majority support for the proposed reforms. An analysis of the reasons for these failures sheds considerable light on the limits of *mamlakhtiut* and on the nature of the political system during the founding period.

Health Services

At the end of 1948, just over half the Jewish population was insured in various health funds, mostly controlled and directed by political parties. By far the largest and most important of these was the Histadrut's Kupat Holim, which accounted for about 81 percent of the insured, with the balance in five other funds, some of which were controlled by parties and some by doctors.[50]

Kupat Holim provided a complete network of health services: hospitals, medical and radiological clinics, laboratories, pharmacies, and convalescent and rest homes. It employed a large medical, paramedical, nursing, scientific, technical, and administrative staff; 2,237 in 1948 and 16,136 in 1968, of whom about one-sixth were in administration.

The growth in staff paralleled the rapid expansion of membership and facilities that took place after independence. Between 1948 and 1955 the number of Kupat Holim insurees more than tripled, from 328,000 to 1,050,000. But even more significant, its insured proportion of the total population grew from 46.5 percent in 1948 to 66 percent in 1955, and to nearly 75 percent in 1968, when its membership numbered 1,990,000.

The rapid and disproportionate expansion in the early years was due mainly to immigration. Under the terms of an agreement between the Histadrut and the Jewish Agency, the immigrants were immediately accepted as full members of Kupat Holim without the usual initial waiting period for eligibility for services and benefits. The Jewish Agency paid their dues for the first three months, after which the immigrants received reduced rates for one year. Membership in Kupat Holim, however, was not acquired independently and directly but was available only to Histadrut members. To receive health care, it was thus necessary to join the Histadrut.

Only a portion of Histadrut membership fees was transferred to Kupat Holim—about 40 percent until the mid-1960s, after which it was nearly 60 percent. Despite this increase, Histadrut membership fees constituted a steadily decreasing proportion of Kupat Holim's income, dropping to 33.4 percent in 1968 from a high of 42.7 percent in 1952. Employers' contributions were consistently about one-third of its income, reaching 37.4 percent in 1968. The major change was in the contribution of the third partner, the government, which grew from 7.4 percent in 1950 to 13.1 percent in 1968. (Subsequently, the proportions changed dramatically: by 1975 only 18.0 percent of Kupat Holim's expenses were covered by the Histadrut; 35.6 percent came from employers' contributions, and 36.9 percent from the government.

Professional relations with Kupat Holim's clients—the membership—were not politicized. Neither were partisan considerations relevant to the provision of health care, its quality, or scientific and professional decisions. This was in direct contrast with the situation in labor exchanges, in which political favoritism and partisan considerations expedited the provision of services. The administration, finances, and membership of Kupat Holim, however, were extensively politicized, deriving from the fact that access to the largest and best-equipped health service in the country entailed membership in a political body and financial support for all its other activities. Thus, Kupat Holim served as an attractive incentive and a vital conduit for the mobilization of workers into the Histadrut.

Once inside the Histadrut, members were exposed to the political views and activities of its constituent parties, and effectively shielded from the influence of parties outside it. This gave the Histadrut parties considerable advantages at the national level by cementing their ties with their supporters in immediate and tangible ways. Conversely, Histadrut members who were supporters of parties not in the Histadrut were at a distinct disadvantage. They not only were under the constant pressure of the Histadrut parties but lacked the political support and opportunities that came with party representation on Histadrut executive bodies.

The administrative aspect of the politicization of health services stemmed from majority Mapai control of the Histadrut, which enabled it to deny the other parties positions of administrative and executive power. As with other Histadrut institutions, Kupat Holim was controlled by one party: Mapai. Although its top representative body reflected the percentages the parties gained in the elections to the Histadrut Convention, at the administrative and executive levels, the Mapai proportions were considerably greater. In 1965, for example, fourteen of the fifteen regional directors of Kupat Holim and twelve of the sixteen administrative heads of Kupat Holim hospitals were Mapai members and activists. Moreover, most other administrative positions, especially the significant ones, were held by Mapai members.

The third key aspect of politicization stemmed from the government's financial support for Kupat Holim. This could clearly be justified on economic, moral, and pragmatic grounds; after all, three-quarters of Israeli society were covered by its health services, and the cost to the government of providing these services itself would be far greater than the cost of the subsidies. Nevertheless, the net result was to subsidize a body controlled by a political party, and effectively to free for political purposes Histadrut resources that might otherwise have been allocated to health care.

After independence, the state established a Ministry of Health that undertook the overall supervision and regulation of health services, and built and ran hospitals where none existed. But these came to supplement, not replace, existing services. The recommendations of at least two official committees of inquiry, and legislative proposals were based upon the rationalization and improvement of the voluntary health funds, which were to be maintained, not taken over.

At first, Ben-Gurion and other Mapai leaders supported the direct transfer of health services to the state. A Mapai committee set up in 1947 to prepare for the establishment of the state concluded that Kupat Holim should be handed over to the state.[51] Similarly, Ben-Gurion in 1949 advocated the same solution: "There are things that should be done by the power of the state, and by its power alone, such as opening up the country's gates to every Jew who wishes to return to the homeland, the provision of basic education to every boy and girl in Israel, health services and the like."[52] By 1956 his position had altered. *Mamlakhtiut* was no longer interpreted to mean the state takeover of existing voluntary health services but the provision of comprehensive health insurance. Although the general principle was that every service required by all citizens should be provided by the state, health services were excluded:

> When I say the state the intention is not specifically the government administration. Many services can be provided more efficiently by organizations of beneficiaries and consumers, such as, for example, health services. It would be a serious mistake, and a social and public loss, if, for example, the whole health service would be administered by the official bureaucracy of the state, once the vast majority of the citizens of the state, led by the members of the Histadrut, have by their own efforts organized medical services on the basis of mutual assistance, which have reached a high level. But the state must guarantee general medical insurance for the whole population in the state, and everyone who is not insured in a Sick Fund, will receive medical aid directly from state institutions. But the autonomy of the organizations of insurees in Sick Funds must be preserved, and the balance of the population should be encouraged to join these organizations.[53]

Ideological uncertainty went hand in hand with partisan interest. To nationalize health services was to weaken the Histadrut. The health services of Kupat Holim were a major attraction of the Histadrut and a critical factor in its successful recruitment of the vast majority of workers in Israel, particularly the new immigrants. Workers would have far less incentive to join it because, given the allocation of Histadrut membership fees, they would in all likelihood receive health services from the state more cheaply. It would change the nature of industrial relations in Israel, and create a free-rider problem of considerable proportions as even unorganized workers received benefits negotiated by the Histadrut that by law were made national.

Mapai had a clear political interest in a strong Histadrut with the widest possible membership because it was one of the main sources of Mapai's national power. Once within the Histadrut net, workers were subject to Mapai's dominant political strength within it, which reached right down to the grass roots through the Histadrut's organizational structure. They were also exposed to Mapai's ideological values and political message within the shared assumptions of the labor movement. Moreover, during the founding period, the right-wing parties within the Histadrut were minuscule. Not only in Kupat Holim but throughout the Histadrut's organizational structure, administrative network, and economic enterprises there existed an abundance of employment opportunities and political offices—patronage—to be distributed to loyal party members, who could then be relied upon to maintain this system and pattern of relationships.

Needless to say, not only Kupat Holim but the Histadrut as a whole, including the opposition labor parties, were adamantly opposed to the transfer of health services to the state. This contrasts with the transfer of labor exchanges, which as noted, gained the support of both the Histadrut and the officials directly involved. United and uncompromising Histadrut opposition presented the proponents of the transfer of health services within Mapai with an almost insuperable problem: in 1954, 34 percent of the members of the Mapai Central Committee were employed in Histadrut institutions, and by 1965 the proportion was over 40 percent. Members of labor settlements brought this figure to just over 50 percent.

Mapai as government also had a strong interest in not transferring health services to the state and keeping Kupat Holim within the Histadrut. Party government was facilitated by a strong and united Histadrut controlled and directed by Mapai. In that way, coordination between the Histadrut and the government was facilitated by means of the practices of primacy of party. Control of Kupat Holim was therefore a linchpin of Mapai's capacity to govern. The party benefited directly to the extent that the resulting governmental effectiveness was a major element in Mapai's continuing electoral success.

There was considerable economic advantage to the state in the founding period in not taking over the direct provision of health services. It was considerably cheaper for the government to make budgetary allocations to existing voluntary health services rather than bear the considerable capital and operational costs of providing health services. As a result, right through to the end of the 1960s, Kupat Holim's budget was larger than that of the Ministry of Health.[54] It was still cheaper for the government, even when account is taken of the additional financial benefits to Kupat Holim, such as convenient loans, land grants for building clinics, subsidies, the payment of insurance dues of new immigrants and welfare cases, and the transfer of employers' contributions.

Kupat Holim's close political relationships with Mapai and the government gave it considerable leverage. It consistently sought to increase its income from Histadrut membership dues. This could be achieved either by increasing the proportion of the Histadrut's membership fees that it was allocated or by increasing its membership fees. However, the party and the Histadrut were opposed politically and electorally to increased Histadrut levies from the workers. The Histadrut leadership was opposed to increasing the percentage allocated to Kupat Holim because this would leave less for all other Histadrut activities.

The stock solution, therefore, was to mobilize special governmental assistance. In 1954, for example, Minister of Finance Eshkol, and Minister of Trade and Industry Pinhas Sapir agreed to make an additional direct grant to Kupat Holim from government sources to obviate the need to raise Histadrut membership fees. On the other hand, such grants enabled the government to extract something from the Histadrut in return. The most striking example occurred toward the end of the 1960s, when, in exchange for additional direct governmental financial support for Kupat Holim, the Histadrut agreed to freeze its wage demands.[55]

This coincidence of party, Histadrut, and government interest is aptly expressed in a statement attributed to Sapir: "Every pound that I invest in Kupat Holim is worth more to me than the same pound that I invest in the Ministry of Health. Approximately everything that I do via the Ministry of Health is not as good and costs me more. If you introduce health insurance, and if you make a Health Law, they will leave the Histadrut. And I warn you, do not rush."[56]

Toward the end of the 1950s, the ideological drive to transfer health services to the state in the name of *mamlakhtiut* was rekindled by many of Ben-Gurion's younger followers within Mapai, the Zeirim, as they were collectively known. The most sustained and searching statement of this point of view argued that by preventing the transfer of these services to the state, Kupat Holim, which had been founded on principles of human brotherhood, a community of fate, mutual help, and solidarity, was responsible for maintaining a situation in which 30 percent of the population did not enjoy adequate and comprehensive health coverage. "In order to receive health services, the Israeli worker should not be obliged to belong to a particular organization, nor to adopt a particular ideology; his right is to enjoy them as a free citizen."[57]

By then it was no longer simply an ideological question of *mamlakhtiut* and the desired role of the Histadrut; it had become intertwined in a complex set of personal, political, and ideological conflicts between the Zeirim, who were thought to have Ben-Gurion's support and blessing, and the party's older leadership waiting to succeed him. The issue of health services, in consequence, was difficult for the party to tackle on its merits. By 1965 it became impossible because most of the proponents of *mamlakhtiut* led by Ben-Gurion split off from Mapai to form a rival party, Rafi, that made *mamlakhtiut* a central plank in its platform. Mapai was now less willing than previously to act to apply the principles of *mamlakhtiut* to health services.

Thus, the health services administered by the party-controlled health funds were not taken over directly by the state for a number of reasons. First, the necessity for this in terms of *mamlakhtiut* was, after an initial bout of enthusiasm, not abundantly clear even to the major proponents of *mamlakhtiut*, including Ben-Gurion. In fact, within a few years not to act was justifed and explained in terms of *mamlakhtiut*, in the view that applying its principles to health care did not require direct state control or takeover. Second, it would have drastically weakened the Histadrut as an institution. A takeover was, then, opposed by all the major Histadrut parties, with Mapai in the lead, and conversely, it was strongly supported by all the parties outside the Histadrut, especially those that were avowedly anti-Histadrut. Whereas Mapai was prepared to transfer specific Histadrut services to the state (education, and labor exchanges), it was not willing to undermine the basis of the Histadrut's power. Third, Mapai's partisan interests were directly affected. During the founding period, the complex combination of relations of patronage, dependency, and political persuasion that it had established with the new immigrants in particular, which brought it considerable electoral support, was facilitated by the almost universal membership of the Histadrut.

Electoral Reform

In the debate over the type of electoral system, the question was not whether in theory a particular system was or was not compatible with the values of *mamlakhtiut* but what happened in practice—how proportional representation operated in the specific context of Israeli society and politics. In Ben-Gurion's view, it stood in the way of the full development of *mamlakhtiut* by entrenching undesirable political characteristics at the core of the political system. By the same token, he believed that structural change to a majoritarian constituency system would avoid the undesirable characteristics and thus permit the values of *mamlakhtiut* to take root by encouraging parties and leaders to act in ways that transcended their narrow partisan interests.

After his initial unsuccessful attempts to have the British system introduced before the elections to the Constituent Assembly (see chapter 2), Ben-Gurion did not pursue electoral reform again in earnest until he left office at the end of 1953, when he made it one of his main goals. By this time, his general views had been strongly reinforced by more than five years of experience with proportional representation, multipartyism, extreme fragmentation, and the trials and tribulations of cabinet coalitions under such conditions. The essence of his argument was that the electoral system had to be changed because it, more than anything else, stood in the way of the development of *mamlakhtiut*.

The ideal political system, in his view, was a two-party system like that in Britain because this bred stable government and an accountable opposition. Knowing that it was likely to be called upon to act as the government in the foreseeable future, the opposition acted responsibly and kept its promises within the realm of possibility. Multipartyism, fragmentation, and the ensuing pattern of coalition government, according to Ben-Gurion, produced disintegration, prevented long-term policy planning, and militated against the development of a sense of national and political responsibility.

Opposition parties in multiparty systems that are not in danger of being called upon to govern tended to outbid each other in making unrealistic promises that they would never have to fulfill. Other than Mapai, which was consistently at the head of government, the parties did not demonstrate a concern for the general and universal, they lacked the very basis of the *mamlakhti* approach, and were guided by narrow partisan considerations. The electoral system promoted unnecessary divisiveness instead of encouraging unity, prevented parliamentarians from establishing a link of representation and accountability with their electorates, and made them beholden to party officials. These practices were deemed to have a destructive effect upon the political system, upon the parties, the civil service and the electorate. "Small parties which are not capable of, and not obliged to be concerned with interests of the state as a whole, and turn at election time initially only to a restricted number of citizens in the name of a party interest or principle, regard the government ministries that are handed to their party members as a means for imposing their rule upon their party membership, or upon their internal rivals." The civil servants take a cue from their political masters, and are loyal to the party that placed the minister at the head of the office, and not to the service of the state and the good of the citizen.[58]

Narrow concern with party interest reinforced by the blackmail capability of coalition partners, irresponsible opposition, negativism, fantastic promises, opposition for the sake of opposition, a pathological exaggeration of party conflict, the blowing up of nonexistent differences, division, divisiveness, and party fanaticism, which inevitably result from proportional representation and multipartyism, had, in Ben-Gurion's view, a corrosive effect upon the public, educating it to prefer narrow and selfish interests over the needs of *mamlakhtiut*.[59] What Israel needed was the opposite: "mutual understanding, friendship, maximum internal unity, education to democratic responsibility, nurturing of the shared, the reinforcement of governmental stability, the strengthening of the ideal of the state, closer connection between elector and elected, and preferring the *mamlakhti* interest over the party interest." Ben-Gurion believed that all this would be achieved by a two-party system, and therefore became the main advocate of reform of the electoral system along the line of the British pattern of first-past-the-post, constituency elections.[60]

The responsibility for government would, Ben-Gurion argued, force both parties to adopt general values and goals that met the criteria of *mamlakhtiut*. This was exactly the opposite of the situation under proportional representation, wherein multipartyism and coalition politics forced the smaller parties to adopt a narrow self-interested approach, even when subjectively they believed that they promoted a *mamlakhti* approach attuned to the general interest of the country as a whole.[61]

He did not restrict himself to educating the party and the public. While still in Sdeh Boker, he persuaded the Mapai party leadership to support his proposed reform, and in December 1954 this was approved by the Mapai Council by an overwhelming majority. It became part of the Mapai electoral program for the elections to the Third Knesset in July 1955 and remained there subsequently. Mapai raised the question in the Knesset in October 1956, but its proposal was roundly rejected, being supported only by Mapai members.

The other parties defended proportional representation in terms of democracy and the political system as a whole. It accurately reflected social reality and enabled the representation of distinctive political ideologies and groups. The two-party system was not suited to Israel because it could not adequately cater to such social diversity and fundamental disagreements. The smaller parties, and the religious parties in particular, opposed electoral reform because it threatened their extinction as autonomous entities, and at the very least, seemed certain to reduce their Knesset representation below the seemingly safe minimum representation under the current system. The larger parties on the right were potential beneficiaries of a two-party system, and for a short time the General Zionists supported electoral reform as suggested by Ben-Gurion, later settling on a mixed proportional-constituency system because like the other parties they believed that a two-party system was certain to produce a Mapai majority. And in those days, that appeared to mean a permanent Mapai majority.

In fact, when the issue was brought up again in the Knesset in February 1958, all the parties that opposed any electoral reform united not only to defeat the proposals of Mapai and the General Zionists but also to give extra protection to the existing system of proportional representation by amending the Basic Law. Henceforth any change in the electoral system would need an absolute majority of the Knesset (at least sixty one members) and not a majority of those present.[62] Mapai sought a referendum on the issue but was once more defeated.

In rejecting electoral reform and entrenching proportional representation, the other parties provided Ben-Gurion with striking, if not conclusive, proof of his arguments for the need to reform the electoral system and made them into self-fulfilling prophecy. Electoral reform failed, in his view, because all parties except Mapai put their immediate and narrow partisan interests above those of *mamlakhtiut*, above the long-term general benefits to the political system of replacing proportional representation.

Here, as in all the other issues relating to implementation of the principles of *mamlakhtiut*, general and partisan considerations were closely intermingled. Acting to meet its general and universal considerations was also the most likely way to produce the single-party Mapai majority that Ben-Gurion had sought from the outset.[63] As such, the case for electoral reform in terms of the values and principles of *mamlakhtiut* is difficult to disentangle from Mapai's partisan advantage, and as noted, Mapai's opponents saw it in this light. Even so, here as elsewhere, the fact that Mapai may have stood to gain does not detract from the independent status and validity of the argument for *mamlakhtiut* in principle. What is more, in the long term a two-party system increased the chances of a party other than Mapai receiving a majority. Compared with Mapai's dominating position under proportional representation, this was to its partisan disadvantage.

But if it is difficult to disentangle the commitment to the values of *mamlakhtiut* per se from Mapai's partisan advantage, there can be no argument about the long-term political impact of the retention of proportional representation. Retaining this nonmajoritarian structural element was critical because it left the political system poised between two opposing sets of structural elements. A permanent tension between majoritarian and nonmajoritarian structural elements was thus built into the system. Moreover, the effects of proportional representation were potentially strong enough to counteract the majoritatian structural elements. As a result, political strategies and arrangements that reflected a certain balance between the majoritarian and nonmajoritarian elements could be upset by changes resulting from the operation and impact of proportional representation. We saw in previous chapters how Mapai-led coalition cabinets succeeded in limiting the impact of the nonmajoritarian elements to achieve a high degree of centralized policy-making and party government more characteristic of majoritarian systems.

In addition to the coalition strategies specifically employed, this balance was conditional upon a number of specific political factors relating both to Mapai and to its rivals. By the end of the founding period, major changes had taken place. Some of Mapai's main rivals sought to replace it at the head of government by adopting a radically new strategy specifically suited to the conditions of proportional representation. At the same time, Mapai itself underwent dramatic internal conflict that it could not contain and was therefore greatly exacerbated by proportional representation. Together, these changes weakened its capacity to maintain the previous arrangements, and they gave way to a new resolution of the tension between the majoritarian and nonmajoritarian structural elements in which the balance swung more in the nonmajoritarian direction. It is to an analysis of this changing balance that we now turn.

Notes

1. For different analyses of *mamlakhtiut*, see Dan Horowitz and Moshe Lissak, *Miyishuv limdinah* (Tel Aviv: Am Oved, 1977), pp. 277–80; Charles S. Liebman and Eliezer Don-Yehiya, *Civil Religion in Israel* (Berkeley: University of California Press, 1983), chap. 4; Mitchell Cohen, *Zion and State: Nation, Class and the Shaping of Modern Israel* (Oxford: Basil Blackwell, 1987), chaps. 11, 12: Natan Yanai, "*Hatefisah hamamlakhtit shel Ben-Gurion*," *Cathedra* 45 (1987): 169–89. Horowitz and Lissak's brief discussion contrast *mamlakhtiut* with the values of *tenu'atiut* (broadly speaking, the achievement of social goals by socialist-Zionist means), in particular *haluziut*, which emphasized personal self-realization within voluntary collectivism, and the maintenance of the institutional structures that embodied those values, as against the achievement of social goals by externally imposed, nonvoluntary, nonpioneering state frameworks. Liebman and Don-Yehiya focus upon the symbols, style, and beliefs associated with statism, those that served to accord it legitimacy and mobilize the population to serve its goals, and upon its role as a civil religion and a substitute for traditional religion. Cohen and Yanai both trace the historical origins of *mamlakhtiut* in Ben-Gurion's thinking in his writings in the 1920s and 1930s. Cohen sees it in terms of class and the relation of class to the state. By making the state the universal category, Ben-

Gurion, in Cohen's view, abandoned his own earlier ideas of a future classless nation. It is the issue of class (not party or partisan interests) that *mamlakhtiut* attacks, and therefore the state is not, or cannot be, "neutral" or impartial. Yanai broadens Horowitz and Lissak's distinction, and sees *mamlakhtiut* as standing in opposition to *yishuviut*, the whole set of political arrangements as they were practiced in the Yishuv. He also states what he considers to be the main principles of *mamlakhtiut* as practiced by Ben-Gurion, with which I agree in the main, although as will become clear later, there are some major differences in emphasis and interpretation.

2. As both Cohen and Yanai point out and illustrate, Ben-Gurion called for *mamlakhti* values in the 1920s and 1930s as being necessary for the transition to, and maintenance of, statehood, and was concerned as to whether such qualities were to be found in the Jewish people.

3. See Cohen's interesting citations from Ben-Gurion's own writings in the 1920s, 1930s, and early 1940s as he explores differences between the nuances of state, kingdom, and commonwealth in the meaning and translation of *mamlakhtiut* and *mamlakhti*, Cohen, *Zion and State*, pp. 201–3.

4. It has also been suggested that *mamlakhtiut* was an unfortunate choice of term by Ben-Gurion because it opened him up to his critics' unfounded charges of "etatism," "which places the state and government at the center at the expense of voluntary bodies that constitute the foundations of democracy. . . . Despite the fact that his emphasis on the term *mamlakhtiut* sometimes created the perception that Ben-Gurion's concept identified the state as the ultimate end of national existence, that was not Ben-Gurion's view." Shlomo Avineri, *Hara'ayon hazioni ligvanav* (Tel Aviv: Am Oved, 1980), pp. 243, 245.

5. 4.4. 1949, David Ben-Gurion, *Hazon vederekh*, 5 vols. (Tel Aviv: Mapai, 1951–57), 1:97–98.

6. Ben-Gurion, 15.10.1954, ibid., 5:90.

7. Ben-Gurion repeated this formulation often. See, for example, ibid., 1:177 (22.6.1949); ibid., 3:48 (26.5.1950); ibid., 5:164 (10.4.1955).

8. Ibid., 1:265 (16.9.1949); ibid., 5:27 (7.1.1954).

9. Ibid., 3:261–62 (29.11.1951).

10. Ibid., 1:177–79 (22.6.1949).

11. Ibid., 5:100 (27.10.1954).

12. Ben-Gurion, 10.4.1955, ibid., 5:164.

13. Ibid., 5:141 (16.9.1954).

14. Ibid., 1:216 (15.8.1949).

15. Ibid., 1:98 (8.4.1949).

16. "Yoman Ben-Gurion" (unpublished diaries), 7.8.1948, p. 638. Emphasis added.

17. Ben-Gurion, speech to the Knesset on the proposal to adopt a constitution, 20.2.1950, *Hazon vederekh*, 2:147.

18. In his diary entry for 14.9.48, Ben-Gurion reports "meeting with Palmach commanders at Na'an. All sixty four Palmah commanders were there. Of them 60 are members of Mapam." Cited in David Ben-Gurion, *Medinat yisrael hamehudeshet* (Tel Aviv: Am Oved, 1969), p. 270. For his general views on the Palmah question see pp. 177–179; 267–80.

19. Ibid., p. 178.

20. Ben-Gurion at the meeting of the Histadrut Executive Committee, 14.10.1948, cited in Yoav Gelber, *Lama pirku et hapalmah* (Tel Aviv: Schocken, 1986), p. 231.

21. The whole subject has recently been surveyed in Anita Shapira, *Mipiturei harama 'ad piruk hapalmah: Sugyot bemaavak 'al hahanhagah habithonit, 1948* (Ha-

kibbutz Hameuhad, 1985). The analysis there tends to be sympathetic to Galili and Ahduth Ha'avodah.

22. Yoram Peri, *Between Battles and Ballots: Israeli Military in Politics* (Cambridge: Cambridge University Press, 1983), p. 159.

23. Daniel Shimshoni, *Israeli Democracy: The Middle of the Journey* (New York: Free Press, 1982), p. 186.

24. Ibid.

25. Peri, *Between Battles and Ballots*, pp. xx–xx.

26. See Eliezer Don-Yehiya, "Shituf vekonflikt ben mahanot politiyim: hamahaneh hadati uten'uat ha'avodah umashber hahinukh beyisrael," (Ph.D diss., The Hebrew University, 1977), pp. 497–501.

27. Ibid., p. 498.

28. These charges, and the Frumkin committee, which investigated them, are analyzed in considerable detail, ibid., and also in Tom Segev, *1949: hayisraelim harishonim* (Jerusalem: Domino Press, 1984), pp. 198–218.

29. Cited, ibid., p. 198.

30. State Education Law, 1953, para. 2.

31. Minutes, Mapai Central Committee, 17.5.1963, 24.5.1963.

32. See Giora Goldberg, "*Lishkhot ha 'avodah kemakhshir politi behevrah mithavah*" (M. A. thesis, Tel Aviv University, 1975) pp. 49–63.

33. Ben-Gurion, *Hazon vederekh*, 1:70.

34. Pinhas Lavon, *'Arakhim utemurot* (Am Oved, Tel Aviv: 1960), p. 158.

35. *Haaretz*, 2.11.1955.

36. Minutes, 8th Histadrut Convention, March 1956, p. 73.

37. *Report, Mapai 8th Conference, 1956*, p. 374.

38. *Report, 70th Histadrut Council*, December 1956. See also the discussion in Goldberg, "The Labour Exchanges," pp. 77–79.

39. I. Harari, *Divrei Hakenesset*, 3.6.1953, p. 1445.

40. Ben-Gurion, *Hazon vederekh*, 1:70.

41. D. Arian, "The First Five Years of the Israel Civil Service", in Robert Bachi, ed., *Scripta Hierosolymitana*, 3 (1958): 356.

42. Harari, *Divrei Haknesset*, p. 1445.

43. *Divrei Haknesset*, 4.8.1959, p. 2871.

44. Arian, "The First Five Years," p. 367.

45. *Divrei Haknesset*, 1.6.1953, p. 1442.

46. *The Laws of Israel 1959*, p. 190.

47. See Donna Robinson, "Patrons and Saints: A Study of Career Patterns of Higher Civil Servants in Israel" (Ph.D. diss., Columbia University, 1970), p. 95.

48. Robinson, "Patrons and Saints," p. 135.

49. Ibid., pp. 167–68; all the above data are from chap. 5, pp. 133–68.

50. See the table in Yair Zalmanovitch, "Histadrut, kupat holim, memshalah" (M. A. thesis, Haifa University, 1981), p. 56.

51. Ibid., p. 59.

52. Ben-Gurion, *Hazon vederekh*, 1:265.

53. Excerpts from Ben-Gurion's speech to the 8th Histadrut Convention, March 1956, cited in Zalmanovitch, "Histadrut, kupat holim, memshalah," p. 135.

54. Zalmanovitch, "Histadrut, kupat holim, memshalah," p. 86.

55. Ibid., p. 85.

56. Ibid., p. 83.

57. Ahuviah Malkin, "Hahistadrut bamedinah," *Ovnayim*, (1961), pp. 29–47.

58. Ben-Gurion, *Hazon vederekh*, 5:90 (15.10.1954).

59. Ibid., 5:27ff., 90ff., 136–45.

60. Ibid., 5:146 (16.9.1954).

61. Ibid., 5:27, 90, 135–46.

62. See the discussion in Yanai, "Hatefisah hamamlakhtit shel Ben-Gurion," p. 185.

63. Just after the 1949 elections, Ben-Gurion, in a meeting with party leaders devoted to a discussion of the role of the party in the new state, put it this way: "It is possible to establish a . . . party that rules by the force of persuasion. It convinces the majority of the people that its path and vision are the path and vision of the people. That is the party which we must maintain. . . . The main goal must be to turn the party into a majority within three to four years, for without this the state will not accomplish its mission. This is possible, because most of the voters who went with Herut, Mapam and the religious parties should go with us." "*Meeting of Party Members with David Ben-Gurion*, 8.4.1949," Labor Party Archives, Bet-Berl, file 15/49, pp. 1, 10.

8

The Political Dynamics of the Founding Period

In previous chapters the relative stability of government in Israel during the founding period was attributed to the pattern of party government led by Mapai, which established and directed the new state structures, headed all cabinets, chose its coalition partners, manned the important ministries, set national priorities, determined the political agenda, and centralized and controlled policy-making and its implementation. In successfully meeting the political, military, economic, and social challenges that accompanied newly acquired statehood, the government demonstrated considerable capacity to rule under difficult conditions.

The government's stability and capacity were achieved despite multidimensional issue differences, extreme multipartyism, proportional representation, and coalition government, which are generally associated with instability and immobilism, because Mapai was able to maximize the majoritarian and power-concentrating elements within the political structures. This, in turn, depended on the interaction between the major political actors.

In this chapter the focus is on two aspects of that interaction: Mapai's internal unity and cohesion; and the political situation and response of the right-wing opposition parties. Major changes within both led to a fundamental realignment in political forces. The breakdown in Mapai's internal unity and cohesion undermined the prevailing pattern of party government and lessened its capacity to control the political structures in a manner that maximized the majoritarian and power-concentrating elements. The split in Mapai and the formation of a rival party, on the one hand, and the adoption of a new strategy of political competition by the parties of the Right, and Herut in particular, fundamentally altered the distribution and intensity of issue differences, upset the existing balance of forces between the parties, and reshaped the party system. As a result, the majoritarian elements were weakened and it was no longer possible to operate the major political structures as before. Together, these developments set the stage for the end of the founding period.

The End of the Ben-Gurion Era and Mapai's Internal Disunity

At the 1959 Knesset elections Mapai was at its peak, receiving forty-seven seats, more than ever before or after. Its nearest rival, Herut, was thirty seats behind. In these elections, Mapai gave a prominent place on the list and wide exposure in the campaign to a number of younger leaders who already had had distinguished careers: Moshe Dayan as chief of staff, Abba Eban as ambassador to the United States and the UN, Shimon Peres as director-general of the Ministry of Defense, and Giora Josephtal in the Jewish Agency and as secretary-general of Mapai. The public responded to Mapai's forward-looking image of promise and dynamism, as well as to its record of experience and performance directed by Ben-Gurion.

After the elections the sense of renewal and change was maintained by the appointment of Dayan, Eban, and Josephtal as ministers, and Peres as a deputy-minister. This represented the culmination of a period of internal friction between the party's younger group, the Zeirim, and older party leaders, the Vatikim, such as Pinhas Lavon, Golda Meir, Zalman Aranne, Levi Eshkol, Moshe Sharett, and Pinhas Sapir, who enjoyed the strong support of the party machine. The issue was participation in party decision-making bodies, and access to positions of influence within and on behalf of the party, which the Zeirim asserted were closed to them. In this conflict, the Zeirim, had the general but not the unqualified support of Ben-Gurion, who urged that the party be opened up to younger talents, as he himself had opened up the areas under his direct control.

But Ben-Gurion did not control the inner workings of the party, and in fact was quite distant from what went on inside it, having left this to an informal party machine. As he said somewhat disingenuously on one occasion, "I don't know very well what has been going on inside the party except for what I read in the newspapers."[1] As prime minister and minister of defense, he devoted himself to policy and high matters of state and society. He was involved in and mobilized only those representative and executive party bodies he needed to support him in his leadership and control of the government. Most of the myriad personnel matters and party appointments were handled by the formal party executive bodies, after first having been discussed and coordinated by the informal party machine, although if the appointments were significant, there is no doubt that he was consulted and had something to do with them. By and large, however, there was a clear division of function: the affairs of state were for Ben-Gurion; the task of the informal party machine was to give loyal support on these matters and look after the affairs of the party.

This intraparty conflict had many elements. It was ultimately about succession, about the character and identity of the party's leadership group after Ben-Gurion. One possibility that greatly disturbed the other party leaders was that the Zeirim sought to supplant them totally as the leadership group. Another possibility was that the Zeirim would be integrated into the older existing leadership group, which still presented some succession problems to the extent that some of the older leaders would be forced to step aside to make room for the newcomers, and others who had slowly worked their way up the party ladder and were waiting their turn just below the top might never make it. It also presented problems of ideological and personal integration.

In challenging the Vatikim, Dayan and Peres, in the name of *mamlakhtiut*, adopted a strident anti-Histadrut tone. For example, they proposed the transfer to the state of Kupat Holim, efficiency dismissals for workers, and the disbanding of Histadrut sports teams. The Vatikim and their supporters charged the Zeirim with wanting to undermine the Histadrut completely by dismantling some of its most important structures. According to Lavon and those close to him, *mamlakhtiut* was now shown in its true light, as etatism, state worship, an ideology that valued the state as an end in itself, and was opposed to all independent and voluntary social activity, and in particular, the values and goals and institutions of *haluziut*, which had created a new society and brought the state into being. Moreover, the Zeirim were portrayed as pragmatists and technocrats with no ideological direction or commitment who were concerned only with getting things done, for which they were prepared to sacrifice the sacred values of the movement and the party.

Personal relations between some members of the two groups were bad. The conflict between Lavon, and Dayan and Peres, stemming from the 1954–55 Lavon Affair, had not abated. To the contrary, before it became public in 1960, it had gathered considerable momentum within the party leadership. Lavon, now secretary-general of the Histadrut, in 1958 accused Dayan and Peres in party leadership forums of organizing a "Dreyfusade" against him. There were also strained relations between Meir, the foreign minister, and Peres. She charged that Peres conducted an independent foreign policy on behalf of the Defense Ministry, and with the blessing of Ben-Gurion, particularly with regard to France and Germany.

This was not merely a jurisdictional dispute as to which ministry should be in charge of foreign policy, although that alone was sufficient to engender considerable resentment on her part; in the case of Germany there were fundamental policy differences. Meir opposed and resisted the relations with Germany maintained by the Defense Ministry. Although these stemmed from Ben-Gurion's desire to normalize relations between Israel and Germany, and his stated belief in the "new Germany," Peres bore the brunt of the resentment. Meir maintained a strong emotional and moral opposition to establishing normal relations with Germany, and saw all interim relationships as paving the way to that end. There was some support within Mapai for her position, but much more outside it, from Herut and Ahdut Ha'avodah.

The intergenerational and succession conflict was contained within Mapai until a series of events beginning with the 1960–61 Lavon Affair and ending with the party split of 1965[2] turned it into a major national crisis. By the time it was over, it had taken its toll; its victims included Ben-Gurion, Lavon, Mapai, the Zeirim, and *mamlakhtiut*.

On the basis of new evidence that surfaced in 1958 and 1959, Lavon requested Ben-Gurion to issue a personal statement exonerating him from the responsibility for the 1954 mishap, which would amount to a complete political rehabilitation. Ben-Gurion refused on the grounds that this would effectively place the blame upon Gibly, the former chief of military intelligence, and that this could be done only in a court of law or through some other judicial process. Nothing could move Ben-Gurion from this position, and Lavon took his case to the Knesset Foreign Affairs and Defense Committee. As we noted above, Ben-Gurion had always, in the name of *mamlakhtiut* and correct civil-military relations, defended secrecy in defense matters, exercised close personal control over decision making, not discussed these questions within party institutions, and involved the cabinet only at the formal stages of decision making.

During the Lavon Affair of 1960–61, these practices broke down. The leaking to the press by all sides resulting in wide coverage, and Lavon's appearance before the Knesset Foreign Affairs and Defense Committee exposed security matters for the first time, to MKs from all the political parties, including those traditionally in opposition such as Herut, and to the public as well. Many, including some from Mapai and other parties in the coalition, sided with Lavon; others welcomed the opportunity to criticize Ben-Gurion or Mapai or both. Moreover, the press, perhaps for the first time, became an active and independent participant in the events.

The published details of what went on in 1954 indicated not only that political and personal relations at the top had been bad but that intrigue, forgery and other criminal acts had also played a part. The obvious implication was that this had been to the benefit of Ben-Gurion's protégés, Dayan and Peres, even if they were not personally implicated. With such revelations, defense matters lost the sacrosanct status that in the past had helped to keep them out of public discussion.

Ben-Gurion's behavior gave added weight to his critics' assertions. He refused to make a personal statement exonerating Lavon, opposed establishment of a ministerial committee to recommend the procedures to be followed, and then attacked its findings and its members for reaching a substantive conclusion exonerating Lavon, which he regarded as exceeding its authority. When this was subsequently approved by the cabinet, Ben-Gurion resigned as prime minister rather than be bound by collective responsibility for that decision. He also brought the full weight of his influence to bear to have Lavon dismissed from his position as Histadrut secretary-general.

The statesman who spoke in the name of a *mamlakhtiut* that was above party and faction, and behind whom his party was generally united, was now portrayed as being involved in a petty, narrow, vengeful, and vindictive personal dispute, and as an autocrat intolerant of opposition. He was accused of putting partisan interests above justice for Lavon, and of preferring the interests of his personal favorites over those of state and party. In particular, Ben-Gurion was subjected to immense personal criticism, not just from rival parties but from within his own party, and from wide sections of the public, the press, and the intellectual community. One group of prominent academics issued a public statement of concern:

Those close to the Prime Minister explain their stand on the grounds that the existence of the state depends upon a certain person standing at its head. A point of view that makes the fate of the state dependent upon any individual is in opposition to the very principles of democracy, and is liable, sooner or later, to lead to the rise of a single leader in the state. . . . It is currently accompanied by the application of mechanisms of pressure and the creation of an emotional and hysterical atmosphere, which denigrate the elected institutions of the state.[3]

The message was clear: Ben-Gurion was not only the enemy of, and a threat to, democracy but an autocrat on the verge of establishing totalitarian rule. The disparagement wounded him deeply.[4] But the criticisms did not remain at the theoretical academic level. To the contrary, they had an immediate and major political impact: saving Israeli democracy from Ben-Gurion and Mapai was made the central issue of the 1961 election campaign.

Ben-Gurion's own view, needless to say, was radically different. On the two major questions—judicial inquiry or personal rehabilitation; and collective responsibility for a ministerial committee conclusion that was by definition political, if not partisan—only the approach he advocated met the demands of *mamlakhtiut*. Yet even within the party he had difficulty in persuading all his colleagues of this, and many openly supported Lavon. The fact that some of those who did so later voted for Lavon's dismissal (for breaking all the rules of accepted party behavior, and for publicly airing the issue and thus paving the way for widespread opposition and press criticism of the defense establishment, previously taboo) did nothing to improve Ben-Gurion's image. To the contrary, it was taken as further evidence of the immense pressure he brought to bear to bring down a personal rival and thereby maintain his autocratic rule.

There is more than an element of political tragedy in this situation because Ben-Gurion's demand for a judicial committee of inquiry and his refusal to bear responsibility for the findings of the ministerial committee could be defended substantively. But at the critical moment when the issue first came before the cabinet, Ben-Gurion inexplicably did not mobilize the full force of his political authority to establish the type of inquiry he favored, particularly because there was no existing provision in Israeli law for such a judicial commission, and its rules and mandate hence needed to be spelled out specifically. Instead, he appeared to go along with the idea of a ministerial committee to make procedural recommendations. Given Ben-Gurion's attitude favoring a judicial inquiry, Eshkol's initiative aimed at settling the issue once and for all by extending this procedural mandate and exonerating Lavon was quite surprising and unexpected, and what is more, was counterproductive. Once the ministerial committee made its decision, Ben-Gurion's reaction was both predictable and inescapable. The tragedy was that not having prevented the establishment of the committee, he was damned if he did and damned if he did not accept its findings. In both cases *mamlakhtiut* was the loser.

Because it was not a judicial inquiry, in Ben-Gurion's view the committee's decision was a rejection of *mamlakhtiut*, and thus there was no way in which he could accept it. But not to accept it allowed the issue to be portrayed as a personal vendetta against Lavon to bring about his dismissal. As events turned out, most damaging of all to Ben-Gurion was his inability to persuade Mapai and the cabinet to reverse the ministerial committee's decision because this underlined their clear and continuing rejection of both *mamlakhtiut* and his leadership. He refused to take back his resignation and to attempt personally to reestablish the same or a similar cabinet, probably preferring to go to new elections.

Ben-Gurion's failure to have the critical decision accord with his views suggests that his leadership had begun to wane, and that he had lost his grip somewhat. His party, however, itself badly weakened, was not keen to go to new elections under these conditions, nor was it prepared to dispense with his services. It preferred to enter into coalition negotiations, and these were conducted on behalf of Mapai by Eshkol.

One possibility was that the other coalition partners would join a Mapai-led cabinet in which Ben-Gurion was not prime minister. There was some support for this within Mapai, particularly if Ben-Gurion could be persuaded to stay on as defense minister, with Eshkol as prime minister, because it would have obviated the need for elections at which Mapai was likely to sustain considerable losses. Eshkol, too, seemed to be prepared to go along with it, but Ben-Gurion's attitude was not clear. He himself suggested that Eshkol should replace him as prime minister, but whether this meant that he would agree to serve as defense minister or would step aside completely was never clarified. In the event, nothing came of the idea because Mapai was not prepared to let its partners veto its candidate for prime minister.[5] Moreover, most of the other parties, sensing—rightly, as it turned out—that both Ben-Gurion and Mapai had been severely weakened, preferred to go to the polls.

After the 1961 elections, in which Mapai lost five seats, it seemed for a while that things had returned to normal. Mapai, as we saw, withstood the combined demands of the Club of Four, and was able to reestablish a government headed by Ben-Gurion. The Lavon Affair was put in the background. Whereas the Zeirim supported Ben-Gurion and most of the leading Vatikim continued to accept his leadership either because they agreed with him or for the sake of party unity and the need to govern, a small group within the party continued to back Lavon and to oppose Ben-Gurion and *mamlakhtiut*. In June 1963 Ben-Gurion retired, and Eshkol became prime minister, retaining more or less the same cabinet. But soon after his election, the old conflict between the Zeirim and the Vatikim was rekindled.

In 1964 Eshkol sought to dissuade the Lavon group from leaving the party by sending it a personal letter stating that he no longer regarded the dismissal of Lavon by the Mapai Central Committee as operative. Simultaneously, he entered into open negotiations with Ahdut Ha'avodah aimed at a joint list for the 1965 elections and eventual reunification. Among its conditions was agreement by Mapai to drop the idea of electoral reform. Ben-Gurion and the Zeirim, and a large group within the party opposed both moves strongly. A third front was reopened at the end of 1964, when Ben-Gurion once more returned to the Lavon Affair. Based on the results of a reexamination by lawyers of Ministry of Defense documents relating to the events of 1954–55, which he had commissioned before his retirement, he demanded establishment of a judicial inquiry to determine whether the government's handling of the inquiry in 1960 had been correct. The Mapai institutions led by Eshkol rejected this, as well as a compromise suggestion to investigate only the events of 1954.

Eshkol argued that the existing narrow coalition would fall if a new inquiry was agreed to. (Most of the ministers of the smaller parties had all personally been members of the 1960 ministerial committee that Ben-Gurion had so severely criticized.) He therefore demanded that the Mapai institutions give the Mapai ministers the authority and freedom to decide this matter and not bind them by a party decision. Ben-Gurion's supporters wanted the party institutions to express an opinion before the cabinet met, but without binding the ministers. Before the party institutions reached a decision, Eshkol announced his resignation and that of the government. He thus avoided the question of whether Mapai institutions should instruct Mapai ministers, and prevented an open vote. Although he probably would have won it narrowly, the vote would have brought matters to a head. Eshkol also made it clear to the party institutions that for Ben-Gurion to succeed, he would have to be prepared to return as prime minister, which he declared he was not. As a result, the party institutions immediately renominated Eshkol as their candidate for prime minister and called upon him to reestablish the same coalition. They simultaneously authorized the ministers to decide on a judicial inquiry, and rejected a recommendation to look into the events of 1954.

This was not the end of the matter; it came up again at the 1965 Mapai Party Conference. A majority of about 60 percent, led by Eshkol and the Vatikim, rejected the demand for a judicial inquiry, and supported alignment with Ahdut Ha'avodah, even though this meant abandonment of the commitment to electoral reform. With these decisions, Mapai embarked on a new political course involving a major change in value orientation, and a new electoral and coalitional strategy.

Ahdut Ha'avodah had been Ben-Gurion's most outspoken critic over the years, and the staunchest opponent of *mamlakhtiut* as it was given institutional expression during the founding period. An alignment with Ahdut Ha'avodah based on the specific condition that Mapai drop electoral reform—the as-yet-unachieved but critical element in the maintenance of *mamlakhtiut*—was, in Ben-Gurion's view, a clear indication that Mapai had moved away from further pursuit of *mamlakhtiut* as a policy guide. This was reinforced by the continuing refusal to endorse the demand for a neutral, nonpartisan *mamlakhti* judicial inquiry.

At the leadership level, the decisions of the 1965 conference were a further rejection of Ben-Gurion, and they also had direct and important implications for the succession struggle within Mapai. They injected into Mapai a group of leaders (Yigal Allon, Yisrael Galili, Moshe Carmel, Izhak Ben-Aharon) who in age were between the Vatikim and the Zeirim, and ideologically were even more strongly opposed than the Vatikim to the views of the Zeirim. What is more, some of them had distinguished military records and prestige from their days in the Palmah. Even if the Zeirim were not displaced completely, they would find it much more difficult to gain control of the party in the future.

For Ben-Gurion, these decisions were morally unacceptable, representing as they did the rejection of some of his most cherished values and goals. Just prior to the 1965 elections he established a rival list (Rafi) to fight for the principles that he held dear, and succeeded in bringing many of his supporters at the conference with him, including the leading Zeirim. At first, he maintained the facade that he had not left the party but that the party had left its principles, which he was now seeking to restore. Mapai would not accept this legalism, and the country was treated to the unusual spectacle of Ben-Gurion's being formally disciplined by his party colleagues and expelled from Mapai. This put the final seal on the party split and the establishment of Rafi as a separate party.

Although the decline and rejection of Ben-Gurion were apparent for all to see, the weakening of Mapai was masked somewhat by the results of the 1965 elections. For Mapai, now joined together with Ahdut Ha'avodah in the Alignment, to fight elections against Ben-Gurion was a major trauma engendering considerable apprehension and fear that he would regain at the polls what he had not been able to achieve within the party. Akin to this was the fear that even if Rafi did not succeed in gaining more seats than the Alignment, it might still gain enough to prevent the Alignment from establishing a coalition. Heightening these fears was the appearance of Gahal, an electoral alliance on the right of Herut and the General Zionist section of the Liberal party.

In the event, Mapai's fears seemed unfounded: the Alignment was clearly the largest party, with forty-five seats, about the Mapai average; Rafi not only did not replace Mapai but gained only ten seats and was not large enough to prevent the Alignment from establishing a coalition, or to ensure its own participation. Neither did Gahal prove to be a great threat; it won fewer seats than its constituent parties had received in 1961.

But the apparent electoral success of the Alignment in 1965 in the face of this dual challenge masked a fundamental weakening of Mapai and the decline of its capacity to play the same controlling and directing role in the political system that it had played in the past. To begin with, its electoral success was only relative; together the two parties in the Alignment had incurred significant absolute losses, winning five seats fewer than in 1961 and seven seats fewer than in 1959. Second, the formation of the Alignment and the battle with Rafi involved a significant value reorientation. Rafi portrayed itself in an aggressive campaign as a forward-looking party of special defense and security experience, *mamlakhtiut*, electoral change, modernization, scientific development, fair representation for the younger segments of society, and opposition to party bureaucratization. Mapai, at the head of the Alignment, was forced to be on the defensive and was portrayed as backward-looking, fossilized, and stay-put, neglecting and rejecting important values in order to return to an outmoded and outdated brand of bureaucratized socialism. Thus, as Mapai moved left, Rafi moved into the center.

The apparent electoral success of the Alignment diverted attention from the changed situation of Herut. In contrast to the Alignment, the two parts of Gahal together were significantly larger than either had been individually; as a bloc, they held more than 20 percent of the seats in the Knesset. And the fact that the Alignment–Gahal ratio was now only 1.73:1, compared with the Mapai-Herut ratio of 2.75:1 in 1959, further underlined these changes. But even more important, the new bloc gave clear expression to Herut's movement toward the center. To gain greater public support and political acceptability, Herut in the previous few years had adopted a strategy of adaptation and change and muted its protest.

Herut—The Dilemma of the Permanently Excluded Opposition Party: The Quest for Electoral Support and Political Acceptance

When Begin converted the Ezel from an underground military organization into a political party, Herut, it embarked upon a course of seeking power through the electoral process. Its goal was to gain sufficient public support to accede to power, either by establishing a government based upon a single-party majority or at the head of a coalition. Herut not only failed to gain this electoral support but also did not succeed in achieving political acceptance among rival parties. Thus, it was never among the ten parties that were included in government coalitions at various times during the founding period, even though it was the second-largest party for much of it. But to understand Herut's role in the political dynamics of the founding period, the major question is not simply to explain Herut's failure but, rather, to reveal the basic features of the overall political situation (that led to that failure) and analyze Herut's response to it.

One can explain Herut's noninclusion in coalition cabinets in the most elementary democratic terms: it did not receive enough public and electoral support and Knesset seats, and Mapai could therefore afford to ignore it in coalition formation. Nor was Herut's express exclusion from governmental coalitions an infringement of democratic rules or procedures. In the absence of constitutional provisions or accepted political formulas specifying how coalitions are to be constituted, their establishment depends entirely upon voluntary agreements among the participants to enter into partnership. Under these conditions, size is not the only criterion, and no party, not even the largest, can claim a *right* to cabinet membership that is infringed by noninclusion.

What is more, parties do not always have equal chances to participate. To the contrary, polarized multiparty systems do not share the "assumptions of a system where all relevant groups are seen to have 'allegemeine Koalitionsfahigkeit,'" a general and equal eligibility for coalition participation. This is because "the polarization of the major components of some party systems . . . makes most of the theoretically possible coalitions—which according to coalition theory increase with the number of parties—politically impossible."[6] To explain Herut's consistent exclusion from cabinet coalitions, therefore, we must go beyond the numbers that made its participation theoretically possible to an examination of the factors that made its participation politically impossible, and rendered it unacceptable to Mapai and other parties as a coalition partner.

The political undesirability of Herut participation in Mapai-led coalitions was recognized by both parties: its inclusion was at least as unacceptable to Herut as it was to Mapai. From Herut's point of view, accession to a share in governmental power could come only through the ballot box, and hence was directly in the hands of the public. The greatest concern of Herut leaders during the founding period, therefore, was not their rejection by Mapai but their rejection by the public, its failure to gain enough public and electoral support to elect them into office.

Herut, as noted, was established by the Ezel, and its early political development cannot be disentangled from the legacy of the Ezel's situation in the Yishuv. According to the majority, the Ezel were *porshim*, dissidents and separatists who not only rejected but actively challenged the authority of the decisions of the voluntarily organized majority, denied the legitimacy of the very basis upon which the state was established, and attempted to impose their views by resort to the independent use of force. They excluded themselves from collective decision making, showed by their actions that they were unfit to govern, and demonstrated that they could not be relied upon to exercise political power responsibly.

Herut viewed the role of the Ezel very differently. Its leaders fully expected that that role would help them win the support and trust of the population, "given that our striking power defeated Britain, that all the right is on our side, and that there is no other element that aims to serve the people with the same honesty with which we served it during the underground."[7]

Would Herut as a political party seeking power through the electoral process follow in the footsteps of its predecessor body? and would it be subjected to the same treatment? were the principal questions that accompanied its entry into politics. Clearly, to Herut's leaders, the answers depended both on the party's behavior as well as on the attitude of the other parties. The first indication came when its underground military organization was finally disbanded, and Herut competed in elections as a political party. Parliamentary opposition gave it further opportunities to establish prosystem credentials by its continually demonstrating its acceptance of the legitimacy of the state and its institutions, the development of shared goals and values, and its willingness to undertake political responsibility.

The integration of Herut into the political system and the establishment of credentials were set back by events surrounding the *Altalena* in June 1948, and those at the time of the decision to accept German reparations in January 1952. These rekindled or reinforced doubts about the genuineness and permanence of Herut's acceptance of majority rule and democratic politics, and its renunciation of the use of force to impose its views upon those of the majority—in short, was it an antisystem opposition party?

The impact of the events was dimmed over time by the steady integration of Herut into the parliamentary system, where it fulfilled its role in a highly formal and avowedly constitutional manner. It characterized itself, in fact, prided itself, on being a responsible opposition ready to criticize or praise the government as it saw fit.[8] Unlike Maki, Herut had representation on all Knesset committees, including the prestigious and politically sensitive Finance Committee and Foreign Affairs and Defense Committee, and one of its members served as chairman of the Economics Committee. From the mid-1950s onward, it participated in the Knesset Presidium, and one of its Knesset members was a deputy speaker.

Herut came to be accepted and recognized by many, including Mapai, as one of a number of parties that at various times were in opposition. The difference was that Herut's opposition was based on principle and seemed permanent. But Herut's opposition behavior was not regarded by Mapai as being qualitatively different from that of other parties in opposition in the Knesset. To the contrary, Ben-Gurion commonly linked Mapam, Agudat Yisrael, General Zionists, Herut, and Maki:

> Mapam . . . has become devoid of all *haluzic* content and all *haluzic* responsi-
> bility, and in its behavior in the Knesset is not very different from Maki and
> Herut. Mapam representatives have thrown off all *mamlakhti* responsibility,
> except for defense matters, and have done all within their power to sabotage
> state activities. . . . In actual fact, these three parties (together with the
> General Zionists, until the latter joined the government at the end of 1952)
> constituted an opposition coalition within the Knesset, and jointly conducted
> an unproductive sabotage campaign against the government.[9]

Even though Ben-Gurion linked together these five parties in opposition in this way, he nevertheless made a distinction between them in terms of principle; not between Mapai and Herut, however, but between Maki and all the others. The effect was obvious: it served to separate Herut from Maki, and to nullify somewhat the impact of their linked exclusion from Mapai-led coalitions ("without Maki and without Herut"). In essence, it put Herut on a par with all the other parties, including Mapai itself. Thus, a line was drawn between the Communists and every other party, including Herut, on the basis of the Zionist consensus. Ben-Gurion expressed this in 1954: "If we exclude the open and the hidden communists, who are slaves to the Kremlin, and operate according to the orders of the Cominform, the people are fundamentally united on the major questions of the state: security, the ingathering and integration of the exiles, upbuilding the land and economic independence."[10] The Communists were both antidemocratic and opposed to the Zionist and Jewish consensus; Herut both was democratic and also embodied that fundamental Zionist and Jewish consensus, and from that point of view, unlike Maki, was theoretically fit to be in a coalition. Moreover, Herut's patriotism was explicitly recognized by Mapai and Ben-Gurion, who on occasion publicly praised Begin's genuine Jewish patriotism.[11]

Practical evidence of the distinction Ben-Gurion made between Herut and Maki, and of his regard for Herut's trustworthiness and patriotism can be found in Ben-Gurion's behavior just prior to the Sinai Campaign. After the cabinet had approved the decision, he informed the leaders of the parties in opposition. Maki was not included among the parties summoned. Not only was Begin invited on behalf of Herut but reports of the meeting suggest that an extremely warm atmosphere, and an almost idyllic understanding accompanied Begin's predictably wholehearted support for the decision.[12]

Herut, unlike Maki, was thus included within the national consensus, accepted at the parliamentary level as a partner in legitimate discourse; it was a rival to be contended with, not an irrelevant political entity. Whereas we may still be able to explain the exclusion of Maki from coalition participation on the grounds that it was outside the shared democratic and Jewish-national political consensus, this does not apply to Herut, and we need an alternative explanation.

Herut's exclusion from Mapai-led governmental coalitions resulted from the special character of its opposition role in the party, electoral, and parliamentary systems. In its policies and political style, Herut manifested many of the features of the "protest party," which has been defined as "a party representing relatively diffuse protest against the present society, either from the right or the left."[13] Whereas, in general, protest parties "find government participation difficult to negotiate,"[14] in Herut's case this was reinforced by the specific antisystem elements in its approach, its desire not only to replace the government but also to change major features of the political regime and social system. As such (and in contrast to Maki), it may be characterized as a democratic antisystem protest party.[15]

As a democratic antisystem protest party on the extreme right of the Israeli party continuum, Herut advocated radical institutional change to dismantle the existing structure of Israeli society upon which its rivals' political power was based. It appealed directly in a populist manner to the disadvantaged and disaffected sections of society, and advocated policies that were rejected by its opponents as irresponsible, imprudent, unrealistic, militarist, and adventurist, and if implemented, likely to endanger the state's security and well-being. In their eyes, and in those of its supporters, Herut should not be given power because its policies would have disastrous results for the state and society, and in that sense its rule was undesirable—it was simply not "fit to govern."

This multifaceted conflict between Mapai and Herut was not tempered by shared agreements on specific policies, by common institutional loyalties, or by a history of cooperation, as was the case with Mapai's relations with the parties of the Left, the center, the moderate Right, and the religious parties. To the contrary, it was set against the history of deep distrust, political rivalry, and mutual rejection, which was discussed earlier. Thus, what distinguished Mapai's relations with Herut from its relations with the other parties were not the intensely expressed disagreements and public attacks upon each other and each other's leaders (which were characteristic of the public political discourse in the founding period) but the fact that after such strong mutual discreditation Mapai sat down to negotiate with Mapam (and the General Zionists and religious parties) but not with Herut. The crucial distinction was not that Herut was discredited and the other parties were not; it was the pattern and substance of the principle and policy divergences, which maximized the overall ideological distance between Herut and Mapai.

In forming governments, as noted, Ben-Gurion sought consistently to establish stable governments based on clear policy agreements and maintained by collective responsibility. The reaching of policy agreements consisted in the main of compromises made by the minor coalition partners in accepting the major elements of Mapai's election program and policies. By including those parties closest to it on the central issues from among the Left, center, Right, and religious parties, Mapai occupied the center of ideologically balanced and policy-connected coalitions. On no occasion did Mapai take into the cabinet a party representing an extreme point of view on any major policy in preference to a party representing a more moderate policy. The more extreme party participated in the coalition only if the moderate party intermediated between it and Mapai.

Ben-Gurion's aim was to narrow the policy range to be bridged to make compromise, coalition formation, and coalition maintenance possible. Thus, Mapai was generally unwilling to deal with Herut as a potential coalition partner because the major policy differences and its antisystem stance and protest style created such a vast distance between them that agreement on the central policy issues was highly unlikely, if not impossible. In Ben-Gurion's view, therefore, to include Herut without first reaching agreement was to introduce sharp internal disagreements into the coalition governments that would throw them into unnecessary and steady political crisis.[16]

Herut's exclusion stemmed, accordingly, from the calculation that it would be difficult to reach and maintain agreement with it on fundamental policy questions. Because of the shared democratic and Jewish-national consensus, however, its exclusion, unlike that of Maki, was not an absolute principle. Rather, the question of its inclusion or exclusion—was agreement with it possible or workable?—was in the last resort pragmatic, even if the negative answer stemmed from an intense ideological and policy conflict that created a seemingly unbridgeable distance between the parties, heightened by and expressed in Herut's goal of replacing Mapai, not serving as its coalition partner.

That Herut's exclusion from the list of potential coalition contenders, and hence from coalition negotiations, was pragmatic rather than an absolute principle was confirmed three times during the founding period when Mapai was in difficulty in forming a coalition majority. On each occasion the possibility of Herut participation was actually mooted and discussed by the leaders of Mapai and Herut, albeit in an extremely preliminary fashion. How serious these overtures were, and how far they were directed to the goal of softening the resistance of other more likely coalition partners is hard to judge because in no case did actual negotiations between Mapai and Herut take place.[17]

The first occasion occurred in September 1952. After the coalition lost its narrow majority due to the resignation of the Aguda parties, Yohanan Bader, a Herut leader, was approached by Pinhas Lavon, at Ben-Gurion's instigation, and urged to accept a "realistic proposal" that Herut join the cabinet and that he accept one of the economic portfolios. Ben-Gurion himself also alluded to this possibility in discussions with the leaders of the Progressive party, who during the previous year had remained outside the coalition. But at Begin's insistence the idea was quickly quashed.[18] The new coalition included the General Zionists for the first and only time.

After the General Zionists left the cabinet in 1955, Ben-Gurion suggested to Bader that the time was opportune for Herut to renounce permanent opposition and join the coalition because, in his view, Herut would probably get only eight to ten seats at the forthcoming elections. Begin again rejected the idea strongly, this time publicly. "The principles upon which the collapsing Mapai regime rest are in direct conflict with those of Herut, which is fighting to establish a new regime in Israel. We are not General Zionists, we do not trade in principles, we believe in them. We shall oppose the Mapai regime until it falls." [19]

The third occasion occurred in 1961, when Mapai's coalition discussions with the Club of Four were deadlocked; Eshkol formally raised with Bader the possibility of Herut's entering the coalition together with the religious parties. As it had twice before, Herut refused to participate in a Mapai-led coalition.

At the very least, the three coalition overtures indicate that from Mapai's point of view, Herut's exclusion was not absolute, and that when policy disagreements with other parties made coalition formation difficult, Mapai acted pragmatically to explore the possibility of Herut's inclusion, and did not dismiss it out of hand on grounds of absolute principle.

As an antisystem protest party that did not participate in Mapai-led coalitions, Herut sought power by portraying itself to the electorate as the alternative to Mapai. Its consistent failure to achieve power indicated that it did not manage to gain sufficient public support to serve as an alternative government because its public image of political irresponsibility led many to the conclusion that its policies were likely to produce disastrous results, and therefore it was not fit to govern. Herut's poor public image was aptly captured in the independent *Haaretz* some weeks before the 1961 elections. Even the widespread criticism of Mapai and Ben-Gurion and the political damage they had suffered because of the Lavon Affair, had not improved Herut's chances or its public image: "Herut which has tried for years to create the impression that it is able to fulfill the role of an alternative has proved that it is not capable of this. A nationalist party with an anti-Histadrut character that cultivates a worship of leadership and subscribes to an unrealistic and at times adventuristic foreign policy, is certainly not able and not fit to be an alternative government. For the last thirteen years the people has passed such a judgment. . . ." [20]

Short of winning an election and then proving its capacity to govern, a permanently excluded opposition party can improve its public image by gaining the acceptance of rival parties, preferably the major ones. It may, on the one hand, maintain its principles, policies, and tactics but seek to convince its opponents that their previous judgment was wrong. It may, on the other hand, seek greater acceptance by its rivals of its fitness to govern by a process of adaptation and change, distancing itself from the policies and tactics that led to its poor public image and lack of acceptability in the first place. In the case of an extreme protest party, this involves moderating its political stance and moving closer to the center of the political spectrum in order to be perceived as a responsible party with realistic policies.

For Herut, the acceptance of two parties—Mapai and the General Zionists—was particularly significant. That of Mapai was important because a public signal that its inveterate opponents, Mapai, no longer regarded Herut's policies as irresponsible and potentially dangerous would give Herut's public image a tremendous boost. Similarly, willingness on the part of the General Zionists to cooperate closely with Herut in establishing a joint opposition to Mapai could create greater public acceptance of Herut and help to remove the image of political irresponsibility. Herut's quest to improve its public image and standing by gaining the acceptance of rival parties falls into two separate periods: pre-1961 and post-1961, each characterized by its own distinctive political stance.

During the pre-1961 period, Herut sought on its own to replace Mapai, and this influenced the manner in which it sought the acceptance of Mapai and the General Zionists. It sought acceptance on its own terms, on the basis of its past actions and of its principles. At this time, Herut and its leaders emphasized their direct organizational continuity with the Ezel. The cornerstone of their program was an expansionist foreign and defense policy aimed at liberating the historic homeland, and extending the borders of the Israeli state to include both sides of the Jordan. This was to be achieved by the use of Israel's military power at the opportune moment, which, if their spokesmen were to be believed, was at any time.

The acceptance Herut sought from Mapai was *ex post facto* approval of its behavior during the period of the Yishuv. This was not a matter of getting Mapai to forget, condone, or forgive what had taken place before the establishment of the state, for all these would have implied that the Ezel was in the wrong. What Herut wanted, even if only symbolically, was no less than an admission by Mapai that it had erred in its policies toward the underground and in its condemnation of its members as separatists and terrorists. In short, this was no less than retroactive justification and acceptance of the Ezel, and its complete political rehabilitation.

Such political approval, the terms of which were set by Herut, Mapai adamantly refused to confer. It assiduously avoided acts or statements that could be interpreted as indicating that it had changed its judgment about the Ezel's past acts. In short, it steadfastly refused to grant Herut retroactive rehabilitation. In Ben-Gurion's words, "There are acts which we disapproved of in the past, and we continue to disapprove of them now." [21]

Even indirect and symbolic approval of the Ezel's past actions was avoided. Thus, Ezel members disabled in Ezel actions before the state were not covered under legislation establishing the rights of the demobilized soldiers of the IDF, although they were later included by administrative order. Similarly, while he was prime minister, Ben-Gurion refused to agree to state action to bring

Vladimir Jabotinsky's remains to Israel for reinterment, as the latter had specified in his will. He also opposed Herut's participation on the executive of the Jewish Agency because he believed that this would be perceived as granting retroactive approval to the Ezel.

This was not just a battle over historical memory; it also had an impact on the battle for power in the present. Mapai's refusal to grant retroactive rehabilitation to the Ezel for the past reinforced its claim that Herut's policies in the state were irresponsible and potentially dangerous. Herut's noninclusion in governmental coalitions had the same result. That is to say, Herut did not receive the retroactive rehabilitation and the positive public image of responsibility that the sharing of power would have bestowed upon it. It should not be inferred, however, that this was the reason that Herut was not included in Mapai-led governmental coalitions. As we saw earlier, the fundamental and intense policy differences and structural conflicts between the two parties precluded coalition negotiations. Consequently, the likely effects of Herut's cabinet participation upon its image and political standing did not even come into play as a factor in determining coalition membership.

Nevertheless, Mapai's refusal to grant Herut the acceptance it sought was not permanent or immutable. Rather, it placed the onus for bringing about a change in its attitude firmly upon Herut. In Ben-Gurion's view, the only way that Herut might remove the image of political irresponsibility would be for it to alter the policies that had created that public image in the first place.[22]

The case of the General Zionists was quite different, since their relations with Herut from the outset were far better than those of Mapai. They had tried to mediate between the government and the Ezel after the sinking of the *Altalena*, and had voted with Herut against German reparations. Although sharing Mapai's views on foreign and defense policy, the General Zionists were in opposition for all but two and one-half years between 1949 and 1965. Moreover, their economic policies were quite similar to those of Herut, particularly after the latter adopted a conventional free-enterprise approach in 1951. By and large, the General Zionists represented the settled and bourgeois component of the middle class: the private entrepreneurs in agriculture, industry, and commerce, and independent professionals and corporate executives.

Between 1950 and 1961 there was a series of abortive unity discussions between the General Zionists and Herut. The General Zionists could bestow upon Herut the promise of greater political acceptability, the stamp of social prestige, and the end of political isolation. As the leader of a formerly separatist underground, illegal both in the eyes of the British and the majority of the Yishuv, Begin was particularly concerned to demonstrate his group's social respectability. For example, he often described publicly how the Ezel fighters who had participated in the capture of Yafo had been received: "That morning Tel-Aviv was amazed to discover that among the Ezel there are to be found doctors, lawyers, men of position, and famous people. . . . We are not riff-raff."[23] Begin later asserted in his autobiography that Ben-Gurion had been met by an Ezel platoon that saluted him, and visibly moved, he had remarked to those accompanying him, "I did not know that they had young men like this." Little was he aware that in his diary Ben-Gurion had written, "I met an Ezel guard unit, and received their salute. Maybe it is coincidental, but all its members looked as if they were from the underworld." [24]

For their part, the General Zionists were encouraged to try to unite with Herut by the promise of greater strength; by the possibility of attracting a much broader and more diverse base of support rather than competing directly for the support of the same sections of society; and eventually by its own shrinking membership and electoral base. Many factors militated against agreement: determining who would stand at the head of the united list; the number of members each party would get in the joint Knesset list; the General Zionists' greater preference for coalition partnership with Mapai than unification with Herut; the possibility of arrangements between the General Zionists and the Progressives; and the strong opposition of some General Zionists to Herut. But the most important factor preventing agreement was Herut's demand for a foreign and defense policy dedicated to the liberation of the homeland on both sides of the Jordan. Very few General Zionists were prepared to agree to this extreme position, which for Herut was an ultimative policy principle.

By the time the 1961 elections were over and the coalition had been established, the situation had changed for both parties. Herut still had not succeeded in gaining sufficient electoral support to enable it to replace Mapai, and with seventeen seats in the Knesset had managed a net gain of only three since 1949. The General Zionists had joined with the Progressives to form the Liberal party, but this had not fulfilled any of their hopes. Although they had the same number of seats as Herut, they were regarded as the smaller Knesset faction because they had received fewer votes. Not only had the General Zionists not succeeded in unseating Mapai but they had not even been invited to participate in the Mapai-led coalition. Particularly chastening for both parties was the failure of the Club of Four, despite Mapai's weakness and the damage to Ben-Gurion's leadership as a result of the Lavon Affair. The Liberals, together with the other parties, had lost in their attempt to dictate coalition terms to Mapai. Moreover, Herut had proved to be the barrier to the establishment of a coalition without Mapai.

Mapai's decision in 1961 to prefer a narrow coalition with Ahdut Ha'avodah rather than a broad coalition that included the Liberals had historic consequences. Ben-Gurion had urged the inclusion of the Liberals in keeping with his general strategy of ideologically balanced, oversized cabinets to ensure governmental stability and protect the government from excessive demands and coalition blackmail by the minor parties. He also warned that rejection of the Liberals would drive them into the arms of Herut and bring about the consolidation and unification of the right-wing opposition.[25] But for reasons having to do with the dynamics of the internal succession struggle and the possibility of labor unity, the Mapai party institutions, led by Eshkol and Meir, did not heed his counsel and preferred a narrow coalition with Ahdut Ha'avodah.

Immediately after the 1961 elections, Begin suggested to the Liberals the establishment of a joint parliamentary bloc in the Knesset. "More important than all these ideological differences," he wrote to them, "there exists the national and *mamlakhti*—and I do not hesitate to say historic—necessity, to establish in time an alternative force to the ruling party . . . that is capable of moving Mapai into second place."[26] The Liberals quickly and decisively turned down the idea, and among them the strongest opposition came from the former Progressives. Undaunted, Begin approached them again in 1963, after Mapai continued to reject the Liberals as coalition partners, but once more the Liberal leadership refused the offer.

In parallel with his overtures to the Liberals, Begin embarked on a more radical course of change and adaptation, and proposed that a Herut faction be set up in the Histadrut. Internally, this was important to keep in check the intraparty influence of *Histadrut Ha'ovdim Haleumiyim* (Union of National Workers). Originally set up as the Herut answer to the Histadrut, its growing power within Herut had given it the capacity to place limitations upon the party leadership.[27] Not surprisingly, the union's leaders were instrumental in having the proposal defeated when it was first brought to the Herut Central Committee in 1961–62, and the full weight of Begin's authority in support of the proposal was necessary to have it passed at the 1963 Herut Convention, 324 to 257. (Not long afterward, the union's leaders and many activists left Herut to form a separate party.)

But even more important was the external motivation for, and impact of, the proposal. The aim was simple and clear: to deprive Mapai of its majority in the Histadrut. For Aryeh Ben-Eliezer, one of Begin's leading associates, this would have direct effects upon Mapai's capacity to rule the state:

> Since the state was established over a million new citizens have arrived. They go straight from the boat to the Histadrut, for housing and employment. . . . A new people has grown up in Israel, a new movement has arisen, and it must develop new activists. It cannot exist only with a party faction in the Knesset. . . . Mapai would not be able to rule in the state as it does, were it not for its control over the Histadrut. Its majority is known. There is a serious and real possibility of depriving it of this majority, and then things will be entirely different.[28]

Begin referred to the fact that the General Zionists have already paved the way by establishing a nonsocialist faction within the Histadrut, and explained that combining forces with them was the way to weaken Mapai: "If only we had a labor faction, and if it were possible to present a joint list of these two factions, and it received 80,000 or perhaps 100,000 votes—that is the possibility—then this would be a tremendous demonstration, both internally and externally. . . . In every election Mapai receives an absolute majority. . . . Why must we give such a gift to Mapai?"[29] For Begin, even more important than the possibility of upsetting the Mapai majority was the public psychological effect of a group associated with Herut receiving the support of 100,000 workers in the bastion of the labor parties, the Histadrut. More than anything else this would bring about a radical change in Herut's image, and enhance its political acceptability as a realistic contender and alternative government.

This decision, early in 1963, to enter the Histadrut put further pressure on the Liberals to enter into negotiations with Herut, but under the counterpressure of the former Progressives, and the real hesitations of most former General Zionist leaders about the desirability of a partnership with Herut, they continued to resist. Despite their relative failure in 1961 and their exclusion from the government, they still harbored hopes of making inroads in the center of the political spectrum and among Mapai supporters, and thereby create the conditions for coalition with Mapai rather than be pulled to the right by alliance with Herut.

Even the eventual establishment early in 1964 of a Herut Histadrut organizational framework did little to bring about renewed negotiations. But over the next few months the internal struggles within Mapai, the secession of the Lavon group, the growing conflict between Ben-Gurion and Eshkol over a whole range of issues, and the likelihood of unity between Mapai and Ahdut Ha'avodah reinvigorated the possibilities of a merger. The idea of a government in Israel without Mapai seemed increasingly real to the leaders of Herut and the Liberals, and in January 1965 discussions between them began, despite the continuing adamant opposition of the former Progressives in the Liberal party.

Events moved rather quickly, and in April 1965 agreements were reached between the two parties for joint blocs in the Histadrut and Knesset elections due later that year, and joint factions in these institutions after the elections. Their substance clearly indicated the lengths to which Herut had gone along the path of change and adaptation to secure political acceptability in order to come closer to its goal of replacing Mapai.

Rather than continue to oppose the Histadrut from the outside, Herut had decided to join it, which demanded considerable institutional integrity, even if it sought to reform it from within. Moreover, Herut compromised significantly on the issue that more than anything else characterized the party, set it aside from all other parties, and led to its being branded as adventurist and irresponsible: the foreign and defense policies that sought the liberation of the whole homeland on both sides of the Jordan River and the advocacy of armed force to achieve that end. This, as we saw, had long been a major obstacle to agreement with the General Zionists, and in view of its inability to bring the Liberals around to its position, Herut itself retreated on policy to make progress with regard to organizational unification.

The parties could not agree on a joint foreign policy plank to be included in the body of the document establishing the merger. The compromise that was reached was the insertion of a clause in the preamble to the document that read as follows:

> 1. Herut and the Liberal Party have agreed to establish a joint parliamentary bloc, in order to constitute, in place of the existing regime, a national–liberal regime in Israel.
> 2. Herut will continue to uphold within the nation the principle of the wholeness of the homeland, that is to say, the eternal and unchallengeable right of the Jewish people to Eretz Israel in its historical totality.[30]

One of the Liberal participants in the negotiations later explained that this formulation had been placed in the preamble in that form because the Liberals had opposed placing it in the body of the document, and in this way it would be clearly understood that only Herut supported it.[31]

Although it continued to maintain its ideals, Herut entered a political union that was not committed to its previous policies, and in which it would be under consistent pressure from its partner to moderate them. The change was registered immediately in the foreign policy plank of the Gahal bloc. As Michael Brecher put it, "Herut joined forces with the General Zionists in Gahal. The effects on Herut's foreign policy demands were striking. The tone was more moderate throughout the Gahal platform. There was no reference to the 'historic boundaries of Eretz Yisrael.'"[32]

Herut also gave in to the Liberal party with regard to the number of members of each party in the joint Knesset list. At first the Liberals had demanded parity with Herut because each had seventeen members in the Fifth Knesset. But the refusal of the Progressives to go along with the merger meant that in effect the arrangement was being made between Herut and the General Zionists, and the latter alone could not sustain a demand for parity. A complicated formula was eventually arrived at, allotting fourteen places to the Liberals in the first thirty-one, compared with the eight seats the General Zionists had won in 1959. Of the twenty-six seats that the Gahal bloc won in 1965, the Liberals received eleven, indicating clearly the extent of the concession that Herut made to them to enable the agreement to be consummated. In later years the concession increased as the Gahal bloc did better in elections.

Begin had to overcome considerable opposition from his parliamentary colleagues to the idea of giving away hard-won Herut electoral gains to the Liberals, which later actually cost some of them their place in the Knesset. The fact that he was prepared to concede such tangible assets to the Liberals to bring about the merger serves to underline the significance that he attached to improving Herut's public image and political acceptance. This was understood by the Liberals, and they pressed their advantage hard. At one critical stage, the negotiations nearly broke down completely over this very issue. The Liberals freely admitted that they did not bring a united electoral force to the merger, but justified their claim to greater parliamentary representation than their apparent electoral base on the grounds that "as dowry they were bringing their good name." This incensed Begin, who was affronted, and only a speedy apology by the Liberals enabled the negotiations to resume.[33]

That Begin was personally insulted by the Liberals' comment does not alter the fact that this is precisely what the merger was about: Herut had come to the point where it had decided to adapt and change, and to make policy and political concessions to improve its public image and political acceptability. In its own eyes, it was politically respectable, and right and justified in its policies all along, but by the mid-1960s it had come to the realization that the other parties and the Israeli electorate did not similarly perceive it, and that so long as it persisted in its old approach it would not be able to persuade the public to give it the reins of power.

Herut needed dramatic public evidence of the extent of its change and adaptation, and what better than a merger with one of its key rivals to bestow a new image of political responsibility? Without such a new image Herut could not hope to capitalize upon the real possibility, available for the first time, of replacing Mapai at the head of the government. Begin eventually overcame the strong opposition of his parliamentary party by emphasizing that "the issue was that of the possibility of a change of direction and transformation of the political scene." Bader put it even more succinctly: "By ourselves we do not constitute an alternative." This had come about, argued Begin, "because something significant had occurred—behold, men like [Yosef] Sapir, are prepared to leave the Liberal Party and to go with Herut." Most revealing of all, however, was the argument in support of Begin's position by Yosef Shofman: "We must not treat with disdain the factor of breaking down the psychology of our isolation among the public."[34]

At the end of the four-year process of adaptation and change, Herut was no longer an antisystem protest party on the extreme right of Israeli politics. Following the 1965 elections, it had moved much closer to the center as the major element in a single parliamentary opposition bloc commanding twenty-six seats in the Knesset. Although no such official position existed, Begin was indisputably the leader of the opposition. Even more symptomatic of the change was Herut's presence in the Histadrut, where the new bloc gained nearly 100,000 votes (15 percent). Herut had changed its public image, gained greater credibility as an alternative government, and broken the psychological barrier between it and large sections of the public.

Was Herut Delegitimated?

It has become increasingly common in recent years to explain Herut's political situation during the founding period—its failure to gain power through elections, its nonparticipation in governmental coalitions, and the process of adaptation and change that it underwent—in terms of its delegitimation and subsequent legitimation. On the basis of our earlier discussion, we are in a position to assess the validity of what has become the conventional wisdom.

According to one formulation, the delegitimation of Herut was a "brilliant political strategy" on the part of Ben-Gurion and Mapai "to discredit the most serious political challenger to the Labor movement's dominance." Without believing it all, they accused Herut of being "an antidemocratic, repressive, fascist type of movement that posed the gravest threat to the core values of Jewish society and the Israeli state. . . . Even more important, however, was its persistent public image as an untrustworthy, irresponsible, and therefore illegitimate political organization." The outcome of this delegitimation was that "Herut was effectively excluded from power. . . . This exclusion is particularly striking when one realizes that it took place not only in the face of Herut's large electoral base but also in the context of Mapai's continual need for coalition partners in order to secure a parliamentary majority."[35]

In its essence the theory consists of three propositions. First, Ben-Gurion and Mapai cynically discredited Herut; second, this created a public image that delegitimated Herut; third, as a result Mapai could exclude Herut from coalition partnership. As to the first, there is no evidence to suggest that Ben-Gurion and Mapai did not believe their own criticisms of Herut and its leaders. To the contrary, all the evidence points to the conclusion that Ben-Gurion implicitly believed the substance of his criticisms of Herut, and their intensity reflected his attitude. What is more, Mapai's condemnations of Herut were fully reciprocated by Herut and its leaders, in keeping with the pattern of ideological polarization and highly charged political conflict between leaders and parties that characterized the founding period. To be sure, the conflict between Mapai and Herut was particularly intense, uncompromising, and prolonged, but this was precisely because leaders on both sides recognized that on major value, policy, and institutional questions they were at opposite poles, and not because they did not believe what they said about each other. On the contrary, it was the direct outcome of Herut's stance of fundamental and uncompromising antisystem protest.

As to the second proposition, clearly Herut had a negative image for those who shared the views of Mapai and the other Left parties that Herut's policies were irresponsible and, if implemented, were likely to produce disastrous results for the state, and that for this reason it was not fit to govern and therefore should not be entrusted with power. Herut was discredited to the extent that its policies were cast in an unfavorable light. Whether or not this criticism was fair or was unjustifiably applied as part of an overall strategy to weaken Herut is a more difficult question and open to conflicting interpretations. On the one hand, it can be argued that the criticism was justified because it reflected reality and was corroborated by Herut's actions and behavior— Herut got its just political deserts. On the other hand, those who charge that Mapai's leaders did not even believe their own criticisms suggest that these were extreme exaggerations of the facts, if not outright fabrications, and therefore conclude that criticisms were not justified but were an undemocratic exploitation of the resources made available by political dominance to maintain that dominance.

Paradoxically, Herut's process of adaptation and change—its care, after 1952, to adhere implicitly to the letter and spirit of democratic parliamentary opposition, and project an image as the opposition guardian of democracy; its policy modification and compromise in moving toward the center; its alliance with a more moderate party; and its entry into the Histadrut, which for so long it had sought to smash—indicates that Herut itself, in some measure, accepted the argument that the criticism was justified.

Does Herut's negative public image and lack of public support and political acceptance constitute delegitimation? The answer to this question involves matters of both definition and concept, and of fact. At the conceptual level, the view cited above—a party that was perceived as "an untrustworthy, irresponsible, and therefore illegitimate political organization"—simply does not follow.

Parties commonly charge their opponents with advocating policies that are irresponsible or likely to prove disastrous, or with not fully living up to democratic practices, and that in consequence they are not fit to govern and therefore should not be entrusted with power. A clear distinction must be made between a democratic party within the fundamental consensus that is rejected as unfit to govern on the grounds that its policies challenge major aspects of political, economic, and social structure and relations, and are deemed likely to have disastrous results, and a party that is rejected as unfit to govern and, in fact, is untrustworthy because its antisystem policies are antidemocratic, outside the fundamental consensus, and seek to overturn the very principles upon which the regime rests. The first is antigovernment, the second antiregime. The distinction, therefore, is between "fit to govern" and the "right to govern." If the concept of delegitimation is to have any meaning, it should be applied only in the latter case, denying such parties the right to govern. Unless such a distinction is made, every time one party criticizes another severely, it delegitimates the other. Not only would Mapai be said to delegitimate Herut, but Herut would be said to delegitimate Mapai, and so forth, and the concept would be devoid of all meaning.[36]

A concept of delegitimation is needed to distinguish it clearly from intense political criticism and opposition in general, such as that characteristic of polarized political conflict, or that which questions another party's fitness to govern, and restricts it to a special and extreme type of political criticism that denies a party's right to govern. This is not simply a semantic issue: the distinction is central to an understanding of the nature of party competition and of the reasons for the exclusion of certain parties from a share in government. A useful definition of delegitimation based upon a similar distinction is offered by Ehud Sprinzak, who points out that delegitimation occurs when

> the political entity under attack comes to be seen, not only as misguided or wrong, but as altogether undeserving of existence. . . . The political entity . . . has lost its right to exist. . . . The loss of legitimacy effectively means the loss of the right to speak or debate in certain forums. . . . When a political entity is subject to widespread delegitimation, whatever its spokesmen may have to say . . . is perceived as irrelevant. They are no longer accepted as partners in legitimate discourse, for they themselves are illegitimate.[37]

The earlier discussion made it clear that, on the one hand, Herut's public image was poor, to say the least; that criticism and opposition to it and its policies were extremely intense; that it was subjected to effective public and parliamentary political ridicule; and that it responded in kind, acting stridently as an antisystem protest party. On the other hand, it was included in the Jewish-national consensus, it participated in all legitimate political discourse, its parliamentarians were members of all the major (and sensitive) Knesset committees, chaired at least one Knesset committee, served on the Knesset Presidium, and were consulted or informed of major military acts. Moreover, the views of Herut's spokesmen may have been criticized trenchantly, opposed vehemently, and rejected totally, both inside the Knesset and outside it, and in election campaigns, but they never were perceived as irrelevant. To cap it all, tentative overtures were made with regard to the possibility of Herut's joining a Mapai-led coalition. However strong the opposition to, and rejection of, Herut, the overall picture does not amount to a pattern of delegitimation.

Obviously, therefore, Herut's exclusion from coalition cabinets could not have resulted from delegitimation. By the same token, neither was Herut's exclusion an act of delegitimation (because there existed no right of participation that was withheld). Nevertheless, as we have noted, the effect of its exclusion was to help maintain Herut's image as an irresponsible party not to be entrusted with power. By not being included in cabinets, it was denied access to a most definitive means of overcoming its negative public image: to prove its responsibility by sharing in the exercise of governmental power.

There can be no doubt that Ben-Gurion and other Mapai leaders were aware that coalition participation per se would indicate acceptance of Herut and greatly enhance its general public standing and reputation, but its significance as a consideration in Mapai's exclusion of Herut never came to be tested during the founding period because the policy, value, and institutional gap was so vast that it was never relevant. The logic underlying Herut's process of adaptation and change after 1961 was therefore to try to close the gap, but by the time that it had done so, Mapai was no longer strong enough to be able to keep it out for this or any other reason.

The decline in Mapai's capacity to operate the cabinet coalition as if it were a majoritarian single-party government, and Herut's new location much closer to the center of the political map indicated that some of the fundamental conditions of the founding period had changed in their essentials. We return to this issue in chapter 9 after we analyze the distinctive features of the founding period and examine the changes that brought it to an end.

Notes

1. Cited in Peter Y. Medding, *Mapai in Israel: Political Organisation and Government in a New Society* (Cambridge: Cambridge University Press, 1971), p. 255.

2. Many works have been written about this and subsequent events. My intention here is to analyze their implications and consequences rather than provide specific historical detail, which can be found in Yehoshu'a Arieli, *Hakenuniah* (Tel Aviv: Kadimah, 1965); Natan Yanai, *Ker'a bazameret* (Tel Aviv: Levin-Epstein, 1969); Natan Yanai, *Mashberim politiyim beyisrael* (Jerusalem: Keter, 1982); Haggai Eshed, *Mi natan et hahoraah* (Jerusalem: 'Idanim, 1979); Michael Bar-Zohar, *Ben-Gurion*, 3 vols. (Tel Aviv: Am Oved, 1975–78), pp. 1427–1604.

3. *Davar*, 11.1.1961.

4. According to the most detailed analysis of Ben-Gurion's relationships with the intellectual community, "till his dying day, Ben-Gurion never got over the surprise and anguish he had suffered as a result of the position taken by the intellectuals." See Michael Keren, *Ben-Gurion and the Intellectuals: Power, Knowledge and Charisma*, (DeKalb: Northern Illinois University Press, 1983), p. 4.

5. Yanai, *Mashberim*, pp. 125–26.

6. Klaus Von Beyme, "Governments, Parliaments and the Structure of Power in Political Parties," in Hans Daalder and Peter Mair, eds., *Western European Party Systems: Continuity and Change* (Beverly Hills, Calif.: Sage Publications, 1983), p. 342.

7. Yohanan Bader, *Herut*, 26.1.1949, cited in Tom Segev, *1949: hayisraelim harishonim* (Jerusalem: Domino Press, 1984), p. 262.

8. *Haaretz*, 3.1.49; see also a long speech by Begin on the role of the opposition, *Herut*, 4.2.49.

9. 20.1.55, David Ben-Gurion, *Hazon vederekh*, 5 vols. (Tel Aviv: Mapai, 1951–57), 5:287; see also 5:144–45.

10. Ibid., 5:138–39. By "open communists," he means Maki; "hidden" ones, it is important to note in view of the argument below, refers to Mapam!

11. This is reported in a speech by Begin, *Herut*, 15.8.55, 19.8.55.

12. Bar-Zohar, *Ben-Gurion*, p. 1257. Bader reports that Ben-Gurion subsequently received him and Begin during the war while in bed with fever, and that so much harmony reigned between them that Begin sat at the edge of Ben-Gurion's bed holding his hand, and "they spoke as a pair of lovers." Yohanan Bader, *Haknesset veani* (Jerusalem: 'Idanim, 1979), p. 102.

13. G. Bingham Powell, Jr., *Contemporary Democracies: Participation, Stability, and Violence*, (Cambridge: Harvard University Press, 1982), p. 94.

14. Powell, *Contemporary Democracies*, p. 183.

15. Luebbert makes this important distinction. "Many parties have been antisystem parties without being antidemocratic. They reject a particular set of democratic arrangements but not democratic arrangements as such. . . . By antidemocratic, I mean that the party would, if it could, change not only the policies and personnel of the government, but would bring an end to competitive politics." Gregory M. Luebbert, *Comparative Democracy: Policymaking and Governing Coalitions in Europe and Israel* (New York: Columbia University Press, 1986), pp. 12–13.

16. As we saw earlier, this is why Ben-Gurion rejected Revisionist participation in the Provisional Government when it was first mooted in March 1948.

17. Judging by the Ben-Gurion–Jabotinsky agreement in the 1930s at the height of the bitter conflict between the Revisionists and the left parties, negotiations and agreements between leaders and parties that opposed and attacked each other in the most intense fashion were not entirely far-fetched or unknown, however surprising they might have appeared to be.

18. Bader, *Haknesset veani*, pp. 71–73.

19. Ibid.

20. *Haaretz*, 3.8.1961.

21. Cited in Bader, *Haknesset veani*, p. 26.

22. Ben-Gurion made this clear as early as May 18, 1948, in a discussion with a Revisionist leader, Dr. Shimon Yunichman, who sought Revisionist representation in the Provisional Government. Ben-Gurion refused, adding, "They must alter their image in the consciousness of our public: in matters of labor, security and Zionism." David Ben-Gurion, *Yoman hamilhamah: milhemet ha'azmaut*, 3 vols., ed. Gershon Rivlin and Elhanan Orren (Tel Aviv: Ministry of Defense, 1982), p. 437. He repeated the same message on August 15, 1948 to another Revisionist leader, Dr. Aryeh Altman, who sought mutual respect, not enmity, between Mapai and the Revisionists. "I told him that the attitude of our public towards them, would be determined by their behavior . . . the attitude to them will not change, as long as they do not change." Ibid., pp. 648–49.

23. Aryeh Ziv, "Hademut shel Herut," in *Miflagot baarez erev habehirot laknesset hashniyah* (Tel Aviv: Pirsumer Haaretz, July 1951), p. 49.

24. Cited in Bar Zohar, *Ben-Gurion*, p. 779.

25. *Davar*, 29.10.1961.

26. Cited in Aryeh Avneri, *Hakesher haliberali* (Tel Aviv: Zmora, Bitan, 1984) p. 75.

27. Yoram Lichtenstein, "*Tn'uat haherut: mivneh vetahalikhim politiyim*" (M.A. thesis, The Hebrew University, 1974), p. 15.

28. Cited in Avneri, *Hakesher haliberali*, p. 76.

29. Cited ibid., p. 76.

30. Cited ibid., p. 86.

31. Ibid.

32. Michael Brecher, *The Foreign Policy System of Israel* (London: Oxford University Press, 1972), p. 174.

33. Avneri, *Hakesher haliberali*, p. 77.

34. These are all taken from the transcript of the meeting of the Herut parliamentary faction, 2.2.1965, cited by Giora Goldberg, "*Haopoziziyah haparlementarit beyisrael* (1965–1977) (Ph.D. diss., The Hebrew University, 1980), p. 71.

35. Ariel Levite and Sydney Tarrow, "The Legitimation of Excluded Parties in Dominant Party Systems: A Comparison of Israel and Italy," *Comparative Politics* 15 (1983): 295–327, at 300–301.

36. For a helpful discussion of some of these issues, see Raphael Zariski, "The Legitimacy of Opposition Parties in Democratic Political Systems: A New Use for an Old Concept," *Western Political Quarterly* 39(1986): 29–47.

37. Ehud Sprinzak, "Anti-Zionism: From Delegitimation to Dehumanization," *Forum* 53 (1985): 2–5.

9

Conclusion

This book has focused upon the establishment and operation of the political structures of Israeli democracy during the founding period that were a hybrid of two diametrically opposed models of democracy: the majoritarian and the consensus models. As we noted, the former tended to concentrate and central-ize executive power in the hands of a single-party majority: the latter promoted restraints upon simple majority rule by sharing, dispersing, distributing, and limiting executive power.

The balance of forces within the political system during the founding period resulted in the relative dominance of the majoritarian political struc-tures, which, as we saw, were generally able to overcome many of the restraints of the consensus political structures, such as coalition cabinets. For much of the founding period Mapai controlled the executive and made policy almost as if it had no coalition partners, with the result that the pattern of coalition government was not very different from the Westminster model of single-party cabinets.

Clearly, this was an unusual outcome in a multiparty system with propor-tional representation. Not only was it not replicated by coalition governments elsewhere, it was not maintained in Israel for very long after the founding period. In this concluding chapter, we shall seek to explain how this came about. We shall do so first in terms of the comparative analysis of political structures, which will enable us to demonstrate the implications of the empiri-cal case of Israel for the comparative study of democracies, and in particular, its relevance for Lijphart's theoretical models of democracy.

Following this we shall relate the dominance of the majoritarian elements to the prevailing political and social conditions during the founding period, partic-ularly the choices and actions of the political leaders and parties in operating the political structures. Although the specific political structures established during the founding period remained essentially the same after it ended, changes in the balance of political forces, political leadership, and social and economic condi-tions transformed the processes that took place within these structures and altered the balance between them. As a result, the dominance of the majoritar-ian elements that characterized the founding period was undermined, enabling the consensus elements that restrained majoritarian executive power to come to the fore. Thus, the coalition-forming party lost its ability to operate the cabinet coalition, control the executive, and centralize policy in a majoritarian manner, as had been the case during much of the founding period.

The Political Structures in Comparative Perspective

Firm empirical verification of the hybrid character of the political structures of Israeli democracy during the founding period is provided by Lijphart's comparative study of twenty-two democracies (including Israel) over the period 1945–80. (This is, of course, considerably longer than the period under consideration here, and we shall make the necessary allowances, but in general his basic findings are not affected by the differences in time frame.) Lijphart conducted a factor analysis of the strength of the various majoritarian and consensual democratic elements that isolated two different and unrelated empirical clusters of variables. One cluster more or less coincided with a low effective number of parties, and was closely related to minimum winning cabinets, executive dominance (as measured by average cabinet durability), and a limited number of issue dimensions. The second cluster grouped together unicameralism, a centralized unitary system (as measured by the proportion of taxes collected by the central government), and constitutional flexibility.

In each case a high positive correlation indicated majoritarianism; a negative correlation was regarded as consensual. A system scored high on majoritarianism if it had two parties, single-party cabinets, maximal cabinet durability, not more than two issue dimensions, a single legislative chamber, a unitary system, and an unwritten constitution. High negative scores indicating consensus democracy correlated with many parties, large or oversized cabinet coalitions, low cabinet durability, balanced executive–legislative relationships, multiple issue dimensions, two legislative chambers, decentralization or federalism, and a rigid, written constitution with judicial review.

TABLE 2. Varimax Rotated Factor Matrix of the Nine Variables Distinguishing Majoritarian from Consensus Democracy

Variable	Factor I	Factor II
Minimal winning cabinets	.85	.04
Executive dominance	.72	−.06
Effective number of parties	.99	−.10
Number of issue dimensions	.75	.02
Electoral disproportionality	.42	−.03
Unicameralism	.01	.65
Centralization	−.14	.51
Constitutional flexibility	−.12	.76
Referendums	−.01	−.02

Source: Arend Lijphart, *Democracies: Patterns of Majoritarian and Consensus Government in Twenty-One Countries* (New Haven: Yale University Press, 1984), p. 214.

TABLE 3.   Standardized Factor Scores for 22 Democratic Regimes

	Factor I	Factor II
Majoritarian		
New Zealand	1.42	2.11
United Kingdom	1.16	1.56
Ireland	.61	.20
Luxembourg	.08	.75
Sweden	.48	.31
Norway	.42	.09
Majoritarian-federal		
United States	1.11	−1.38
Canada	.81	−1.01
Germany	.68	−1.55
Austria	1.50	−.65
Australia	.67	−.97
Japan	.12	−.98
Consensual-unitary		
Israel	−1.07	1.75
Denmark	−.78	.56
Finland	−1.49	.33
France IV	−1.52	.29
Iceland	−.06	1.05
Consensual		
Switzerland	−1.65	−1.19
Belgium	−.55	−.48
Netherlands	−1.69	−.06
Italy	−.10	−.66
France V	−.18	−.09

Source: Lijphart, *Democracies*, p. 216.

Not unexpectedly, two countries, the United Kingdom and New Zealand (the Westminster models), were found to have strong positive correlations on both factors, and were prototypical of the majoritarian group. At the other extreme, only one country, Switzerland, had strong negative correlations on both factors, and was prototypical of the consensus group. The United States was found to be strongly positive on the first dimension, and strongly negative on the second, and became the prototype of a mixed majoritarian-federal category.

Israel was the only country found to be strongly consensual on all variables of the first dimension (multiparty, oversized cabinets, low average cabinet life, and multi-issue), "but even more majoritarian or unitary on the second dimension, as a result of its highly centralized government, unicameral legislature, and unwritten constitution."[1] Accordingly, Lijphart made it the prototype of an unexpected consensual-unitary category, although it might just as well have been named the consensual-majoritarian category, or the consensual-centralized category.

Lijphart's findings with regard to Israel bear closer analysis because with suitable amendment and restatement they provide valuable insights into the structural underpinnings of the dominance of the majoritarian elements during the founding period. According to Lijphart's calculations, Israel's majoritarian score on the second factor was much stronger than its consensual score on the first factor. As can be seen from Table 2, Israel had the second-highest majoritarian score of all twenty-two countries on the centralization factor, behind New Zealand *but ahead of the United Kingdom*, the other prototypical majoritarian country. But we can go even further in this direction.

In keeping with its high majoritarian score on the second factor, Israel's score was the lowest of the five countries that were strongly consensual on the first factor, well behind the Netherlands, Switzerland, the Fourth French Republic, and Finland. Moreover, this consensual score may not adequately reflect the Israeli experience. In light of our discussion of the founding period, two variables that contribute significantly to this factor, cabinet size and executive dominance, need to be reexamined.

In Lijphart's analysis the smaller the cabinet size in terms of the number of participating parties, the higher the majoritarian score. Thus, minimal winning (including single-party) cabinets are majoritarian, and oversized cabinets are consensual. Consequently, Ben-Gurion's preference for oversized cabinets that characterized the founding period (and continued for some time after its end) make a major contribution to Israel's relatively high consensual score. Israel, however, may be an exception to this general relationship because, as we demonstrated earlier, during the founding period oversized cabinets were established specifically for the opposite reason: to reinforce majoritarianism. They facilitated the maintenance of a Mapai majority within the cabinet, and effectively deprived the other parties of veto and blackmail potential.

The second variable making a major contribution to Israel's relatively high consensual score on the first factor was a low level of executive dominance as measured in terms of cabinet durability. Long-lasting cabinets were majoritarian, indicating that the legislature was unable to overthrow the executive; conversely, short-lived cabinets were associated with the absence of executive dominance and consensus democracy. For the purposes of calculating cabinet durability, a cabinet was considered to remain the "same" cabinet if its party composition did not change. (A new cabinet formally installed following elections would be regarded as the "same" cabinet, if its party composition remained the same, which means that when the same party is regularly re-elected, average cabinet life turns out to be longer than the period between elections.)

According to Lijphart's calculations, Israel's average cabinet life was at the low end of the scale, (28 months, compared with countries at the top end with between 64 and 102 months). Here, too, familiarity with the historical realities of Israeli coalition politics in the founding period suggests the need for further analysis and some recalculation. Low durability not only may not be evidence of lack of executive dominance but may, in fact, be a central element in the maintenance of executive dominance. Because almost all cabinet resignations were brought about by the resignation of the prime minister, and not by defeat in the Knesset, the reasons for, and the circumstances of, prime ministerial resignations must be examined more closely before it is possible to assess their relation to executive dominance.

Examination reveals three types of prime ministerial resignation: disciplinary resignation—used by the prime minister as an effective and powerful measure of cabinet control enabling him to bring coalition partners back into line; constructive resignation—when the prime minister was able to create or utilize opportunities to enlarge the cabinet; and personal resignation—the resignation of the prime minister for personal reasons. All of these were generally followed by reconstitution of the same cabinet, or of most of it. *On only one occasion did a cabinet fall as a result of being defeated in parliament.* Even that was not the result of a formal motion of no confidence but, rather, of the government's announcement before a particular vote that it would resign if defeated.

If such realities are taken into account, the defeat or resignation of governments ceases to be an adequate measure of executive dominance, that is, the degree of cabinet control over the legislature and, conversely, of the legislature's capacity to limit or restrain the executive, which clearly is an indication of consensus democracy.

Although it goes part of the way in recognizing these realities, measuring cabinet durability in terms of the precise party composition of the cabinet does not go far enough, and may distort the picture somewhat. It recognizes, on the one hand, that not all governmental defeats or resignations are qualitatively equivalent, and that the reconstitution of the cabinet along precisely the same party lines does not indicate a loss in durability. This is borne out by the figures. Lijphart's calculations indicating an average cabinet life of twenty-eight months relate to the period 1949-77, but if we ignore party composition completely and measure cabinet durability by all governmental resignations, the average cabinet life for the same period was about seventeen months. Similarly, for the period 1949-65, cabinet durability by Lijphart's criteria was about twenty-six months, but if we ignore party composition, average cabinet life was about sixteen months.

Making changes in party composition the measure of cabinet durability does not, on the other hand, go far enough because it does not distinguish between major and minor changes in cabinet composition. The removal of Mapai from the coalition would carry the same weight as the removal of a coalition partner with only a few Knesset seats. Consequently, it registers statistically all the minor cabinet reshuffles but does not give any weight to the fact that during the founding period Mapai established and headed every coalition cabinet, occupied the most important ministries, and had an absolute numerical majority within each one. Anthony King's definition of a new government "as one with a substantially altered partisan composition"[2] does succeed in reflecting these realities. From this perspective, Israel had only *one* government between 1949 and 1965; cabinet durability, therefore, was sixteen years, and the effective degree of executive dominance was much stronger than indicated by Lijphart's measures.

In sum, taking account of the strongly majoritarian impact of oversized cabinets and the greater degree of effective executive dominance would clearly lower Israel's consensus score on Lijphart's first factor for the founding period, and further substantiate the argument that the balance between the majoritarian and consensus elements in Israel during the founding period was weighted heavily in the majoritarian direction.

A number of more general comparative and theoretical conclusions follow from our analysis of the Israeli case. One relates to the limitations by other parties over the leading government party in majoritarian compared with consensus democracies. It suggests that cabinet type alone (minimal winning versus oversized) does not provide a sufficient basis for the conceptualization and measurement of the extent to which majority power is restrained and limited. Although generally the presence of coalition partners limits the power of the party forming the coalition to act as if it were a single-party government, (and the greater the number of partners and the larger the coalition, the greater the limitation), the empirical example of Israel suggests the need to take into consideration not only the size of the coalition but also the relative size of the other coalition partners. Clearly, under certain conditions, as we demonstrated, oversized cabinets can be majoritarian instruments.

The measurement of executive dominance also bears further examination. Conceptually, it relates to the relative power of the executive and the legislature, and the capacity of the cabinet to control the parliament. (This, of course, depends upon their party composition, most notably, as in the case of majority control of both by the same party.) It is evident, however, that the problem is not only that the three measures of cabinet durability examined—number of governments, number of party changes, and substantially altered partisan composition—produced different results but that cabinet durability by any measure is not alone a satisfactory measure of executive dominance.

The lack of cabinet durability can serve as a satisfactory negative test if it unequivocally indicates legislative control of the cabinet, such as the legislature's ability to force the government to resign or change its composition. Passing the test—the absence of such legislative ability—does not, however, necessarily indicate the existence of executive dominance. What is needed is a measure that reflects effective executive dominance: the capacity to control the process of policy-making, that is, the cabinet's ability to make policies and have them adopted by the legislature.

One such pattern of effective executive dominance is that of single-party majority government in a parliamentary system that is not limited or restrained by either coalition partners or legislative opposition. Such executive dominance will be reinforced by a strong pattern of party government, but it can also exist without it, and the extent to which it rests upon party government is a separate question to be investigated empirically. Thus, even in dominant single-party cabinets, ministers may be more or less independent of party institutions and policies. But the case of Israel in the founding period indicates that a high level of executive dominance (including policy control) and a considerable degree of party government were operative even with coalition governments and in the absence of a single-party legislative majority. The challenge for comparative scholars is to develop a measure of effective executive dominance that includes policy control, even in the face of coalition government, and what on the surface appears to be a low level of cabinet durability.

Finally, the relationship between policy control and centralization bears further analysis because executive policy control is itself a form of centralization. Lijphart, however, relates centralization to governmental structure: a unitary system is centralized, whereas a federal system is decentralized. Hence, by definition, a decentralized federal system with a balanced legislative–executive relationship does not permit executive dominance or centralized control of policy. By the same token, although the centralization of governmental structure is a precondition for, and may reinforce, centralized executive control of policy, it does not guarantee it if the executive itself is internally divided. One must not make the error of assuming that because Israel scored extremely high on structural centralization as measured by the proportion of tax receipts collected by the central government, both before and after the founding period, this reflected or implied centralized executive control of policy. To the contrary. This was true, as we saw, of the founding period, but subsequently, the continuing high level of structural centralization was accompanied by a steadily declining capacity for centralized executive policy control as the consensus elements came to the fore.

The implications of this for the study of comparative democratic political structures are twofold. The first is to separate executive policy control from executive dominance as an independent variable, and to seek ways of measuring it. The second is that it reinforces what is implicit in Lijphart's analysis: majoritarianism and centralization are two separate principles that are joined in various combinations to produce four rather than two patterns of democratic government. Thus, by our calculations, if Israel was closer to the majoritarian-centralized pattern during the founding period, it subsequently became closer to the consensual-centralized pattern.

Plainly, the dominance of the majoritarian elements during the founding period was not a structural imperative (as it is in the Westminster model, for example). It stemmed, rather, in no small measure from the combined impact upon these structures of Ben-Gurion's leadership and Mapai's pattern of party government, under what in retrospect turned out to be relatively favorable political and social conditions.

Ben-Gurion and the Founding Period

There can be no doubt, as has been abundantly obvious time and again throughout the book, that Israeli politics during the founding period was uniquely molded by Ben-Gurion, who had a decisive impact upon the establishment and functioning of the political structures, and upon the content of policies. After his retirement, marked social and political strains developed that the political institutions did not seem able to resolve decisively, or at all. Moreover, the majoritarian political structures became weaker and lost their dominance, which both reflected and added to the decline in the capacity and effectiveness of the political system. Should it be concluded, then, that the political structures and processes established during the founding period were insufficiently institutionalized and weak, and that they were held together only by Ben-Gurion's leadership and were unable to function satisfactorily when he retired? And if this is so, was his leadership style responsible for the weakness of the political structures by depriving them of the opportunity to develop autonomous authority, as is implicitly or explicitly claimed by those critical of his leadership? We shall answer these questions by proposing an analytical framework for understanding Ben-Gurion's political leadership that highlights its democratic and institutional character. As such, it differs radically from all other interpretations of his role in the political system during the founding period.

During the period of the Yishuv and in the early years of the state not only was Ben-Gurion strongly opposed by his political rivals and competitors but, among his party colleagues, he was, by all accounts, at most "first among equals." Only some years after the establishment of the state was the extent of his decisive and authoritative leadership recognized and accepted by the party and the public (and grudgingly admitted by his opponents). Although there is widespread agreement on the authoritativeness and decisiveness of Ben-Gurion's leadership, its evaluation and interpretation remain the subjects of an ongoing historiographical and partisan controversy.

One popular view depicts Ben-Gurion positively, as a charismatic political leader with superior judgment who made a unique historical contribution. Within the broad context of this positive view, his last years—described earlier—are mainly explained in two ways. According to one interpretation, he was forced out by an impatient clique of formerly loyal party and ministerial colleagues, who now rejected him and his values, to ensure that they, and not the group of younger leaders whom he appeared to favor, would succeed him at the head of the state and the party.[3] The other (not entirely contradictory) interpretation of his last years is of self-inflicted damage and decline. General fatigue after many years at the helm led to a personal obsession with the Lavon Affair that affected his leadership capacity. This led him to make uncharacteristic tactical mistakes in his conduct in that affair, and more generally, alienated many of his erstwhile party supporters, diverted his attention from the needs of country and party, and resulted in serious errors of judgment in foreign affairs and personnel matters.[4]

The negative view emanates mainly from his principal political opponents: Herut, Mapam, Ahdut Ha'avodah, and Min Hayesod. Its basic theme is Ben-Gurion's underlying quest for personal power and narrow Mapai partisan advantage, which was carefully camouflaged by grand rhetoric about universal goals, collective values, and the common good. His policies and actions on major issues are attributed to an overriding need to remove all opponents, and to weaken all institutions, forces, parties, and individuals standing in the way of personal aggrandizement and partisan advantage.

Herut, led by Begin, as we had occasion to note, consistently attacked Ben-Gurion as a dictator who did not hesitate to use the armed force of the military and the police to maintain personal and party rule. This later mellowed somewhat, and some Herut leaders openly acknowledged Ben-Gurion's personal contribution to the state, despite his errors and faults.[5] Somewhat more damaging were the criticisms emanating from the Left, in particular those from groups within Mapai or formerly within it, because these appeared to be based upon close personal experience and familiarity with Ben-Gurion, and upon many shared values. Over the years, Mapam and Ahdut Ha'avodah leaders were among his most consistent and outspoken critics.

Ahdut Ha'avodah leader Yizhak Ben-Aharon put it in these words:

> Ben-Gurion's concept of an inclusive party, was a concept of unification, of central rule with unlimited authority, and beneath him the mere semblance of people. . . . With him, it was all or nothing.[6]

Or, as he wrote on a later occasion with regard to Mapai:

> He was determined to create a comprehensive, cohesive political body—but only on the condition that it would serve the realization of his goals. The moment he felt that . . . it was not completely under his control—he split it without hesitation. . . . Ben-Gurion dismantled the Palmah because it was influenced by forces he could not dominate.[7]

So, too, when asked why the split took place in Hakibbutz Hameuhad in 1951 between the supporters of Mapai and Ahdut Ha'avodah, Ben-Aharon replied:

> His aim was to break up Hakibbutz Hameuhad. To break up the only force which had the power to stand up against him and to compete with him for ideological supremacy among Israeli workers. This was the express aim. A calculated and conscious attack to destroy Hakibbutz Hameuhad. If it was impossible to subjugate it, and force it to accept the judgement of Mapai, the judgement of Ben-Gurion—then Hakibbutz Hameuhad had to be broken up.[8]

Similarly, as we noted earlier, during the Lavon Affair of 1960–61, Ben-Gurion was widely criticized as a threat to democracy, an autocrat on the verge of establishing totalitarian rule, from which Israeli democracy had to be saved.

A mélange of such views still exists among some leading contemporary historians. For example, Ben-Gurion's leadership was recently described in terms of his "tendency to unlimited rule, through the deprecation of his internal rivals and their representation as malevolent trouble-makers,"[9] and his "singular ability to identify the good of the people with the success of the institution which he headed,"[10] to the extent that "what was good for Ben-Gurion . . . was good for the state."[11] Ben-Gurion, who is described as "a military commander in the style of Lenin,"[12] sought to build a

> party that was intended to fulfill functions similar to those of a communist party in the peoples' democracies. Ben-Gurion did not deviate from formal-democratic conceptions, to the contrary: nobody was more loyal than he to the parliamentary frameworks, elections and majority rule. But beyond the formal-legalistic aspect of democracy Ben-Gurion faithfully represented the ideas of 'guided democracy'. . . and the Russian revolutionary movement. . . . The open political contest was foreign to his spirit. . . . In his world-view, the individual is insignificant as compared with the all-powerful, all-encompassing state, that molds the image of the citizen, his spiritual world, that controls his acts, and subordinates his particular interests to the 'general will.'[13]

The common thread running through all these interpretations of Ben-Gurion's leadership is its personal and individual character. He is, on the one hand, the visionary, the source of ideological and national values, the goal setter, the charismatic figure. On the other hand, he is the dictator, the autocrat, the totalitarian, the Leninist loyal to Bolshevik conceptions of the relation of party and state[14] who pursued the politics of "all or nothing," ruled by coercion not agreement, ruthlessly removed the individuals who opposed him, and crushed the collective political forces that stood in his way or in that of his party in order to maximize his personal power because "what was good for Ben-Gurion was good for the state." This interpretation not only is totally inconsistent with his understanding and practice of *mamlakhtiut* as we explained it above but also completely misses the central significance of the institutional and democratic character of Ben-Gurion's leadership. Rather than contributing to a weakening of the majoritarian political structures during the founding period, through personal and autocratic leadership, as his critics allege, his institutionalized and democratic leadership style actually strengthened and reinforced their dominance.

The analysis offered here rejects the view that the political structures during the founding period were fundamentally weak, and that any apparent strength derived solely from Ben-Gurion's personal leadership qualities, which meant that the institutions lacked the capacity to survive his retirement. Instead, it attributes their strength and capacity to their institutionalization, to which, manifestly, his leadership style made a significant contribution but was not their source, as was demonstrated in 1965 by his personal failure to defeat Mapai and gain control of the key majoritarian political structures. By the same token, his successors would have been able to maintain the existing institutional pattern had conditions been similar, as, indeed, Eshkol did until 1967, despite the problems of internal party conflict and Ben-Gurion's determined opposition.

However, the fact that social and political conditions changed markedly make it impossible to determine whether failure to maintain the same institutional pattern and governmental capacity after Ben-Gurion's departure from an active leadership role resulted from leadership failure on the part of his successors or from institutional inadequacy in the face of new challenges. There is simply no answer to the question of how previous leaders would have fared under the new conditions because it is entirely hypothetical and conjectural. Still, analysis of Ben-Gurion's leadership during the founding period, is not subject to the same limitations.

Ben-Gurion: A Prototypical Democratic Political Leader

Earlier, we examined Ben-Gurion's tremendous influence and control over policy in many areas. Over the years his formal authority as prime minister and minister of defense was reinforced by his personal, if not charismatic, authority as a party and national leader who was deemed to possess uncommon political vision and judgment—special qualities that had been demonstrated in the most difficult circumstances and vindicated by events. In certain key areas this led to a pattern of decision making in which his personal decision was often unquestionably accepted and final.

This, together with his frequent use of the threat of resignation in support of his views and policies, and the fact that he carried it out on many notable occasions, are often pointed to as evidence of autocratic and dictatorial behavior that imposed his personal will on party and government. In short, he coerced members of the majority into decisions against their better judgment and in opposition to their own considered opinions by exploiting their psychological dependence upon him and their need and desire for his continued leadership, or their inability to do without it. From this standpoint, it is irrelevant that generally those decisions were made democratically by majority vote in formally authoritative national and party bodies after discussion in which opposing opinions were freely expressed because the decisions did not represent the "real" views of the majority. In the last resort Ben-Gurion always found the means to override his colleagues even when he was in the minority, in the extreme case, by the threat of resignation.

Such an interpretation must be assessed in the broader context of an analysis of democratic leadership. At the most general level, the unwillingness to dispense with the services of a successful, skilled, and proven leader that is taken as evidence of psychological dependence, undue influence, and coercion may also constitute evidence of readiness to defer to greater experience and better judgment. As his long-time party colleague and fellow minister Zalman Aranne once put it when asked why he supported Ben-Gurion's proposals even when he disagreed with some of his conceptions, "What do you expect of me? He carries a searchlight and I—a pocket torch." Or as Aranne declared on another occasion, "I believe in Ben-Gurion's intuition more than in my own opinion."[15] Similarly, far from being a manifestation of coercion and dictatorship, the threat of resignation, as we explain later, can constitute an important element of responsible and democratic leadership.

In earlier chapters, we noted how Ben-Gurion generally ensured cabinet approval by first mobilizing the united support of fellow Mapai ministers for his key policy proposals. Rather than impose his views in such policy discussions, Ben-Gurion, it seems, was mindful of his influence over his colleagues and therefore often adopted decision-making methods that would enable them to give free rein to their opinions without feeling constrained by his views. According to Bar-Zohar, when Ben-Gurion had clear and firm policy views and was determined to have them passed, he would raise his suggestion at the beginning of a meeting and recommend its acceptance. This usually was sufficient to have the matter decided in accordance with his views, although as we shall see, this did not always work, and how he reacted on such occasions provides an important insight into the character of his leadership.

But when Ben-Gurion was not firmly in favor of a particular proposal, or was not certain in his own mind, or wanted to offer a suggestion but was not committed to its acceptance, he would place it before his colleagues without expressing his own opinion, would listen to the discussion, and would finally sum up, often in a manner that contradicted the original proposal. Moreover, these final decisions were usually preceded by extensive consultation with relevant ministers, civil service officials, military staff, party colleagues, and personal advisers.[16]

The overall pattern, therefore, seems to be one of formal and substantive democratic decision making more than one of imposition, coercion, autocracy, and dictatorship. As Golda Meir put it in 1971, "You made it easier for your colleagues in this, not that they opposed you and accepted your opinion in contradiction to their own opinion, but you made it easier for them to make a decision together with you. In short, Ben-Gurion, it was easier to decide on critical issues when it was together with you."[17] This is further borne out by an analysis of his behavior when he was faced with opposition or was defeated on a vote.

Political Leadership and Political Responsibility

In his analysis of political leadership, Max Weber distinguished between "the directing mind," the "moving spirit" of the political leader, and the "civil-service mentality of the official." According to Weber:

> The difference lies rather in the kind of *responsibility*, and this does indeed determine the different demands addressed to both kinds of positions. An official who receives a directive which he considers wrong can and is supposed to object to it. If his superior insists on its execution, it is his duty and even his honor to carry it out as if it corresponded to his innermost conviction, and to demonstrate in this fashion that his sense of duty stands above his personal preference. . . . This is the ethos of *office*. A political leader acting in this way would deserve contempt. He will often be compelled to make compromises, that means, to sacrifice the less important to the more important. If he does not succeed in demanding of his master, be he a monarch or the people: "You

either give me now the authorization I want from you, or I will resign," he is
. . . not a leader. "To be above parties"—in truth, to remain outside the realm
of the struggle for power—is the official's role, while this struggle for personal
power, and the resulting personal responsibility, is the lifeblood of the politician.[18]

There can be no better example of the Weberian political leader than Ben-
Gurion. His political career was guided by the principle of seeking the authorization that conferred political responsibility and enabled him to act. Before the
establishment of the state, the party was his "master"; afterward, he sought
authorization from the people. The party became the instrument for gaining
and maintaining political power within the state, and was therefore vital in
supporting this type of political leadership. But it was not the "master" and no
longer provided ultimate authorization. *Mamlakhtiut*, as we have seen, defined
the boundaries of this view of political leadership and underpinned it ideologically by insisting that only the separation of neutral state institutions from
partisan party bodies permitted the clear delineation of political responsibility.

In democratic regimes, personal political responsibility may conflict directly with majority decisions, and Israel is no exception. In such cases, Weber
points out, the political leader struggles to have his point of view accepted, to
receive majority authorization for his policies, but is expected to resign if he
fails. One does not know whether Ben-Gurion had read Weber, but he acted in
accordance with this principle. This does not mean that Ben-Gurion resigned
or threatened to resign every time he faced opposition to his policies. To the
contrary, over the years he brought many proposals to the cabinet that were
defeated. In some cases, he accepted majority decisions rejecting the course of
action that he proposed, and dropped the issue. To avoid such difficulties,
however, and to be assured of a majority, he would often, as described earlier,
discuss policies with Mapai ministers before cabinet meetings so as to reach an
agreed-upon and binding policy position. On other occasions, he successfully
reversed initially negative decisions by mobilizing majority support in favor of
his preferred policy among cabinet colleagues and in party bodies. This occurred, for example, on a number of occasions in 1955-56 with regard to
reprisal raids against terrorist incursions, and in the debate over the workers'
flag and hymn in the state educational system.

Ben-Gurion consistently refused, however, to be bound by majority cabinet
decisions to carry out or implement actions that he opposed but for which he,
as prime minister or defense minister, would bear personal political responsibility. His willingness to resign under such conditions rather than carry personal political responsibility for the decisions of others was a central element in
his style of political leadership.

Similarly, Ben-Gurion indicated a readiness to resign if the Provisional
Government insisted on interposing Yisrael Galili between him as minister of
defense and the chief of the General Staff, and again if Sharett had refused to
step down as foreign minister in 1956, in both instances thereby reinforcing the
principle of personal political responsibility. So too in 1960, when the cabinet

approved the findings of the ministerial committee of seven that exonerated Lavon, Ben-Gurion resigned rather than accept responsibility for the cabinet's decision, which in effect had rejected his view that such matters should be dealt with judicially and not politically.

Resignation, moreover, is not the weapon of the autocrat or the dictator, or of the political leader who identifies the good of the state with his own personal power. "Either-or," "all or nothing," and resignation are manifestations of the Weberian concept of political responsibility. When the political leader can neither compromise nor be persuaded to change his mind, he has reached the point where he must seek authorization for his point of view and must say "either-or." Under such conditions, the weapon of resignation is the ultimate exercise of democratic political responsibility.

As we saw previously, when faced with hostile majorities, Ben-Gurion often found it necessary and convenient to seek to influence and persuade the party and government to adopt and follow the policies that he proposed or favored. This involved complex processes of ideological attitude change and institutional policy change. Such a role was not foreign at all to Ben-Gurion; neither was it the outcome of mere necessity. To the contrary, it grew out of another key element of his democratic leadership: its transformative aspect, the success of which depended upon the capacity for education, exhortation, and persuasion.

Transformative Leadership

The second key aspect of Ben-Gurion's democratic leadership was its transformative character,[19] and it is significant that he did not employ the weapon of resignation in his attempts to transform society and polity. Transformative leaders set goals for the society and justify them in terms of ideological values shared by followers. Although transformative leadership shares certain characteristics with revolutionary leadership, and like it may have a dramatic or radical impact upon the society, transformative leadership differs fundamentally. Its characteristic tendency is to create its own structures, to innovate, develop, test, and refine values by way of actual experience rather than seek to smash existing institutions according to a rigid, preconceived ideological scheme. It tends to be evolutionary and incremental, to add to or redirect existing structures rather than destroy them.

Transformative leadership aims consciously to supply society with its "directing mind" and its "guiding spirit." It has a clear notion of the ultimate ends of social and political action, sets intermediate goals, and confers legitimacy upon means and intermediate activities. It gives politics a clear sense of direction, of movement from one historical stage to another. It seeks to mobilize the whole society or large sections of it to assist in the process of transformation, for without such assistance, failure is inevitable. Transformative leadership may thus come to symbolize or characterize a whole period or era.

In direct contrast with charismatic leadership, which is based upon belief in the individual leader as an individual because he is recognized as having special powers—the gift of grace—transformative leadership rests upon shared commitments to values and ends that stand outside and above the qualities of the individual leaders. Leaders are accepted because they represent these values, and not vice versa.

Ben-Gurion's leadership exemplified transformative qualities. During the period of the Yishuv, the regnant collective pioneering values of *Haluziut* focused upon the creation of a new Jewish society through the transformation of individuals and the establishment of new structures. To these Ben-Gurion added the political transformation from "class to nation." After the state was declared, his major emphasis was on the effort to transform society in accord with what he perceived to be the needs and demands of statehood, including the adaptation of the Yishuv structures and processes to the new conditions. Its ideological expression was *mamlakhtiut*, which was at core a theory of social and political transformation.

Throughout the founding period, Ben-Gurion's conception of the leadership role was to set these transformative goals for the society, to go out ahead of the people, to show them the way, to educate by speech and by example in the expectation that they would follow. This included not only the general values of *mamlakhtiut* but also the more specific goals that he consistently stated: the ingathering of the exiles, the integration of the migrants, military security, political independence, economic development, the settlement of the land, and population dispersion. Far from being intensely personal, autocratic, or totalitarian, as is alleged by his critics, Ben-Gurion's leadership in fact depended upon, and derived from, its anchoring in a democratic institutional base, without which it ultimately foundered.

Democratic Institutional Leadership

Formally, all democratic decisions are made by a majority, be it of the cabinet, the parliament, or the people. Hence, democratic polities need procedures and institutions that faciitate majority decision. Majority decision is not mere formality but the culmination of the process of discussion and debate that expresses the democratic commitment to act according to popular will, and to maximize agreement.

Transformative leadership is a special type of democratic leadership and complements it. Both depend upon the support of popular will, and both are involved in its development and formulation. Whereas democratic leadership may be satisfied by the discovery of the popular will that is to be followed, transformative leadership actively seeks to create, define, shape, change, and mobilize that will by education, exhortation, persuasion, and example. In the last resort, however, both are dependent upon institutional rather than personal sources of support.

Within institutions, belief and confidence in the personal qualities and capacity of leaders may be significant in influencing others: in generating support, in persuasion, and in the securing of agreement. But this is only one of a variety of factors that are relevant to institutionalized decision-making processes. When all is said and done, democratic leaders can receive the authorization they seek only by generating agreement and support within specific authoritative institutions, expressed in majority decisions in which the sources of, and motives for, that support are to a large degree irrelevant to the substance of the decision. Thus, in democratic institutions support for charismatic leadership cannot be expressed directly but must be channeled through institutionalized processes aimed at the generation of majority support, and to that extent it loses much of its charismatic quality.

Ben-Gurion's pattern of leadership fits clearly in the democratic institutional mold. Over the years, he developed considerable personal authority within the state and the party. It was based upon his successful and effective performance in dealing with the problems associated with the establishment, defense, and consolidation of the new state, and conferred considerable advantages upon him in the fulfillment of his leadership role. But the most striking thing about his personal authority was the lengths that he went to *not* to base his leadership upon his personal authority, and to set it within a democratic institutional framework.

We encountered this earlier in regard to his approach to decision making. Another striking example was his decision to resign in 1953 and to retire to a kibbutz in the Negev, a key element being, as he wrote to the president, his desire to demonstrate that in democratic regimes no single leader was irreplaceable or indispensable. But perhaps even more significant was the way in which he consistently based his leadership upon decisions made within the relevant institutions, and upon the mobilization of majority support within them. This is evident in his decision to make collective responsibility for majority decisions the determining principle of coalition operation. The various institutional practices associated with the doctrine of the primacy of party enabled him to mobilize the support of a majority of Mapai ministers, anchored in the decisions of the authoritative Mapai party bodies.

When faced with majority decisions against him in cabinet or in party bodies, Ben-Gurion, as we have noted, reacted in a number of ways, depending on the circumstances. But both acceptance of a majority decision against his views, and action to change the decision by gaining a majority among Mapai ministers or the relevant party body are examples of democratic institutional leadership rather than of personal, autocratic rule.

Ben-Gurion's exercise of democratic institutional authority, not personal or autocratic rule, is further adumbrated in his relations with the party. The party apparatus was not appointed by him, although he had considerable influence over some of the appointments to the major positions, but even this was in conjunction with other party leaders. He could, and sometimes did, secure the appointment of some individuals to the party's Knesset team and to the ministry, but in both cases there were clear limits to his influence. Being able to nominate some individuals is very different from being able to nominate whomsoever one wanted or the whole list.

In nominating matters, Ben-Gurion was limited by internal party constraints to the extent that he was not always able to place his own nominees in the cabinet, and often had to bow to the wishes of the party and accept other candidates. If this was so in appointments close to him, it was even more so in those that were at a remove. In fact, there was a clear division of function between persons who dealt with high matters of state and those who looked after the party, who supported his general policies for the state and society but kept him somewhat at arm's distance where it affected their internal party interests. When they eventually found themselves at loggerheads, Ben-Gurion was unable to control those who held sway in the party machine and the alliance between them was shattered. Some put their commitment to the values and policies that he espoused above their internal party interests and supported him; others did the opposite and opposed him.

The party therefore was not an extension of personal rule by Ben-Gurion, loyal to him, at his beck and call, and waiting to do his bidding. It was available to be used to support and promote his policies, provided that he could mobilize it and win its support. But it had considerable autonomy, and to the extent that he could not mobilize the party, it acted as a powerful counterweight to his authority. Once mobilized, however, it provided strong backing for his pattern of democratic and responsible institutional leadership.

For Ben-Gurion's critics, as we mentioned earlier, the ideology and practices of his personal and autocratic rule within a framework of *mamlakhtiut* produced etatism, in which the state took precedence over, replaced, and suppressed all individual and collective voluntary activity, but its ultimate expression was personal: "What was good for Ben-Gurion was good for the state," which was in imminent danger of "rule by a single leader." If our analysis of Ben-Gurion's leadership behavior is correct, the contrary is in fact the case: the values and institutional manifestations of *mamlakhtiut* reinforced and complemented Ben-Gurion's democratic institutional leadership.

To return to the question with which we began this section, namely, the relationship between Ben-Gurion's leadership style and behavior and the strength of the political structures in the founding period, our analysis suggests that Ben-Gurion's leadership behavior contributed to their institutionalization rather than being the source of weakness that could not survive his retirement. Similarly, although Ben-Gurion's acknowledged leadership of the state strengthened Mapai as a party both internally and externally, in many important ways his leadership was dependent upon Mapai's institutional and organizational strength. To round off the explanation of the strength and capacity of the political structures of Israeli democracy during the founding period and their subsequent decline, we must take account of the organizational strength and dominant role of political parties in general, and of Mapai in particular.

The Role of Parties and the Power and Leadership of Mapai

The dominant role of political parties in the political system in the founding period was reflected in, and made possible by, a very high level of party recruitment and membership. More than one-third of the population belonged to political parties, and the ratio of members to voters in elections was therefore high. (In the case of Mapai, for example, the ratio in Knesset elections ranged from 1:1.8 to 1:2.5.[20]) The larger parties, and Mapai in particular, were highly aggregative in their recruitment, leading to considerable internal diversity based upon socioeconomic status, occupation, ethnic origin, religious belief, age, and sex.

The broad aggregative nature of the party was given formal expression in internal party organization, on the one hand, and reflected in policy outcomes, on the other. It was complemented by Mapai penetration and control of the organizational bodies of these groups, which enabled it to channel and temper their demands, to coordinate them with one another, and with party policy and government priorities.

In keeping with this high level of political mobilization, parties played a major role in forming the pattern of public opinion, and voters responded to the views of the parties and their leaders in setting the political agenda and determining their stance upon the issues. On most of the important issues, policy differences were quite clear, and by and large were between parties, not within them. Voting patterns during most of the founding period therefore tended to be relatively stable, with a low floating vote, and switching mainly between parties within the same camp rather than across political camps. (Some of the latter occurred, but the movements seem to have offset one another.) Although there are no firm empirical data to support it, the most widely credited assumption is that until the 1960s there was a high degree of correspondence between party policies and voter attitudes, and the distribution of opinion broadly followed party divisions.

Toward the middle of the 1960s, the identity of views between parties and voters declined to such an extent that according to Arian "there was little evidence of . . . correspondence between party affiliation and party ideological position."[21] The supporters of left parties in general, and Mapai supporters in particular, tended to be to the right of party leaders and official party platforms, that is more concentrated in the center, whereas Liberal supporters were to the right of their leaders and party policies, which were closer to the center. (Only in the case of Herut was there high correspondence between voters' and party positions.) This is indicative of a slow major value transformation that began during the last part of the founding period and continued to gather strength, bursting through with dramatic effect upon the structure and distribution of voting support in 1977.

The relatively minor impact of the change in voter attitudes on support for parties and party camps during the founding period meant that in the six elections between 1949 and 1965 the parties of the noncommunist Left regularly enjoyed an absolute majority in the Knesset, which was even greater if the Arab lists affiliated to Mapai are added. (The exception occurred in 1955, when they fell one seat short of an absolute majority, with fifty-nine seats.) This distribution of opinion and voting support underpinned and reinforced the impact of Mapai's consistent electoral plurality. It was by far not only the largest single party but also the major party (averaging 72 percent) within a camp that enjoyed an absolute majority.

Mapai's policy centrality boosted its electoral plurality considerably. So long as the parties to the left of Mapai in principle vetoed government partnership with the parties to the right of it, no coalition without Mapai was possible. This constituted, as we saw earlier, a dominated party system in which the inescapable result was government headed by Mapai.

In heading all coalition governments during the founding period, Mapai's power did not rest solely upon its position in the Knesset. Its simultaneous control and coordination of all major institutions in the state—the government, the Histadrut, the Jewish Agency, and most local government authorities, including the major municipalities—gave it unique advantages. These provided a firm institutional basis for Mapai's political dominance, and facilitated Ben-Gurion's distinctive style of responsible, democratic, transformative leadership. During the founding period, Mapai, led by Ben-Gurion, was able to set the political agenda, determine national priorities, make the major policy decisions, and mobilize public opinion in support of them. At the same time, it was effective in maintaining a high degree of policy coherence in decision making, and in achieving many of the goals that it set for itself and the state.

Mapai's major values and goals achieved a higher degree of acceptance within the society as a whole than the level of support it achieved in elections. But herein lies a paradox: its success at instilling in Israeli society the general, public, and universal values of *mamlakhtiut* undercut its own partisan, socialist-Zionist and pioneering values, and as a result it lost its ideological distinctiveness.

Although in some instances Mapai acted to instill its own particular socialist-Zionist and pioneering values, as, for example, in their incorporation as major goals of the state education system, and in the integration of new immigrants in moshavim, Mapai's main ideological drive was directed to changing, transforming, and adapting its own values and goals to the needs and constraints of the new situation created by independence and statehood—not to the preservation and maintenance of the values that it had promoted in the Yishuv. In the process, many of the particular and partisan goals with which it had previously been identified were either rejected or subsumed within broader state and national goals.

The popular view has it that Mapai achieved ideological dominance by identifying itself with the state, and by conveying this identification to the public.[22] There were, of course, very close connections between Mapai and the state, and as we have indicated, Mapai was boosted by being perceived as having made the major contribution to the establishment, defense, and development of the state. But the assertion that Mapai identified itself with the state does not take proper account of the fundamental distinction between state and party that lay at the core of the values of *mamlakhtiut*, which guided Mapai in this regard.

Mapai did not seek to base its claim to power upon an ideology that identified Mapai with the state, or upon the credo "that what was good for Mapai was good for the state." On the contrary, Mapai felt it acted according to the credo "that what was good for the state was good for Mapai." Mapai, led by Ben-Gurion, regarded the state as the collective embodiment of Zionist national and social aspirations. However significant their functions, the state took precedence over all partial and partisan organizations and institutions, including the labor movement and political parties. Mapai conceived its role in terms of the political responsibility that had been conferred upon it by elections; it was to lead the state and all other major institutional frameworks on behalf of all citizens, and not just on behalf of its own members and supporters. Mapai was not the state, but it acted on behalf of the state.

Nor did Mapai seek to portray itself as the "state party." Rather, as was most prominent in its electioneering, it presented itself and its leaders as having played the decisive role in the establishment of the state, in its successful defense, and subsequently in all major social, economic, and political institutions and policies for which it had been given the political responsibility. Initial successes reinforced by continuing public response to assertions of demonstrated effectiveness reinforced the sense of leadership of, and responsibility for, the state that most accurately characterizes Mapai's own views of its relations with the state. These are clearly evident in its approach to party government.

Party government as institutionalized by Mapai enabled it to develop to the full the majoritarian and centralizing elements of the political structures. The doctrines and practices of the primacy of party facilitated the determination of party policy, and enhanced the capacity of Mapai ministers to act as a united group in the promotion of party policy within state institutions. Their application was posited upon acceptance of the ultimate precedence of state authority, and it was most effective where ministers deferred to them in policy determination and coordination, and in conflict resolution. Moreover, they were a necessary precondition for efficient coalition functioning, and collective responsibility. Thus, despite coalition conditions, the practices of the primacy of party underpinned a pattern of party government that significantly enhanced the system's majoritarian and centralizing elements, and, in effect, the power and authority of the political structures of the state.

This pattern of party government also pervaded the other main institutional structures of the society: municipal government, the Histadrut, the individual trade unions, the Jewish Agency. Political and electoral competition within them was between the political parties that competed in Knesset elections. In each of these institutional frameworks, the party representatives were directed and coordinated by central and local party bodies, and reproduced the main outlines of party government as practiced in the national government.

Mapai's simultaneous leadership and control of all these bodies promoted policy integration and institutional coordination, which facilitated the national policy-making through Mapai's capacity to bring into line potentially conflicting elements, such as the Histadrut. On the other hand, it often introduced extraneous national considerations into electoral and political competition in these institutions, such as defense policies in Histadrut or municipal elections.

The Weakness of Nonparty Groups
and the Substance of Democracy

Our analysis has emphasized the central and directive role of the political parties in the political process during the founding period. Conversely, other groups and processes situated between government and individual citizen lacked autonomy, were weak, or were simply nonexistent, and this had a significant impact upon the character and substance of Israeli democracy in the founding period.

Perhaps the most direct and powerful effect was upon interest representation and the various groups that sought to promote and protect interests and influence policy. By far the largest and most powerful of these was the Histadrut, which, because of its inclusiveness, encountered problems of role and interest definition, internal organization and discipline, and external effectiveness. Thus, it simultaneously sought to represent workers in general and particular groups of workers, which inevitably aroused internal disagreements and brought out declarations by one group or another that it was disadvantaged. Similarly, the interests of industrial labor and of agriculture were not clearly separated because the Histadrut also included agricultural workers, and collective and cooperative agricultural producers within its ranks. What is more, it ran a vast network of industrial enterprises, which obliged it to take account of the interests of capital.

Under such conditions it was almost impossible to give adequate voice and representation to the specific needs of the disparate interests included within the Histadrut. The solution adopted was centralization. Within the Histadrut, industrial, craft, local, and national unions, and local labor councils were all relatively weak. So, too, were the representatives of Histadrut agricultural and industrial capital. The central executive bodies and departments in Tel Aviv made and administered overall national policies. Yet however centralized and powerful it was, as an organization of workers, it had little autonomy. These arrangements worked effectively only so long as it was controlled and directed by a single political party, Mapai.

The major collective and cooperative agricultural movements—the kibbutzim and moshavim—not only were part of the Histadrut network but were each also closely identified with a political party. The larger private agricultural producers were connected to the parties of the right and enjoyed a greater degree of autonomy but were relatively weak when compared with the combined weight of the Histadrut agriculture sector. Private industry, too, was relatively weak during the founding period, as was clear from wage negotiations in which the Manufacturers Association was often effectively represented by the Ministry of Finance.

The net result of this lack of autonomy was that during the founding period, groups that sought to promote the interests of their members needed close connections with, or to be incorporated into, political parties, and groups that lacked such relationships took steps to be formally included under a party umbrella. Economic groups were not the only ones that followed this pattern.

The major religious institutions were closely allied to political parties, and in many cases controlled by them. Sex, ethnicity, and age all formed the bases of group organization, but in almost all cases the major organizations were closely integrated into a political party. Consumers' groups, and public interest groups hardly existed.

Nor were the mass media an independent factor for most of the founding period. Television did not exist. Radio was directly administered by the government through the Prime Minister's office until an independent semigovernmental authority was established in 1965; there were no commercial radio stations. Even if news reporting fairly and accurately represented the events and issues with which the media dealt, competing news sources, independent and critical reporting, and incentives to "discover" news rather than report what was on the surface were not a structural feature of the system.

During this period, the radio acted as the government's official spokesman, conveying only what it wished to make public, which clearly meant a high degree of news management, particularly in security matters and foreign affairs but also in avoidance of controversial social issues, and in the banning of certain politicians from the air waves. Overall the radio was regarded as an educational instrument, serving the purposes of nation-building and national integration. Significantly, in light of the foregoing discussion of *mamlakhtiut* and Ben-Gurion's leadership style, Ben-Gurion, whose office administered and controlled the radio, almost never intervened personally in deciding what should or should not be broadcast. Nor, it seems, was the radio used to promote Mapai's partisan interests. In fact, "the Prime Minister's office in charge of the radio was more concerned with using this powerful instrument to reinforce statehood than partisan interests." [23]

The only area in which there was some built-in independence and autonomy was that of the press. Although each party published its own newspaper that featured its own views, there were a number of privately owned newspapers. These sought to adopt a more independent and critical stance regarding the government and the major parties, although at various times they were more or less identified with particular parties or points of view.

A noteworthy breakthrough in the direction of independence and autonomy occurred during the Lavon Affair of 1960, when the independent press was active in bringing the issues before the public and in shaping public opinion. The fact that these papers took different points of view and supported different key personalities heightened their independent and critical impact. Interestingly, in this case, party discipline and self-control broke down; large-scale leaks and disclosure of information brought matters previously not the subject of public discussion into the open. Subsequently both the media and public opinion regularly played a more autonomous role in Israeli politics. Nevertheless, the media were subject to formal legal limitations that raised fundamental questions about the practice and institutionalization of democratic values of liberty and equality during the founding period. And in particular, the capacity of individual citizens to realize democratic rights, on the one hand, and citizen protection against infringement of such rights by the state, on the other.

The Israeli government possessed (and still possesses) very wide emergency powers inherited in the main from the British Mandate, including powers of censorship, restriction of movement, detention, deportation and closed areas. Yet according to one analysis,[24] the emergency powers did not affect the normal functioning of government or of the Knesset, which, in any event, has the power to change the emergency laws, which are subject to limited review by the courts as well. Moreover, the actual application of the emergency powers fell far short of what could be done legally, with some not utilized and others moderated by administrative self-restraint, so that over the years the balance between security considerations and the regular processes of law and justice tipped more in the direction of the latter.

Throughout the period the most widely applied restrictions were the censorship provisions, which form the legal basis for control of the media. Although these represent a serious potential threat to freedom of speech and freedom of information, they were applied mainly in cases of sensitive security matters. What is more, their application was cushioned by voluntary consultative arrangements between the media, the military, and the public.

The emergency powers provided the legal basis for the regulations in force between 1948 and 1966, which established military government over the areas in which most of the Arab citizens of Israel lived. They reflected both aspects of the issue. On the one hand, because of the security situation, Arab citizens were deprived of some fundamental political and social rights and liberties, and were subjected to close administrative control that facilitated political manipulation by the government and the parties. On the other hand, the removal of the restrictions is a good example of the process described above, of a balance tipping steadily in the direction of justice and rights and less reliance on security considerations. In the final analysis, "considering the amount of discretion available, and the absence of firm institutional obstacles in a system without a written constitution or Bill of Rights, the use of emergency powers in Israel has been modest."[25]

Overall, then, in all the various spheres, the trend during the founding period was in the direction of greater democratization. Political competition was heightened, various social groups became more autonomous, the media became less controlled, the judiciary slowly undertook a more active role in protecting rights and liberties, major applications of the emergency regulations were repealed, and remaining pockets of politicization in the civil service, military, and security services either disappeared completely or shrunk considerably.

The End of the Founding Period

Nothing more poignantly symbolized the end of the founding period than the events surrounding the 1967 War. The government, led by Mapai with Levi Eshkol as prime minister, literally could not make up its mind what to do. Increasing pressure from coalition members, political opponents, the General

Staff, and public opinion demanded that the government act. Public morale fell alarmingly. Menachem Begin, at the head of Gahal, proposed no less than the return of Ben-Gurion as prime minister.

Mapai's incapacity to act decisively led to its loss of control over the coalition and the process of coalition formation, and it was effectively dictated to by the other parties. A dominated party system no longer existed, as indicated by the fact that for the first time Mapai was forced to give up the portfolio of minister of defense. Amid mounting media pressure and public demonstrations, Mapai's partners and rivals, and some leading party members demanded the appointment of Moshe Dayan, the architect of the successful 1956 Sinai Campaign but now a Rafi leader, as minister of defense. A last-ditch attempt by Mapai stalwarts to bring about the appointment of Ahdut Ha'avodah minister Yigal Allon was thwarted by the pressure, and in the event Mapai was obliged to accept Dayan.

But this was not all. Dayan made his acceptance conditional upon Mapai's agreement to a radical departure from customary Israeli coalition practice: formation of a national unity government that included Gahal, and Begin as a minister without portfolio. Such dramatic events not only indicated clearly that a Mapai-dominanted party system no longer existed but that the founding period of Israeli democracy was also over, as a result of significant changes in political and social conditions that had been slowly gathering strength since the early 1960s. These disturbed the previous balance of political forces and this, in turn, undid the pattern of democratic government that characterized the founding period. As if to underline the fundamental nature of the shift in the balance of political forces, within one week the Israeli army stood on the banks of the Jordan River, and in control of all the territory between it and the 1949 armistice lines.

The first significant change was electoral restructuring, which by the end of the founding period caused the loss by the parties of the noncommunist Left (Mapai, Mapam, Ahdut Ha'avodah, and later Rafi) of their long standing absolute majority in the Knesset.[26] Thus, in 1969, although the joint Alignment list of Labor and Mapam was still more than twice as large as Gahal, it received only fifty-six seats. Subsequently, the loss accelerated: by 1973 the noncommunist left Alignment bloc was less than one-third larger than the right (Likud) bloc. By 1977 it was over one-third smaller.

The second significant change concerned policy and ideology. Following its joint list with Ahdut Ha'avodah and the split with Rafi in 1965, Mapai began to lose political and ideological centrality. The process was further accentuated by the 1969 Alignment with Mapam, which was further to the left. Whereas previously Mapai had occupied the center of the political spectrum and had two noncommunist parties to its left, after 1969 it headed a single noncommunist left electoral bloc. This placed it further to the left than Mapai had been. (By way of contrast, Gahal on the right was now closer to the center than Herut had been in the past.) As a result, the Alignment was deprived of Mapai's firm control of the center which was now unoccupied and therefore available for capture by the Right. Moreover, Mapai lost its policy centrality, which previously had been based upon its capacity to determine policy preferences that both distinguished it from its major rivals and enjoyed majority support. This was replaced by a new distribution of opinion and policy that produced major policy differences *within* parties. The formation of multiparty blocs, with guaranteed representation for the constituent parties, supplemented by formal and informal vetoes aimed at maintaining their previous separate identities severely reduced the chances of internal policy unity, and created structural obstacles for decisive policy determination.

The changed distribution of opinion and policy resulted in part from the development of new social and economic interests, and political issues, which altered the political agenda. The most obvious and dramatic of the issues stemmed from the outcome of the 1967 War: what should Israel do with the territories and inhabitants that had come under its control? And what should be the borders of the State of Israel? These issues, which had been settled in the past in a status quo that even Herut had seemed to come to terms with, were reopened. But now both major blocs were internally divided over them. The greatest divisions were within the noncommunist left bloc, within which the solutions ranged from unilateral withdrawal to annexation; it was therefore unable to agree upon or formulate a clear and definitive policy preference without jeopardizing recently achieved unity. On the right, Herut's traditional policies seemed to have been finally vindicated, and this set the tone for the bloc, although many of its Liberal partners did not share its enthusiasm for maximalist territorial policies and were closer to the mainstream of the Labor party.

Similarly, on major economic and social questions the Alignment bloc increasingly became internally divided. The Histadrut had lost much of its control over some of the strongest and most strategically situated groups of workers, and consequently its centralizing capacity and authority declined. Furthermore, the needs and interests of Histadrut-industry-as-capital began to make their mark within the Histadrut, and the former began to develop common interests with those of private capital, which as a result of economic growth had become much stronger.

The split in Mapai in 1965; the bitter conflict with Rafi and Ben-Gurion, involving not only the loss of Ben-Gurion's leadership but his relentless opposition to, and criticism of, Mapai and its leaders; Mapai's success in achieving widespread public acceptance of the values of *mamlakhtiut*, on the one hand, and the criticism that Mapai and Labor had regressed and had betrayed these values for narrow partisan and personal advantage, on the other—all further weakened Labor's capacity to control and centralize policy-making, and to determine policy decisively. They also provided fertile ground for the media and public opinion to strengthen and reinforce their own autonomy.

In sum, Mapai and later Labor steadily lost the capacity to set the political agenda and to order national priorities, and no longer appeared to promote and represent national values. Together with a marked decline in party government, these limited the ability to control the processes of coalition formation and operation, as Mapai had done during the founding period. Consequently, the majoritarian elements were severely weakened while the consensus elements were correspondingly being reinforced.

Afterword: Beyond the Founding Period

We began this book with an analysis of relations between polity and society in the Yishuv. We end it with an analysis of relations between polity and society at the end of, and after, the founding period. In the Yishuv, it was argued, politics had primacy, that is to say, political forces were stronger than social forces, and as a result, in the main, society was controlled and directed by them. Put somewhat differently, major aspects of social structure lacked autonomy; rather, they were penetrated and directed by political actors, particularly the parties.

In its essentials this pattern was maintained during the founding period by the parties and the political leaders by means of the new political structures, especially those that promoted the concentration of executive power, executive dominance, party government, and centralization, and in some respects, as we saw, the pattern was even extended to additional areas of social life. At the same time, values were introduced and processes were set in motion, particularly those associated with *mamlakhtiut*, democracy, and with the establishment of central state structures, that limited the extent and legitimacy of direct partisan political control. This strengthened the autonomy of neutral state political structures but did not, at first, increase the autonomy of social forces or greatly alter the direction of relations between the polity and society. It did, however, involve a change in the character and identity of the political structures that controlled and directed the social forces.

After the founding period, the autonomy of social forces increased considerably, amounting to what might be termed the breakthrough of society, bringing with it reduced ability on the part of the political structures to control and direct society. Moreover, despite continued high structural centralization, a considerable loss in governmental capacity has occurred. At the same time, new issues and demands placed on the political agenda by the breakthrough of society and by the extended boundaries of Israeli military control raised serious questions about the maintenance of the democratic values of liberty and equality, and commitment to the rule of law. These questions were exacerbated by serious economic problems, by dependence upon the United States, by the extent of governmental incapacity, and by sheer overload.

One social breakthrough was the continued development and growing influence of competing, independent, and nonparty media sources that operated in the main according to professional journalistic criteria. Legislation put radio and television outside the legitimate spheres of direct party direction and government control, and together with an increasingly independent press they began to take on a significant investigative, evaluative, critical role as watchdog. In important ways they took over some of the functions formerly fulfilled by the Knesset and the opposition parties. Moreover, they became major sources of political information and socialization that competed with and in many ways took the place of the political parties. No longer did the public or party members get their information or political guidance from party-controlled sources, or solely from these. Most significant, even politicians received much of their information from the mass media.

A second breakthrough of social forces resulted from the heightened salience of ethnic origins and religious observance as bases of political organization, sources of demands, and foci of division, all of which intensified political and social conflict. This attests the growing independence, self-reliance, assertiveness, and confidence of two formerly dependent or relatively passive groups in Israeli society: Sephardim and the religiously observant, particularly the ultra-Orthodox. In both cases they sought to correct what they perceived to be an earlier pattern of deprivation and disadvantage, and made more and more demands of an economic, symbolic, and occasionally value nature that were economically costly and could not be met without changes in resource priorities. These new or heightened demands were expressed both in the existence of separate parties and also cut across party lines as the major parties sought to cater to these interests and to meet their needs.

Ethnicity and religion made a major contribution to the restructuring of the party system and the coalition system. The move from majority support for Mapai among the first-generation Sephardi immigrants in the founding period to even greater support for the Likud among their children in the 1970s and 1980s completely altered the relative strengths of the two major party blocs, deprived the Alignment bloc of its previous overwhelming plurality, and left them evenly matched. The size of the respective parties, the balance of power in coalition formation held by the religious parties, and the transfer of their support from the Left to the Right restructured the pattern of coalition government.

The growth and diversification of the economy that contributed to the increased significance of both public and private capital constituted the third breakthrough of social forces. In particular, it strengthened the private sector, including corporations, and individual entrepreneurs in industry, commerce and services, and agriculture. This stimulated the growth of independent professions, and led to the expansion of a managerial and executive stratum, a trend further reinforced by the spread of university education. The result was a new salaried and independent middle class comprising individuals who possessed free-floating resources that conferred a high degree of occupational mobility, and personal autonomy, and for whom political party membership generally provided little economic incentive or advantage.

Not only had the parties and blocs become divided internally on some major issues, but issues that were previously separate now became inextricably intertwined. The NRP, which formerly supported Mapai's position on foreign policy and defense issues came under considerable pressure from militant and activist youth circles, led by Gush Emunim, which promoted a maximalist territorial policy, and spearheaded the movement to settle on the West Bank, often prodding the government to act by establishing a series of illegal and semilegal settlements that later gained *ex post facto* recognition. In adopting an increasingly militant territorial policy, the NRP based its stance in the main on religious beliefs and Scriptural promises, thereby injecting a powerful theological and messianic element into what till then had been primarily a security issue. Eventually, when the NRP and, in fact, the Likud seemed too moderate and accommodating (as at Camp David), the territorial maximalists, both religious and secular, established movements and political parties committed to the continued maintenance of Jewish settlement in the territories.

The direct link of the parties to the settlers further mixed the issues by introducing competition for scarce economic resources between the needs of settlement as a means of maintaining control over the West Bank and all other claims upon the government budget (development towns, health, agriculture, the Negev, social services, education, the roads, and so on), all of which encountered shrinking allocations. And when more militant settlers took the law into their own hands, as in the case of the Jewish underground, the issue became closely entwined with key aspects of the application of the rule of law. Similarly, the whole question of continued Israeli military occupation of the territories and rule over their inhabitants raised a set of fundamental questions about democratic values. These in turn reopened basic questions about the identity of the state (Judaism versus democracy), and about the territory and borders of the state, that had been settled during the founding period.

Significant change also took place in a number of key political organizations and structures. The most obvious has been a marked decline in the significance of party institutions in all major parties, an absolute and relative decrease in party membership, and a contraction of the level of party activity. Party institutions meet less frequently and have far less policy input. Parties also play a less significant role in socialization, goal setting, and providing an identification that locates individuals in society. As a result, former party affiliations and loyalties were loosened, voter volatility increased, and the electorate was destructured. The rapid rise (and fall) of new parties established to give expression to new issues, or in protest against the incapacity of the old parties to meet pressing problems, introduced a further element of instability into the electoral and party systems and heightened fractionalization.

Major changes also took place in the autonomy of interest groups and in the pattern of interest representation, as evidenced by the growth of an interest group system that operates across parties and beyond party control. At the same time, the Histadrut's pattern of centralized organizational control by national executive bodies broke down, and it was confronted by an upsurge of competing, militant workers' committees, which it eventually incorporated at the top, at further cost to direct party control. Moreover, the growth of Histadrut enterprises, some of which are among the country's largest companies in a variety of spheres, and are listed on the stock exchange, sometimes in partnership with other companies, have made it increasingly difficult for the Histadrut to develop a coherent, centralized policy reflecting its interests—

particularly when these companies face liquidation or the mass dismissal of employees. It has thus found it more and more trying, if not impossible, to play the central coordinating and restraining role it played in the founding period.

Collective responsibility broke down except at the very formal level of ministers and their parties not voting against the government in the Knesset. Ministers criticized their colleagues publicly and disagreed with government policy openly. They discussed policies outside their realm of formal responsibility, and even the prime minister was not always immune to criticism. In short, the cabinet as a collective body, barely existed; it became at best a federation of ministries, and at worst it represented the feudalization of collective responsibility, with each minister regarding his ministry as a private fiefdom in which policy was made with little reference to that of his colleagues or the cabinet as a whole. Hence, in the extremely important area of economic policy, for example, gaining support for the budget and producing a coordinated policy generally proved extremely hard to do, if not often impossible, because individual ministers and ministries, and not only those controlled by minor coalition partners, would not agree to budget cuts.

All of this was fertile ground for reinforcing the process of the personalization of politics, decision making, and political conflict. It arose in part from the impact of television upon politics: its need to simplify matters, to apportion instant blame or praise, to identify heroes and villains, and to avoid complex, involved, or lengthy explanation. The rise of investigative reporting further promoted this process. But the main contribution came from the character of the internal leadership contests in both major parties, which reflected personality differences more than policy disagreements. Similarly, in national elections personality contests between the two top leaders assumed such increased prominence that national issues were often overshadowed.

In all these regards, party government, which had played such a central role in maintaining the structural pattern of the founding period, has declined. But, paradoxically, in other respects, party government has been strengthened. In a clear reversal of the policies and practices of depoliticization and *mamlakhtiut* of the founding period, and a return to some of the practices of that period's very earliest days and of the Yishuv, there has been a recrudescence of direct partisan influence in administration in a number of ways. It took the form of open politicization—the replacement of experienced middle-level and upper-level civil servants by unqualified party appointees, often from outside the civil service and lacking professional expertise. It was also apparent in the large increase in the number of personal advisers and personal staff of ministers, who in most cases are outside the civil service framework. Often such appointments were rewards for, or inducements to, support ministers in internal party conflicts. Another manifestation has been the wholesale farming out of public funds to leaders of minor parties by means of coalition agreements; the funds are allocated by them personally, and at their sole discretion, without any universal criteria of allocation or disbursement, and are not subject to public supervision and oversight, even when formally passed by the Knesset Finance Committee and listed in the Budget Bill.

There are two factors that, in the main, account for the recrudescence of direct partisan influence and the decline of *mamlakhtiut*. Because the party system was no longer dominated by a single party, coalition formation became much more difficult. One way of resolving the problems of coalition formation was to resort to minimum winning coalitions, but as a result of the extreme party fractionalization this bestowed considerable veto and blackmail power on a large number of tiny parties. It also reinforced the general loss of government capacity to make policy decisively, referred to earlier. Thus payoffs to coalition partners were demanded and made in highly visible and symbolic areas, and in appointments and budget allocations, which the smaller parties needed to demonstrate to their supporters and constituencies that they were successful in achieving party goals. The second factor stems from allegations by certain small coalition parties of long-standing patterns of ethnic and religious discrimination: here the public, expressive, and symbolic elements are of the essence. The legitimation of demands in terms of broader public interests and the common good gave way to blatant justification in terms of narrow partisan interests or those of a particular constituency.

Subsequently, although the veto and blackmail power of the small parties within the cabinet declined somewhat with the establishment of the grand coalitions in 1984 and 1988 that joined the increasingly diametrically opposed large Likud and Labor blocs, it did not disappear completely. The veto power was a significant element in the agreement to set up such grand coalitions and became even more so after they were formed with the inclusion of the smaller parties; in the event of the breakup of the grand coalitions, both large parties would need the support of the smaller parties to establish and lead a narrow minimum winning coalition. As the possibility of breakup was never far below the surface, the large parties were careful not to offend or alienate the smaller coalition parties they might need in the future, which, of course, had the effect of increasing their veto and blackmail power.

Moreover, apart from one or two major exceptions, these grand coalitions further weakened the government's capacity for coherent and decisive overall policy-making in every sphere. The parity within the cabinet of the two opposing party blocs and their satellites, which was structured and institutionalized in the rules of cabinet operation, produced mutual veto and paralysis at the top and encouraged further feudalization and independent policy-making at the level of individual ministries. In addition, the absence of a strong parliamentary opposition and mounting succession conflict within the Likud led Herut ministers to signficiantly widen and deepen the pattern of politicization and partisan appointment in spheres in which *mamlakhtiut* had previously made considerable strides.

Twenty years after the end of the founding period, both the political structures and the values of Israeli democracy are under severe challenge. Little could be further from the structural pattern of the founding period than the joint Likud-Alignment, mutual-veto, grand-coalition cabinets that were established in 1984 and 1988. And little could be further from the values of Israeli democracy as expressed in the Declaration of Independence than continuing military occupation of, and rule over, the territories and their inhabitants.

Notes

1. Arend Lijphart, *Democracies: Patterns of Majoritarian and Consensus Government in Twenty-One Countries* (New Haven: Yale University Press, 1984), p. 218.

2. Anthony King, "What Do Elections Decide?" in David Butler, Howard R. Penniman, and Austin Ranney, eds., *Democracy at the Polls: A Comparative Study of Competitive National Elections* (Washington, D.C.: American Enterprise Institute, 1981), pp. 293–324, at 299. In a separate article Lijphart compares seven different measures of cabinet durability and their effects, but not that suggested by King. See Arend Lijphart, "Measures of Cabinet Durability: A Conceptual and Empirical Evaluation." *Comparative Political Studies* 17 (1984): 265–79.

3. The sharpest expression of this point of view appears in Hagai Eshed, *Mi natan et hahoraah* (Jerusalem: 'Idanim, 1979), pp. 282–302. It also appears intermittently, but less pointedly, in Michael Bar-Zohar, *Ben-Gurion*, 3 vols. (Tel Aviv: Am Oved, 1975–78), especially pp. 1425–1560.

4. Bar-Zohar, *Ben-Gurion*, places considerable weight on this interpretation. See also Natan Yanai, *Mashberim politiyim beyisrael* (Jerusalem: Keter, 1982), especially pp. 141–51.

5. See, for example, Yohanan Bader, *Haknesset veani* (Jerusalem: 'Idanim, 1979), pp. 144–46.

6. Yizhak Ben-Aharon, interview, *Arkhion Ha'avodah*, no. 114, 15.9.1977, a copy of which is held in the archives of the Oral History Division of the Institute of Contemporary Jewry, The Hebrew University, pp. 149–50.

7. Yizhak Ben-Aharon, "Remembering Ben-Gurion," *Jerusalem Quarterly* 16 (Summer 1980): 41, 44.

8. Ben-Aharon interview, *Arkhion Ha'avodah*, p. 152.

9. Anita Shapira, *Mipiturei harama 'ad piruk hapalmah* (Hakibbutz Hameuchad Publishing House, 1985), p. 9.

10. Ibid., p. 60; in this she echoes Ben-Aharon, who declared that "Ben-Gurion always saw himself as standing at the centre of events, the focus of the world. When he moved from the Histadrut to the Zionist Federation, he took the centre of gravity with him and began to regard the Histadrut and its needs as unimportant." Ben-Aharon, "Remembering Ben-Gurion," p. 42.

11. Shapira, *Mipiturei harama 'ad piruk hapalmah*, p. 64.

12. Ibid., p. 9.

13. Ibid., p. 64.

14. Anita Shapira emphasizes this aspect in another essay, "Ben-Gurion u'Berl: Shenai tipusei manhigut," in Shlomo Avineri, ed., *David Ben-Gurion: demuto shel manhig tn'uat po'alim* (Tel Aviv: Am Oved, 1988), pp. 46–72.

15. Cited in Bar-Zohar, *Ben-Gurion*, p. 1403.

16. Ibid., pp. 1401–4.

17. Meir made the statement at a reunion of colleagues at Sde-Boker on the occasion of Ben-Gurion's eighty-fifth birthday. At the time she was prime minister. It will be recalled that she had been a long-time close colleague of Ben-Gurion; she, Aranne, and Sapir were among his main Mapai opponents during the events of the 1960s. Meir and Ben-Gurion were reconciled after Ben-Gurion's retirement from the Knesset in 1969, to which he had been elected in 1965 on the Rafi ticket. The event was broadcast on Israel Television, which provided a transcript.

18. Max Weber, *Economy and Society*, ed., Guenther Roth (New York: Bedminster Press, 1968), 3:1403–4.

19. I have here adapted James MacGregor Burns's concept of transformational leadership. See James MacGregor Burns, *Leadership* (New York: Harper and Row, 1980).

20. For a discussion and analysis of this and related phenomena, see Itzhak Galnoor, *Steering the Polity: Communication and Politics in Israel* (Beverly Hills, Calif.: Sage Publications, 1982), pp. 165–73.

21. Alan Arian, "Voting and Ideology in Israel," in Moshe Lissak and Emanuel Gutmann, eds., *Political Institutions and Processes in Israel*, (Jerusalem: Academon, 1971), pp. 257–86, at 266.

22. See, for example, Segev, who asserts that "in Mapai there were those who tended to identify their party with the state, and the struggle against its rule as an attack on the state itself." Tom Segev, *1949: hayisraelim harishonim* (Jerusalem: Domino Press, 1984), p. 264.

23. Galnoor, *Steering the Polity*, pp. 218–50. The citation is on p. 247, and is based upon N. Mishal, "The Broadcasting Authority: Political Dynamics" (M.A. thesis, Bar-Ilan University, 1978).

24. Alan Dowty, "The Emergency Powers in Israel: The Devaluation of Crisis," undated manuscript kindly made available to me by the author.

25. Ibid., p. 43.

26. Except for 1955 and 1961, when these parties were one short of a majority with fifty-nine seats.

APPENDIX A

Israel's Declaration of Independence*

The Land of Israel was the birthplace of the Jewish people. Here their spiritual, religious and national identity was formed. Here they achieved independence and created a culture of national and universal significance. Here they wrote and gave the Bible to the world.

Exiled from Palestine, the Jewish people remained faithful to it in all the countries of their dispersion, never ceasing to pray and hope for their return and the restoration of their national freedom.

Impelled by this historic association, Jews strove throughout the centuries to go back to the land of their fathers and regain their Statehood. In recent decades they returned in their masses. They reclaimed the wilderness, revived their language, built cities and villages, and established a vigorous and ever-growing community, with its own economic and cultural life. They sought peace yet were prepared to defend themselves. They brought the blessings of progress to all inhabitants of the country.

In the year 1897 the First Zionist Congress, inspired by Theodor Herzl's vision of the Jewish State, proclaimed the right of the Jewish people to national revival in their own country.

This right was acknowledged by the Balfour Declaration of November 2, 1917, and reaffirmed by the Mandate of the League of Nations, which gave explicit international recognition to the historic connection of the Jewish people with Palestine and their right to reconstitute their national home.

The Nazi holocaust, which engulfed millions of Jews in Europe, proved anew the urgency of the reestablishment of the Jewish State, which would solve the problem of Jewish homelessness by opening the gates to all Jews and lifting the Jewish people to equality in the family of nations.

The survivors of the European catastrophe, as well as Jews from other lands, proclaiming their right to a life of dignity, freedom and labor, and undeterred by hazards, hardships and obstacles, have tried unceasingly to enter Palestine.

In the Second World War the Jewish people in Palestine made a full contribution in the struggle of the freedom-loving nations against the Nazi evil. The sacrifices of their soldiers and the efforts of their workers gained them title to rank with the peoples who founded the United Nations.

---

*The official title is The Proclamation of the State of Israel. Reprinted in Itamar Rabinovich and Jehuda Reinharz, eds., *Israel in the Middle East: Documents and Readings on Society, Politics and Foreign Relations 1948-Present* (New York: Oxford University Press, 1984), pp. 12–14.

On November 29, 1947, the General Assembly of the United Nations adopted a Resolution for the establishment of an independent Jewish State in Palestine, and called upon inhabitants of the country to take such steps as may be necessary on their part to put the plan into effect.

This recognition by the United Nations of the right of the Jewish people to establish their independent state may not be revoked. It is, moreover, the self-evident right of the Jewish people to be a nation, like all other nations, in its own sovereign state.

Accordingly, we, the members of the National Council, representing the Jewish people in Palestine and the Zionist movement of the world, met together in solemn assembly today, the day of the termination of the British Mandate for Palestine, and by virtue of the natural and historic right of the Jewish people and of the resolution of the General Assembly of the United Nations, hereby proclaim the establishment of the Jewish State in Palestine, to be called Israel.

We hereby declare that as from the termination of the Mandate at midnight, this night of the fourteenth to the fifteenth of May, 1948, and until the setting up of the duly elected bodies of the State in accordance with a Constitution, to be drawn up by a Constituent Assembly not later than the first day of October 1948, the present National Council shall act as the Provisional State Council, and its executive organ, the National Administration, shall constitute the Provisional Government of the State of Israel.

The State of Israel will be open to the immigration of Jews from all countries of their dispersion, will promote the development of the country for the benefit of all its inhabitants; will be based on the precepts of liberty, justice and peace taught by the Hebrew Prophets; will uphold the full social and political equality of all its citizens, without distinction of race, creed or sex; will guarantee full freedom of conscience, worship, education and culture; will safeguard the sanctity and inviolability of the shrines and Holy Places of all religions; and will dedicate itself to the principles of the Charter of the United Nations.

The State of Israel will be ready to cooperate with the organs and representatives of the United Nations in the implementation of the Resolution of the Assembly of November 29, 1947, and will take steps to bring about the Economic Union over the whole of Palestine.

We appeal to the United Nations to assist the Jewish people in the building of its State and to admit Israel into the family of nations.

In the midst of wanton aggression, we yet call upon the Arab inhabitants of the State of Israel to return to the ways of peace and play their part in the development of the State, with full and equal citizenship and the representation in all its bodies and institutions, provisional or permanent.

We offer peace and amity to all the neighboring states and their peoples, and invite them to cooperate with the independent Jewish nation for the common good of all. The State of Israel is ready to contribute its full share to the peaceful progress and development of the Middle East.

Our call goes out to the Jewish people all over the world to rally to our side in the task of immigration and development and to stand by us in the great struggle for the fulfillment of the dream of generations—the redemption of Israel.

With trust in the Rock of Israel, we set our hand to this Declaration, at this Session of the Provisional State Council, in the city of Tel Aviv, on this Sabbath eve, the fifth of Iyar, 5708, the fourteenth day of May, 1948.

APPENDIX B

TABLE A1. Knesset Elections, 1949–65: Votes, Percentages, and Seats by Party

	KNESSET					
	I *25.1.1949*	*II* *30.7.1951*	*III* *26.7.1955*	*IV* *3.12.1959*	*V* *15.8.1961*	*VI* *2.11.1965*
Population	872,700	1,370,100	1,789,100	2,088,700	2,179,500	2,598,400
Eligible voters	506,567	924,885	1,057,795	1,218,413	1,271,285	1,499,709
Voters	440,095	695,007	994,306	1,037,030	1,244,706	1,427,981
Turnout (%)	86.9	75.1	82.8	81.6	81.6	83.0
Parties						
Mapai						
Votes	155,274	256,456	274,375	370,585	349,330	
Percentage	35.7	37.3	32.2	38.2	34.7	
Seats	46	45	40	47	42	
Ma'arakh (a)						
Votes	—	—	—	—	—	443,379
Percentage	—	—	—	—	—	36.7
Seats	—	—	—	—	—	45
Rafi						
Votes	—	—	—	—	—	95,323
Percentage						7.9
Seats						10
Mapam						
Votes	64,018(b)	86,095(b)	62,401	69,469	75,654	79,985
Percentage	14.7	12.5	7.3	7.2	7.5	6.6
Seats	19	15	9	9	9	8
Ahdut Ha'avodah						
Votes	(b)	(b)	69,475	58,043	66,170	(a)
Percentage			8.2	6.0	6.6	
Seats			10	7	8	
Arab Lists (Mapai affiliated)						
Votes	13,413	32,288	37,777	37,782	35,376	39,894
Percentage	3.0	4.7	4.4	3.9	3.5	3.3
Seats	2	5	5	5	4	4

TABLE A1.   (*continued*)

	I 25.1.1949	II 30.7.1951	III 26.7.1955	IV 3.12.1959	V 15.8.1961	VI 2.11.1965
KNESSET						
Maki						
Votes	15,148	27,334	38,492	27,374	42,111	13,617
Percentage	3.5	4.0	4.5	2.8	4.2	1.2
Seats	4	5	6	3	5	1
Rakah						
Votes	—	—	—	—	—	27,413
Percentage						2.3
Seats						3
Left Parties						
Percentage	56.9	58.5	55.5	58.1	56.5	58.0
Seats	71	70	70	71	68	71
Mizrachi parties (NRP) (c)						
Votes	52,982	56,730	77,936	95,581	98,786	107,966
Percentage	12.2	8.3	9.1	9.9	9.8	8.9
Seats	16	10	11	12	12	11
Aguda parties (c)						
Votes		24,993	39,836	45,569	56,606	61,861
Percentage		3.6	4.7	4.7	5.6	5.1
Seats		5	6	6	6	6
Religious Parties						
Percentage	12.2	11.9	13.8	14.6	15.2	14.0
Seats	16	15	17	18	18	17
General Zionists						
Votes	22,661	111,394	87,099	59,100	(d)	(e)
Percentage	5.2	16.2	10.2	6.2		
Seats	7	20	13	8		
Progressives/ Independent Liberals						
Votes	17,786	22,171	37,661	44,889	(d)	45,299
Percentage	4.1	3.2	4.4	4.6		3.8
Seats	5	4	5	6		5
Liberals						
Votes	—	—	—	—	137,255	(e)
Percentage					13.6	
Seats					17	
Herut						
Votes	49,782	45,651	107,190	130,515	138,599	(e)
Percentage	11.5	6.6	12.6	13.5	13.8	
Seats	14	8	15	17	17	
Gahal						
Votes	—	—	—	—	—	256,957
Percentage						21.8
Seats						26

TABLE A1. (*continued*)

	KNESSET					
	I *25.1.1949*	*II* *30.7.1951*	*III* *26.7.1955*	*IV* *3.12.1959*	*V* *15.8.1961*	*VI* *2.11.1965*
Center-Right Parties						
Percentage	20.8	26.0	27.2	24.3	27.4	25.1
Seats	26	32	33	31	34	31
Other lists						
Votes	43,620	24,380	20,618	29,891	7,077	20,905
Percentage	10.1	3.6	3.5	3.0	0.7	1.8
Seats	7	3	—	—	—	—

[a]Ma'arakh (Alignment) formed by Mapai and Ahdut Ha'avodah in 1965.

[b]In 1949 and 1951, Mapam and Ahdut Ha'avodah constituted Mapam.

[c]All the religious parties appeared together on a joint list—the United Religious Front—in 1949.

[d]The Liberal party was formed by the General Zionists and the Progressive party before the 1961 elections.

[e]Gahal was formed in 1965 by Herut and the Liberals, although some of the latter (mainly former Progressives) refused to join, and formed the Independent Liberals.

TABLE A2. Israel's Coalition Cabinets, 1949–67

Year	*Prime Minister*	*Coalition Parties*	*Total Knesset Seats*
First Knesset			
1949	Ben-Gurion	Mapai (46), Religious Front (16), Progressives (5), Sephardim (4)	73*
1950	Ben-Gurion	Mapai (46), Religious Front (16), Progressives (5), Sephardim (4)	73*
Second Knesset			
1951	Ben-Gurion	Mapai (45), Mizrachi-Hapo'el Hamizrachi (10), Agudat Israel-Po'alei Agudat Israel (5)	65*
1952	Ben-Gurion	Mapai (45), Mizrachi-Hapo'el Hamizrachi (10), General Zionists (20), Progressives (4)	84*
1954	Sharett	Mapai (45), Mizrachi-Hapo'el Hamizrachi (10), General Zionists (20), Progressives (4)	84*
1955	Sharett	Mapai (45), Mizrachi-Hapo'el Hamizrachi (10), Progressives (4)	64*
Third Knesset			
1955	Ben-Gurion	Mapai (40), Mizrachi-Hapo'el Hamizrachi (NRP)** (11), Ahdut Ha'avodah (10), Mapam (9), Progressives (5)	80*
1958	Ben-Gurion	Mapai (40), (NRP) (11), Ahdut Ha'avodah (10), Mapam (9), Progressives (5)	80*
1958	Ben-Gurion	Mapai (40), Ahdut Ha'avodah (10), Mapam (9), Progressives (5)	69*

TABLE A2. (*continued*)

Year	Prime Minister	Coalition Parties	Total Knesset Seats
Fourth Knesset			
1959	Ben-Gurion	Mapai (47), NRP (12), Mapam (9), Ahdut Ha'avodah (7), Progressives (6)	86*
Fifth Knesset			
1961	Ben-Gurion	Mapai (42), NRP (12), Ahdut Ha'avodah (8), Po'alei Agudat Israel (2)	68*
1963	Eshkol	Mapai (42), NRP (12), Ahdut Ha'avodah (8), Po'alei Agudat Israel (2)	68*
1964	Eshkol	Mapai (42), NRP (12), Ahdut Ha'avodah (8), Po'alei Agudat Israel (2)	68*
Sixth Knesset			
1966	Eshkol	Ma'arakh*** (45), NRP (11), Mapam (8), Independent Liberals (5), Po'alei Agudat Israel (2)	75*
1967	Eshkol	Ma'arakh*** (45), Gahal (26), NRP (11), Rafi (10), Mapam (8), Independent Liberals (5), Po'alei Agudat Israel (2)	111*

*Includes the Knesset members of the Arab parties affiliated to Mapai.

**The two Mizrachi parties joined in 1956 to form the National Religious Party (NRP).

***In 1965, Mapai presented a joint Knesset list with Ahdut Ha'avodah, which was called the Ma'arakh (Alignment).

SELECT BIBLIOGRAPHY

Primary Sources

Official Records and Reports

State of Israel. Central Bureau of Statistics. *Statistical Abstract of Israel*. Jerusalem (annual).

State of Israel. *Divrei Haknesset*. Jerusalem: Government Printer, 1949–67.

State of Israel. *Moezet Hamedinah Hazemanit* (Protocols). Tel Aviv, 1948–49.

State of Israel. State Archives. *Minhelet-Ha'am* (Protocols, 18.4.1948–13.5.1948). Jerusalem, 1978.

State of Israel. *Sefer Hahukkim*. Jerusalem.

Mapai, Protocols of Veidah, Merkaz, Mazkirut, and various other party bodies and ad hoc committees and meetings, 1948–67, held in the party archives—Arkhion Mifleget Ha'avodah, Bet Berl.

Newspapers

'Al Hamishmar
Davar
Ha'aretz
Haboker
Hador
Hamodi'a
Hapo'el Haza'ir
Hazofeh
Herut
Jerusalem Post
Lamerhav
Ma'ariv
Yedi'ot Aharonot

Miscellaneous Written Sources

Ben-Gurion, David. *Hazon vederekh*. 5 vols. Tel Aviv: Mapai, 1951–57.

———. *Israel: A Personal History*. New York and Tel Aviv: Funk and Wagnalls and Sabra Books, 1971.

———. *Medinat yisrael hamehudeshet*. Tel Aviv: Am Oved, 1969.

———. *Yoman hamilhamah: milhemet ha'azma'ut*. 3 vols. Ed., Gershon Rivlin and Elhanan Orren. Tel Aviv: Ministry of Defense Publications, 1982.

————. "Yoman Ben-Gurion." Unpublished, Ben-Gurion Archives, Sedeh Boker. (These are Ben-Gurion's handwritten diaries, which he generally wrote daily. They are available to researchers at these archives either in typescript or in their original handwritten form. The only part published to date are those for the period 1948–49, which appear elsewhere as *Yoman hamilhamah.*)

Sharett, Moshe. *Yoman ishi* 9 vols. Tel Aviv: Sifriat Ma'ariv, 1978.

Oral Interviews

Bader, Yohanan. 23.3.1968, Project (33) 9, Interviews 6, 7. Oral Documentation Division, Institute of Contemporary Jewry, The Hebrew University.

Ben-Aharon, Izhak. 15.9.1977, Project (114) 105, Oral Documentation Division, Institute of Contemporary Jewry, The Hebrew University. (The original is housed in Arkhion Ha'avodah—the Histadrut archives in Tel Aviv.)

Secondary Sources

Books and Pamphlets

Akzin, Binyamin. *Sugyot bemishpat uvimdinaut.* Jerusalem: Magnes, 1966.

Akzin, Benjamin, and Yehezkel Dror. *Israel: High-Pressure Planning.* Syracuse, N.Y.: Syracuse University Press, 1966.

Almogi, Yosef. *Be'ovi hakorah.* Jerusalem: 'Idanim, 1980.

Arian, Alan. *Ideological Change in Israel.* Cleveland, Ohio: Case Western Reserve University Press, 1968.

————. *The Choosing People: Voting Behavior in Israel.* Cleveland, Ohio: Case Western Reserve University Press, 1973.

————, ed. *The Elections in Israel, 1969.* Jerusalem: Jerusalem Academic Press, 1972.

Arieli, Yehoshu'a. *Hakenuniah.* Tel Aviv: Kadimah, 1965.

Aronson, Shlomo. *Conflict and Bargaining in the Middle East: An Israeli Perspective.* Baltimore, Md.: Johns Hopkins University Press, 1978.

Avihai, Avraham. *Ben-Gurion: State-Builder.* Jerusalem and New York: Israel Universities Press and John Wiley, 1974.

Avineri, Shlomo. *Hara'ayon hazioni ligvanav.* Tel Aviv: Am Oved, 1980.

————, ed. *David Ben-Gurion: demuto shel manhig tenu'at po'alim.* Tel Aviv: Am Oved, 1988.

Avneri, Aryeh. *Hakesher haliberali.* Tel Aviv: Zmora, Bitan, 1984.

Avrech, Israel, and Dan Giladi. *Labor and Society in Israel.* Tel Aviv: Histadrut and Tel Aviv University, 1973.

Bader, Yochanan. *Haknesset veani.* Jerusalem: 'Idanim, 1979.

Bar-Zohar, Michael. *Ben-Gurion.* 3 vols. Tel Aviv: Am Oved, 1975–78.

Berenson, Zvi. *Megilat ha'azmaut: hazon umeziut.* Jerusalem: Ministry of Education and Culture, 1988.

Bernstein, Marver H. *The Politics of Israel: The First Decade of Statehood.* Princeton, N.J.: Princeton University Press, 1957.

Bernstein, Peretz. *Sefer Peretz Bernstein.* Tel Aviv: 1961.

Bialer, Uri. *"Our Place in the World"—Mapai and Israel's Foreign Policy Orientation, 1947–1952.* Jerusalem Papers on Peace Problems, 33. Jerusalem: Leonard Davis Institute, The Hebrew University, 1981.

Binder, Leonard, et al. *Crises and Sequences in Political Development.* Princeton, N.J.: Princeton University Press, 1971.

Braslavski, Moshe. *Tnu'at hapo'alim haerez-yisraelit.* 4 vols. Hakibbutz Hameuchad Publishing House, 1958–62.

Brecher, Michael. *Decisions in Israel's Foreign Policy.* London: Oxford University Press, 1974.

———. *The Foreign Policy System of Israel: Setting, Images, Process.* London: Oxford University Press, 1972.

Brenner, Uri. *Altalena: mehkar medini uzevai.* Hakibbutz Hameuchad Publishing House, 1978.

Brichta, Avraham. *Demokratiah ubehirot.* Tel Aviv: Am Oved, 1977.

Burns, James M. *Leadership.* New York: Harper and Row, 1980.

Cohen, Mitchell. *Zion and State: Nation, Class and the Shaping of Modern Israel.* Oxford and New York: Basil Blackwell, 1987.

Daalder, Hans, and Peter Mair, eds. *Western European Party Systems: Continuity and Change.* Beverly Hills, Calif.: Sage Publications, 1983.

Dahl, Robert A. *Polyarchy: Participation and Opposition.* New Haven: Yale University Press, 1971.

Dayan, Moshe. *Avnei Derekh.* Jerusalem and Tel Aviv: 'Idanim and Dvir, 1976.

Diskin, Avraham. *Boharim ubehirot.* Tel Aviv: Am Oved, 1988.

Eisenstadt, Shmuel N. *Israeli Society.* London: Weidenfeld and Nicolson, 1968.

———. *The Transformation of Israeli Society.* London: Weidenfeld and Nicolson, 1985.

Eisenstadt, Shmuel N., Hayim Adler, Rivka Bar-Yosef, and Reuven Kahane, eds. *Yisrael—hevrah mithavah: nituah soziologi shel mekorot.* Jerusalem: Magnes Press, 1972.

Eshed, Hagai. *Mi natan et hahoraah.* Jerusalem: 'Idanim, 1979.

Friedrich, Carl J. *Man and His Government: An Empirical Theory of Politics.* New York: McGraw-Hill, 1963.

Galnoor, Itzhak. *Steering the Polity: Communication and Politics in Israel.* Beverly Hills, Calif.: Sage Publications, 1982.

Gelbar, Yoav. *Lamah pirku et hapalmah.* Tel Aviv: Schocken, 1986.

Gutmann, Emanuel, and Yehezkel Dror. *Mishtar medinat yisrael: osef mekorot.* Jerusalem: Academon, 1969.

Ha'aretz. *Miflagot baaretz erev habehirot laknesset hashniyah.* Tel Aviv: Pirsumei Ha'aretz, 1951.

Hacohen, David. *Et lesaper.* Tel Aviv: Am Oved, 1974.

Horowitz, Dan, and Moshe Lissak. *Miyishuv limdinah.* Tel Aviv: Am Oved, 1977. English edition: *Origins of the Israeli Polity: Palestine under the Mandate.* Chicago: University of Chicago Press, 1978.

Isaac, Rael Jean. *Party and Politics in Israel: Three Visions of a Jewish State.* New York: Longmans, 1981.

Kantor, Levi. *Lelo maso panim: hitpathut yahasei 'avodah beyisrael.* Tel Aviv: Yahad, 1977.

Keren, Michael. *Ben-Gurion and the Intellectuals: Power, Knowledge and Charisma.* DeKalb: Northern Illinois University Press, 1983.

Krausz, Ernest, ed. *Politics and Society in Israel.* New Brunswick, N.J.: Transaction, 1985.

Landau, Jacob M. *The Arabs in Israel.* London: Oxford University Press, 1969.

Laqueur, Walter Z. *Communism and Nationalism in the Middle East.* London: Routledge and Kegan Paul, 1956.

Lavon, Pinhas. *'Arakhim utemurot*. Tel Aviv: Am Oved, 1960.

Liebman, Charles S., and Eliezer Don-Yehiya. *Civil Religion in Israel*. Berkeley: University of California Press, 1983.

——. *Religion and Politics in Israel*. Bloomington: Indiana University Press, 1984.

Lijphart, Arend. *Democracies: Patterns of Majoritarian and Consensus Government in Twenty-one Countries*. New Haven: Yale University Press, 1984.

Likhovski, Eliahu S. *Israel's Parliament: The Law of the Knesset*. Oxford: Clarendon Press, 1971.

Lissak, Moshe, and Emanuel Gutmann, eds. *Political Institutions and Processes in Israel*. Jerusalem: Academon, 1971.

——. *Hama'arekhet hapolitit hayisraelit*. Tel Aviv: Am Oved, 1977.

Lucas, Noah. *The Modern History of Israel*. London: Weidenfeld and Nicolson, 1974.

Luebbert, Gregory M. *Comparative Democracy: Policymaking and Governing Coalitions in Europe and Israel*. New York: Columbia University Press, 1986.

Lustick, Ian. *Arabs in the Jewish State*. Austin: University of Texas Press, 1980.

Mahler, Gregory, ed. *Readings on the Israeli Political System*. Washington, D.C.: University Press of America, 1982.

Medding, Peter Y. *Mapai in Israel: Political Organisation and Government in a New Society*. Cambridge: Cambridge University Press, 1972.

Nakdimon, Shlomo. *Altalena*. Jerusalem: 'Idanim, 1978.

Peri, Yoram. *Between Battles and Ballots: Israeli Military in Politics*. Cambridge: Cambridge University Press, 1983.

Perlmutter, Amos. *Israel: The Partitioned State*. New York: Scribner's, 1985.

Powell, G. Bingham, Jr. *Contemporary Democracies: Participation, Stability and Violence*. Cambridge: Harvard University Press, 1982.

Rubinstein, Amnon. *Hamishpat hakonstituzioni shel medinat yisrael*. 3d ed. Jerusalem: Schocken, 1980.

Safran, Nadav. *Israel: The Embattled Ally*. Cambridge: Harvard University Press, 1981.

Sager, Samuel. *The Parliamentary System of Israel*. Syracuse, N.Y.: Syracuse University Press, 1985.

Sartori, Giovanni. *Parties and Party Systems: A Framework for Analysis*. Cambridge: Cambridge University Press, 1976.

Schiff, Gary S. *Tradition and Politics: The Religious Parties of Israel*. Detroit, Mich.: Wayne State University Press, 1977.

Segev, Tom. *1949: hayisraelim harishonim*. Jerusalem: Domino Press, 1984.

Shapira, Anita. *Mipiturei harama 'ad piruk hapalmah: sugyot bemaavak 'al hahanhagah habithonit, 1948*. Hakibbutz Hameuhad, 1985.

Shapiro, Yonatan. *Hademokratyah beyisrael*. Ramat-Gan: Masadah, 1977.

Sherf, Ze'ev. *Shloshah yamim*. Tel Aviv: Am Oved, 1981.

Shimshoni, Daniel. *Israeli Democracy: The Middle of the Journey*. New York: Free Press, 1982.

Sprinzak, Ehud. *Ish hayashar be'eninav: i-legalism bahevrah haysrealit*. Tel Aviv: Sifriat P'oalim, 1986.

Unna, Moshe. *Bidrakhim nifradot*. Jerusalem: Moreshet Yad Shapira, 1983.

Weber, Max. *Economy and Society*. Guenther Roth. New York: Bedminster Press, 1968.

Ya'acobi, Gad. *Hamemshalah*. Tel Aviv: Zmorah, Bitan Modan, 1980.

Yanai, Natan. *Mashberim politiyim beyisrael*. Jerusalem: Keter, 1982.

——. *Ker'a bazameret*. Tel Aviv: Levin-Epstein, 1969.

Zidon, Asher. *Haknesset*. Tel Aviv: Ahiasaf, 1950.

Articles and Essays

Antonovsky, Aron. "'Amadot politiyot-sozialiyot beyisrael." *Amot* 6 (June–July 1963): 11–22.

———. "Idiologiah uma'amad beyisrael." *Amot* 7 (August–September 1963): 21–28.

Arian, Alan. "Voting and Ideology in Israel." In *Political Institutions and Processes in Israel.* Edited by Moshe Lissak and Emanuel Gutmann, pp. 257–86. Jerusalem: Academon, 1971.

Arian, Alan, and Samuel H. Barnes. "The Dominant Party System: A Neglected Model of Democratic Stability." *Journal of Politics* 36 (1974): 592–614.

Arian, David. "The First Five Years of the Israel Civil Service." *Scripta Hierosolymitana* (edited by Robert Bachi) 3 (1958): 351–67.

Ben-Aharon, Yizhak. "Remembering Ben-Gurion." *Jerusalem Quarterly* 16 (Summer 1980): 37–48.

Bergman, Dubi. "'Tnu'at Haherut'—Meirgun mahteret lemiflagah politit." *Kivunim* 21 (November 1983): 55–95.

Beyme, Klaus von. "Governments, Parliaments and the Structure of Power in Political Parties." In *Western European Party Systems: Continuity and Change.* Edited by Hans Daalder and Peter Mair, pp. 341–68. Beverly Hills, Calif.: Sage Publications, 1983.

Don-Yehiya, Eliezer. "Pitaron ha'status quo' bithum yahasei dat umedinah beyisrael." *Medinah, mimshal vihasim benleumiyyim* 1 (Summer 1971): 100–112.

Etzioni, Amitai. "Alternative Ways to Democracy: The Example of Israel." *Political Science Quarterly* 74 (1959): 196–214.

Goldberg, Giora. "The Struggle for Legitimacy—Herut's Road from Opposition to Power." In *Conflict and Consensus in Jewish Political Life.* Edited by Stuart E. Cohen and Eliezer Don-Yehiya, pp. 146–69. Comparative Jewish Politics, vol. 2. Ramat-Gan: Bar-Ilan University Press, 1986.

Gutmann, Emanuel, "Miflagot umahanot - yezivut veshinui." In *Ham'arekhet hapolitit hayisraelit.* Edited by Moshe Lissak and Emanuel Gutmann, pp. 122–70. Tel Aviv: Am Oved, 1977.

King, Anthony. "What Do Elections Decide?" In *Democracy at the Polls: A Comparative Study of Competitive National Elections.* Edited by David Butler, Howard R. Penniman, and Austin Ranney, pp. 293–324. Washington, D.C.: American Enterprise Institute, 1981.

Levite, Ariel, and Sydney Tarrow. "The Legitimation of Excluded Parties in Dominant Party Systems: A Comparison of Israel and Italy." *Comparative Politics* 15 (1983): 295–327.

Lijphart, Arend. "Measures of Cabinet Durability: A Conceptual and Empirical Evaluation." *Comparative Political Studies* 17 (1984): 265–79.

Mahler, Gregory, and Richard Trilling. "Coalition Behavior and Cabinet Formation: The Case of Israel." *Comparative Political Studies* 8 (1975): 200–233.

Malkin, Ahuviah. "Hahistadrut bamedinah." *Ovnayim* (1961): 29–47.

Nachmias, David. "Coalition Politics in Israel." *Comparative Political Studies* 7 (October 1974): 316–33.

———. "The Right-Wing Opposition in Israel." *Political Studies* 24 (1976): 268–80.

Sager, Samuel. "Pre-State Influences on Israel's Parliamentary System." *Parliamentary Affairs* 25 (1972): 29–49.

Sani, Giacomo, and Giovanni Sartori. "Polarization, Fragmentation and Competition in Western Democracies. In *Western European Party Systems: Continuity and*

Change. Edited by Hans Daalder and Peter Mair, pp. 307–40. Beverly Hills, Calif.: Sage Publications, 1983.

Shapira, Anita. "Ben-Gurion u'Berl: shenai tipusei manhigut." In *David Ben-Gurion: demuto shel manhig tenu'at po'alim.* Edited by Shlomo Avineri, pp. 46–72. Tel Aviv: Am Oved, 1988.

Sprinzak, Ehud. "Anti-Zionism: From Delegitimation to Dehumanization." *Forum* 53 (1985): 2–5.

Weiss, Shevah, and Avraham Brichta. "Private Members' Bills in Israel's Parliament—The Knesset." *Parliamentary Affairs* 23 (1969): 21–33.

Wolf-Phillips, Leslie. "The 'Westminster Model' in Israel?" *Parliamentary Affairs* 26 (1973): 415–39.

Yanai, Natan. "Hatefisah hamamlakhtit shel Ben-Gurion." *Cathedra* 45 (1987): 169–89.

Zahor, Ze'ev. "Aharei 20 shanah." *Monitin* (October 1980): 52–55.

Zariski, Raphael. "The Legitimacy of Opposition Parties in Democratic Political Systems: A New Use for an Old Concept." *Western Political Quarterly* 39 (1986): 29–47.

Unpublished Sources

Don-Yehiya, Eliezer. "Shituf vekonflikt ben mahanot politiyim: hamahaneh hadati uten'uat ha'avodah umashber hahinukh beyisrael." Ph.D. diss., The Hebrew University, 1977.

Goldberg, Giora. "Lishkot ha'avodah kemakhshir politi behevrah mithavah." Master's thesis, Tel Aviv University, 1975.

———. "Haopoziziyah haparlementarit beyisrael (1965–1977)." Ph.D. diss., The Hebrew University, 1980.

Lichtenstein, Yoram. "Tnu'at haherut: mivneh vetahalikhim politiyim." Master's thesis, The Hebrew University, 1974.

Milkov, Avi. "Mo'adon ha'arba." Seminar paper for my course Parties and Party Politics in Israel, 1984.

Paltiel, Khayyam Ze'ev. "The Progressive Party: A Study of a Small Party in Israel." Ph.D. diss., The Hebrew University, 1961.

Robinson, Donna. "Patrons and Saints: A Study of Career Patterns of Higher Civil Servants in Israel." Ph.D. diss., Columbia University, 1970.

Sirkin, R. "Coalition, Conflict, and Compromise: The Party Politics of Israel." Ph.D. diss., Pennsylvania State University, 1971.

Yanai, Yizhak. "Haidiolgiyah hahevratit shel mapai leor medinyutah bamedinah uvahistadrut bashanim 1948–1953." Ph.D. diss., Tel Aviv University, 1987.

Yishai, Ya'el. "Si'atiyut bitnu'at ha'avodah beyisrael." Ph.D. diss., The Hebrew University, 1976.

Zalmanovitch, Yair. "Histadrut, kupat holim, memshalah." M.A. thesis, Haifa University, 1981.

Index